AF519008

GLOBAL
CARGO MANAGEMENT
Concept, Typology, Law and Policy

GLOBAL CARGO MANAGEMENT

Concept, Typology, Law and Policy

Prem Nath Dhar

KANISHKA PUBLISHERS, DISTRIBUTORS
NEW DELHI-110 002

KANISHKA PUBLISHERS, DISTRIBUTORS
4697/5-21A, Ansari Road, Daryaganj
New Delhi-110 002
Phones : 2327 0497, 2328 8285
Fax : 011-2328 8285
e-mail: kanishka_publishing@yahoo.co.in

First Published 2008

ISBN 978-81-8457-029-8

PRINTED IN INDIA

Published by Madan Sachdeva for Kanishka Publishers, Distributors, 4697/5-21A, Ansari Road, Daryaganj, New Delhi-110 002; Typeset by Sunshine Graphics, Delhi, and Printed at Chaudhary Offset Process,

Preface

"Global Cargo Management: Concept, Typology, Law and Policy" covers the subject area of cargo management in its totality and provides readers with an introductory overview of related themes both at basic and advanced levels. For instance, an extensive glossary on the subject area of aviation management is very helpful in creating basic understanding of all possible terms, themes or sub-themes. The book provides in detail an introductory overview of major cargo classification systems and cargo management in general, where themes like containerization, bulk cargo, cargo agent etc., are described briefly. This book deals with the much important themes of supply chain management, performance management, and logistics management in great detail, besides briefly touching upon related areas of company; reporting; integrated planning solutions; distributed order management; warehouse management; labour management; slotting optimization; load management; billing management; transportation management, procurement, planning and execution; carrier management; and trading partner management. A brief overview of air cargo management is provided with extensive discussions on cargo airline, International Air Transport Association, Cargo Agency Registration Services, Cargo Claims Management, and liability related to international air carriers. A brief introduction is also given to Air Cargo World. Also, the latest 2007 Directory on Airports Around the World is provided. Other chapter deals with Marine Cargo Ships and Marine Shipping industry. Details have been given regarding cargo ship, uship, import-export consolidation in this sector and international marine insurance management. The international "Convention for the Unification of Certain Rules Relating to International Carriage by Air" is documented, popularly known as the Warsaw Convention. Also the Montreal Protocol with respect to marine cargo and shipping is given. Select Case Studies have been presented regarding the subject area of cargo management law and policy, both from India and abroad. Brief detail of The Cargo Law Network of Legal Services has been provided. An elaborate appendix deals with the management and supervision of cargo and the issues related to staffing and human resources management in this industry.

In sum, this book introduces readers with the subject area of cargo management in a rather user friendly and informative way and helps them develop a sound understanding of the subject in question.

Prem Nath Dhar

Contents

Preface *v*

1. **Introduction to Cargo Classification and Management** **1**
   - Marine Cargo Types
   - Containerization
   - Containers Used for Housing and Other Architecture
   - Case Study of a Contatiner Leasing and Chassis Leasing Company
   - Bulk Cargo
   - Freight
   - Less Than Truckload
   - Cargo Agent
2. **Conceptual Study of Supply Chain, Performance and Logistics Management** **23**
   - Company : An Introduction
   - Supply Chain
   - Supply Chain Management
   - Performance Management
   - Reporting
   - Logistics Planning and Execution
   - Reverse Logistics Management
   - Integrated Planning Solutions
   - Distributed Order Management
   - Warehouse Management
   - Labour Management
   - Slotting Optimization
   - Load Management
   - Billing Management
   - Transportation Management
   - Transportation Procurement
   - Transportation Planning and Execution
   - Carrier Management
   - Trading Partner Management
3. **Air Cargo Management: A Brief Overview** **43**
   - Cargo Airline
   - International Air Transport Association (IATA)
   - Cargo Agency Registration Services
   - Effective Cargo Claims Management
   - Air Cargo World
   - Airports Directory
   - International Air Carrier Liability: The Montreal Convention

4. Marine Cargo Ships and Ocean Shipping 94

- Cargo Ship
- Uship
- Import/Export Consolidation
- International Marine Insurance Managers
- Convention for the Unification of Certain Rules Relating to International Carriage by Air
- Montreal Protocol

5. Cargo Management Policy and Law: Select Case Studies 125

- Evergreen Seal Management Policy
- Gati International: An Overview
- The Law Offices of Countryman and McDaniel
- The Cargo Law Network of Legal Services

Appendix

- ***Introduction to Management and Supervision*** **156**
  - What is "Management"?
  - Core Skills in Management and Supervision Problem Solving and Decision Making
  - Define the Problem
  - Planning
  - Effective Delegation
  - Basics of Internal Communications
  - Meeting Management
  - Managing Yourself
  - Designing Organization and Staff
- ***Staffing*** **177**
  - Defining a New Job Role
  - Hiring (Advertising, Screening and Selecting)
  - Building Teams
  - Training
  - Job Training
  - Employee Performance Management Setting Goals
  - Supporting Employee Motivation
  - Observing and Giving Feedback
  - Addressing Performance Issues
  - Conducting Performance Appraisals/Reviews
  - Firing Employees
  - Personnel Policies
  - Developing an Employee Manual
  - Sample List of Personnel Policies
  - Additional Free Resources

Glossary of Terms 207

Index 357

1

Introduction to Cargo Classification and Management

Cargo is a term used to denote goods or produce being transported generally for commercial gain, usually on a ship, plane, train, van or truck. Nowadays containers are used in all intermodal long-haul cargo transport.

MARINE CARGO TYPES

There is a wide range of marine cargoes at seaport terminals operated. The primary types are these:

- Containers are the largest and fastest growing cargo category at most ports worldwide. Containerized cargo includes everything from auto parts and machinery components to shoes, toys, and frozen meat and seafood.
- Automobiles are handled at many ports.
- Project cargoes and heavy lift cargoes may include items such as manufacturing equipment, factory components, power equipment such as generators and wind mills, military equipment or almost any other oversized or overweight cargo too big or too heavy to fit into a container.
- Break bulk cargo is typically material stacked on wooden pallets and lifted into and out of the hold of a vessel by cranes on the dock or aboard the ship itself. The volume of break bulk cargo has declined dramatically worldwide as containerization has grown.
- Bulk cargoes, such as salt, oil, tallow and scrap metal, are usually defined as commodities that are neither on pallets nor in containers, and which are not handled as individual pieces, the way heavy-lift and project cargoes are. Alumina, grain, gypsum, logs and wood chips, for instance, are bulk cargoes.

CONTAINERIZATION

Containerization is a system of intermodal freight transport cargo transport using standard ISO containers (also known as isotainers) that can be loaded and sealed intact onto container ships, railroad cars, planes, and trucks.

Container Dimensions

There are five common standard lengths, 20 ft (6.1 m), 40 ft (12.2 m), 45 ft (13.7 m), 48 ft (14.6 m), and 53 ft (16.2 m). US domestic standard containers are generally 48 ft and 53 ft (rail and truck). Container capacity is measured in twenty-foot equivalent units (TEU, or sometimes teu). A twenty-foot equivalent unit is a measure of containerized cargo capacity equal to one standard 20 ft (length) × 8 ft (width) × 8 ft 6 in (height) container. In metric units this is 6.10 m (length) × 2.44 m (width) × 2.59 m (height), or approximately 39 m³. These sell at about US$2,500 in China, the biggest manufacturer.

Most containers today are of the 40-ft (12.2 m) variety and thus are known as 2 TEU. 45 foot (13.7 m) containers are also designated 2 TEU. Two TEU are referred to as one forty-foot equivalent unit (FEU). These two terms of measurement are used interchangeably. High cube containers have a height of 9 ft 6 in (2.9 m), while half-height containers, used for heavy loads, have a height of 4 ft 3 in (1.3 m). When converting containers to TEUs, the height of the containers typically is not considered.

History

Containers produced a huge reduction in port handling costs, contributing significantly to lower freight charges and, in turn, boosting trade flows. Almost every manufactured product humans consume spends some time in a container. Containerization is an important element of the innovations in logistics that revolutionized freight handling in the 20th century.

Containerization was a Canadian innovation, the world's first purpose-built container ship was the *Clifford J. Rodgers* built in Montreal in 1955 and owned by the White Pass & Yukon Route. Based in Vancouver, it carried 600 containers between North Vancouver, British Columbia and Skagway, Alaska. It started its first trip on November 26, 1955.

Containerization has revolutionized cargo shipping. Today, approximately 90 per cent of non-bulk cargo worldwide moves by containers stacked on transport ships; 26 per cent of all containers originate from China. As of 2005, some 18 million total containers make over 200 million trips per year. There are ships that can carry over 9,000 TEU, and designers are working on freighters capable of 14,000 TEU. It has even been predicted that, at some point, container ships will be constrained in size only by the Straits of Malacca, one of the world's busiest shipping lanes. Such a ship would be as long as one-quarter of a mile (400 m) and 190 feet (58 m) wide.

However, few initially foresaw the extent of the influence containerization would bring to the shipping industry. In the 1950s, Harvard University economist Benjamin Chinitz predicted that containerization would benefit New York by allowing it to ship industrial goods produced there more cheaply to the Southern United States than other areas, but did not anticipate that containerization might make it cheaper to import such goods from abroad. Most economic studies of containerization merely assumed that shipping companies would begin to replace older forms of transportation with containerization, but did not predict that the process of containerization itself would have some influence on producers and the extent of trading.

The widespread use of ISO standard containers has driven modifications in other freight-moving standards, gradually forcing removable truck bodies or swap bodies into the standard sizes and shapes (though without the strength needed to be stacked), and changing completely the worldwide use of freight pallets that fit into ISO containers or into commercial vehicles.

Improved cargo security is also an important benefit of containerization. The cargo is not visible to the casual viewer and thus is less likely to be stolen and the doors of the containers are generally locked (or rather "sealed") so that tampering is more evident. This has reduced the "falling off the truck" syndrome that long plagued the shipping industry.

Use of the same basic sizes of containers across the globe has lessened the problems caused by incompatible rail gauge sizes in different countries. Most of the trains in the world operate on 1,435 mm (4 ft 8½ in) gauge track known as standard gauge but many industrialized countries like Australia, Russia, Finland and Spain use broader gauges while many countries in Africa and South America use narrower gauges on their networks. The use of container trains in all these countries makes trans shipment between different gauge trains easier, with automatic or semi-automatic equipment.

Effect of Development of Containerization on Status Quo

In the United States, at first, containerization grew through cracks in the rigid regulatory structure of the 1960s. But the United States' present fully integrated systems became possible only after the Interstate Commerce Commission's regulatory oversight was cut back (and later abolished in 1995), trucking and rail were deregulated in the 1970s and maritime rates were deregulated (with very little fanfare) in 1984.

In some ways, Malcom McLean's vision was nothing new. Beginning in 1929, Seatrain Lines had carried railroad boxcars on its sea vessels to transport goods between New York and Cuba. Likewise, the idea of putting truck trailers on railroad flatcars was a method of moving less-than-railroad carload shipments economically. This integrated transport concept held the hope of competing with trucks, which were taking more and more of this business from the railroads. From 1926 to 1947, the Chicago North Shore and Milwaukee Railway carried motor carrier vehicles and shippers' vehicles loaded on flatcars between Milwaukee and Chicago.

In the mid-1930s, the Chicago Great Western Railway Company and then the New Haven railroad began piggy-back service limited to their own railroad. By 1953, the CB&Q, the Eastern Illinois and the Southern Pacific railroads had joined the innovation. Most cars were surplus flatcars equipped with new decks. By 1955, an additional 25 railroads had begun some form of piggy-back trainler service. What was new about McLean's innovation was the idea of using large containers that were never opened in transit between shipper and consignee and that were transferable on an intermodal basis, among trucks, ships and railcars.

Using these concepts, McLean initially favoured the construction of "trailerships"-—taking trailers from large trucks and stowing them in a ship's cargo hold. This method of stowage, referred to as roll-on/roll-off, was not adopted because of the large waste in potential cargo space onboard the vessel, known as broken stowage. Instead, he modified his original concept into loading just the containers, not the chassis, onto the ships, hence the designation container ship or "box" ship.

Double-stack Containerization

The advent of "double-stacked" container transport has changed the entire intermodal freight distribution industry in North America. It has resulted in more cost-effective, secure and reliable freight shipments, and provided domestic intermodal rail capacity that could not otherwise have been possible.

The double-stack rail car's unique design also significantly reduced damage in transit, and provided greater cargo security by cradling the lower containers so their doors cannot be opened. A succession of large, new domestic container sizes was introduced to further enhance shipping productivity for customers.

Origins of Double-stack

As early as the 1970s, doublestack designs and equipment were introduced, but the cars were heavy and uneconomical to operate. While always deflecting credit to the many contributors who enabled the introduction of Stacktrain rail service, Pacer International's chief executive officer Donald Orris is widely considered the "Father of Stacktrain Service." He earned that moniker for his role in the early 1980s, as the head of APL's intermodal department, in sponsoring the development and implementation of lightweight, fuel-efficient equipment and the first successful operating network.

With Orris' system, launched in 1984, container trains were finally able to break cost, capacity and service barriers by using specially engineered rail cars that could carry two tiers of containers instead of one—significantly reducing the locomotive power, track capacity and train crews required by conventional intermodal trains to move a comparable payload.

In 1999, Pacer International acquired the original double-stack network that Orris and his colleagues had helped develop and named it "Pacer Stacktrain." Pacer remains the largest wholesale provider of double-stack rail service in North America.

Impact on Transportation

For freight intermediaries—the intermodal marketing companies, ocean carriers, and other third parties that market end-to-end transportation services to businesses that ship product worldwide—introduction of double-stack changed their business. It was more cost-effective than basic container-on-flat car, piggyback or truck for cross-country moves; also, it significantly reduced cargo damage and claims, helping the intermediaries better sell intermodal services to skeptical prospects.

Pacer Stacktrain now (2006) carries more than one million containers per year and purchases over $1 billion of rail transportation annually. The company accounts for more than 20 per cent of all domestic container moves in North America. Overall, the double-stack market has grown more than 100-fold since 1984, and now accounts for about 70 per cent of intermodal shipments.

Container Types

Various container types are available for different needs:

- general purpose "dry van" for boxes, cartons, cases, sacks, bales, pallets, drums in standard, high or half height
- high cube palletwide containers for europallet compatibility
- temperature controlled from -25°c to +25°c "reefer (container)"
- open top "bulktainers" for bulk minerals, heavy machinery
- open side for loading oversize pallet
- flushfolding flat-rack containers for heavy and bulky semi-finished goods, out of gauge cargo
- platform or bolster for barrels and drums, crates, cable drums, out of gauge cargo, machinery, and processed timber
- ventilated containers for organic products requiring ventilation
- tank containers for bulk liquids
- rolling floor for difficult to handle cargo
- Gas Bottle
- Generator
- Collapsible ISO
- Swapbody

Biggest Container Companies

Table 1.1: Top 10 Container Shipping Companies in Order of TEU Capacity, January 1, 2006

Company	TEU capacity	Market share	Number of ships
A.P. Moller-Maersk Group	1,665,272	18.2%	549
Mediterranean Shipping Company S.A.	784,248	8.6%	299
CMA CGM	507,954	5.6%	256
Evergreen Marine Corporation	477,911	5.2%	153
Hapag-Lloyd	412,344	4.5%	140
China Shipping Container Lines	346,493	3.8%	111
American President Lines	331,437	3.6%	99
Hanjin-Senator	328,794	3.6%	145
COSCO	322,326	3.5%	118
NYK Line	302,213	3.3%	105

Other Container Systems

- Haus-zu-Haus (Germany)
- RACE (Container) (Australia)

CONTAINERS USED FOR HOUSING AND OTHER ARCHITECTURE

In North America, containers are in many ways an ideal building material, because they are strong, durable, stackable, cuttable, movable, modular, plentiful and relatively cheap. It is not surprising then that architects as well as laypeople have utilized them to build homes, offices, apartments, schools, dormitories, artists' studios, emergency shelters and many other uses. They are also used to provide temporary secure spaces on construction sites and other venues on "as is" basis instead of building shelters.

During the 1991 Gulf War ("Desert Storm"), containers saw considerable non-standard uses, not only as makeshift shelters but also for the transportation of Iraqi prisoners of war. Holes were cut in the containers to allow for ventilation and there were no reported ill effects from this method. Containers continue to be used for military shelters, often additionally fortified by adding sandbags to the side walls to protect against weapons such as rocket-propelled grenades ("RPGs").

The abundance and relative cheapness during the last decade comes from the deficit in manufactured goods coming from North America in the last two decades. These manufactured goods come to North America from Asia and, to a lesser extent, Europe, in containers that often have to be shipped back empty ("deadhead"), at considerable expense. It is often cheaper to buy new containers in China and elsewhere in Asia, and to try to find new applications for the used containers that have reached their North American cargo destination.

In the middle of Central Asia in the country of Kyrgyzstan, the huge shopping bazaar Dordoi is made entirely of shipping containers stacked in a vast labyrinth. Dordoi is the main market for all kinds of goods, especially clothes, purchased in Bishkek, Kyrgyzstan's capital and largest city. Travellers come from Kazakhistan to take advantage of the cheap prices and plethora of knock-off designers. The large Seventh-Kilometer Market in Odessa, Ukraine is constructed out of double-stacked shipping containers.

CASE STUDY OF A CONTATINER LEASING AND CHASSIS LEASING COMPANY

Interpool, Inc. is one of the world's leading lessors of intermodal dry containers, and the largest lessor of intermodal container chassis in the U.S.

Our market remains very strong with continued significant demand for both new and used chassis and containers. As the global economy expands, and newly manufactured ships come online, our new business opportunities remain excellent.

We are poised to capitalize on continued industry growth. With fleet utilization above 95 per cent, we offer investors a unique opportunity to participate in economic globalization and the resulting container and chassis market growth.

Interpool Overview

Interpool, Inc. originally founded in 1968 is one of the world's leading suppliers of equipment and services to the transportation industry. With a chassis fleet of 208,000 units and a container fleet of 808,000 twenty-foot equivalent units (TEU's) with a utilization rate in excess of 97 per cent as of December 31, 2004, Interpool is the largest lessor of intermodal container chassis in the United States and a world leading lessor of intermodal dry freight standard containers used in international trade.

Interpool is well positioned to benefit opportunities creat growing global eco and a more efficier shipping industry.

Interpool's Businesses

Founded in 1968, Interpool is the largest lessor of intermodal container chassis in the United States and one of the world's leading lessors of intermodal dry freight containers. We lease our chassis and containers to over 600 shipping and transportation companies throughout the world, including nearly all of the world's 25 largest international container shipping lines and major North American railroads. The customers for our chassis include a large number of domestic lessees, many of which are domestic subsidiaries or branches of international shipping lines to which we also lease containers. With a network of offices and agents covering major ports in the United States, Europe and the Far East, we have been able to supply containers in nearly all locations requested by our customers.

Leasing companies own a significant portion of North America's chassis and of the world's container fleet and we believe the balance is owned predominantly by shipping lines and railroads. Leasing companies have maintained this market position because container shipping lines and railroads receive both financial and operational benefits by leasing a portion of their equipment. Our objective is to continue to expand on our market position as a leading long-term lessor of intermodal transportation equipment. To achieve this objective, we intend to continue to:

- Focus on our core business of North American chassis and international marine container leasing. Our strong market positions in the chassis and container leasing businesses provide us with economies of scale that benefit our customers. Our equipment and operations are located worldwide to meet our domestic and international customers' needs in a timely manner. In addition, we are able to focus our management and financial resources to compete effectively for equipment leasing requirements of all quantities.
- Concentrate on long-term leasing to achieve high utilization rates and to minimize the impact of economic cycles on earnings. We concentrate on long-term leases in order to minimize the impact of economic cycles on our equipment leasing revenues and to achieve high utilization and more stable and predictable earnings. The lower rate of turnover provided by long-term leases enables us to concentrate on the expansion of our asset base through the purchase and lease of new equipment, rather than on the repeated re-marketing of our existing fleet.

- Re-marketing of equipment when returned by lessees. When long-term leases reach their termination date, we make every effort to extend the lease with the customer that originally leased the equipment, or in lieu of that, to lease the equipment to another customer for an extended term. Containers may also be made available to our 50 per cent-owned consolidated subsidiary, CAI, which manages our containers in the short-term marketplace. This allows us to maintain our focus on long-term leasing while CAI expands its fleet of equipment that it manages for us and for others, providing CAI with further economies of scale.

"Poolstat"™ Chassis Management Services

Our chassis customers are turning to outside service companies to help them manage chassis that they own and lease. We offer management services under the trademarked name "PoolStat"™. "PoolStat"™ aggregates chassis activity data from over 400 locations around the country and reports on this activity, processing more than two million transactions monthly. Customers contract with us to track their chassis nationally and determine usage patterns, ongoing requirements, and overall fleet efficiencies. Reports are provided using a "PoolStat"™ proprietary Internet based report generator. "PoolStat"™ services also include the use of field staff under contract where field management of chassis operations is involved. Under the Trac Lease "PoolStat"™ chassis management programme, Interpool's chassis customers participate in pools which provide improved availability of chassis and reduce their overall investment in equipment. "PoolStat"™ represents additional revenue opportunities for Interpool and allows the Company to forge closer relationships with our chassis customers.

Outlook

Interpool is well positioned to take advantage of a current market environment. Strong demand, coupled with increases in new container prices during 2004, continued to facilitate lease renewals at attractive rates and increase residual value realization on used equipment sales. As the global economy continues its projected expansion, particularly in China, and anticipated newly manufactured ships come off production lines, our prospects for continued healthy growth remain extremely positive.

We are continuing to build depth in the organization as well as upgrade our information technology capabilities to meet an expanding asset base and attain the highest levels of accountability and corporate governance practices.

BULK CARGO

Bulk cargo is cargo that is unpacked (un-bundled or un-bound) and is of the same or a similar kind or nature (homogeneous). These cargos are usually dropped or poured, with a spout or shovel bucket, as a liquid or solid, into a bulk carrier's hold, railroad car, or truck/trailer/semi-trailer body. Bulk cargos are classified as liquid or dry.

The largest bulk carrier cargo ship in the world is the iron ore carrier Berge Stahl, weighing a massive 364,768 dead-weight-tons (metric).

The busiest bulk cargo port in the world is the New Orleans-area based Port of South Louisiana.

Dry Bulk Cargos

- coal
- grain (wheat, maize, rice, barley, oats, rye, sorghum, soybeans, etc.)
- iron ore (ferrous and non-ferrous ores, ferroalloys, pig iron, scrap metal, etc.)
- wood chips
- cement
- chemicals (fertilizer, plastic granules and pellets, resin powder, synthetic fiber, etc.)
- dry edibles (for animals or humans: alfalfa pellets, citrus pellets, livestock feed, flour, peanuts, raw or refined sugar, seeds, starches, etc.)
- bulk mine (sand and gravel, copper, iron (ores in pellet form), salt, etc.)

Liquid Bulk Cargos

- oil
- liquefied natural gas (LNG)
- gasoline
- chemicals
- liquid edibles (vegetable oil, cooking oil, fruit juices, etc.)

Large Bulk Sea-going Companies

- Aasen Shipping and Aasen Chartering (Norway)
- ALL-Transport A/S (Norway)
- American Steamship Company (United States)
- Canada Steamship Lines (Canada)
- Commercial Trading and Discount (Greece)
- Czech Ocean Shipping (Czech Republic)
- Daeyang Shipping (China-Greece-Japan)
- Fednav (Canada)
- Gearbulk (Norway-Japan)
- M/S Fjordbulk (Norway)
- NOL Services (Singapore)
- OAM Coal Trade and Bulk Shipping (Germany)
- Österströms Rederi AB (Sweden)
- SMC Marine Services (Singapore)
- Samsun Logix (South Korea)
- The Skaarup Group (United States)

- Zhejiang Ocean Shipping Company (China).

Large Ports Specializing in Bulk Cargo

- Port of South Louisiana
- Port of Rotterdam.

FREIGHT

Freight is just a description of the cargo, Cargo on the shipment. Items being shipped typically fall into various categories depending on (1) what the item is, (2) how large the shipment is, both in terms of item size and in terms of how many items make up the shipment, and (3) how fast the shipment needs to get to where it is going. Shipments are typically categorized as household goods, express, parcel, and freight shipments.

Furniture, art, or similar items are usually classified as "household goods" and are transported by specialized household goods (HHG) carriers like Bekins and North American Van Lines.

Very small business or personal items like envelopes are considered "overnight express" or "express letter" shipments, and are transported by carriers like UPS, FedEx Express, and DHL. These shipments are rarely over a few pounds, and almost always travel in the carrier's own packaging. Service levels are variable, depending on the shipper's choice. Express shipments almost always travel some distance by air. An envelope may go coast to coast overnight or it may take several days, depending on the service options and prices chosen.

Slightly larger items like small boxes are considered "parcel" or "ground" shipments, and are transported by carriers like UPS and FedEx Ground. These shipments are rarely over 100 pounds, with no single piece of the shipment weighing more than about 70 pounds. Shipments are always boxed, sometimes in the shipper's packaging and sometimes in carrier-provided packaging. Service levels are again variable; but most "ground" shipments will move about 500-700 miles per day, going coast to coast in about four days. Parcel shipments rarely travel by air, and typically move via road and rail. Parcels represent the majority of business-to-consumer (B2C) shipments.

Beyond HHG, express, and parcel shipments, you get into the category of "freight shipments."

Less-than-truckload (LTL) Freight

The first category of freight shipment is "less than truckload" (LTL), which represents the majority of "freight" shipments and the majority of business-to-business (B2B) shipments. LTL shipments are also often referred to as "motor freight." LTL shipments range from 100 pounds to about 15,000 pounds, and are always less than 28′ long because LTL carriers' trailers are typically 28′ long. The shipments are usually palletized and packaged for a mixed-freight environment. Unlike express or parcel, LTL shippers must provide their own packaging, as LTL carriers do not provide any packaging supplies or assistance. However, crating or other substantial packaging is required for LTL shipments due to the mixed freight environment.

LTL shipments are transported by regional carriers like AAA Cooper or Averett Express, or by multi-regional or national carriers like Roadway, Old Dominion or Southeastern. Shipments may be booked directly with the carriers or through brokers or online marketplace service. Major brokers include CHRobinson, Twin Modal, Hub Group, and Rockwell. Leading online intermediaries are Freightquote.com and Transcore DAT. Service levels are again variable; but most LTL shipments will move about 500 miles per day, going coast to coast in about five business days, travelling by road and rail.

"Air cargo" or "air freight" shipments are very similar to LTL shipments in terms of size and packaging requirements. However, air freight shipments typically need to move at much faster speeds than 500 miles per day. These types of shipments are typically arranged through air freight forwarders like Bax, Eagle, and Pilot. Air shipments may be booked directly with the carriers or through brokers or online marketplace services. While shipments move faster than standard LTL, "air" shipments don't always actually move by air.

Truckload (TL) Freight

Shipments larger than about 15,000 pounds are typically classified as "truckload" (TL). Truckload shipments may be up to 40,000 pounds or 53′ long. While express, parcel, and LTL shipments are always intermingled with other shipments on a single piece of equipment and are typically reloaded across multiple pieces of equipment during their transport, TL shipments usually travel as the only shipment on a trailer and TL shipments usually deliver on exactly the same trailer as they are picked up on. While very large shippers may contract directly with TL carriers like JB Hunt and Schneider, most TL shipments are arranged through freight brokers or online marketplaces. When shipping freight, it is extremely important to understand pricing, claims, and insurance.

How Freight Pricing Works

Express letter and parcel carriers typically have fairly simple pricing based on package size and service level requested; however, freight pricing is considerably more complicated. LTL carriers typically charge by freight "class." The National Motor Freight Traffic Association (NMFTA) issues a publication called the National Motor Freight Classification (NMFC). The NMFC is basically a list of every kind of item that ships via truck. Each item has a class assigned to it based on the item's density, loadability or mixability, value, and other factors. Freight classes range from 50 to 500, and generally indicate the percentage of the base rate that should apply. So class 85 freight should be charged 85 per cent of the full rate between points A and B, theoretically. Denser items such as steel and machinery have low classifications such as Class 50 to 85. Fragile or bulky items fall into freight Classes 125 to 500, and pay higher shipment costs.

LTL rates are quoted "per 100 pounds" or "cwt" or "per hundred weight." Besides the discount off of base rate created by the freight class, there is typically a second discount applied to the calculated transportation rate. So a given LTL lane may have a rate of $50 cwt. If your shipment is class 70, then your adjusted base rate is $35 cwt (70% of 50 cwt); then the carrier applies a negotiated discount of 50 per cent for example, to give you a rate of $17.50 cwt. So a 1,000 class 70 shipment would have a base rate of $175.

Besides class, rates, and discounts, an LTL carrier will apply a wide range of surcharges and accessorial charges that will affect the final price of the shipment. Most shipments will receive a fuel surcharge, which is always a significant proportion of the overall cost, possibly as much as 30 per cent or more. Some common accessorial charges are:

- Liftgate: this is a service that assists the driver in loading or unloading his truck when a loading dock or forklift is not available. The trailer is equipped with a hydraulic ramp that lowers to the ground. Liftgate service is almost always billed on residential pickups or deliveries and in commercial pickup and deliveries where loading docks or forklifts are not available. Only a small percentage of most trucking companies' trailers are equipped with liftgates, so be sure to notify them of your need for one in advance.
- Residential pickup or delivery: anytime a carrier must pickup or delivers into a residential area an extra fee is charged, because in most cases the local laws restrict the size of delivery trucks, causing the carrier to utilize a smaller truck to service a residential area. These requirements equal less shipments per day picked up and delivered, so these fees are assessed to offset the carrier's costs.
- Appointments or notification before pickup or delivery: by default, carriers make pickups and deliveries in order arranged by geographic location (a route). If your shipment requires the carrier to call ahead, or schedule and appointment, the carrier will charge an additional fee for this service.
- Inside pickup or delivery: by requiring the truck driver to pickup or deliver inside a building his route takes longer to complete. The carrier will charge an additional fee for this service.

Also, charges for additional insurance or literally hundreds of other possibilities may be added to the final freight bill. It is extremely important that the LTL shipper works with the carrier or intermediary to completely understand all of the requirements of their shipment in order for an accurate price to be quoted.

Often, an LTL shipper may realize significant savings by utilizing a freight "broker," online marketplace, or other intermediary instead of contracting directly with a trucking company. Brokers can shop the marketplace and obtain lower rates than most smaller shippers can directly. In the Less-than-Truckload (LTL) marketplace, intermediaries typically receive 50 per cent to 80 per cent discounts from published rates, where a small shipper may only be offered a 5 per cent to 30 per cent discount by the carrier.

Truckload (TL) carriers usually charge a rate per mile. The rate varies depending on the distance, items being shipped, equipment type required, and service times required. TL shipments usually receive a variety of surcharges very similar to those described for LTL shipments above. In the TL market, there are thousands more small carriers than in the LTL market; so the use of transportation intermediaries or "brokers" is extremely common.

One other cost-saving method is facilitating pickups or deliveries at the carrier's terminals. By doing this, you remove any accessorial fees that might normally be charged for liftgate, residential pickup/delivery, inside pickup/delivery or notifications/ appointments. Your carrier or intermediary should be able to provide you the address and phone number for the closest shipping terminal to the origin and destination.

Shop smart when pricing your shipment cost by sampling rates from several carriers, brokers, and online marketplaces. When obtaining rates from different providers, you may find quite a contrast in the pricing offered. If you use a broker, freight forwarder, or other transportation intermediary, ask for a copy of their Federal Operating Authority. Freight intermediaries are required by Federal Law to be licensed by the Federal Highway Administration. Avoid unlicensed brokers and forwarders; if they working outside the law by not having a Federal Operating License, you will have no protection in the event of a problem. Also ask for a copy of their insurance certificate and any specific insurance that applies to your shipment. The internet is full of websites operated by unlicensed and inexperienced brokers, forwarders, and other intermediaries who come and go and come again overnight. Stick to major brokers and established online marketplaces that have been in business a while and manage thousands of shipments annually, in order to get the best service and price.

Cargo Insurance

Whether you deal directly with a carrier or use an intermediary, be sure to question the amount of cargo insurance coverage they will be providing on the shipment. Don't make an assumption that full-coverage insurance is provided, as it almost never is. Many carriers offer minimal cargo coverage, typically pennies per pound, and intermediaries typically just pass along the carrier's coverage. In the event of a damage claim, you may find yourself without enough coverage and you mind yourself having to file a claim with the carrier directly without the assistance of the broker. Ask the broker about the procedure they have in place regarding freight loss or damage claims. Responsible carriers and intermediaries will always have additional insurance available for purchase; and they will have fast and easy ways to manage claims.

About 10 per cent of all freight shipments will experience some significant loss or damage. It is a common misconception that a freight rate includes full coverage insurance, when in fact a base freight rate typically includes only a bare minimum of cargo insurance. A shipper should always ask their carrier or intermediary what the insurance coverage is for every specific shipment. LTL shipments will often be insured for less than 25 percent pound, and TL shipments will often be insured for only slightly more than LTL shipments. Most good TL carriers have maximum cargo insurance of $100,000 for the entire load; but for a 40,000 load, that's only about $2.50 per pound.

Furthermore, cargo insurance only covers significant loss or damage to the cargo only. Carriers' insurance does not cover "consequential" damages like lost sales or downtime on a production line. Also, carrier insurance does not cover the cost of returning damaged cargo to the shipper. Again, cargo insurance is very low and very tightly defined; so package your shipment extremely well and be sure to clarify the specific insurance that will apply to your shipment.

Carriers and intermediaries do typically offer "additional insurance" though known insurance companies like Fireman's Fund. Rates vary widely depending on the item to be covered and the amount of additional insurance that the shipper would like to purchase.

Tips to Avoid Shipping Loss, Damage, and Claims

Unlike small parcel shipping via Fed EX or UPS, shipping freight has a much higher likelihood of damage. Trucking companies pack lots of different types of freight onto lots of different trailers using forklifts and other heavy equipment, creating a harsh and dirty environment for freight. Other shipments will be packed around and on top of your shipment; so all freight shipments should be packaged very carefully. All shipments should be palletized and wrapped in plastic, at a minimum. Most shipments should be fully crated in order to ensure a damage free delivery. Ask the carrier or intermediary for the specific packaging requirements for your shipment—then exceed them. Also, since shipments may be reloaded several times, it is important that the packaging has all of the shipper and consignee info clearly noted on at least two sides of the shipment. Filing claims with freight companies is a huge hassle and claims are almost always denied; so you want to do as much as possible to avoid freight claims.

Freight Shipping Summary

As a shipper, you should first be sure that you are using the best type of carrier for your type of shipment: use an LTL carrier for an LTL shipment, for example. While parcel carriers will accept LTL shipments, and LTL carriers will accept TL shipments, shippers will typically realize lower service at higher rates.

Once you have chosen the right kind of carrier, shop several carriers in order to find the best service and price. Be sure to ask for an "all-inclusive" quote that includes all surcharges and accessorial fees.

When you are ready to ship, over-package your freight and verify insurance coverage.

If you are not a freight shipping expert, try using a freight intermediary to help you find the best carrier, service, and price for your shipment. If you are shipping items sold on online marketplaces like eBay, you should seriously consider using the preferred freight carrier of that particular marketplace.

LESS THAN TRUCKLOAD

Less-Than-Truckload (LTL) shipping is the transportation of relatively small freight. The alternatives to LTL carriers are parcel carriers or full truckload carriers. Parcel carriers usually handle small packages and freight that can be broken down in to units less than 150 US pounds. Full truckload carriers move freight that is loaded into a semi trailer. Semi trailers are typically between 26 and 53 US feet and thereby require a substantial amount of freight to make such transportation economical.

Less than Truckload Carrier Operations versus Full Truckload Operations

Full Truckload

Full truckload carriers normally delivers a semi trailer to a shipper who will fill the shipment with freight for one destination. After the trailer is loaded the driver returns to the shipper to collect the required paperwork (i.e. Bill of lading, Invoice, Customs paperwork) and depart with trailer containing freight. In most cases the driver then proceeds directly to the consignee and delivers the freight him or herself. Occasionally, a driver will transfer the trailer to another driver who will drive the freight the rest of the way. Full Truckload (FTL) transit times are normally constrained by the drivers availability according to Hours of Service regulations and distance. It is normally accepted that Full Truckload drivers will transport freight at an average rate of 47 US miles per hour (including traffic jams or queues at intersections).

One advantage Full Truckload carriers have over Less than Truckload carriers is that the freight is never handled in route whereas an LTL shipment will typically be transported on several different trailers.

Less than Truckload

Less than truckload carriers typically have several drivers in a city where a shipper is located to collect freight from various shippers. Usually the same driver will visit the same shipper each time a shipment goes by a particular carrier. Once the driver has made several stops and has picked up enough freight to fill his trailer with either enough volume or weight, he returns to his terminal to have his trailer unloaded. The trailer is unloaded and the individual shipments are then weighed and rated for billing purposes. Next, the freight is then loaded onto an outbound trailer which will forward the freight to either a breakbulk or other terminal. Once the freight arrives at its next stop along its way it will be transferred to another trailer and forwarded to the terminal in its destination city where it will be transferred to the trailer that will deliver it to the consignee. A shipment may be handled four or more times by the carrier, not including the initial loading and unloading.

Transit times for LTL freight is much slower than for FTL. Transit times in LTL shipments are not exactly related to the direct distance from shipper to consingee. LTL transit times are solely dependent upon the makeup of the network of Terminals and Breakbulks that are operated by a carrier. For example, if a carrier offers a next day service region shipments ranging from 0 to approximately 500 miles will most likely be delivered at similar times during the next day.

The main advantage to using an LTL carrier is that a shipment may be delivered at a very small percentage of the cost if it had to be sent on a large trailer by itself. Also, LTL carriers typically offer guarantees whereas Full Truck Load carriers normally do not.

Integrating FTL and LTL Carriers for Shipper Cost Savings

Shippers with enough volume of LTL freight may choose to use a Full Truckload Carrier to move the freight directly to a break-bulk facility of an LTL carrier. For example, if a North Carolina shipper has a large quantity of shipments for Western US States such as CA, NV, OR, WA, and ID then the shipper can realize significant cost savings by having an FTL carrier, known as a Linehaul carrier, transport the freight to a breakbulk facility nearest the centre of such shipments in terms of the carriers network. In this case the shipper may choose to send the freight to a break-bulk in CA. The use of an FTL carrier to transport this freight is a cost savings because the freight will not have to be unloaded and reloaded as many times.

Less than Truckload Operations versus Parcel Carrier Operations

Parcel Carrier Operations

A parcel carrier traditionally only handles shipments weighing less than approximately 150 US Pounds. Parcel carriers typically still compete with LTL carriers by convincing shippers to break larger shipments down to smaller packages. Parcel carriers typically refer to multipiece shipments as "Hundredweight" shipments as the rating is based on 100 US Pounds. The Hundredweight rate is multiplied by the shipment's weight and then divided by 100 and then rounded up to the nearest hundred.

LTL Carrier Operation

LTL carriers prefer to handle shipments with the least amount of handling units possible. LTL carriers prefer a shipment of 1 pallet containing 100 boxes shrinkwrapped to form one piece than 100 individual pieces. This reduces handling costs and the risk of damage during transit. Typically the rates of LTL carriers per pound is less than the rate of parcel carriers.

Similarities

Both LTL carriers and parcel carriers are similar in the fact that they both use a network of hubs and terminals to deliver freight. Delivery times by both types of service providers are not directly dependent upon the distance between shipper and consingee. Also, using an LTL carrier is very similar to that of using a parcel carrier. The shipper often has a regular, if not daily, pickup schedule and can log onto the carriers homepage to schedule pickups, track shipments, print paperwork, and manage billing information.

Integrating LTL and Parcel Carrier for Shipper Cost Savings

If a shipper has a large number of parcels to distribute it may be able to save shipping costs by using LTL carriers to feed parcels to parcel carriers. If the shipper has a large number of parcels going to different destinations within one region then the shipper can load the parcels onto a pallet and have an LTL carrier transport the parcels to a parcel carrier's hub near the destinations.

An example of this is a shipper in NC that has 500 parcels destined for CA, 250 destined for NY, and 250 destined for IN. The shipper will segregate the parcels by their destination. All the Southern California shipments will be separated and loaded on a pallet that would be delivered to a parcel carriers hub in Los Angeles; The Northern California parcels will be loaded on a pallet for San Francisco; New York parcels loaded on a pallet for New York City; and the Indiana parcels will be loaded for Indianapolis.

The LTL carrier will pick up the skids containing these parcels and transport them to the appropriate hub of a parcel carrier. The parcel carrier will take the parcels off of the skid and inject them into the parcel distribution system and deliver them to their final destination.

Another name for this operation using both LTL and Parcel carriers is known as zone skipping. The LTL carrier is being used to skip several parcel zones as the costs of using a parcel carrier solely for long distance transportation of parcels is more costly per pound than an LTL carrier.

Many shippers prefer to not use such methods as they prefer to only contract with one service provider. Using an LTL carrier and a parcel carrier does add another point of failure for the shipper's operations.

Preparing Shipments for LTL Carriers

Since freight sent via LTL carriers must be handled several times during transit it must be packaged to withstand unintentional drops from dockworkers or forklifts. It is normally good practice to load freight onto pallets or package freight into crates. Cardboard boxes are normally acceptable as well.

Since freight sent via LTL carriers is subject to misrouting or misloading it is a good practice to put the Tracking number on each side of each piece of freight. If the Destination State and Zipcode are affixed to each side as well misloading is less likely to occur. Even though it is not required it is good practice to affix a relatively large label including four letter Carrier Code, Tracking Number, Destination Station, and Destination Zipcode of the shipment (i.e. ABFS123456789 GA 30301). The easier it is for dockworkers to identify an individual shipment the less likely it is to be put in the wrong place. If the only piece of identification is the tracking number the dockworker will have a harder time identifying the shipments pieces and as such the chances of freight being loaded onto the wrong trailer is greater thereby increasing the transit time and also increasing the chances of the shipment being lost.

Factors of LTL Operation

Factors Relating to Profit Margin

LTL shipping is a thin-margined business, so costs must be minimized. Two of the biggest costs for LTL carriers are fuel and labour. As many LTL carriers have unionized labour, labour costs are relatively fixed, so minimizing fuel usage is a significant goal. This translates to maximizing the utilization of every trailer for every mile driven—ideally, every trailer carrying freight would contain a maximum level of freight by both weight and volume. The weight and volume characteristics of a set of freight is referred to as "freight mix".

Density of Freight/Freight Mix

To achieve a good freight mix on average, one method employed by the industry is the use of a two-tiered transportation network involving a clique of large freight way-stations (called "breakbulks", for example), with smaller freight "terminals" fanning out from each breakbulk facility.

The philosophy behind the "breakbulk approach" is that by consolidating a large amount of freight from dispersed locations (i.e. from the connected terminals), a larger and more diverse pool of freight is available to choose from so as to achieve better freight mix for the long haul between breakbulks. For example, the freight coming from one terminal location may be relatively light and bulky, whereas the freight from another terminal location may tend to be much denser. Some freight may be irregular in shape. By consolidating the freight originating from multiple terminals in one location, there is a wider range of freight to choose from, so as to efficiently pack each trailer for the long inter-breakbulk journey.

In this terminal-breakbulk network, a typical shipment would first be picked-up from a customer location and dropped off at the local terminal. It would then be trucked a relatively short distance (a couple hundred miles, for example) to the terminal's associated breakbulk. From there, the shipment would be trucked a relatively long distance to the breakbulk associated with the destination terminal, and then finally trucked to the destination terminal, to be delivered to the customer. The continual goal in this network is, however, to minimize transfers of freight. Ideally, only one or even no break bulks are involved in the process.

Intermodal Transportation of LTL Freight

Not all LTL shipments travel by truck solely. LTL carriers rely on rail or air to forward some freight toward its destination. LTL carriers are normally able to deal with railroads more effectively than small shippers are able to as LTL carriers typically send a large volume of freight each and every day. LTL carriers are able to monitor railroad performance to ensure delivery of freight within the specified delivery window. An Intermodal freight transport shipment employs several methods of transporting goods from start to finish. For instance, one shipment will start out on the railroad, then be transferred to an ocean carrier, and end up on a truck before delivery.

Intermodal shipping is considered advantageous by some shippers because there is no handling of the freight when it changes from one carrier to the next. Pallets are used to consolidate many things into one easy-to-move container. Because handling is reduced, it also reduces damage and loss, increases security, and allows the items to be transported more quickly.

Examples of LTL Carriers

- YRC Worldwide Inc.
- Yellow Transportation.

CARGO AGENT

Significant Points

- Many jobs are entry level and do not require more than a high school diploma.
- Although cargo traffic is expected to grow faster than in the past, employment of cargo and freight agents will not keep pace because of technological advances.

Nature of the Work

Cargo and freight agents arrange for and track incoming and outgoing cargo and freight shipments in airline, train, or trucking terminals or on shipping docks. They expedite shipments by determining the route that shipments are to take and by preparing all necessary shipping documents. The agents take orders from customers and arrange for the pickup of freight or cargo for delivery to loading platforms. Cargo and freight agents may keep records of the cargo, such as its amount, type, weight, and dimensions. They keep a tally of missing items, record the condition of damaged items, and document any excess supplies.

Cargo and freight agents arrange cargo according to its destination. They also determine the shipping rates and other charges that can sometimes apply to the freight. For imported or exported freight, they verify that the proper customs paperwork is in order. Cargo and freight agents often track shipments electronically, using bar codes, and answer customers' inquiries on the status of their shipments.

Working Conditions

Cargo and freight agents work in a wide variety of businesses, institutions, and industries. Some work in warehouses, stockrooms, or shipping and receiving rooms that may not be temperature controlled. Others may spend time in cold storage rooms or outside on loading platforms, where they are exposed to the weather.

Most jobs for cargo and freight agents involve frequent standing, bending, walking, and stretching. Some lifting and carrying of smaller items also may be involved. Although automated devices have lessened the physical demands of this occupation, their use remains somewhat limited. The work still can be strenuous, even though mechanical material-handling equipment is employed to move heavy items.

The typical workweek is Monday through Friday; however, evening and weekend hours are common in some jobs and may be required in other jobs when large shipments are involved.

Employment

Cargo and freight agents held about 70,000 jobs in 2004. Most jobs were in transportation. Approximately 20 per cent worked in the air transportation industry and 8 per cent worked in the truck transportation industry. Couriers employed another 11 per cent. In addition, about 43 per cent worked for firms engaged in support activities for the transportation industry.

Training

Many jobs are entry level and do not require more than a high school diploma. Employers, however, prefer to hire those familiar with computers. Typing, filing, recordkeeping, and other clerical skills also are important.

Cargo and freight agents start out by checking items to be shipped and then attaching labels to them and making sure that the addresses are correct. Training in the use of automated equipment usually is done informally, on the job. As this occupation becomes more automated, however, workers may need longer periods of training in order to master the use of the equipment. Advancement opportunities for cargo and freight agents vary with the place of employment.

Other Qualifications (Advancement)

Job Outlook

Employment of cargo and freight agents is expected to decline through 2014. Although cargo traffic is expected to grow faster than in the past, employment of cargo and freight agents will not keep pace because of technological advances. For example, the increasing use of bar codes on cargo and freight allows agents and customers to track these shipments quickly over the Internet, rather than manually tracking their location. In addition, customs and insurance paperwork now can be completed over the Internet by customers, reducing the need for cargo and freight agents.

Despite these advances in technology that dampen job growth among cargo and freight agents, job openings will continue to arise due to increases in buying over the Internet, which will result in more shipments. Jobs also will open up because of the increasing importance of same-day delivery, which expands the role of agents. In addition, many job openings will be created to replace cargo and freight agents who leave the occupation.

Earnings

Median annual earnings of cargo and freight agents in May 2004 were $34,250. The middle 50 per cent earned between $25,720 and $43,250. The lowest 10 per cent earned less than $20,700, and the highest 10 per cent earned more than $54,480.

These workers usually receive the same benefits as most other workers. If uniforms are required, employers generally provide them or offer an allowance to purchase them.

Related Occupations

Cargo and freight agents plan and coordinate shipments of cargo by airlines, trains, and trucks. They also arrange freight pickup with customers. Others who do similar work are couriers and messengers; shipping, receiving, and traffic clerks; weighers, measurers, checkers, and samplers, recordkeeping; truck drivers and driver/sales workers; and Postal Service workers.

Types of Packers and Movers, Shipping, Forwarding and Clearing Agents

- Cargo and Shipping Agents.
- Clearing and Forwarding Agents.
- Courier, Parcel and Other Postal Services.
- Custom Agents and Consultants.
- Indenting Agents.
- Packers and Movers.
- Passport, Visa and Other Immigration Services.
- Transport Agents, Bulk Carriers and Transport Contractors.
- Warehouses, Warehousing Agents and Consultants.

2

Conceptual Study of Supply Chain, Performance and Logistics Management

COMPANY : AN INTRODUCTION

A *company* in the broadest sense is an aggregation of people who stay together for a common purpose. Such usage includes people assembled:

- For commercial or judical purposes, organized as a type of business organization. See company (law) or the term corporation which may have the same meaning, depending on the jurisdiction.
- For military purposes. See company (military unit).
- As the officers and crew, collectively, of a ship.
- As firefighters stationed in one location or even more specifically, firefighers associated with a single fire engine.

SUPPLY CHAIN

A fixed mobile, or transportable structure, including (*a*) all installed electrical and electronic wiring, cabling, and equipment and (*b*) all supporting structures, such as utility, ground network, and electrical supporting structures.

A Network-provided service to users or the network operating administration.

Types of Customer

Customers can be classified into two main groups—internal and external customers. An internal customer is someone who works for the organization, possibly in another department or another branch. External customers are essentially the general public.

A supply chain essentially has three main parts—the supply, manufacturing and distribution:

- The *supply* side concentrates on how, where from and when raw materials. *Materials* are inputs to production or manufacturing. They are often raw—that is unprocessed, but are sometimes processed before being used in more advanced production processes. In general technologically advanced societies, the materials are not finished consumer goods.

- *Manufacturing* converts these raw materials to finished products.
- *Distribution* ensures that these finished products reach the final customers through a network of distributors. In the ignition system of an internal combustion engine, the *distributor* is a device which routes the spark to the correct cylinder.

It consists of a rotating arm or *rotor* inside the distributor cap, on top of the distributor shaft. The rotor contacts the central high voltage cable from the coil via a spring loaded carbon brush. The rotor arm passes close to (but does not touch) the output contacts which connect via high tension cables to the spark plug of each cylinder. Within the distributor, the high voltage energy is able to jump the small gap from the rotor arm to the contact.

A warehouse is a commercial building for storage of goods. Warehouses are used by manufacturers, importers, exporters, wholesalers, transporters, customs, etc. They are usually large plain buildings in industrial parts of towns. They come equipped with loading docks to load and unload trucks; or sometimes are loaded directly from railways, airports, or seaports. They also often have cranes and forklifts for moving goods, which are usually placed on ISO standard pallets.

In commerce, a *retailer* buys goods or products in large quantities from manufacturers or importers, either directly or through a wholesaler, and then sells individual items or small quantities to the general public or end user customers, usually in a *shop*, also called *store*. Retailers are at the end of the supply chain. Marketers see retailing as part of their overall distribution strategy.

The chain can be said to start with the suppliers of your suppliers and ends with the customers of your customer.

Distribution is one of the four aspects of marketing. The other three parts of the marketing mix are product management, pricing, and promotion. Distribution deals with how to get the product or service to the customer. It must answer questions such as:

- What kind of distribution channel to use?
- Should the product be sold through a retailer?
- Should the product be distributed through wholesale?

Logistics: In military and business, *logistics* experts manage how and when to move resources to the places they are needed. In military science, maintaining ones supply lines while disrupting those of the enemy is a crucial, and some would say the most crucial element, of military strategy.

There are two fundamentally different forms of logistics. One optimizes a steady flow of material through a network of transportation links and storage nodes. The other coordinates a sequence of resources to carry out some project.

Marketing: Marketing is the craft of linking the producers (or potential producers) of a product or service with customers, both existing and potential. Some form of marketing arises naturally in all capitalist societies but is not limited to capitalist societies. Marketing techniques are also applied in politics, religion, personal affairs, and many other aspects of life.

Marketing methods are informed by many of the social sciences, particularly psychology, sociology, and economics. Marketing research underpins these activities. Through advertising, it is also related to many of the creative arts.

Manufacturing: Manufacturing is the transformation of raw materials into finished goods for sale, or intermediate processes involving the production or finishing of semi-manufactures. It is a large branch of industry and of secondary production. Some industries, like semiconductor and steel manufacturers use the term fabrication.

Although handicraft production has been with us for many millennia, modern-style manufacturing is generally regarded as beginning around 1780 with the British Industrial Revolution, spreading thereafter to Continental Europe and North America, and subsequently around the world.

Supply chain management (SCM) deals with the planning and execution issues involved in managing a supply chain.

The components of SCM are:

- Demand planning: forecasting.
- Demand collaboration: collaborative resolution process to determine consensus forecasts.
- Order promising: when can one promise a product to a customer taking account lead times and constraints.

Trade item: Any item (product or service) upon which there is a need to retrieve pre-defined information and that may be priced or ordered or invoiced at any point in any supply chain. It is a term used primarily by people in supply chain management and logistic engineering.

Transportation

- For the movement of people or objects, see transport.
- For the shipping of convicted criminals to penal colonies, see penal transportation.

SUPPLY CHAIN MANAGEMENT

Supply chain management (SCM) deals with the planning and execution issues involved in managing a supply chain. A supply chain is a network of facilities and distribution options that performs the functions of procurement of materials; transformation of these material into intermediate and finished products; and distribution of these finished products to customers. (*Source*: Ganeshan and Harrison—Introduction to Suppply Chain Management).

A supply chain essentially has three main parts—the supply, manufactureing and distribution:

- The *supply* side concentrates on how, where from and when raw materials are procured and supplied to manufacturing.
- *Manafacturing* converts these raw materials to finished products.
- *Distribution* ensures that these finished products reach the final customers through a network of distributors, warehouses and retailers.

The components of SCM are:

- *Demand planning*: forecasting.
- *Demand collaboration:* collaborative resolution process to determine consensus forecasts.
- *Strategic network optimization*: what plants and DC's should serve what markets for what products (monthly-yearly).
- *Production and distribution planning:* (Coordinate the actual production and distribution plans for a whole enterprise) (daily).
- *Production scheduling*: For a single location create a feasible production schedule (minute by minute).
- *Transportation planning*: For multiple supply, manufacturer, distributor and warehousing points in a network.
- *Tracking and measuring*: An ever increasing aspect of supply chain management designed to highlight potential against the plan and possible process improvements.
- *Plan of reduction of costs and management of the performance:* Diagnosis of the potential and the indicators, the organization and planification strategic, masters dysfunctions in real time, evaluation and accounting reporting, evaluation and reporting quality.

PERFORMANCE MANAGEMENT

Leverage Data, Identify Trends, Improve Performance, Maximize Profitability

Managing your enterprise effectively involves more than simply moving goods from place to place. Effective management requires accurate insight into every link of your supply chain—from source to consumption—to know how your suppliers, carriers, customers and workers are performing. It takes reliable, actionable information to help you evaluate processes and identify inefficiencies.

Leverage KPIs to Make Informed, Strategic Decisions

Manhattan Associates' Performance Management solutions support an Integrated Logistics Solutions™ platform by providing a dashboard that monitors and scores supply chain performance—within and beyond the four walls. The measurement and analysis capabilities of performance management solutions will enable you to track trends based on key performance indicators (KPIs) and make informed, strategic decisions to optimize your supply chain performance—to take your enterprise to new levels of productivity and profitability.

Performance management solutions include:

- Event Management
- Analysis
- Reporting.

Monitor Performance at a Glance

Our unique scorecard functionality provides a highly-effective method of evaluating and improving performance. Create KPIs using performance management data and measure them against your specific company goals. KPIs can be weighted based on company-defined importance and combined into role-specific and enterprise-wide scorecards. Calculate the performance index to get a high-level look at performance. To keep senior management and key decision makers informed, take advantage of the solution's subscriber capability to automatically distribute alerts on a pre-determined schedule.

Better Measurement, Greater Visibility

The integration of performance management solutions simplifies data sharing and provides a single view of your entire enterprise. Real-time graphical displays present a clear picture of metrics and KPIs that can impact your bottom line. Flexible reporting ensures delivery of results in a user-friendly format. And event management functionality enables rapid problem resolution by alerting users to exceptions—before they have a chance to impact your operations.

With performance management, you can achieve company goals by focusing your entire organization on its most critical areas. Increase employee efficiency by directing more attention to the issues that impact performance. Strengthen relationships with your trading partners through proactively identifying and resolving problem areas. And reduce time and costs associated with collecting, organizing and communicating KPIs.

A Powerful Integrated Yet Modular Approach

Optimize your supply chain performance with performance management solutions or streamline your entire logistics network by implementing Integrated Logistics Solutions™ for source-to-consumption supply chain execution and optimization. This comprehensive set of solutions provides a new perspective on the supply chain by optimizing supply chain processes and viewing them as a single, synchronized business process that can boost your overall corporate performance.

REPORTING

Clear, Concise Reporting for Intelligent Decision-Making

Manhattan Associates' *Reporting* solution captures real-time information on the vital aspects of your fulfillment operation and presents it in a clear and concise format. A comprehensive, highly-configurable reporting tool, our Reporting solution monitors supply chain activities at a granular level in real-time to eliminate guesswork and enable tactical decision-making.

Real-time Access to Vital Business Information

The Reporting solution presents vital business information in a concise, user-friendly format enabling users to easily monitor changes in operations—down to the most detailed level. With more than 30 standard report options, you have the information you need right at your fingertips. Custom reports can also be easily created, minimizing IT involvement and costs.

Schedule reports to be posted, printed or e-mailed on a scheduled basis, so critical business information is disseminated directly to those who need it. Managers can quickly access information about activities within the warehouse, including the number of orders to be picked by the end of a shift, outstanding cycle count tasks and how many cartons have been packed and are waiting to ship. Answer questions regarding profitability and transportation, such as the amount of revenue generated by an individual SKU, shipping costs by state, revenue shipped or the number of returns by customer.

Minimal Effort Maximum Value

As a Web-based tool, our Analysis solution requires minimal installation effort. Because implementation is typically completed within a matter of days, you will realize a return on investment almost immediately—to deliver substantial value across your enterprise and extended enterprise.

LOGISTICS PLANNING AND EXECUTION

- Serve as your dedicated conference specialist... your single source for all your conference needs
- Serve as liaison between all service providers and your planning committee
- Provide advance scheduling and coordination of meeting facilities, audiovisual equipment, hotel accommodations, food services, travel/transportation, parking, and recreational activities/tours
- Provide on site management and trouble-shooting
- Arrange for services to meet the needs of those with disabilities
- Provide and arrange for simultaneous translation services
- Arrange for academic credit or continuing education units (CEUs)

- Design and produce professional programme signs
- Prepare and organize handout materials
- Produce custom certificates of programme completion
- Provide for floral and table decorations for special events
- Arrange and provide for security services
- Arrange for VIP services

REVERSE LOGISTICS MANAGEMENT

Streamline Returns, Increase Visibility and Grow Profits

Your reverse supply chain is full of potential opportunities—enhanced customer service, higher net asset recovery, maximized call centre resources, streamlined operations, improved bottom line—all you need is the right solution. Manhattan Associates' *Reverse Logistics Management* solution manages the entire returns process, turning your reverse supply chain into a source of profit and customer satisfaction.

Reverse Logistics Management solution uses a sophisticated workflow engine to automate every step of the return and disposition process—minimizing unauthorized returns, transportation costs and call center administrative burdens. This Web-based solution ensures that critical product and shipping information is tracked, stored, referenced and reported. With this valuable information, you can take better care of your customers throughout the returns process by giving them the information and the credit they deserve.

Manage Your Supply Chain in Reverse

Gain control over which products are accepted for return and how they are sent back using rules-based decision capabilities. A centralized repository for return merchandize authorizations (RMAs) facilitates invoice matching so proper credit is given for returned goods.

Reverse Logistics Management determines the optimal carrier for each return, ensuring the package arrives at the correct processing location to avoid double handling charges. Once the product is picked up, you receive notification when products move from receiving to inspection to pre-disposition—even when goods are in process or en route.

An Integrated Yet Modular Approach

Improved asset recovery is enabled by integration between our Reverse Logistics Management and Warehouse Management solutions. Your distribution centre knows exactly what returned products to expect, can allocate resources accordingly and get that product where it belongs—whether that's back on the shelf for resale or to scrap inventory for liquidation. This visibility improves use of valuable warehouse space and decreases inventory-holding costs.

INTEGRATED PLANNING SOLUTIONS

A New Outlook on Supply Chain Solutions

Manhattan Associates provides solutions to help you manage your entire supply chain more efficiently.

From Integrated Planning Solutions™ to Integrated Logistics Solutions™—Manhattan Associates provides complete supply chain solutions so you can drive down inventory levels, reduce costs and increase customer service.

Connecting Every Link in the Supply Chain

Developed for companies of every size and across key industries, Manhattan Associates' Supply Chain Solutions can be implemented as an integrated whole for maximum value or may be deployed as individual point solutions.

Either way, our best-of-value solutions can help you reduce costs and target opportunities for continuous improvement.

By making the right decisions in advance, you can ensure efficiency throughout your supply chain. These solutions enable optimal supply chain planning through the development of strategic and tactical plans.

Each of these solutions help you lower costs and build revenue by knowing how much product to order and when you need it.

Integrated Planning Solutions include:

- Advanced Planning
- Financial and Item Planning
- Catalogue Planning
- Web Planning
- Promotion Planning
- Demand Forecasting
- Promotion Forecasting
- Replenishment
- Vendor Managed Inventory.

Integrated Logistics Solutions

By knowing where your goods are at any location in the world, you can respond to the demands of your customers quickly and effectively.

These supply chain execution solutions allow you to balance supply and demand and ensure the timely and profitable movement of goods from demand to consumption.

Integrated Logistics Solutions include:

- Distributed Order Management
- Warehouse Management

- Slotting Optimization
- Labour Management
- Yard Management
- Transportation Management
- Trading Partner Management
- Reverse Logistics Management
- RFID Solutions

Business Process Platform

Manhattan Associates' Logistics Event Management Architecture™ (LEMA) provides a business process platform that manages the flow of data between Manhattan Associates' solutions and facilitates integration and interoperability with other solutions.

This advanced engine gathers and coordinates data and alerts you to any problems if inconsistencies occur.

Logistics Event Management Architecture includes:

- Enterprise Integration Management
- Enterprise Data Management
- Advanced Exception Management.

Manhattan Associates' Supply Chain Solutions are further supported by services that help you assess, generate and measure the return on your investment. Whether you require a quick implementation, 24-hour customer support, associated hardware or hands-on training courses—our service offerings dramatically increase the value of our solutions and impact throughout your organization.

DISTRIBUTED ORDER MANAGEMENT

Supply and Demand: Balance Your Supply Chain

In a customer-driven supply chain, globalization, outsourcing and the increasing number of order channels are impacting the way you match demand to inventory—so how do you balance the two? Manhattan Associates' Distributed Order Management solution dramatically improves order fill rates while reducing inventory and operational costs.

This powerful distributed order management solution coordinates the entire order fulfillment cycle. In real time, you can experience seamless customer order fulfillment through inventory visibility, sourcing, allocation and delivery scheduling at each stage of the fulfillment process and across your entire supply chain.

Adapting quickly to market conditions is key to success. Manhattan Associates' distributed order management solution:

- Gives you precise understanding of product demand and backlog in each of your markets.

- Provides "intelligent" inventory deployment information.
- Has configurable routing, sourcing and allocation rules.
- Replaces the need for unwieldy spreadsheets.
- Immediately lets you know what inventory you need to procure, source or manufacture.
- Considers your entire multi-stage distributed supply chain network, enabling true ATP and CTP responses.

Manage Multiple Order Fulfillment Channels

Customer demand is constantly changing, products are flowing from factories to distribution centres around the world, inventory availability is fluctuating by the hour and customer orders are strewn across divisions and order channels. We can help you adapt to these changes by providing a single view into customer orders and supply. With Manhattan Associates' Distributed Order Management solution, you can have complete control over orders, suppliers and worldwide trading partners while gaining complete visibility into your inventory network.

Dynamic Sourcing and Allocation

With our Distributed Order Management solution, you know what you have in stock, what has been committed and what is scheduled to arrive at your warehouse. Using configurable rules, our solution aggregates orders as they are placed, considers your global inventory, including in-transit shipments and purchase orders and then optimally matches demand to the supply within or outside your enterprise. This dynamic sourcing capability makes it possible to improve order execution speed, accuracy, fill rate and ultimately customer service.

Manhattan Associates' Distributed Order Management solution is built on a standards-based, pure Java (J2EE) platform. The solution, which works warehouse and transportation planning and execution systems for fulfillment, also integrates with your existing ERP (Enterprise Resource Planning) and supply chain execution software.

An Integrated Yet Modular Approach

The impact of Manhattan Associates' Distributed Order Management solution is maximized when used with our Warehouse Management and Transportation Management solutions to streamline overall distribution centre and transportation processes. The result is a dramatic improvement in customer service levels that harnesses the benefits of operating a global and distributed supply chain. You can take a modular approach to implementation to address specific pains or opportunities within your enterprise. Our solution seamlessly integrates with Manhattan Associates' Integrated Logistics Solutions™ as well as your existing business systems so you can build out your supply chain execution and optimization strategy as your company's needs evolve.

WAREHOUSE MANAGEMENT

Improve Performance at Every Stage of the Fulfillment Process

Your warehouse plays a key part in ensuring that your company meets its productivity goals. With our Warehouse Management solution, you can move goods and information through your warehouse at maximum speed. And, with our Billing Management solution, your warehouse can become more profitable by eliminating hidden costs that can add up over time.

Warehouse Management enhances inventory management by decreasing inventory levels, improving order fulfillment and reducing order cycle time. Designed to control all of your warehouse activities, this powerful solution allows you to track every unit down to the lowest level of detail—country of origin, lot number, serial number and date code. Warehouse Management:

- Improves warehouse facility layout
- Increases inventory accuracy
- Increases order fulfillment and accuracy
- Calculates item velocity to ensure inventory is optimally located
- Provides picking, packing and replenishment tools
- Increases billing accuracy and boosts profitability
- Identifies hidden costs of doing business.

LABOUR MANAGEMENT

Increase Productivity, Not Headcount

Your employees are your company's greatest resource—they are also its most expensive. For most distribution centres, labour represents 65 per cent of costs, so leveraging your workforce will maximize productivity and your bottom line. But with so many variables to consider—shifts in demand, types of equipment, location of products, tasks performed—accurately assessing and maximizing workforce performance can be complicated.

Optimize Your Workforce

Manhattan Associates' Labour Management solution offers an advanced approach to resource allocation to help you realize the full potential of your workforce. This comprehensive and flexible solution can be configured to track all warehouse activities, providing objective performance monitoring, as well as analysis and reporting of labour activity. With accurate data, you can better allocate resources to increase productivity—not headcount—and reduce labour costs.

Leverage the Power of Integration

Maximize your warehouse operations with Manhattan Associates' Integrated Warehouse

Management solution—Warehouse Management, Labour Management, Slotting Optimization, Load Management, Billing Management and Performance Management. Or streamline your entire supply chain by implementing our Integrated Logistics Solution™ for source-to-consumption execution and optimization.

SLOTTING OPTIMIZATION

Improve Workforce Efficiency through Optimal Facility Layout

To achieve optimal productivity in your warehouse, products need to be placed strategically. Manhattan Associates' Slotting Optimization solution increases workforce efficiency, shortens order fulfillment cycles and minimizes damage by determining the best place for inventory in your warehouse.

Before you actually slot goods, our Slotting Optimization solution calculates ROI of the new position to ensure that the time and labour you invest pays off. Using a genetic algorithm, the solution considers millions of move combinations against user configured strategies to determine the optimal layout.

Once your pickline is at peak productivity, the daily maintenance feature keeps it that way—regardless of how your inventory changes from day to day or month to month. Slotting optimization:

- Determines the best location for every product in your facility
- Organizes your facility to decrease bottlenecks and product damage
- Adjusts slotting criteria as products, locations and demand change
- Prevents worker fatigue and accidents
- Maintains peak productivity of your pick line
- Integrates with Labour Management for optimal cost-efficiency.

LOAD MANAGEMENT

Schedule Efficiently, Maximize Yard Capacity and Turn Loads Quickly

Effectively managing the yard is a challenge. With Hours of Service in the U.S., the Working Time Directive in the EU and other worldwide regulations, carriers today have less tolerance for costly delays. Carriers need on-time reliability—to know their scheduled slot is available when they arrive. And you need real-time visibility—to know what's on which truck and where it is located in your yard. That is why it is critical that your shipping and receiving operation is timely, reliable and synchronized—from dock to door.

Up-to-the-Minute Information for Proactive Yard Management

With Manhattan Associates' Load Management solution, you can generate an efficient plan for yard and dock door management while addressing the complex requirements associated with shipping and receiving. With appointment scheduling, carrier communications and coordinated yard management, you can plan, execute, track and audit all incoming and outgoing loads. Identify and expedite critical loads, such as those at detention risk or needed to replenish out-of-stocks. Comprehensive yard management capabilities—complete with an up-to-the-minute graphical display of yard capacity—provide inbound and outbound visibility and security, while enabling maximum productivity and throughput.

Your carriers and suppliers can schedule appointments or requests easily using electronic data interchange (EDI) or a Web interface so you can turn loads more quickly. Task and movement algorithms optimize product flow to improve utilization of assets and yard capacity. Our solution also sends alert notifications that enable you to proactively correct issues before they cause delays.

Leverage the Power of Integration

Maximize your warehouse operations with Manhattan Associates' integrated Warehouse Management solutions— Warehouse Management, Labour Management, Slotting Optimization, Load Management, Billing Management and Performance Management. Or streamline your entire supply chain by implementing our Integrated Logistics Solutions ™ for source-to-consumption execution and optimization.

BILLING MANAGEMENT

Improve Performance at Every Stage of the Fulfillment Process

With Manhattan Associates' Billing Management solution, you can identify hidden operational costs and boost profitability. This dynamic solution allows you to track all inventory handling, storage fulfillment and transportation activities by business unit or client. If you are a logistics service provider, this tool can help you improve billing accuracy and service, preview invoices and ensure the appropriate discounts are taken into account on a client-by-client basis. Also, Billing Management audits charges and makes adjustments prior to final invoicing.

Pulling real-time data from warehouse management and transportation management systems, Billing Management uses rules-based logic to evaluate transactions and create billing records so you can easily track and assign charges to virtually any warehouse event—giving you a clear understanding of your cost drivers and protecting your profitability.

- Provides activity-based billing
- Increases billing accuracy and boosts profitability
- Tracks all inventory handling, storage and fulfillment activities by unit or client
- Affixes charges to all internal or client-driven activities
- Applies billing rules at the client level.

TRANSPORTATION MANAGEMENT

Running an efficient transportation network depends on many variables of product delivery—including speed, accuracy and cost. Manhattan Associates' Transportation Management solutions enable you to automate, standardize and optimize critical processes—streamlining planning and execution and substantially reducing procurement time and associated transportation costs.

Our Transportation Management solutions can be leveraged on demand or as licensed solutions and offer comprehensive functionality covering the entire spectrum of processes related to your global intra-enterprise transportation network.

- Transportation Procurement
- Transportation Planning and Execution
- Load Management
- Performance Management.

Control Costs, Grow Margins and Improve Customer Service

Transportation Management bridges the gap between planning and execution for efficient day-to-day operations. This solution for transportation optimization enables manufacturers, retailers and logistics service providers to maximize supply chain efficiency and strengthen the bottom line. As a result, both shippers and carriers benefit from easier management of bids, the ability to quickly adapt to changes, an increase in on-time deliveries, a reduction in out-of-route miles and better visibility into the transportation network—including operations within the yard.

An Integrated Yet Modular Approach

Manage your transportation network with Manhattan Associates' Integrated Transportation Management solutions—Transportation Procurement, Transportation Planning and Execution and Load Management. Or, target specific operational opportunities through a modular approach. Either way, you will benefit from improved operations and seamless integration with other Manhattan Associates solutions or with your existing legacy or back-office systems. Streamline your entire supply chain by implementing our Integrated Logistics Solutions™ for source-to-consumption execution and optimization.

TRANSPORTATION PROCUREMENT

Distribute, Receive and Analyze Bids—Entirely Online

Excessive transportation costs, capacity constraints, bid refusals and carrier unreliability can become obstacles to executing your transportation strategy and achieving profitability. Manhattan Associates' Transportation Procurement solution enables a reliable, financially astute carrier procurement process—providing a firm foundation for a profitable transportation strategy.

With our Transportation Procurement solution, you can automate and standardize your entire bid process to identify and secure the most cost-efficient transportation providers for each lane within your worldwide network and across all transportation modes—ocean, air, rail, and road.

Reliable Capacity, On-time Deliveries, Reduced Time, Lower Costs

Our Web-native Transportation Procurement solution is solely focused on transportation contract sourcing and goes well beyond pricing—taking into account both your business priorities and your carriers' capabilities. Intelligent optimization functionality models all of your critical business factors—from freight variability and seasonal surges, to equipment requirements, carrier rates and service level rankings. Real-time data and efficient processes will enable you to optimize the way you project, procure and perform transportation services—resulting in a carefully engineered avenue for connecting point to point.

Leverage the Power of Integration

Manage your transportation network with Manhattan Associates' Integrated Transportation Management solutions—Transportation Procurement, Transportation Planning and Execution and Load Management. Or, target specific operational opportunities through a modular approach. Either way, you will benefit from improved operations and seamless integration with other Manhattan Associates solutions or with your existing legacy or back-office systems. Streamline your entire supply chain by implementing our Integrated Logistics Solutions™ for source-to-consumption execution and optimization.

TRANSPORTATION PLANNING AND EXECUTION

Optimize Day-to-Day Efficiency and Productivity

Moving goods in the global transportation network is complex, dynamic and often unpredictable. Businesses must be able to adapt quickly and cost-effectively to unforeseen changes in their shipping networks. Manhattan Associates' Transportation Planning and Execution solution enables you to formulate a strategic transportation plan to dynamically optimize efficiency and productivity of your transportation network, no matter how large or complex it may be. You can make the best possible trade-off between quality, and cost and quickly secure capacity across multiple transportation modes—to get goods into your customers' hands faster.

Best Carrier, Best Route, Best Plan

As a Web-native solution, Transportation Planning and Execution allows you to easily bridge the gap between planning and execution with real-time global visibility into shipping activities. Automatic event management alerts allow you to quickly identify delays or changes in your transportation network flows and respond proactively to avert potential delivery problems. Our solution also supports seamless communications with trading partners so you can better synchronize operations for maximum efficiency.

Leverage the Power of Integration

Manage your transportation network with Manhattan Associates' Integrated Transportation Management solutions—Transportation Procurement, Transportation Planning and Execution and Load Management. Or, target specific operational opportunities through a modular approach. Either way, you will benefit from improved operations and seamless integration with other Manhattan Associates solutions or with your existing legacy or back-office systems. Streamline your entire supply chain by implementing our Integrated Logistics Solutions™ for source-to-consumption execution and optimization.

CARRIER MANAGEMENT

In the transportation industry fast lane, the needs of your fleet are constantly changing based on customer demands, fluctuating fuel prices and regulatory requirements. Manhattan Associates' Carrier Management solutions can help you overcome the challenges in your transportation network—enabling you to maximize asset utilization and drive profits without compromising efficiency and quality. On any given day, there are more than 125,000 power units on the road being optimized by our solutions.

Designed for motor carriers, our Driver&Load®, Drop&Swap®, Fuel&Route®, Profit Analyzer and Load Analyzer solutions facilitate optimal driver-to-load assignments and en route swapping, generate profit analysis reports and present the most favourable fuel and route plans—putting carriers in the driver's seat of a competitive marketplace.

Increase Control, Profitability and Customer Satisfaction

Driver & Load will enable you to fully utilize your transportation assets by considering your entire network—beyond region-based decision-making—and optimally matching a specific driver to the best possible load combinations. These driver-to-load assignments are continually updated as the Driver&Load solution evaluates real-time driver positions and incoming requests for capacity. This translates into better customer service, reduced driver turnover and improved bottom line performance.

Drop & Swap ensures the unexpected doesn't impact your service with real-time en-route swapping optimization. Drop&Swap considers all potential drivers and loads—whether already dispatched or still available—and evaluates each scenario. Once an optimal swap is determined, the driver is informed and a new ETA is automatically recalculated for each load. Built-in ETA monitoring allows you to monitor your fleet 24/7 and receive alerts of impending service failures and recommended swaps—before they occur. With Drop&Swap, you can avoid late pick-ups and deliveries, intercept potential failures and meet last-minute customer demands while balancing driver and equipment capacity requirements.

Load Analyzer can help globally balance your transportation network and ensure customer satisfaction by enabling you to intelligently respond to load requests, proactively solicit freight in markets with surplus capacity and optimally position equipment to enhance not only revenue, but also profit. Reduce deadhead miles and dwell time. With Load Analyzer's demand forecasting, optimization and commitment management capabilities, you can maintain network balance, improve decision-making, enhance service and drive profit margins.

Profit Analyzer will help you assess the long-term value of each lane and shipper in your network. Proprietary mathematical algorithms enable activity-based costing, reporting, mapping and data-mining. The Profit Analyzer solution also uses regional metrics to depict the relative value of lanes and customer lanes within your network. These areas are calculated along with regional value, lane value, customer-lane value and opportunity costs. Built-in scorecards provide a report customized for your desired metrics. The Network Dashboard offers easy access to profit analysis metrics from any Web browser—run multiple scenarios with profit per cent options to select the best possible outcome. The Bid Response component provides a standardized, universal process for analyzing and responding to shippers' complex bid requests. This information can be used to set lane capacities or adjust bid rates in order to achieve network balance.

Fuel & Route optimizes routing and fuel recommendations—while balancing driver requests and preferences—reducing out-of-route miles and lowering overall fuel-related costs. The solution takes into account both fixed and variable costs and also factors in carrier- and driver-specific criteria. After analyzing this data in conjunction with route information and real toll costs from ALK's PC*Miller®—and daily fuel prices from your existing fuel network provider—the Fuel&Route solution determines the optimal fuel and detailed routing plan for each dispatch to meet the individual needs of every driver.

TRADING PARTNER MANAGEMENT

Synchronize Processes with Your Business Partners

Each day, you deal with trading partners that can be miles away—in different time zones and even on other continents, speaking different languages and with varying business practices. How can you maintain control of information, products and shipments in such a vast and disjointed supply chain?

Manhattan Associates' Trading Partner Management solution connects you with your business partners so you can improve the movement of goods through your facilities and throughout the entire supply chain.

Trading Partner Management includes:

- Supplier Enablement

- Logistics Hub Management
- Carrier Enablement
- Customer/Store Enablement.

With Trading Partner Management, your partners can be anywhere in the world using any type of technology and still exchange essential business documents through a Web browser or direct integration with back-end systems. Data is converted into usable information, so you can ensure your products reach their destinations accurately and on time. Trading Partner Management:

- Synchronizes key business processes
- Enables the exchange of critical business information in real time
- Increases inventory and order accuracy levels
- Allows quick response to supply chain events
- Improves on-time delivery percentages
- Speeds time-to-market
- Enhances in-stock positions and profitability.

Supplier Enablement

Extend Supply Chain Capabilities to Your Suppliers

Moving goods through the supply chain can be complex. You need tight integration with vendors to enable real-time communication and synchronize business processes.

With Supplier Enablement—a component of Manhattan Associates' Trading Partner Management solution—you can extend supply chain execution capabilities to your suppliers. With stronger collaboration, you can speed time to market, reduce errors, increase inventory turns and lower costs.

Supplier Enablement makes it possible to manage the entire lifecycle of supplier POs. With electronic integration, your suppliers always have the most current documentation. Suppliers can electronically generate and send ASNs, providing accurate information about the content of inbound shipments. Manufacturers and other suppliers can use this tool to print compliant bar coded shipping labels, retail item tickets and shipping documentation via the Web. Supplier Enablement:

- Extends execution capabilities to suppliers
- Manages routing and updates of supplier POs electronically
- Enables suppliers to generate ASNs and print compliant bar coded shipping labels, retail item tickets and shipping documentation
- Streamlines receiving by supporting partner-direct programmes and cross docking.

Logistics Hub Management

Get Visibility into Your Hubs and Logistics Service Providers

Logistics hubs support shipment consolidation from multiple suppliers and manage the flow of goods to distribution centres, customers and stores. Yet they often don't have automation systems to give them visibility into receipts and shipments.

Logistics Hub Management—a component of Manhattan Associates' Trading Partner Management solution—gives you visibility into the activities of your hubs and third-party logistics providers.

Hubs can manage inbound and outbound ASNs electronically and support partner-direct shipping programmes. When goods are shipped directly to stores and customers—yet fully managed and tracked—your operations can be streamlined.

With just an Internet connection, hubs get real-time visibility into orders, shipments and inventory flowing through their facilities—anywhere in the world. Key inbound and outbound processes can be automated, resulting in productivity gains in your distribution network and throughout the entire supply chain. Logistics Hub Management:

- Provides visibility into hubs, logistics service providers and consolidators
- Enables hubs to manage inbound and outbound ASNs electronically
- Supports partner-direct shipping programmes
- Provides information sharing via the Web
- Improves yard management and appointment setting capabilities.

Carrier Enablement

Improve On-Time Delivery and Customer Service

Keeping track of goods in transit is often easier said than done. Businesses can lose sight of shipments when they are on the road, in the air or crossing the sea—resulting in limited control over delays and reduced profit margins.

Carrier Enablement—a component of Manhattan Associates' Trading Partner Management solution—can give you visibility into inventory that is en-route, improving on-time delivery and customer service.

With Carrier Enablement, you will get real-time visibility into inventory in transit. Whether it is a small carrier with limited technology or a large carrier with advanced systems. Carrier Enablement can provide shipment status via an online browser screen. With real-time shipment status, you can reduce safety stock and alert users when shipments are delayed.

When integrated with Manhattan Associates' Transportation Planning and Execution solution, Carrier Enablement enables comprehensive business process management. It:

- Allows shipment status to be updated online.

- Provides visibility into domestic and international shipments.
- Facilitates data via a Web browser or integrates with carriers' standard electronic data interchange (EDI) transactions.
- Alerts users immediately to delayed shipments for proactive resolution.

Customer / Store Enablement

Enable Your Customers and Stores to Manage their Orders Online

Whether you sell to business partners, corporate-owned stores or consumers, providing first-rate service is what keeps you in business.

Customer/Store Enablement—a component of Manhattan Associates' Trading Partner Management solution—gives your customers and stores the information and control they need to place, update, track and confirm orders online. This eliminates service issues so you can ensure your customers have a positive experience—and keep coming back.

Orders can be placed electronically through Customer / Store Enablement and flow directly into back-end systems. Your customers will have controlled access to order status and can confirm goods received, providing proof of delivery and feedback on the quality of service provided. Invoicing is based on actual customer receipts. This information can then be used to measure fill rates, order cycle time and on-time percentages against key performance indicators (KPIs).

- Enables stores to enter and update POs and requisitions online.
- Provides customers with order status online.
- Enhances stock position, merchandize plans and customized promotions for buyers.

3

Air Cargo Management: A Brief Overview

CARGO AIRLINE

Cargo airlines (or airfreight carriers, and derivatives of these names) are airlines dedicated to the transport of cargo. Some cargo airlines are divisions or subsidiaries of larger passenger airlines.

Aircraft Used

Larger cargo airlines tend to use new or recently built aircraft to carry their freight, but many use older aircraft, like the Boeing 707, Boeing 727, Douglas DC-8, Ilyushin Il-76. Examples of the 60-year-old Douglas DC-3 are still flying around the world carrying cargo (as well as passengers). Short range turboprop airliners such as the Fokker Friendship and British Aerospace ATP are now being modified to accept standard air freight pallets to extend their working lives. This normally involves the replacement of glazed windows with opaque panels, the strengthening of the cabin floor and insertion of a broad top-hinged door in one side of the fuselage. A number of cargo airlines carry a few passengers from time to time on their flights, and UPS once unsuccessfully tried a passenger charter airline division.

Notable Cargo Airlines

All-cargo

- ABX Air
- Airnet Express
- Air Hong Kong
- American International Airways/Kalitta
- Atlas Air
- Burlington Air Express
- Cargo 360
- Cargojet Airways
- Cargolux
- Challenger Air Cargo

- DAS Air Cargo
- DHL Aviation
- Emerald Air
- Emery Worldwide
- Emirates Sky Cargo
- FedEx
- Fine Air
- Flying Tiger Line
- Gemini Air Cargo
- Heavylift Cargo Airlines
- Kalitta Air
- Kelowna Flightcraft (on behalf of Purolator)
- Martinair
- National Air Cargo
- Polar Air Cargo
- Seaboard World Airlines
- TNT
- Tol Air
- UPS
- Volga-Dnepr

All-cargo Subsidiary

- Aeromexpress
- Thai Airways Cargo
- Air France Cargo
- American Airlines Cargo
- Avianca Cargo
- British Airways World Cargo
- Delta Cargo-Delta operated hercules airplanes on cargo only routes during the 1970's
- Emirates SkyCargo
- KLM Cargo
- LAN Cargo
- Lufthansa Cargo
- Malaysia Airlines Kargo
- Nippon Cargo Airlines (NCA, an associate of ANA)
- Northwest Cargo
- Pan Am Cargo
- SAS Cargo Group
- Singapore Airlines Cargo
- Qatar Airways Cargo

Non-separate entity

- Cathay Pacific
- China Airlines

World's Largest Freight Carriers by Scheduled Freight Tonne-kilometres Flown

2004 Total Scheduled Freight Tonne-kilometres Flown

1. Federal Express 14.579 million
2. Korean Air 8.264 million
3. Lufthansa Cargo 8.040 million
4. United Parcel Service 7.353 million
5. Singapore Airlines Cargo 7.143 million
6. Cathay Pacific 5.876 million
7. China Airlines 5.642 million
8. Eva Airways 5.477 million
9. Air France 5.388 million
10. Japan Airlines 4.924 million

2004 International Scheduled Freight Tonne-kilometres Flown

1. Korean Air 8.164 million
2. Lufthansa Cargo 8.028 million
3. Singapore Airlines Cargo 7.143 million
4. Cathay Pacific 5.876 million
5. China Airlines 5.642 million
6. Federal Express 5.595 million
7. Eva Airways 5.477 million
8. Air France 5.384 million
9. British Airways 4.771 million
10. Cargolux 4.670 million

2004 Domestic Scheduled Freight Tonne-kilometres Flown

1. Federal Express 8.984 million
2. United Parcel Service 4.260 million
3. Northwest Airlines 0.949 million
4. China Southern Airlines 0.860 million
5. American Airlines 0.576 million
6. Delta Air Lines 0.557 million
7. Air China 0.531 million
8. United Airlines 0.525 million
9. Cargojet Airways 0.517 million
10. China Eastern Airlines 0.458 million

INTERNATIONAL AIR TRANSPORT ASSOCIATION (IATA)

The IATA that has emerged since 1979 has put an increasing share of its resources into Trade Association activities.

At the same time, IATA has changed the basis of its funding. Much of the Association's funding requirements are through the marketing of its products and services to Member airlines, other airlines and others in the travel, transport and tourism industry. This has given the Members greater "a la carte" choice of what to buy from the Association and it gives IATA greater flexibility in the way it approaches its tasks.

In many ways, those tasks remain the same as in 1945, or even in 1919. But IATA gave them new relevance and focus by re-defining its mission and goals in 1994.

Taking account of its present size and average annual world growth rates in the range of 5-6 per cent—typically, twice the rate of general economic growth—air transport has a dynamism undiminished from its pioneering days. IATA's role in it remains central.

The market for air transport has changed beyond recognition during the history of the modern IATA. The industry continues to change and IATA is adapting to meet the new needs. However, one thing has not changed—the necessity to provide service. IATA helps the airlines to achieve this objective as they meet the new demands of the 21st century. In large measure, the airlines have created a modern, interdependent world over the past 50 years. IATA is working to ensure that the world's most exciting industry meets its greatest possible potential.

IATA—The International Air Transport Association—was founded in Havana, Cuba, in April 1945. It is the prime vehicle for inter-airline cooperation in promoting safe, reliable, secure and economical air services—for the benefit of the world's consumers. The international scheduled air transport industry is now more than 100 times larger than it was in 1945. Few industries can match the dynamism of that growth, which would have been much less spectacular without the standards, practices and procedures developed within IATA. At its founding, IATA had 57 Members from 31 nations, mostly in Europe and North America. Today it has over 270 Members from more than 140 nations in every part of the globe. The modern IATA is the successor to the International Air Traffic Association founded in the Hague in 1919—the year of the world's first international scheduled services.

IATA at the Air Transport Industry's Side

Air transport is one of the most dynamic industries in the world. The International Air Transport Association (IATA) is its global trade organization.

Over 60 years, IATA has developed the commercial standards that built a global industry. Today, IATA's mission is to *represent, lead and serve the airline industry*. Its members comprise some 260 airlines—the world's leading passenger and cargo airlines among them—representing 94 per cent of international scheduled air traffic.

Representing

IATA seeks to improve understanding of the industry among decision makers and increase awareness of the benefits that aviation brings to national and global economies. It fights for the interests of airlines across the globe, challenging unreasonable rules and charges, holding regulators and governments to account, and striving for sensible regulation.

Leading

IATA's aim is to help airlines help themselves by simplifying processes and increasing passenger convenience while reducing costs and improving efficiency. The groundbreaking simplifying the business initiative is crucial in this area. Moreover, safety is IATA's number one priority, and IATA's goal is to continually improve safety standards, notably through IATA's Operational Safety Audit (IOSA). Another main concern is to minimize the impact of air transport on environment.

Serving

IATA ensures that people and goods can move around the global airline network as easily as if they were on a single airline in a single country. In addition, it provides essential professional support to all industry stakeholders with a wide range of products and expert services, such as publications, training and consulting. IATA's financial systems also help carriers and the travel industry maximize revenues.

For the benefit for all parties involved:

- For *consumers*, IATA simplifies the travel and shipping processes, while keeping costs down. Passengers can make one telephone call to reserve a ticket, pay in one currency and then use the ticket on several airlines in several countries.
- IATA allows *airlines* to operate safely, securely, efficiently and economically under clearly defined rules.
- IATA serves as an intermediary between airlines and *passenger* as well as *cargo agents* via neutrally applied agency service standards and centralized financial systems.
- A large network of *industry suppliers* and *service providers* gathered by IATA provides solid expertize to airlines in a variety of industry solutions.
- For *governments*, IATA seeks to ensure they are well informed about the complexities of the aviation industry to ensure better, long-term decisions.

CARGO AGENCY REGISTRATION SERVICES

Introduction

IATA is a trade association of the world's scheduled airlines and its major purpose is to ensure that airline traffic worldwide moves with the greatest possible speed, safety, convenience and efficiency. Through IATA, airlines work towards developing worldwide industry standards that ensure safe, speedy and economic international air transportation.

The relationship between Member Airlines and their registered Cargo Agents are regulated and administered under a set of IATA Resolutions. These Government-approved rules establish the rights and obligations of the parties, as well as the procedures and requirements for agents wishing to obtain and to maintain industry accreditation and become a part of the airlines global cargo distribution network.

Simplified procedures and conditions for agency accreditation have been developed to meet regional requirements. IATA conducts regular dialogue with FIATA (International Federation of Freight Forwarders Association) as well as with national cargo agent's federation, who work together at all levels for the common benefit of the air cargo industry.

In today's market being recognized as an IATA agent has became a hallmark of quality for the airlines and public at large. So why hesitate? *It's about time for you to come forward and join a Global Freight Business Club!* If you would like to receive a set of Application Form to register an an IATA Cargo Agent, a copy of the Request Form is enclosed.

Guide for Changes to Cargo Agency Registration

The rights enjoyed by a registered IATA Cargo Agent cannot be assigned or transferred, wholly or in part except in accordance with the Cargo Agency Rules.

In the event that a Cargo Agent wishes to make changes to its ownership, shareholding, legal status, name or address, the Cargo Agent must notify the Agency Administrator.

Notification is mandatory. Failure to notify may either result in the Cargo Agent being placed on commissionable-cash basis or removal from the Cargo Agency List.

Two forms have been designed to assist in the Notifications. They are:

- A three-page Notice of Change of Ownership or Shareholding or Legal Status or Name or a combination of either of the changes,
- A one-page Notice of Change of Address.

Complete it and send the original copies to:

Assistant Director, Agency Accreditation Services
Asia/Pacific 77, Robinson Road
#05-00, SIA Building Singapore 068896

Upon receipt, IATA would guide you through the necessary steps in compliance with the Cargo Agency Rules.

EFFECTIVE CARGO CLAIMS MANAGEMENT

It's all here in the Cargo Claims and Loss Prevention Handbook. Packed with practical information, this new guide is the complete resource for airlines, freight forwarders, and all who share an interest in cost-effective claims handling and loss prevention.

- A convenient, single source for international cargo claims information
- The most up-to-date reference for industry best practices
- Written in plain language with clear, detailed explanations

An effective new tool for any cargo team's toolkit!

The Cargo Claims and Loss Prevention Handbook topics include:

- Industry definitions
- Cargo claims processing instructions
- Explanations of international legal regimes
- Worldwide liabilities converted to local currencies
- US domestic claims handling regulations
- Carrier-specific claims policies and procedures
- Airline contact information
- Loss prevention best practices

Don't Let Cargo Claims Turn into Cargo Problems!

Order your Cargo Claims and Loss Prevention Handbook!
Visit the IATA Online Store at:
www.iataonline.com, or call our Customer Care Center:
Tel: +1 (514) 390-6726 or *Tel*: +1 (800) 716-6236 toll free in USA and Canada.

Send us a fax or e-mail order with contact information, method of payment and quantity. *E-Mail*: custserv@iata.org *Fax:* +1 (514)874-9659.

AIR CARGO WORLD

2007 World Airports Directory is divided into two sections—the first lists United States airports by state; the international section lists airports in Europe, Asia, South America and the Middle East by country. Information is based on responses to questionnaires.

Alabama	Louisiana	New York
Alaska	Maine	North Carolina
Arizona	Maryland	Ohio
California	Massachusetts	Oregon
Colorado	Michigan	Pennsylvania
Connecticut	Minnesota	Puerto Rico

District of Columbia
Florida
Georgia
Hawaii
Idaho
Illinois
Indiana
Iowa
Kentucky
Mississippi
Missouri
Montana
Nebraska
Nevada
New Hampshire
New Jersey
New Mexico
South Carolina
South Dakota
Tennessee
Texas
Utah
Virginia
Washington
Wisconsin

AIRPORTS DIRECTORY

ARGENTINA

Aeropuerto Internacional DE Ezeiza

Ezeiza, Buenos Aires, Argentina, B180 2

Identifier: EZE.

Phone: +54 11 80 2500

Fax: +54 11 5480 2597.

WWW.Buenos-aires-eze.com

Air Service: Total Carriers: 21, All-Cargo: 10, Non-Scheduled Charter: around 3.

Cargo Space: Total Ramp/Tarmac Surface for Cargo Handling: 15,314 s.m. Warehouse Space: 67,734 s.m. Occupied: 50 per cent.

FTZ: No

Special Services/Facilities: Handling for large animals, equine; refrigeration for cut flowers, perishable food, frozen goods; quarantine, HazMat, bonded and secure storage.

Customs: Yes

Agriculture Inspector: Yes

Traffic: Total '05 Tonnage: 177,358 m.t, +1.4 per cent. Total '05 Aircraft Movements: 62,048, +6.1 per cent.

ARUBA

Aruba Airport Authority

Aeropuerto Internacional Reina Beatrix Aruba, Wayaca z/n, Oransestad, Aruba.

Identifier: AUA.

Contact: Peter Steinmetz.

Phone: +297 524 2424.

Fax: +297 583 4229.

E-Mail: p.steinmetz@airportaruba.com

WWW.airportaruba.com

Air Service: Total Carriers: 22; All-Cargo: 4; Non-Scheduled Charter: 4.

Cargo Space: Warehouse Space: 2,700 s.m./540s.m. office space. Occupied: 229 s.m./319 s.m. office space.

FTZ: Yes.

Special Services/Facilities: Refrigeration for cut flowers, perishable food, frozen goods.

Customs: Yes.

Agriculture Inspector: Yes.

Traffic: Total '05 Aircraft Movements: 2,493, -6 per cent. Distance to Connecting Transportation: Ocean Port: 10 minutes.

AUSTRALIA

Sydney (Kingsford Smith) Airport

Locked Bag 5000, Sydney International Terminal, NSW, Australia 2020.

Identifier: SYD.

Contact: Michelle Turcotte.

Phone: + 61 2 9667 9111.

Fax: +61 2 8338 4919.

E-Mail: feedback@syd.com.au

WWW.sydneyairport.com.au

Air Service: Total Carriers: 56, All-Cargo: 8.

Cargo Space: Total Ramp/Tarmac Surface for Cargo Handling: 34 gates, 90,000 s.m. apron space. Warehouse Space: 4 international and 2 domestic cargo facilities in use.

Special Services/Facilities: Handling for large animals, equine; refrigeration for cut flowers, perishable food, frozen goods; quarantine, HazMat, bonded and secure storage.

Customs: Yes Avg. Customs Clearance Time: most cargo pre-cleared, if not < 2 hrs.

Agriculture Inspector: Yes Freight Forwarders: >150.

Traffic: Total '05 Aircraft Movements: 286,827. +2.5 per cent.

Distance to Connecting Transport (kms): Rail Terminal: On Site, Ocean Port: 4, Highway: 1, Truck Terminal: 2.

Perth Airport

Baker Rd., Perth, WA, Australia, 6105.

Identifier: PER.

Contact: Jennifer Walsh.

Phone: +61 8 9478 8888.

Fax: +61 8 9277 7537.

E-Mail: perthairport@wac.com.au

WWW.perthairport.com

Customs: Yes

Agriculture Inspector: 1 km.

Traffic: Total '05 Aircraft Movements: 89,054, +7.3 per cent.

Distance to Connecting Transport (kms): Rail Terminal: 4, Highway: Adjacent, Ocean Port: 22, Truck Terminal: 1.

AUSTRIA

Innsbruck Airport

Fuerstenweg 180, Innsbruck, A-6020, Austria.

Identifier: INN.

Contact: Peter Doerfler.

Phone: +43 512 290292.

Fax: +43 512 290 29420.

E-Mail: doerfler.ilug@innsbruck-airport.com

WWW.innsbruck-airport.com.

Air Service: Total Carriers: approximately 60

Cargo Space: Total Ramp/Tarmac Surface for Cargo Handling: 400 s.m. Occupied: 100 per cent.

Special Services/Facilities: Refrigeration for cut flowers, perishable food; HazMat, bonded and secure storage.

Customs: Yes Avg. Customs Clearance Time: 1 hr

Agriculture Inspector: 500 km.

Traffic: Total '05 Tonnage: 4,141 tons, +6 per cent. Total '05 Aircraft Movements: 40,140, +2 per cent.

Distance to Connecting Transport (kms): Rail Terminal: 6 Highway: 2

Vienna International Airport

Flughafen Wien, Postfach 1, Vienna, Austria A-1300

Identifier: VIE

Phone: +43 1 7007 0

Fax: +43 1 7007 11 120.

E-Mail: cargoservices@viennaairport.com

WWW.viennaairport.com

Cargo Space: Total Ramp/Tarmac Surface for Cargo Handling: 12,000 s.m. Warehouse Space: 20,500 s.m. Occupied: 100 per cent Foreign Trade Zone: Yes

Customs: Yes

Agriculture Inspector: Yes

Traffic: Total '05 Tonnage: 180,067 m.t., +12.8 per cent. Total '05 Aircraft Movements: 252,983, +3.4 per cent.

BAHRAIN

Bahrain International Airport

PO Box 586, Manama, Bahrain.

Identifier: BAH.

Contact: David Ryan.

Phone: +973 17 32 1094.

Fax: +973 17 32 1139.

E-Mail: dryan@ aa.gov.bh

WWW.bahrainairport.com

Air Service: Total Carriers: 41, All-Cargo: 6, Non-Scheduled Charter: 4-5.

Cargo Space: Total Ramp/Tarmac Surface for Cargo Handling: 90,000 s.m. Warehouse Space: 30,000 s.m. Occupied: 80 per cent

FTZ: No

Customs: Yes

Agriculture Inspector: On Site

Traffic: Total '05 Tonnage: 334,831 m.t., +10.8 per cent. Total '05 Aircraft Movements: 73,891, +1.9 per cent.

Distance to Connecting Transport (kms): Ocean Port: 5, Hwy: 2, Intermodal Centre: 4.

BELGIUM

Brussels International Airport

Building 706—Box 31, Brucargo, Belgium BE-1931

Identifier: BRU.

Contact: Alain Bertrand.

Phone: +32 2 753 7200.

Fax: +32 2 753 7201.

E-Mail: info@brucargo.be

WWW.brusselsairport.be

Air Service: Total Carriers 125, All-Cargo: 20.

Cargo Space: Total Ramp/Tarmac Surface for Cargo Handling: 120,000 s.m. Warehouse Space: 160,000 s.m. Occupied: 75 per cent Foreign Trade Zone: Yes Special Services: Handling for large animals, equine; refrigeration for cut flowers, perishable food, frozen goods; HazMat, bonded and secure storage.

Customs: Yes Avg. Customs Clearance Time: 90 minutes.

Agriculture Inspector: Yes Freight Forwarders: 150

Traffic: Total '05 Tonnage: 702,819 tons excl RFS, +5.8 per cent. Total '05 Aircraft Movements: 253,255, +0.5 per cent.

Distance to Connecting Transport (kms): Ocean Port: 35, Hwy: 0.5, Inland Waterway Port: 10.

Comments: Planned new cargo facilities to be completed in 2008 adding 100,000 s.m. of ramp space and 119,000 s.m. of warehouse space.

Liege Airport

Building 44, Grace-Hollogne, Liege, Belgium B-4460.

Identifier: LGG

Contact: Eric Gysen.

Phone: +32 4 234 8411.

Fax: +32 4 234 8404.

E-Mail: liegeairport@sab.be

WWW.liegeairport.com

Air Service: Total Carriers: 16, All-Cargo: 6, Non-Scheduled Charter: 10

Cargo Space: Total Ramp/Tarmac Surface for Cargo Handling: 180,000 s.m. (160,000 s.m. under construction) Warehouse Space: 22,000 s.m. Occupied: 80 per cent.

Special Services/Facilities: Handling for large animals, equine; refrigeration for cut flowers, perishable food, frozen goods; quarantine, HazMat, bonded and secure storage.

Customs: Yes. Avg. Customs Clearance Time: less than 1 hr.

Agriculture Inspector: Yes.

Traffic: Total '05 Tonnage: 325,713 tons, -14 per cent. Total '05 Aircraft Movements: 42,369, +11 per cent.

Distance to Connecting Transport (kms): Rail Terminal: 2, Ocean Port: 130, Hwy: 200m, Truck Terminal: 2, Inland Waterway Port: 10, Intermodal Centre: 2.

Comments: A dedicated cargo airport, open 24/7, with all infrastructure, equipment and services to handle general and perishable cargo.

Ostend-bruges Int'l Airport

Nieuwpoortsesteenweg 887, Oostende, B-8400 Belgium.

Identifier: OST.

Contact: Gino Vanspauwen.

Phone: +32 59 551288.

Fax: +32 59 551213.

E-Mail: ceo@ost.aero

WWW.ost.aero

Air Service: Total Carriers: +/-10, All-Cargo: +/-7 plus ad-hoc carriers, Non-Scheduled Charter: 3.

Cargo Space: Total Ramp/Tarmac Surface for Cargo Handling: 193,187 s.m. Warehouse Space: 16,536 s.m.

FTZ: Yes.

Special Services/Facilities: Handling for large animals, equine; refrigeration for cut flowers, perishable food, frozen goods; quarantine, HazMat.

Customs: Yes Avg. Customs Clearance Time: 1-2 hrs.

Agriculture Inspector: Yes. Freight Forwarders: 7.

Traffic: Total '05 Tonnage: 108,260 tons, +11 per cent. Total '05 Aircraft Movements: 25,132, -24 per cent. Distance to Connecting Transport (km): Rail Terminal: 6, Ocean Port: 6, Highway: Adjacent, Truck Terminal: On Site

Comments: New cargo facilities to add additional ramp space for six widebodies and 4,000 s.m. of warehouse space. New apron has been opened.

BRAZIL

Rio De Janeiro Int'l Airport

Avenida 20 de Janeiro S/No, Ilma Do Governador, Rio de Janeiro, Brazil, 21942-900.

Identifier: GIG.

Phone: +55 21-398 6400.

Fax: +55 21-393-6301.

Air Service: Total Carriers: 26; All-Cargo: 10.

Cargo Space: 112,000 s.m. Warehouse Space: 8,000 s.m. Avg. Customs Clearance Time: 1-3 days

Agriculture Inspector: Yes

Traffic: Total '05 Tonnage: 112,200 m.t., -7.1 per cent. Total '05 Aircraft Movements: 97,332, +25.5 per cent.

Sao Paulo/Guarulhos International Airport

Guarulhos, Sao Paulo, Brazil 07141-970.

Identifier: GRU.

Phone: +55 11 945 2945.

Fax: +55 11 912 3335.

Cargo Space: Total Ramp/Tarmac Surface for Cargo Handling: 30,000 s.m. Warehouse Space: 32,530 s.m. Foreign Trade Zone: Yes Avg. Customs Clearance Time: 11 days

Agriculture Inspector: Yes

Traffic: Total '05 Tonnage: 475,182 tons, +8.3 per cent. Total '05 Aircraft Movements: 154,336, +3.2 per cent.

CANADA

Calgary Airport Authority

2000 Airport Road NE, Calgary, AB, Canada, T2E 6W5.

Identifier: YYC.

Contact: Katherine Witwicki.

Phone: 403-735-5325.

Fax: 403-735-1286.

E-Mail: Katherk@yyc.com

WWW.calgaryairport.com

Air Service: Total Carriers: 25, All-Cargo: 12, Non-Scheduled Charter: 15

Cargo Space: Total Ramp/Tarmac Surface for Cargo Handling: 781,500 s.f. Warehouse Space: 687,487 s.f. Occupied: 90 per cent.

FTZ: Yes.

Special Services/Facilities: Handling for large animals, equine; refrigeration for cut flowers, perishable food, frozen goods; quarantine, HazMat, bonded and secure storage.

Customs: Yes

Agriculture Inspector: Yes.

Traffic: Total '05 Tonnage: 125,500 m.t, +2 per cent. Total '05 Aircraft Movements: 105,821, +2 per cent.

Distance to Connecting Transport (kms): Rail Terminal: 15, Ocean Port: 1000, Hwy: 1, Truck Terminal: 5, Inland Waterway Port: 500, Intermodal Centre: 1.

Comments: Began new cargo facilities to be completed in April 2007 adding 400,000 s.f. of ramp space and 300,000 s.f. warehouse space.

Edmonton Airport Authority

PO Box 9860, Edmonton, Alberta, Canada, T5J 2T2

Identifier: YEG

Contact: Glen Vanstone

Ph: 780-890-8543

Fax: 780-890-8215

e-mail: gvanstone@edmontonairports.com

WWW.edmontonairports.com

Air Service: Total Carriers: 22, All-Cargo: 5, Charter: 5

Cargo Space: 350,000sq ft

Warehouse: 240,000sq ft

FTZ: Yes

Customs: Yes

Agriculture Inspection: Yes

Special Services: Indoor fwd main-deck and (747) nose-load facility, Large animal handling, perishables, Bonded and secure storage.

Traffic: Total 2005 Tonnage: 342.000m.t. + 9.6 per cent

Total 2005 Aircraft Movements: 78,000 +4 per cent

Distance to connecting transport: Highway: 1,

Rail/Intermodal: 5,

Truck Terminal: 2

Comments: Port Alberta development initiated with approx 100,000 Sqm of Apron over two phases, Cat F taxiway and full truck & rail intermodal on site.

Gander International Airport

PO Box 400, Gander, NF, Canada, A1V 1W8.

Identifier: YQX.

Contact: Reg Wright.

Phone: 709-256-6668.

Fax: 709-256-6725.

E-Mail: wrightr@giaa.nf.ca

WWW.ganderairport.com

Air Service: Total Carriers: 53, All-Cargo: 12, Non-Scheduled Charter: 36

Cargo Space: Total Ramp/Tarmac Surface for Cargo Handling: 250,000 s.f. Warehouse Space: 27,000 s.f. Occupied: 20 per cent

FTZ: Yes

Special Services/Facilities: Refrigeration of cut flowers, perishable food, frozen goods; HazMat, bonded and secure storage. Planned handling for large animals, equine and quarantine.

Customs: Yes.

Agriculture Inspector: Yes.

Traffic: Total '05 Tonnage: 26,000 m.t. Total '05 Aircraft Movements: 11,000.

Distance to Connecting Transport (kms): Ocean Port: 60, Hwy: 2

Comments: Planned new cargo facilities.

Greater Moncton Int'l Airport

777 Aviation Avenue, Unit 12, Dieppe, NB, Canada, E1A 7Z5.

Identifier: YQM.

Contact: Johanne Gallant.

Phone: 506-856-5444.

Fax: 506-856-5431.

E-Mail: office@gma.ca

WWW.gmia.ca

Air Service: Total Air Carriers: 6, All-Cargo: 3

Cargo Space: Warehouse Space: 6,000 s.f. Occupied: 60 per cent. Special Serevices/ Facilities: HazMat.

Customs: 10 km away.

Traffic: Total '05 Tonnage: 23,684 m.t., +5.90 per cent. Total '05 Aircraft Movements: 68,290, +5.43 per cent.

Distance to Connecting Transport (miles): Rail Terminal: 10, Ocean Port: 160, Hwy: 50 meters, Truck Terminal: 2.

Halifax International Airport

1 Bell Boulevard, Enfield, NS, Canada, B2T 1K2.

Identifier: YHZ.

Contact: Andy Lyall.

Phone: 902-873-4422.

Fax: 902-873-4750.

E-Mail: info@hiaa.ca

WWW.halifax-airport.com

Air Service: Total Carriers: 25, All-Cargo: 5.

Cargo Space: Total Ramp/Tarmac Surface for Cargo Handling: 1.2 million s.f. Occupied: 100 per cent

FTZ: No

Special Services/Facilities: Refrigeration for cut flowers, perishable food; bonded & secure storage.

Customs: Yes Avg. Customs Clearance Time: 2 hrs.

Agriculture Inspector: Yes Freight Forwarders: 7.

Traffic: Total '05 Tonnage: 26,229 m.t., -17.6 per cent. Total '05 Aircraft Movements: 34,946, -3.6 per cent.

Distance to Connecting Transport (miles): Rail Terminal: 35, Ocean Port: 35, Interstate Hwy: 1, Truck Terminal: 15.

Comments: Planned new cargo facilities estimated additional 125,000 s.f. of ramp space and 45,000 s.f. of warehouse space.

Montreal Mirabel Int'l Airport

1100 Rene-Levesque Blvd West, Ste 2100, Montreal, Quebec, Canada, H3B 4X8.

Identifier: YMX.

Contact: Daniel Boileau.

Phone: 514-394-7254.
Fax: 514-394-7356.
E-Mail: cargo@admtl.com
WWW.admtl.com
Air Service: Total Carriers: 59, All-Cargo: 18.
Cargo Space: 18 hectares. Warehouse Space: 64,000 s.m.
Special Services/Facilities: Handling for large animals, equine; refrigeration for cut flowers, perishable food, frozen goods; quarantine, HazMat, bonded and secure storage.
FTZ: No
Customs: Yes
Agriculture Inspector: Yes
Traffic: Total '05 Tonnage: 117,784 m.t., +3.7 per cent. Total '05 Aircraft Movements: 23,640, -20.6 per cent.
Distance to Connecting Transport (kms): Rail Terminal: 3, Ocean Port: 20, Interstate Hwy: 1, Truck Terminal: on site, Inland Waterway Port: 20, Intermodal Centre: 1.

Toronto Pearson Int'l Airport

PO Box 6031, 3111 Convair Drive, Toronto AMF, ON, Canada, L5P 1B2.
Identifier: YYZ.
Contact: Guy Maynard.
Phone: 416-776-3000.
Fax: 416-776-3555.
E-Mail: guy.maynard@gtaa.com
WWW.gtaa.com
Air Service: Total Carriers: 65, All-Cargo: 8.
Cargo Space: 700,000 s.f. Warehouse Space: 1,200,000 s.f. Occupied: 85 per cent.
FTZ: Yes.
Special Services/Facilities: Handling for large animals, equine; refrigeration for cut flowers, perishable food, frozen goods; quarantine, HazMat, bonded and secure storage.
Customs: Yes Avg. Customs Clearance Time: Electronic Clearance, 24 hr. service.
Traffic: Total '05 Tonnage: 410,000 m.t., +39 per cent. Total '05 Aircraft Movements: 409,645, +1.5 per cent.

Vancouver Int'l Airport

PO Box 23750, Airport Postal Outlet, Richmond, BC, Canada, V7B 1Y7.
Identifier: YVR.
Contact: John Korenic.
Phone: 604-276-6326.
Fax: 604-232-6220.
E-Mail: john_korenic@yvr.ca
WWW.yvr.ca
Air Service: Total Carriers: 59, All-Cargo: 5

Cargo Space: Total Ramp/Tarmac Surface for Cargo Handling: 986,783 s.m. Warehouse Space: 96,156 s.m. Occupied: 85 per cent.

Special Services/Facilities: Handling for large animals, equine; refrigeration of cut flowers, perishable food, frozen goods; HazMat, bonded and secure storage.

Customs: Yes Avg. Customs Clearance Time: Less than 45 minutes

Agriculture Inspector: Yes

Traffic: Total '05 Tonnage: 223,608 m.t., -3 per cent. Total '05 Aircraft Movements: 322,763, +2.5 per cent.

Distance to Connecting Transport (miles): Rail Terminal: 13, Ocean Port: 13, Highway: 2, Truck Terminal: 13, Intermodal Centre: 13

Winnipeg International Airport

Winnipeg Airports Authority, 2000 Wellington Ave., Room 249 Admin. Bldg., Winnipeg, MB, Canada, R3H 1C2.

Identifier: YWG.

Contact: Michael Rodyniuk, Sr VP.

Phone: 204-987-2737.

Fax: 204-987-2029.

E-Mail: mrodyniuk@waa.ca

WWW.waa.ca

Air Service: Total Carriers: 31, All-Cargo: 11, Non-Scheduled Charter: 3

Cargo Space: 55,288 s.m. Warehouse Space: 33,921 s.m. Occupied: 75 per cent.

Customs: Yes

Agriculture Inspector: Yes Freight Forwarders: 29

Traffic: Total '05 Tonnage: 150,000 m.t., +6 per cent. Total '05 Aircraft Movements: 137,787, -2 per cent.

Distance to Connecting Transport (kms): Rail Terminal: 10, Hwy: 1, Truck Terminal: <1

Comments: Two facilities scheduled to be completed in November 2006 adding 12,900 s.m. of apron space and 3,380 s.m. of warehouse space.

CHILE

Arturo Merino Benitez Airport

Comuna Pudahuel, Casilla 61, Correo Central, Santiago, Chile.

Identifier: SCL.

Phone: +56 2 676 3210.

Fax: +56 2 601 9416.

E-Mail: oym@dgac.cl

WWW.dgac.el

Air Service: Total Carriers: 29, All Cargo: 6, Non-Scheduled Charter: 2

Cargo Space: 181,776 s.m. Warehouse Space: 32,124 s.m.

Customs: Yes Avg. Customs Clearance Time: 1 hr

Agriculture Inspector: Yes

Traffic: Total '05 Tonnage: 279,426 m.t., +3.9 per cent. Total '05 Aircraft Movements: 76,330, +2.3 per cent.

Distance to Connecting Transport (miles): Rail Terminal: 20, Ocean Port: 120, Hwy: 10

CHINA

Hong Kong Int'l Airport

Airport Authority of Hong Kong, 1 Cheong Yip Road, Lantau, Hong Kong, China.

Identifier: HKG.

Phone: +852 2188 7111.

Fax: +852 2824 0717.

E-Mail: kayd@hkairport.com

WWW.hongkongairport.com

Air Service: Total Carriers: 75, All-Cargo: 17, Non-Scheduled Charter: 17.

Cargo Space: Total Ramp/Tarmac Surface For Cargo Handling: 412,936 s.m. Warehouse Space: 470,791 s.m. Occupied: 100 per cent.

FTZ: No.

Special Services/Facilities: Handling for large animals, equine; refrigeration for cut flowers, perishable food, frozen goods; quarantine, HazMat, bonded and secure storage.

Customs: Yes.

Agriculture Inspector: Yes

Traffic: Total '05 Tonnage: 3,437,050 m.t.s, +10.1 per cent. Total '05 Aircraft Movements: 273,407, +10.4 per cent.

Distance to Connecting Transport (km): Rail Terminal: 30, Ocean Port: 25, Hwy: On Site, Truck Terminal: On Site, Inland Waterway Port: On Site, Intermodal Centre: On-Site.

Beijing Capital Int'l Airport

Beijing Capital Int'l Airport Authority, Airport Road, Beijing, China 10062

Identifier: PEK.

Fax: +86 10 645 70487.

E-Mail: webmaster@bcia.com.cn

WWW.bcia.com.cn

Traffic: Total '05 Tonnage: 782,066 m.t., +17 per cent. Total '05 Aircraft Movements: 241,543, +12.1 per cent.

Guangzhou Baiyun Int'l Airport

Guangzhou, Guangdong, 510405, China.

Identifier: CAN.

Phone: +86 20 861 24518

Fax: +86 20 8665 0804

E-Mail: qualit@gahco.com.cn

WWW.gahco.com.cn

Traffic: Total '05 Tonnage: 750,552 m.t., +18.7 per cent. Total '05 Aircraft Movements: 211,309, +15.6 per cent.

Macau International Airport

Cam Macau Int'l Airport Company, 29/F, Bank of China Bldg. Av. Dr. Mario Soares, Macau, China.

Identifier: MFM.

Phone: +853 598 8888.

Fax: +853 785 465.

E-Mail: camlgd@macau.ctm.net

WWW.macau-airport.gov.mo

Air Service: Total Carriers: 11, All-Cargo: 5, Non-Scheduled Charter: 3

Cargo Space: Total Ramp/Tarmac Surface for Cargo Handling: 22,300 s.m Warehouse Space: 8,500 s.m. Occupied: 133.84 per cent.

Special Services/Facilities: Handling for large animals, equine; refrigeration for cut flowers, perishable food, frozen goods; bonded and secure storage.

Customs: Yes.

Agriculture Inspector: Yes.

Traffic: Total '05 Tonnage: 227,694 m.t., +3.1 per cent. Total '05 Aircraft Movements: 45,002, +11.1 per cent.

Distance to Connecting Transport (kms): Ocean Port: 5, Hwy: 3, Truck Terminal: On Site, Inland Waterway Port: 5

Nanjing Lukou Int'l Airport

Lukou Town, Jiangning District, Nanjing, Jiangsu, China, 210029.

Identifier: NKG.

Contact: Mr. Chen Bangchang.

Phone: +86 25 2480195.

Fax: +86 25 2480025.

E-Mail: marketing@nliairport.com

WWW.nliariport.com.

Air Service: Total Carriers: 20, All-Cargo: 3, Non-Scheduled Charter: 1

Cargo Space: Total Ramp/Tarmac Surface for Cargo Handling: 401,000 s.m. Warehouse Space: 2,000 s.m.

FTZ: Yes

Special Services/Facilities: Refrigeration for cut flowers, perishable food, frozen goods; quarantine, HazMat, bonded and secure storage. Planned handling for large animals and equine.

Customs: Yes Avg. Customs Clearance Time: 30 mins to 1 hr.

Agriculture Inspector: Yes

Traffic: Total '05 Tonnage: 139.368 m.t., +16.2 per cent. Total '05 Aircraft Movements: 55,507, +7.7 per cent.

Shenzhen Baoan Int'l Airport

Office 603, Airport Hoter, Shenzhen Baoan Int'l Airport, Shenzhen, China 518128

Identifier: SZX.

Contact: Jack Wu.

Phone: +86 755 2777 6047.

Fax: +86 755 2777 6313.

E-Mail: sacabd@public.szptt.net.cn

WWW.szairport.com

Air Service: Total Carriers: 22, All-Cargo: 7

Cargo Space: Total Ramp/Tarmac Surface for Cargo Handling: 588,000 s.m. Warehouse Space: 64,797 s.m. Occupied: 76 per cent.

Special Services/Facilities: Refrigeration for cut flowers, perishable food, frozen goods; quarantine, bonded and secure storage. Planned handling for large animals, equine.

Customs: Yes

Agriculture Inspector: Yes Freight Forwarders: 65

Traffic: Total '05 Tonnage: 463,763 m.t., +9.6 per cent. Total '05 Aircraft Movements: 151,398, +7.8 per cent.

Distance to Connecting Transport (kms): Rail Terminal: 35, Ocean Ports: 50 & 20, Highway: 500 meters, Inland Waterway Port: 20.

CZECH REPUBLIC

Airport Ruzyne

Leglerove 1075/4, Airport Ruzyne, Prague, Czech Republic 16008.

Identifier: PRG.

Phone: +420 2 2011 3512.

Fax: +420 2 2428 1035.

E-Mail: cargo@csa.cz

WWW.csacargo.com

Air Service: Total Carriers: 45. All-Cargo: 3, Non-Scheduled Charter: 10

Cargo Space: 8,000 s.m. Warehouse Space: 3,500 s.m. Occupied: 43 per cent.

Special Services/Facilities: Handling for large animals, refrigeration for cut flowers, perishable food, frozen goods, quarantine, HazMat, bonded and secure storage.

Customs: Yes

Agriculture Inspector: Yes

Traffic: Total '05 Tonnage: 51,712 m.t., -0.7 per cent. Total '05 Aircraft Movements: 160,213, +10.5 per cent.

Distance to Connecting Transport (kms): Rail Terminal: 20, Ocean Port: On-Site, Hwy: 1, Truck Terminal: On-Site.

DENMARK

Billund Airport

Eksportvej 40, DK-7190 Billund, Denmark.

Identifier: BLL.

Contact: Jan Ditlevsen.
Phone: +45 7650 5151.
Fax: +45 7535 3475.
E-Mail: ccb@bll.dk
WWW.ccb.dk
Air Service: Total Carriers: 98, All-Cargo: 78, Non-Scheduled Charter: 5
Cargo Space: Total Ramp/Tarmac Surface for Cargo Handling: 60,000 s.m. Warehouse Space: 11,000 s.m. Occupied: 40 per cent.
Special Services/Facilities: Handling large animals, refrigeration for cut flowers, perishable food, frozen goods, HazMat, bonded and secure storage. Planned quarantine.
Customs: Yes Avg. Customs Clearance Time: less than 30 minutes.
Agriculture Inspector: Yes.
Traffic: Total '05 Tonnage: 52,000 tons, +5 per cent. Total '05 Aircraft Movements: 53,671, +6.5 per cent.
Distance to Connecting Transport (kms): Rail Terminal: 28, Ocean Port: 50, Hwy: 20, Truck Terminal: On Site, Intermodal Centre: 20.

Copenhagen Airport

Lufthavnsboulevarden 6, Kastrup, DK-2770, Denmark.
Identifier: CPH.
Contact: Lars Korup.
Phone: +45 32 31 25 21.
Fax: +45 32 31 31 66.
E-Mail: l.korup@cph.dk
WWW.cph.dk
Air Service: Total Carriers: 90, Non-scheduled Charter: 6.
Cargo Space: 60,000 s.m. Warehouse Space: 43,700 s.m. Occupied: All, but available land.
FTZ: Yes.
Customs: Yes
Agriculture Inspector: Yes
Traffic: Total '05 Tonnage: 356,000 m.t., +5.8 per cent; Total '05 Aircraft Movements: 268,655, -1.4 per cent.
Distance to Connecting Transport (kms): Rail Terminal: On Site, Ocean Port: 7, Highway: On Site, Truck Terminal: On Site, Intermodal Centre: On Site.
Comments: Planned new cargo facilities. Airport Business Park, 418,000 s.m. and up to 220,000 s.m. building next to cargo aprons.

ECUADOR

Aeropuerto Internacional Simon Bolivar Guayaquil

Tagsa, Av. De Las Americas (Apto. Simon Bolivar), Guayaquil, Guayas, Ecuador
Identifier: GYE.
Contact: Fernando Guerrero

Phone: +593 4 2391603
Fax: +593 4 2391 374
E-Mail: fguerrero@tagsa.aero
Air Service: Total Carriers: 20, All-Cargo: 7, Non-Scheduled Charter: 3.
Cargo Space: Total Ramp/Tarmac Surface for Cargo Handling 86223 s.m. Occupied: 90 per cent.
Customs: Yes.
Traffic: Total '05 Tonnage: 62,860 m.t. +12.8 per cent.
Distance Connecting Transport (km): Ocean Port: 45 minutes, Hwy: 20 minutes, Truck Terminal: 25 minutes.

Aeropuerto Internacional Marscal Sucre

Av. Amazonas s/n y Av. De La Prensa, Quito, Pichincha, Ecuador.
Identifier: UIO.
Contact: Yves Gautier
Phone: +593 2 2944900.
Fax: +593 2 2944906.
E-Mail: yves.gautier@adc-hos.com
WWW.quiport.com
Air Service: Total Carriers: 14, All-Cargo: 5, Non-Scheduled Charter: 9
Cargo Space: Total Ramp/Tarmac Surface for Cargo Handling: 18,800 s.m. Warehouse Space: 12,500 s.m. Occupied: 100 per cent.
FTZ: Yes.
Customs: Yes
Traffic: Total '05 Tonnage: 123,432.83 m.t., +3 per cent. Total '05 Aircraft Movements: 4,927, +8 per cent.
Distance Connecting Transport (km): Ocean Port: 420.

ESTONIA

Tallinn Airport

Lennujaama 2, 11101 Tallinn, Estonia.
Identifier: TLL.
Contact: Martin Grunberg.
Phone: +372 605 8701.
Fax: +372 605 8333.
E-Mail: marketing@tll.aero
WWW.tallinn-airport.ee
Air Service: Total Carriers: 13, All-Cargo: 3, Non-Scheduled Charter: 1 Warehouse Space: 4,100 s.m. Occupied: 100 per cent.
Special Services/Facilities: Refrigeration for frozen goods; quarantine, HazMat, bonded and secure storage.
Customs: Yes
Traffic: Total '05 Tonnage: 9,932 m.t., +89.6 per cent. Total '05 Aircraft Movements: 33,609, +20.2 per cent.

Distance to Connecting Transport (kms): Rail Terminal: 4, Ocean Port: 5, Highway: 100.

FINLAND

Helsinki/Vantaa Int'l Airport

PO Box 29, Vantaa, 01531, Finland
Identifier: HEL.
Contact: Timo Jarvela, Mktg Mgr.
Phone: +358 9-8277 3002.
Fax: +358 9-8277 3089.
E-Mail: airlinerelations@fcaa.fi
WWW.helsinki-vantaa.fi
Air Service: Total Carriers: 70, All-Cargo: 7.
Customs: Yes
Traffic: Total '05 Tonnage: 113,998 m.t., -6.6 per cent. Total '05 Aircraft Movements: 172,355, 0.3 per cent.
Distance to Connecting Transport (kms): Rail Terminal: 10, Ocean Port: 10.

FRANCE

Aeroport De Lille

B.P. 227-59812 Lesquin, Cedex, Lille, France.
Contact: Nicolas De Clercp.
Phone: +33 3 20 49 68 80.
Fax: +33 3 20 49 68 85.
WWW.lille.aeroport.fr
Cargo Space: Total Ramp/Tarmac Surface For Cargo Handling: 70,000 s.m. Warehouse Space: 10,000 s.m.
Customs: Yes. Freight Forwarders: 40.
Traffic: Total '05 Tonnage: 63,000 tons, +13.1 per cent. Total '05 Aircraft Movements: 100.
Distance Connecting Transport (km): Rail Terminal: 20, Ocean Port: 80, Hwy: On Site, Truck Terminal: 1, Inland Waterway Port: 15, Intermodal Centre: On Site.

Chateauroux—Deols Airport

RN 20, Deols 36130, France.
Contact: Eric Boisseau Beharn.
Phone: +33 2 5460 5353.
Fax: +33 2 5460 5354.
E-Mail: e.bouisseaubeharn@chateauroux-airport.com
WWW.chateauroux-airport.com
Cargo Space: Total Ramp/Tarmac Surface for Cargo Handling: 90 hectares.
FTZ: Yes

Special Services/Facilities: Refrigeration for packages meat; HazMat, secure storage.

Customs: 7 km away. Avg. Customs Clearance: 4 hrs.

Agriculture Inspector: 7 km away

Traffic: Total '05 Tonnage: 6,763 tons, +27 per cent. Total '05 Aircraft Movements: 18,108, +13 per cent.

Distance to Connecting Transport (kms): Rail Terminal: 7.

Lyon-Saint-Exupery Aeroport

BP 113, Lyon St Exupery, France, 69125.

Identifier: LYS.

Contact: Eric Burdin.

Phone: +33 4 72 22 81 51.

Fax: +33 4 72 22 72 66.

E-Mail: eric.burdin@lyon.aeroport.fr

Air Service: Total Carriers: 68, All-Cargo: 19, Non-Scheduled Charter: 6

Cargo Space: Total Ramp/Tarmac Surface for Cargo Handling: 200 hectares Warehouse Space: 17,953 s.m. Occupied: 92.55 per cent.

Special Services/Facilities: Handling for large animals, refrigeration for cut flowers, perishable food, frozen goods; HazMat, bonded and secure storage.

Customs: Yes. Avg. Customs Clearance Time: 20 minutes

Agriculture Inspector: Yes Freight Forwarders: 80

Traffic: Total '05 Tonnage: 38,681 m.t., +9.9 per cent.

Distance Connecting Transport (km): Rail Terminal: On Site, Ocean Port: 300, Highway: 2, Truck Terminal: On Site, Inland Waterway Port: 30, Intermodal Centre: 20

Nice Cote D'azur Airport

CCINCA BP 3331, Nice, France 06206.

Identifier: NCE.

Contact: Herue De Place.

Phone: +33 4 8988 9828

Fax: +33 4 9321 3147

E-Mail: info@nice.aeroport.fr

WWW.nice.aeroport.fr

Air Service: Total Carriers: 54, All-Cargo: 4.

Cargo Space: Warehouse Space: 10,000 s.m. Occupied: 100 per cent.

FTZ: Yes

Special Services/Facilities: Refrigeration for cut flowers, perishable food; bonded and secure storage.

Customs: Yes. Avg. Customs Clearance Time: fast.

Agriculture Inspector: 5-10 minutes away. Freight Forwarders: 25.

Traffic: Total '05 Tonnage: 14,651 m.t., -6.5 per cent. Total '05 Aircraft Movements: 168,666, +1.8 per cent.

Distance to Connecting Transport (kms): Rail Terminal: 15, Ocean Port: 20, Hwy: 3, Truck Terminal: On Site.

Paris Charles De Gaule Airport

CDGX—Bat 5720, 6 rue des Bruyeres, BP 24101, Roissy CDG Cedex France 95711.

Identifier: CDG.

Contact: Hughes Potart.

Phone: +33 1 48 62 79 88.

Fax: +33 1 48 62 58 02.

E-Mail: hughes.potart@adp.fr

WWW.adp.fr

Air Service: Total Carriers: 440, All-Cargo: 62, Non-Scheduled Charter: +250.

Cargo Space: Total Ramp/Tarmac Surface for Cargo Handling: 35 h.a. Warehouse Space: 400,000 s.m.

Special Services/Facilities: Handling for large animals, equine; refrigeration for cut flowers, perishable food, frozen goods; quarantine, HazMat, bonded and secure storage.

Customs: Yes. Freight Forwarders: 201

Traffic: Total '05 Tonnage: 1,770,940 m.t., +8.2 per cent. Total '05 Aircraft Movements: 522,619 -0.6 per cent.

Distance Connecting Transport (km): Rail Terminal: On Site, Ocean Port: 300, Truck Terminal: On Site.

Comments: A new common user terminal will open in 2007.

Vatry International Airport

B.P. 80005, Chalons, Champagne, France, 51555.

Identifier: XCR.

Contact: Youssef Sabeh, CEO.

Phone: +33 3 26 64 82 00.

Fax: +33 3 26 64 82 11.

E-Mail: vatry@vatry.com

WWW.vatry.com

Cargo Space: Total Ramp/Tarmac Surface for Cargo Handling: 45,000 s.m. (+60,000 s.m. in 2007).

FTZ: Yes.

Special Services/Facilities: Refrigeration for cut flowers, perishable food, frozen goods, quarantine, bonded and secure storage.

Customs: Yes

Agriculture Inspector: Yes

Traffic: Total '05 Tonnage: 37,670 m.t.; +98 per cent.

Distance to Connecting Transport (kms): Rail Terminal: On Site, Hwy: On Site, Truck Terminal: On Site, Intermodal Centre: On Site

Comments: Additional warehouse space of 8,100 s.m. was completed in December 2006.

GERMANY

Airport Nuernberg

Flughafen Strasse 88a, D-90411 Nuernberg, Bavaria, Germany.

Identifier: NUE.
Contact: Ulrich Buwen.
Phone: +49 911 937 2050.
Fax: +49 911 937 1794.
E-Mail: buwen-ulrich@airport-nuernberg.de
WWW.airport-nuernberg.de
Air Service: Total Carriers: 132, All-Cargo: 2, Non-Scheduled Charter: 8.
Cargo Space: Total Ramp/Tarmac Surface for Cargo Handling: 1,500 s.m. Warehouse Space: 14,000 s.m. Occupied: 95 per cent.
Special Services/Facilities: Refrigeration for cut flowers, perishables, HazMat, bonded and secure storage.
Customs: Yes Avg. Customs Clearance Time: 2 hrs.
Agriculture Inspector: 3 miles away.
Traffic: Total '05 Tonnage: 80,600 tons, +13.6 per cent. Total '05 Aircraft Movements: 76,111, +6 per cent.
Distance to Connecting Transport (kms): Rail Terminal: direct connection to underground, Highway: 1, Truck Terminal: On Site, Inland Waterway Port: 6, Intermodal Centre: On Site.

Berlin International Airport

Berlin Schonefeld Airport, Berlin, Germany D-12521.
Identifier: TXL.
Contact: Torsten Jueling.
Phone: +49 30 6091 1682.
Fax: +49 30 6095 1682.
E-Mail: marketing@bbf.de
WWW.berlin-airport.de
Special Services/Facilities: Handling for large animals, equine; refrigeration of cut flowers, perishable food, frozen goods; quarantine, HazMat, bonded and secure storage.
Customs: Yes Avg. Customs Clearance Time: 2-6 hrs.
Agriculture Inspector: Yes
Traffic: Total '05 Tonnage: 20,068 m.t., -6.1 per cent. Total '05 Aircraft Movements: 143,067, +3.7 per cent.
Distance to Connecting Transport (kms): Rail Terminal: On Site, Ocean Port: 300, Hwy: On Site, Truck Terminal: On Site, Inland Waterway: 10, Intermodal Centre: 10

Cologne/Bonn Int'l Airport

PO Box 98 01 20, D-51129, Koln, Germany.
Identifier: CGN.
Contact: Ute Weber.
Phone: +49 2203 405071.
Fax: +49 2203 405707.
E-Mail: ute.weber@cologne-bonn-airport.de
WWW.cologne-bonn-airport.de

Air Service: Total Carriers: 65, All-Cargo: 17

Cargo Space: Total Ramp/Tarmac Surface for Cargo Handling: 350,000 s.m. Warehouse Space: 70,000 s.m.

FTZ: Yes

Special Services/Facilities: Handling for large animals, equine; refrigeration for cut flowers, perishable food, frozen goods; quarantine, HazMat, bonded storage.

Customs: Yes Avg. Customs Clearance Time: 2.5 hrs

Agriculture Inspector: Yes

Traffic: Total '05 Tonnage: 643,653 m.t., +4.8 per cent. Total '05 Aircraft Movements: 154,593, +1.3 per cent.

Distance to Connecting Transport (kms): Rail Terminal: Cologne 20, Bonn 25, Hwy: On-Site, Truck Terminal: On Site, Inland Waterway Port: 20

Flughafen Hamburg

PO Box Hamburg, Germany D-22331.

Identifier: HAM.

Contact: Siegmar Weegen.

Phone: +49 40 50750.

Fax: +49 40 5075 1234.

E-Mail: cargo@ham.airport.de

WWW.ham.airport.de

Air Service: Total Carriers: 60, All-Cargo: 3.

Cargo Space: Total Ramp/Tarmac Surface for Cargo Handling: 120,000 s.m. Warehouse Space: 16,000 s.m. Occupied: 70 per cent.

FTZ: No

Special Services/Facilities: Handling for large animals; refrigeration for cut flowers, perishable food, frozen goods; HazMat, bonded and secure storage.

Customs: Yes

Agriculture Inspector: Yes

Traffic: Total '05 Tonnage: 82,161 m.t., -3 per cent. Total '05 Aircraft Movements: 156,128, +3.1 per cent.

Distance to Connecting Transport (kms): Rail Terminal: 8, Ocean Port: 10, Highway: 5, Truck Terminal: 300 miles, Inland Waterway Port: 10, Intermodal Centre: 12

Frankfurt Airport

Fraport AG, Frankfurt Airport Services Worldwide, D-60549 Frankfurt/Main, Germany.

Identifier: FRA.

Contact: Volker Antoni.

Phone: +49 69 6900.

Fax: +49 69 69 070081.

E-Mail: info@frankfurt-airport.com

WWW.fraport.com

Air Service: Total Carriers: 106, All-Cargo: 14, Non-Scheduled Charter: Approx. 50.

Cargo Space: Total Ramp/Tarmac Surface for Cargo Handling: 1,340,000 s.m. Warehouse Space: 181,000 s.m Occupied: 90 per cent.

Special Services/Facilities: Handling for large animals, equine; refrigeration for cut flowers, perishable food, frozen goods; quarantine, HazMat, bonded and secure storage.

Customs: Yes

Agriculture Inspector: Yes

Traffic: Total '05 Tonnage: 1,963,141 m.t., +6.7 per cent. Total '05 Aircraft Movements: 490,147, +2.7 per cent.

Distance to Connecting Transport (kms): Rail Terminal: On Site, Ocean Port: Approx 500, Hwy: Approx 1, Truck Terminal: On Site, Inland Waterway Port: Approx 10.

Frankfurt Hahn Airport

Building 667A, Hahn Airport, Germany 55483.

Identifier: HHN.

Contact: Maria Muller.

Phone: +49 6543 509200.

Fax: +49 6543 509204.

E-Mail: info@hahn-airport.de

WWW.hahn-airport.de

Air Service: Total Air Carriers: 50+, All-Cargo: 20+, Non-Scheduled Charter: 15+.

Cargo Space: Total Ramp/Tarmac Surface for Cargo Handling: 337,000 s.m. Warehouse Space: 27,500 s.m.

Special Services/Facilities: Handling for large animals, equine; refrigeration for cut flowers, perishable food, frozen goods; quarantine, HazMat, bonded and secure storage.

Customs: Yes

Agriculture Inspector: Yes. Freight Forwarders: 12

Traffic: Total '05 Tonnage: 228,920 m.t., +20 per cent. Total '05 Aircraft Movements: 37,283, +19 per cent.

Distance to Connecting Transport (kms): Rail Terminal: 24, Ocean Port: 400, Hwy: 30, Truck Terminal: On Site, Inland Waterway Port: 70.

Comments: Runway extension of 3,800 s.m. is completed and cargo apron extension to 337,000 s.m.

Hannover Airport

PO Box 42 02 80, Hannover, Germany, D-30662.

Identifier: HAJ.

Contact: Udo Siedler.

Phone: +49 511 977 1560.

Fax: +49 511 977 1212.

E-Mail: u.siedler@hannover-airport.de

WWW.hannover-airport.de

Air Service: Total Air Carriers: >60, All-Cargo: 1, Non-Scheduled Charter: 18

Cargo Space: Total Ramp/Tarmac Surface for Cargo Handling: 60,000 s.m. Warehouse Space: 6,500 s.m. Occupied: 90 per cent.

FTZ: No

Special Services/Facilities: Refrigeration of cut flowers, perishable food, frozen goods; quarantine, HazMat, bonded and secure storage. Planned handling for large animals, equine.

Customs: Yes Avg. Customs Clearance Time: 6 hrs.

Agriculture Inspector: Yes. Freight Forwarders: > 30.

Traffic: Total '05 Tonnage: 6,552 m.t.(on aircraft)/95,000 m.t. (via truck), +7.5 per cent.

Distance to Connecting Transport (kms): Rail Terminal: 20, Ocean Port: 100, Hwy: 0.5, Truck Terminal: 2, Inland Waterway: 10, Intermodal Centre: 10.

Comments: Planning in the final stages for new cargo facilities to be completed in 2007 adding 10,000 s.m. of warehouse space.

Munich Airport International

PO Box 231755, Munich, Bavaria, Germany, 85326.

Identifier: MUC.

Contact: Markus Heinelt.

Phone: +49 89 975 33524.

Fax: +49 89 975 33106.

E-Mail: markus.heinelt@munich-airport.de

WWW.munich-airport.de

Air Service: Total Carriers: 102, All-Cargo 12, Non-Scheduled Charter: 48.

Cargo Space: Total Ramp/Tarmac Surface for Cargo Handling: 120,000 s.m. Warehouse Space: 53,000 s.m. Warehouse Space Occupied: 100 per cent.

Special Services/Facilities: Refrigeration for cut flowers, perishable food, frozen goods; quarantine, HazMat, bonded and secure storage.

Customs: Yes

Agriculture Insector: Yes

Traffic: Total '05 Tonnage: 352,000 tons, +15 per cent. Total '05 Aircraft Movements: 387,000, +4 per cent.

Distance to Connecting Transport (kms): Rail Terminal: On Site, Ocean Port: 500, Hwy: Adjacent, Truck Terminal: On Site, Inland Waterway Port: 100, Intermodal Centre: 30.

Comments: Planned new cargo facilities adding 35,000 s.m. of warehouse space to be completed by end of 2007. Planned 3rd runway (4,000 meters) and perishable centre to be completed by end of 2007.

GREECE

Athens International Airport

Administration Building (17), Eleftherios Venizelos, Spata GR-19019, Greece.

Identifier: ATH.

Contact: Alexios Sioris

Phone: +30 210 35 37237.

Fax: +30 210 35 37884.

E-Mail: cargo@aia.gr

WWW.aia.gr

Air Service: Total Carriers: 71 scheduled—103 Charter, All-Cargo: 10, Non-Scheduled Charter: approx. 17.

Cargo Space: Total Ramp/Tarmac Surface for Cargo Handling: 130,000 s.m. Warehouse: 30,000 s.m. Occupied: 100 per cent.

FTZ: No

Special Services/Facilities: Handling for large animals, equine; refrigeration for cut flowers, perishables, frozen goods; quarantine, HazMat, bonded and secure storage.

Customs: Yes Avg. Customs Clearance: 60-90 minutes.

Agriculture Inspector: Yes. Freight Forwarders: 40.

Traffic: Total '05 Tonnage: 109,741 m.t., -2.6 per cent. Total '05 Aircraft Movements: 7,523, -21 per cent.

Distance to Connecting Transport (kms): Rail Terminal: On Site, Ocean Port: 30, Hwy: 1, Truck Terminal: On Site, Intermodal Centre: On Site.

Comments: 24 hour airport operation, no slot and night constraints; sea-air cargo link between Port of Piraeus and airport.

HUNGARY

Budapest-Ferihegy Int'l Airport

PO Box 53, Budapest, H-1675, Hungary.

Identifier: BUD.

Contact: Lajos Palos.

Phone: +36 1 296 8010.

Fax: +36 1 296 7506.

E-Mail: lajos.palos@bud.hu

WWW.bud.hu

Air Service: Total Carriers: Over 40, All Cargo: 6, Non-Scheduled Charter: 20 +, varies.

Cargo Space: Warehouse Space: 8,500 s.m. Occupied: 100 per cent.

Special Services/Facilities: Refrigeration for cut flowers, perishable food, frozen goods; HazMat, bonded and secure storage.

Customs: Yes.

Traffic: Total '05 Tonnage: 55,519 m.t., -8.2 per cent. Total '05 Aircraft Movements: 126,359, +13.1 per cent.

Distance to Connecting Transport (kms): Rail Terminal: 2, Ocean Port: 300, Highway: 5, Inland Waterway Port: 20.

ICELAND

Keflavik Airport

Leifur Eiriksson Air Terminal, 235 Keflavik Airport, Iceland.

Identifier: KEF.
Phone: +354 425 0600.
Fax: +354 425 0610.
E-Mail: bikf@caa.is
WWW.keflavikairport.com
Air Service: All-Cargo: 3. Warehouse Space: 5,000 s.m.
Customs: Yes
Agriculture Inspector: Yes
Traffic: Total '05 Tonnage: 59,827 m.t., +7.7 per cent.
Distance to Connecting Transport (kms): Ocean Port: 5, Highway: 5, Truck Terminal: On Site

INDIA

Chennai Airport

Meenambakkam, Airport Authority Chennai Airport, Chennai 600027, India.
Identifier: MAA.
Phone: +91 44 234 0581.
Fax: +91 44 234 8557.
Air Service: Total Carriers: 17, All Cargo: 9,
Cargo Space: Total Ramp/Tarmac Surface for Cargo Handling: 15 acres Warehouse Space: 13,070 sm
FTZ: Yes
Customs: Yes
Agriculture Inspector: Yes Freight Forwarders: 219
Traffic: Total '05 Tonnage: 206,728 m.t., +13 per cent. Total '05 Aircraft Movements: 78,534, +12.1 per cent.

Delhi Indira Gandhi Int'l Airport

Delhi Indira Gandhi Int'l Airport, Delhi 110 037, India
Identifier: DEL.
Phone: +91 11 648 4579.
Fax: +91 11 329 5196.
WWW.delhiairport.com
Air Service: Total Carriers: 6.
Cargo Space: Total Ramp/Tarmac Surface for Cargo Handling: 13,500 s.m.
Traffic: Total '05 Tonnage: 388,609 m.t., +13.1 per cent. Total '05 Aircraft Movements: 157,557, +18.3 per cent.

IRELAND

Shannon Airport

New Terminal Building, Shannon, Co. Clare, Ireland.
Identifier: SNN.

Contact: Eugene Pratt.
Phone: +353 61 71 2000.
Fax: +353 61 71 2284.
WWW.shannonairport.com
Air Service: Total Carriers: 44, All-Cargo: 12, Non-Scheduled Charter: 7
Cargo Space: Warehouse Space: 60,000 s.f. Occupied: 100 per cent.
FTZ: Yes
Special Services/Facilities: Handling for large animals, equine; refrigeration for cut flowers, perishable food; quarantine, HazMat, bonded and secure storage.
Customs: Yes Avg. Customs Clearance Time: 90 minutes
Agriculture Inspector: Yes
Traffic: Total '05 Tonnage: 46,540 m.t., -3 per cent. Total '05 Aircraft Movements: 34,239, +32 per cent.
Distance to Connecting Transport (kms): Rail Terminal: 18, Ocean Port: 26, Interstate Hwy: 2, Truck Terminal: On Site, Inland Waterway Port: 18.

ISRAEL

Tel Aviv/David Ben Gurion International Airport

PO Box 7, Ben Gurion, 70100, Israel
Identifier: TLV.
Phone: +972 3 971 5360.
Fax: +972 3 973 1354.
Air Service: Total Carriers: 40, All-Cargo: 1.
Cargo Space: Total Ramp/Tarmac Surface for Cargo Handling: Approx. 100,000 s.m.
Customs: Yes
Agriculture Inspector: Yes
Traffic: Total '05 Tonnage: 314,810 m.t., -7.9 per cent. Total '05 Aircraft Movements: 62,308, +5.3 per cent.
Distance to Connecting Transport (kms): Ocean Port: 35, Highway: 1, Truck Terminal: On Site.

ITALY

Aeroporto Di Venezia "Marco Polo"

Viale G.Galilei 30, I-30030 Tessera, Venice, Italy.
Identifier: VCE.
Contact: Antonio Prontera.
Phone: +39 041 260 3400.
Fax: +39 041 260 3409.
E-Mail: aprontera@veniceairport.it
WWW.veniceairport.it
Air Service: Total Carriers: 23, All-Cargo Carriers: 1, Non-Scheduled Charter: 3 Warehouse Space: 6,000 s.m. Occupied: 100 per cent

FTZ: No

Special Services/Facilities: Refrigeration of cut flowers, perishable food, frozen goods; bonded and secure storage.

Customs: Yes Avg. Customs Clearance Time: 4 hrs

Agriculture Inspector: Yes

Traffic: Total '05 Tonnage: 19,497 m.t., +2 per cent.

Distance to Connecting Transport (kms): Rail Terminal: 14, Ocean Port: 15, Hwy: 6, Truck Terminal: 35, Inland Waterway Port: 15, Intermodal Centre: 35.

Milan Linate Airport

2090 Aeroporto de Linate Segrate, Milan, Italy 20090, Italy.

Identifier: LIN.

Phone: +39 02 74 85 2319.

Fax: +39 02 74 85 2072.

E-Mail: cargo@sea-aeroportimilano.it

WWW.sea-aeroportimilano.it

Air Service: Total Carriers: 14.

Cargo Space: Total Ramp/Tarmac Surface for Cargo Handling: 50,000 s.m.

Customs: Yes

Agriculture Inspector: Yes

Traffic: Total '05 Tonnage: 25,342 m.t., -1.1 per cent. Total '05 Aircraft Movements: 121,636, -0.1 per cent.

Malpensa Airport

21010 Aeroporto di Malpensa, Milano, Italy

Identifier: MXP.

Phone: +39 02 74 85 2200.

Fax: +39 02 74 85 2010.

E-Mail: relest@sea.aeroportimilano.it

WWW.sea-aeroportimilano.it

Air Service: Total Carriers: 80 (passenger and cargo), All-Cargo: 13, Non-Scheduled Charter: 4.

Cargo Space: Warehouse Space: 55,000 s.m. Occupied: 87 per cent.

Special Services/Facilities: Handling for large animals, equine; refrigeration for cut flowers, perishable food, frozen goods; HazMat, bonded and secure storage.

Customs: Yes

Agriculture Inspector: Yes

Traffic: Total '05 Tonnage: 370,000 tons, +6.3 per cent. Total '05 Aircraft Movements: 230,000, +6.2 per cent.

Distance to Connecting Transport (kms): Rail Terminal 1.5, Ocean Port: Marsiglia 550 & Lisbona 2300, Hwy: 15, Inland Waterway Port: Genova 180.

Comments: New cargo facilities to be completed in 2011 adding 25,000 s.m. of warehouse space.

Rome Fiumicino/Leonardo Da Vinci Airport

CP-00050 Fiumicino, Roma, Italy.

Identifier: FCO.
Phone: +39 6 659 53243.
E-Mail: aviation.marketing@adr.it
WWW.adr.it
Air Service: Total Carriers: 80, All-Cargo: 7, Non-Scheduled Charter: 15.
Cargo Space: Total Ramp/Tarmac Surface for Cargo Handling: 70,000 s.m.
Traffic: Total '05 Tonnage: 170,795 m.t., -2.2 per cent. Total '05 Aircraft Movements: 308,284, -0.4 per cent.

JAPAN

New Tokyo Int'l Airport

Narita Airport, Chiba Prefecture, Narita, Japan 282-8601

Identifier: NRT.
Contact: Tadashi Harnada.
Phone: +81 476 34 5037.
Fax: +81 476 30 1571.
E-Mail: naa-intl@naa.go.jp
WWW.narita-airport.or.jp
Air Service: Total Carriers: 40 (scheduled only), All-Cargo: 4 (scheduled only).
Cargo Space: Total Ramp/Tarmac Surface for Cargo Handling: approx. 300,000 s.m. Warehouse Space: 145,000 s.m. Occupied: 100 per cent.
Customs: Yes
Agriculture Inspector: Yes Freight Forwarders: 100
Traffic: Total '05 Tonnage: 2,290,346 m.t., -3.5 per cent. Total '05 Aircraft Movements: 189,498, +1.7 per cent.
Distance to Connecting Transport (kms): Rail Terminal: 0.5, Highway: Adjacent.

KENYA

Jomo Kenyatta Int'l Airport

P.O. Box 19082 Nairobi, Kenya.

Identifier: NBO.
Contact: William Simbah.
Phone: +82 2 111 x5132.
Fax: +82 2 931.
E-Mail: wsimbah@naa.go.jp
WWW. kenyaairports.com
Air Service: Total Carriers: 20, All-Cargo: 10, Non-scheduled cargo charter 10.
Cargo Space: Total Ramp/Tarmac Surface for Cargo Handling: approx. 140,443 s.f.
Customs: Yes

Agriculture Inspector: Yes

Special Services/Facilities: Handling for large animals, equine; refrigeration for cut flowers, perishable food, frozen goods; quarantine, HazMat, bonded and secure storage.

Traffic: Total '05 Tonnage: 203,210, m.t., +12 per cent.

Distance to Connecting Transport (kms): Rail Terminal: Adjacent, Highway: 2, Ocean Port: 500, Truck Terminal: 4; Inland Waterway Port: 4; Intermodal Centre: 16.

KOREA

Incheon International Airport

2172-1 Woonseo-Dong, Joong-Qu, Incheon, Korea 400-340.

Identifier: ICN.

Contact: Myung Suk Ko.

Phone: +82 32 741 2426.

Fax: +82 32 741 2110.

E-Mail: webmaster@iia.airport.or.kr

WWW.airport.or.kr

Air Service: Total Carriers: 48, All-Cargo: 18

Cargo Space: Total Ramp/Tarmac Surface for Cargo Handling: 180,000 s.m. Warehouse Space: 205,000 s.m. Occupied: 100 per cent.

Customs: Yes Avg. Customs Clearance Time: 4 hrs.

Agriculture Inspector: Yes Freight Forwarders: Approx. 200.

Traffic: Total '05 Tonnage: 2,149,937 m.t., +0.8 per cent. Total '05 Aircraft Movements: 162,575, +7 per cent.

Comments: Incheon Free Economic Zone opened in 2006.

LUXEMBOURG

Findel Airport

P.O. Box 273, Luxembourg L-2013.

Identifier: LUX.

Contact: Gilbert Meyer.

Phone: +352 4798 2003.

Fax: +352 4798 2850.

E-Mail: gilbert.meyer@airport.etat.lu

Air Service: Total Carriers: 73, All-Cargo: 11.

Cargo Space: Total Ramp/Tarmac Surface for Cargo Handling: 90,000 s.m. Warehouse Space: 37,500 s.m. Occupied: 100 per cent.

Customs: Yes

Agriculture Inspector: Upon request.

Traffic: Total '05 Tonnage: 742,758 m.t., +4.2 per cent.

MALAYSIA

Kuala Lumpur Int'l Airport

FCZ Unit, Malaysia Airports (Sepang) SDN. BHD., Level 4, Airport Mgmt Ctr Bldg. KL Int'l Airport, Sepang, Selangor, Malaysia, 64000.

Identifier: KUL.

Contact: Nik Nazlan Nik Jaafar.

Phone: +603 87 766 028.

Fax: +603 87 766 044.

E-Mail: nnazlan@malaysiaairports.com

WWW.fcz.klia.com.my

Cargo Space: Total Ramp/Tarmac Surface for Cargo Handling: Over 92,900 s.m. Warehouse Space: 52,000 s.m. Occupied: 100 per cent.

FTZ: Yes

Special Services/Facilities: Handling for large animals, equine; refrigeration for cut flowers, perishable food, frozen goods; quarantine, HazMat, bonded and secure storage.

Customs: Yes.

Agriculture Inspector: Yes.

Traffic: Total '05 Tonnage: 655,944 m.t., +0.1 per cent. Total '05 Aircraft Movements: 182,386, +10.5 per cent.

Distance to Connecting Transport (kms): Rail Terminal: 20, Ocean Port: 70, Hwy: 20, Truck Terminal: On Site, Intermodal Centre: On Site.

Penang International Airport

Bayan Lepas, Georgetown, Pulau Penang, 11900, Malaysia

Identifier: PEN.

Phone: +60 4 643 4411.

Fax: +60 4 643 5339.

Air Service: Total Carriers: 20, All-Cargo: 10.

Cargo Space: Total Ramp/Tarmac Surface for Cargo Handling: 57,889 s.m. Warehouse Space: 32,507 s.m. Occupied: 60 per cent.

FTZ: Yes

Customs: Yes

Agriculture Inspector: Yes

Traffic: Total '05 Tonnage: 222,123 m.t., +3.8 per cent. Total '05 Aircraft Movements: 34,616, +4.7 per cent.

Senai International Airport

Sultan Ismail Airport, Johor Bahru, Johor, Malaysia 81250.

Identifier: JHB.

Contact: Shaun Kumar, GM Bus. Dev.

Phone: +60 7 599 4500.

Fax: +60 7 599 6624.

Cargo Space: Total Ramp Tarmac Surface for Cargo Handling: 48,047 s.m. Warehouse Space: Under development.

Customs: Yes

Traffic: Total '05 Tonnage: 7,518 m.t., -9.4 per cent.

Distance to Connecting Transport (kms): Rail Terminal: 7, Ocean Port 35, Hwy: 5, Truck Terminal: On Site.

MEXICO

Aeropuerto De Monterrey

Carretera A. Miguel Aleman, KM 24, Apodaca, Nuevo Leon, Mexico, 66600.

Identifier: MTY.

Contact: Raul Gimenez Jimeno.

Phone: 818 156 0900 al 05.

Fax: 818 369 0891.

E-Mail: monterrey@oma.bz

WWW.gacn.com.mx

Air Service: Total Carriers: 21, All-Cargo: 9, Non-Scheduled Charter: 3

Cargo Space: Total Ramp/Tarmac Surface for Cargo Handling: 26,000 s.m. Occupied: 70 per cent.

FTZ: Yes

Customs: Yes

Agriculture Inspector: Yes

Traffic: Total '05 Tonnage: 41,249 m.t., +3.7 per cent. Total '05 Aircraft Movements: 94,292, -0.8 per cent.

THE NETHERLANDS

Amsterdam Airport Schiphol

PO Box 7501, Luchthaven, Schiphol,1118 ZG, The Netherlands.

Identifier: AMS.

Contact: F. Van Der Ent.

Phone: +31 20 601 4530.

Fax: +31 20 601 2936.

E-Mail: cargo@schiphol.nl

WWW.schiphol.nl

Air Service: Total Carriers: 113, All-Cargo: 28, Non-Scheduled Charter: 25.

Cargo Space: Total Ramp/Tarmac Surface for Cargo Handling: 313,950 s.m.Warehouse Space: 373,777 s.m. Occupied: 99 per cent

FTZ: Yes

Special Services/Facilities: Handling for large animals, equine; refrigeration for cut flowers, perishable food, frozen goods; quarantine, HazMat, bonded and secure storage.

Customs: Yes Avg. Customs Clearance Time: immediately.

Agriculture Inspector: Yes Freight Forwarders: >100.

Traffic: Total '05 Tonnage: 1,449,855 m.t., +20 per cent. Total '05 Aircraft Movements: 404,594, +0.5 per cent.

Distance to Connecting Transport (kms): Rail Terminal: 10, Ocean Port: 10, Highway: 0.4, Truck Terminal: 0.1, Inland Waterway Port: 10, Intermodal Centre: 10

Comments: New cargo facilities completed in February 2007, estimated 28,000 s.m. additional ramp space and 15,000 s.m. additional warehouse space.

Maastricht Aachen Airport

PO Box 1, Maastricht Airport, NL 6199ZN, The Netherlands.

Identifier: MST.

Contact: W. Dohmen, Commercial Mgr.

Phone: +31 43 358 9721.

Fax: +31 43 358 9933.

E-Mail: w.dohmen@mhs.nl

WWW.mhs.nl

Cargo Space: Total Ramp/Tarmac Surface for Cargo Handling: 28,000 s.m. Warehouse Space: 11,000 s.m. Occupied: 60 per cent.

FTZ: Yes

Special Services/Facilities: Handling for large animals, equine; refrigeration for cut flowers, perishable food, frozen goods; quarantine, HazMat, bonded and secure storage.

Customs: Yes

Agriculture Inspector: Yes Freight Forwarders: 10

Traffic: Total '05 Tonnage: 57,509 m.t., +30.1 per cent. Total '05 Aircraft Movements: 19,806, -39.2 per cent.

Distance to Connecting Transport (kms): Rail Terminal: 10, Hwy: 1.

NORWAY

Oslo Airport

PO Box 100, N-2061 Gardermoen, Norway

Identifier: OSL.

Contact: Knut Stabaek.

Phone: +47 64812349.

Fax: +47 64812355.

E-Mail: knut.stabaek@osl.no

WWW.osl.no

Air Service: Total Carriers: 96, All-Cargo: 6, Non-Scheduled Charter: 11.

Cargo Space: Total Ramp/Tarmac Surface for Cargo Handling: 200,000 s.m. Warehouse Space: 25,500 s.m.

Special Services/Facilities: Handling for large animals, equine; refrigeration for cut flowers, perishable food, frozen goods; quarantine, HazMat, bonded and secure storage.

Customs: Yes

Agriculture Inspector: Yes

Traffic: Total '05 Tonnage: 201,404 m.t., +2.6 per cent.

Distance to Connecting Transport (kms): Rail Terminal: 35, Ocean Port: 45, Truck Terminal: On Site.

PERU

Jorge Chavez Int'l Airport

Av. Elmer Faucett, Callao, Peru, Callao 01.

Identifier: LIM.

Contact: Peter Schreier.

Phone: +533 575 0912.

Fax: +533 574 2120.

E-Mail: pschreier@lap.com.pe

Cargo Space: Total Ramp/Tarmac Surface for Cargo Handling: 45,000 s.m. Warehouse Space: 12,000 s.m.

FTZ: Yes

Customs: Yes Avg. Customs Clearance Time: 1-3 days

Agriculture Inspector: Yes Freight Forwarders: Approx 250.

Traffic: Total '05 Tonnage: 177,358 +1.4 per cent.

Comments: New cargo facilities to be completed 2008, adding estimated 40,000 ramp and 50,000 s.m. warehouse space.

RUSSIA

Domodedovo Int'l Airport

Domodedovo Airport, Domodedovo District, Moscow Region, Russia, 142015.

Identifier: DME.

Phone: +7 495 363 6111.

Fax: +7 495 795 3825.

E-Mail: dtk@eastline.ru

WWW.domodedovo.ru

Air Service: Total Carriers: 72, All-Cargo: 11, Non-Scheduled Charter: 8. Warehouse Space: 3,600 s.m.

FTZ: Yes

Special Services/Facilities: Handling for large animals, equine; refrigeration for cut flowers, perishable food, frozen goods; quarantine, HazMat, bonded and secure storage.

Customs: Yes.

Agriculture Inspector: Yes

Traffic: Total '05 Tonnage: 115,351 m.t., -38.5 per cent.

Comments: Construction has started on office building to open in 2007 and work will be started on storage area to add 10,000 s.m. of space.

SINGAPORE

Singapore Changi Airport

PO Box 1, Singapore 918141.

Identifier: SIN.

Contact: Damon Wong.

Phone: +65 6541 2179.

Fax: +65 6542 5390.

E-Mail: damon_wong@caas.gov.sg

WWW.changiairport.com.sg

Air Service: Total Carriers: 80, All-Cargo: 8 pure freighter airlines, 10 airlines with both cargo and pax operations, Non-Scheduled Charter: 8-10

Cargo Space: Total Ramp/Tarmac Surface for Cargo Handling: 71,100 s.m. Warehouse Space: 117,000 s.m. (including office area) Occupied: 59 per cent. Free Trade Zone: Yes

Special Services/Facilities: Handling for large animals and equine; refrigeration for cut flowers, perishables, frozen goods; quarantine, HazMat, bonded and secure storage.

Customs: Yes Avg. Customs Clearance Time: 90 per cent within 13 minutes.

Agriculture Inspector: Yes on call 24 hrs. Freight Forwarders: 223 in four cargo agent buildings.

Traffic: Total '05 Tonnage: 1,833,721 m.t., +3.3 per cent. Total '05 Aircraft Movements: 204,138, +10.4 per cent.

Distance to Connecting Transport (kms): Ocean Port: 24, Intermodal Centre: 24 from port.

Comments: Developments underway to enhance capability to handle a wider range of niche cargo.

SPAIN

Barcelona Airport

Centros Logisticos Aeroportuarios, SA, Edifici Serveis Generales of A003, Aeroport De BCN-El Prat, 08820, Barcelona, Spain.

Identifier: BCN.

Contact: Eduardo Rebollo.

Phone: +34 93 298-4291.

Fax: +34 93 298 4292.

E-Mail: afabregas@aena.es

WWW.clasanet.com

Warehouse Space: 50,000 s.m.

Special Services/Facilities:

Handling for large animals, equine; refrigeration for cut flowers, perishable food, frozen goods; quarantine, HazMat, bonded and secure storage.

Customs: Yes

Agriculture Inspector: Yes

Traffic: Total '05 Tonnage: 101,910 tons, +8.3 per cent. Total '05 Aircraft Movements: 307,799, +5.6 per cent.

Distance to Connecting Transport (kms): Ocean Port: 3.

Comments: Developing several areas; others planned to be developed giving a final total area of 62 HA to the cargo centre.

Madrid Airport

Centros Logisticos Aeroportuarios, SA, Edificio Servicios Generales of 701, Aeropuerto de Madrid-Barajas, Madrid, Spain 28042.

Identifier: MAD.

Contact: Anais Fabregas

Phone: +34 91 393 7601.

Fax: +34 91 329 4646.

E-Mail: afabregas@aena.es

WWW.clasanet.com

Warehouse Space: 160,000 s.m.

Special Services/Facilities: Handling for large animals, equine; refrigeration for cut flowers, perishable food, frozen goods; quarantine, HazMat, bonded and secure storage.

Customs: Yes

Agriculture Inspector: Yes

Traffic: Total '05 Tonnage: 365,596 tons, -2.7 per cent. Total '05 Aircraft Movements: 415,677, +3.5 per cent.

Comments: We are expanding the cargo centre with a whole new area which will add 32.5 HA to the current surface.

SWEDEN

Goteborg-Landvetter Airport

SE-438 80 Landvetter, Sweden.

Identifier: GOT

Contact: Bjorn Lennartz, Bus. Dev. Mgr.

Phone: +46 31 941434.

Fax: +46 31 941554.

E-Mail: bjorn.lennartz@lfv.se

WWW.lfv.se

Special Services/Facilities: Handling for large animals, equine; refrigeration for cut flowers, perishable food, frozen goods; quarantine, HazMat, bonded and secure storage.

Customs: Yes. Clearance Time: 30 minutes or less.

Agriculture Inspector: Yes.

Traffic: Total '05 Tonnage: 60,635 m.t., -9.1 per cent.

Distance to Connecting Transport (kms): Rail Terminal: 20, Ocean Port: 30, Hwy: 1, Inland Waterway Port: 30.

Stockholm-Arlanda Airport

Stockholm-Arlanda Airport, Luftfartsverket, SE 19045 Stockholm, Sweden.

Identifier: ARN.

Contact: Karsten Bjarbo, Mgr Cargo Ops.

Phone: +46 8 797 6160.

Fax: +46 8 797 6984.
E-Mail: karsten.bjarbo@lfv.se
WWW.arlanda.com
Air Service: Total Carriers: 69; All-Cargo: 8. Non-Scheduled Charter: 3-4.
Cargo Space: Total Ramp/Tarmac Surface for Cargo Handling: 100,000 s.m. (7 code E-stands plus 11 code G-Stands) Warehouse Space: 60,000 s.m. Occupied: 80 per cent.
FTZ: Yes
Special Services/Facilities: Handling for large animals; refrigeration for cut flowers, perishable food, frozen goods; quarantine, HazMat, bonded and secure storage.
Customs: Yes. Avg Customs Clearance Time: less than 1 hr.
Agriculture Inspector: Yes. Freight Forwarders: 15.
Traffic: Total '05 Tonnage: 299,773 tons, +5.6 per cent. Total '05 Aircraft Movements: 234,044, -4.6 per cent.
Distance to Connecting Transport (kms): Rail Terminal: 40, Ocean Port: 40, Hwy: 1, Truck Terminal: 12, Intermodal Centre: 40.
Comments: New cargo facilities to be completed in 2008 adding 500 s.m. of ramp space and 15,000 s.m. of warehouse space.

SWITZERLAND

Euroairport/Basel-Mulhouse-Freiburg Airport

Flughafen Basel-Mulhouse, CH-4030, Basel, Switzerland.
Identifier: BSL.
Contact: Ingrid Sturzenegger.
Phone: +41 61 325 4337.
Fax: +41 61-325-7566.
E-Mail: isturzeuegger@euroairport.com
WWW.euroairport.com
Air Service: Total Carriers: 27, All-Cargo: 4, Non-Scheduled Charter: 3
Cargo Space: Total Ramp/Tarmac Surface for Cargo Handling: 36,000 s.m. Warehouse Space: 19,600 s.m. Occupied: 20 per cent
FTZ: Yes
Customs: Yes Avg. Customs Clearance Time: 2-3 hrs.
Agriculture Inspector: 2 km away
Traffic: Total '05 Tonnage: 32,205 m.t., -6.1 per cent.

Geneva International Airport

PO Box 100, Geneva, Switzerland, 1215.
Identifier: GVA.
Phone: +41 22 717 71 11.
Fax: +41 22 798 6377.
E-Mail: cargo@gva.ch
WWW.gva.ch

Cargo Space: Total Ramp/Tarmac Surface for Cargo Handling: 70,000 s.m. Warehouse Space: 24,000 s.m. Occupied: 90 per cent.

FTZ: Yes

Customs: Yes Avg. Customs Clearance Time: 1 hr. Freight Forwarders: 38

Traffic: Total '05 Tonnage: 39,118 m.t., -7.6 per cent. Total '05 Aircraft Movements: 170,938, +2.6 per cent.

Zurich Unique Airport

Unique Flughafen Zurich, Postfach, Zurich, Switzerland, CH-8058.

Identifier: ZRH.

Phone: +41 1 816-2211.

Fax: +41 1 816-5747.

E-Mail: fracht@uniqueairport.com.

WWW.uniqueairport.com.

Air Service: Total Carriers: 150, All-Cargo: 2 Warehouse Space: 60,000 s.m. Occupied: 100 per cent.

Customs: Yes

Agriculture Inspector: Yes

Traffic: Total '05 Tonnage: 348,596 m.t., +2.5 per cent. Total '05 Aircraft Movements: 267,369, +0.7 per cent.

TAIWAN

Taipei Chiang Kai-Shek Int'l Airport

PO Box 9, Chiang Kai-Shek Airport, Taoyuan, ROC, Taiwan 337.

Identifier: TPE.

Phone: +886 3-398-2430.

Fax: +886 3-383-4588.

E-Mail: manager@cksairport.gov.tw

WWW.cksairport.gov.tw.

Air Service: Total Carriers: 43, All-Cargo: 9

Cargo Space: Total Ramp/Tarmac Surface for Cargo Handling: 375,800 s.m. Warehouse Space: 208,681 s.m. Occupied: 90 per cent.

FTZ: Yes.

Special Services/Facilities: Handling for large animals, equine; refrigeration for cut flowers, perishable food, frozen goods; quarantine, HazMat, bonded and secure storage.

Customs: Yes Avg. Customs Clearance Time: 52 minutes

Agriculture Inspector: Yes

Traffic: Total '05 Tonnage: 1,705,318 m.t., +0.3 per cent. Total '05 Aircraft Movements: 152,607, +2.4 per cent.

Distance to Connecting Transport (kms): Rail Terminal: 15, Ocean Port: 18, Truck Terminal: 3.

THAILAND

Bangkok International Airport

Airport of Thailand Public Co Ltd, 222 Cargo Terminal 1, Bangkok Int'l Airport, Vibhavadi Rangsit Rd, Seekan Donmuang, Bangkok, Thailand, 10210.

Identifier: BKK.

Phone: +662-996-8561.

Fax: +662-996-8562.

E-Mail: anupong@hotmail.com

WWW.tags.co.th

Warehouse Space: 39,172 s.m.

Customs: Yes

Traffic: Total '05 Tonnage; 1,140,836 m.t., +7.8 per cent. Total '05 Aircraft Movements: 285,434, +9 per cent.

Distance to Connecting Transport (kms): Rail Terminal: est. 2-3, Ocean Port: Over 150, Hwy: 2, Truck Terminal: 1, Inland Waterway Port: est. 50.

TURKEY

Sabiha Gokcen Int'l Airport

Kurtkoy—Pendik, Istanbul, Turkey, 81440.

Identifier: SAW.

Contact: Mr. Tulga Tilev.

Phone: +90 216 585 5174.

Fax: +90 216 585 5281.

E-Mail: tulga.tilev@sgairport.com

WWW.sgairport.com

Air Service: Total Carriers: 13, All-Cargo: 1

Cargo Space: Total Ramp/Tarmac Surface for Cargo Handling: 63,200 s.m. Warehouse Space: 8,000 s.m. Occupied: 5 per cent.

FTZ: Yes

Customs: Yes Avg. Customs Clearance Time: 1 hr

Agriculture Inspector: 25 km away

Traffic: Total '05 Tonnage: 6,505 m.t., +30 per cent.

UNITED ARAB EMIRATES

Abu Dhabi Int'l Airport

Abu Dhabi Airport Services, PO Box 3668, Abu Dhabi, United Arab Emirates 3668.

Identifier: AUH.

Contact: Mohammed Said Al-Hameli.

Phone: +971 2 575 7110.

Fax: +971 2 575 7157.

E-Mail: auhapsvc@emirates.net.ae

WWW.abudhabiairptsvcs.com

Air Service: Total Carriers: 44; All-Cargo: 11; Non-Scheduled Charter: 6

Cargo Space: 15,000 s.m. Warehouse Space: 14,095 s.m. Occupied: 100 per cent.

FTZ: Yes. Special Services: Handling for large animals; refrigeration for cut flowers, perishable food, frozen goods; quarantine, HazMat, bonded and secure storage. Planned handling for equine.

Customs: Yes. Avg Customs Clearance Time: 30 minutes.

Agriculture Inspector: Yes. Freight Forwarders: 28

Traffic: Total '05 Tonnage: 202,000 to 240,000 tons, +40 per cent. Total '05 Aircraft Movements: 23,773, -2 per cent.

Distance to Connecting Transport: Ocean Port: 35 km, Interstate Hwy: 1, Truck Terminal: On Site.

Comments: New cargo facilities to be completed in 2009. Double the capacity of warehouse and tonnage that can be handled.

Dubai Airport

PO Box 522, Dubai, United Arab Emirates

Identifier: DXB.

Contact: Kevin Ennis.

Phone: +971 4 2124100.

Fax: 971 4 2996889.

E-Mail: kennis@dnata.com

WWW.dnata.com

Air Service: Total Carriers: 107, All-Cargo: 10, Non-Scheduled Charter: 45

Cargo Space: Total Ramp/Tarmac Surface for Cargo Handling: Warehouse 40,000 s.m., Warehouse Space: 10,000 s.m. Occupied: 100 per cent.

FTZ: Yes

Special Services/Facilities: Handling for large animals, equine; refrigeration for cut flowers, perishable food, frozen goods; quarantine, HazMat, bonded and secure storage.

Customs: Yes. Avg Customs Clearance Time: 20 mins.

Agriculture Inspector: Yes.

Traffic: Total '05 Tonnage: 1,314,904 m.t., +12.5 per cent. Total '05 Aircraft Movements: 217,165, +12.6 per cent.

Distance to Connecting Transport (kms): Ocean Port: 5, Hwy: 5.

Comments: New cargo facilities completed in January 2007, adding 15,000 s.m. of warehouse space. Separate express handling terminal and separate air cargo terminal at seaport and free zone.

Fujairah International Airport

PO Box 977, Fujairah, United Arab Emirates.

Identifier: FJR.

Phone: +971 9 222 6222.

Fax: +971 9 224 1414.
E-Mail: gm@fujairah-airport.com
WWW.fujairah-airport.com
Cargo Space: Total Ramp/Tarmac Surface for Cargo Handling: 8,645 s.m. Warehouse Space: 4,645 s.m. Occupied: 60 per cent.
Special Services/Facilities: HazMat, bonded and secure storage; planned refrigeration for perishable food and quarantine.
Customs: Yes. Clearance Time: 15 to 30 minutes.
Agriculture Inspector: Yes
Traffic: Total '05 Tonnage: 22,129 m.t., -13.3 per cent.
Distance to Connecting Transport (kms): Ocean Port: 5, Highway: 1, Truck Terminal: On Site, Intermodal Centre: On Site.

Sharjah International Airport

PO Box 8, Sharjah, United Arab Emirates.
Identifier: SHJ.
Contact: Ali H. Kombargi.
Phone: +971 60-558-1252.
Fax: +971 60-558-0449.
E-Mail: mktg@sharjahairport.ae
WWW.sharjahairport.ae
Air Service: Total Carriers: 170, All-Cargo: 110, Non-Scheduled Charter: 64
Cargo Space: Total Ramp/Tarmac Surface for Cargo Handling: 167,575 s.m. Warehouse Space: 32,000 s.m. Occupied: 90 per cent.
FTZ: Yes
Special Services/Facilities: Handling for large animals, equine; refrigeration for cut flowers, perishable food, frozen goods; quarantine, HazMat, bonded and secure storage.
Customs: Yes.
Agriculture Inspector: Yes Freight Forwarders: 48
Traffic: Total '05 Tonnage: 229,472 m.t., +16.4 per cent. Total '05 Aircraft Movements: 40,752, +13.5 per cent.
Distance to Connecting Transport (kms): Ocean Port: 15, Hwy: 300 mtrs, Truck Terminal: 15

UNITED KINGDOM

Edinburgh Airport

BAA, Heathrow Point West, 234 Bath Road, Harlington, Hayes, Middlesex, UK, UB3 5AP
Identifier: EDI.
Contact: Chris Mankelow.
Phone: +44 208 745 4584.
Fax: +44 208 745 7237.

E-Mail: chris_mankelow@baa.com
WWW.baa.com/cargo
Air Services: Total Carriers: 50, All-Cargo: 4.
Cargo Space: Warehouse Space: 9250 s.m. Occupied: 100 per cent.
FTZ: No
Special Services/Facilities: HazMat, bonded and secure storage.
Customs: Yes. Avg. Customs Clearance Time: 1 hr.
Agriculture Inspector: 8 miles away.
Traffic: Total '05 Tonnage: 127,114 m.t., +1.4 per cent.
Distance Connecting Transport (miles): Rail Terminal: 8, Interstate Hwy: 3.6.

Glasgow Airport

BAA, Heathrow Point West, 234 Bath Road, Harlington, Hayes, Middlesex, UK, UB3 5AP
Identifier: GLA.
Contact: Chris Mankelow.
Phone: +44 208 745 4584.
Fax: +44 208 745 7237.
E-Mail: chris_mankelow@baa.com
WWW.baa.com/cargo
FTZ: No
Special Services/Facilities: Quarantine, HazMat, bonded and secure storage. Planned refrigeration for cut flowers, perishable food, frozen goods.
Customs: Yes.
Agriculture Inspector: 20 miles.
Traffic: Total '05 Tonnage: 110.574 m.t., +2.6 per cent.

Glasgow Prestwick International Airport

Aviation House, Prestwick, Ayrshire, Scotland, United Kingdom KA9 2PL
Identifier: PIK.
Contact: Stuart Sinclair.
Phone: +44 1292 511052.
Fax: +44 208 1292 511070.
E-Mail: ssinclair@gpia.co.uk
WWW.gpia.co.uk
Cargo Space: Total Ramp/Tarmac Surface for Cargo Handling: 3 x 747F & substantial remote parking. Warehouse Space: 115,000 s.f. Occupied 75 per cent.
Customs: Yes.
Agriculture Inspector: 30 miles.
Traffic: Total '05 Tonnage: 55,138 m.t., -1.8 per cent. Total '05 Aircraft Movements: 29,706, -13.8 per cent.
Distance to Connecting Transport: Hwy: On-Site, Truck Terminal: On Site.

London Gatwick Airport

BAA, Heathrow Point West, 234 Bath Road, Harlington, Hayes, Middlesex, UK, UB3 5AP.

Identifier: LGW.

Contact: Chris Mankelow.

Phone: +44 208 745 4584.

Fax: +44 208 745 7237.

WWW.baa.com

Cargo Space: Total Ramp/Tarmac Surface for Cargo Handling: 100,000 s.f. Warehouse Space: 250,000 s.f. Occupied: 90 per cent.

Customs: Yes

Agriculture Inspector: Yes

Traffic: Total '05 Tonnage: 232,133 m.t., +2.2 per cent. Total '05 Aircraft Movements: 261,272, +4 per cent.

Distance to Connecting Transport: Hwy 2.

London Heathrow Airport

BAA, Heathrow Point West, 234 Bath Road, Harlington, Hayes, Middlesex, UK, UB3 5AP.

Identifier: LHR.

Contact: Chris Mankelow.

Phone: +44 208 745 4584.

Fax: +44 208 745 7237.

WWW.baa.com

Cargo Space: Total Ramp/Tarmac Surface for Cargo Handling: 56 hectares. Warehouse Space: 2 million s.f. Occupied: 97 per cent.

Special Services/Facilities: Handling for large animals, equine; refrigeration for cut flowers, perishable food, frozen goods; quarantine, HazMat, bonded and secure storage.

Customs: Yes Customs Clearance Time: 1 hr.

Agriculture Inspector: Yes

Traffic: Total '05 Tonnage: 1,389,591 m.t., -1.6 per cent. Total '05 Aircraft Movements: 477,888, +0.4 per cent.

Distance to Connecting Transport (miles): Hwy 2.

London Stansted Airport

BAA, Heathrow Point West, 234 Bath Road, Harlington, Hayes, Middlesex, UK, UB3 5AP.

Identifier: STN.

Contact: Chris Mankelow.

Phone: +44 208 745 4584.

Fax: +44 208 745 7237.

WWW.baa.com

Air Service: All-Cargo: 25, Non-Scheduled Charter: 57 Warehouse Space: 450,000 s.f. Occupied: 100 per cent

Customs: Yes Customs Clearance Time: 1 hr.

Agriculture Inspector: No

Traffic: Total '05 Tonnage: 256,815 m.t., +6.5 per cent. Total '05 Aircraft Movements: 193,508 +0.7 per cent.

Distance to Connecting Transport (miles): Hwy 2.

Manchester Airport

Manchester Airport, Manchester, M90 1QX.

Identifier: MAN.

Contact: Michael O'Connor.

Phone: +44 161 489 5021.

Fax: +44 161 489 2703.

E-Mail: ichael.oconnor@manairport.co.uk

WWW.manchesterairport.co.uk

Air Service: Total Carriers: 100+, All-Cargo: 4, Non-Scheduled Charter: numerous.

Cargo Space: Total Ramp/Tarmac Surface for Cargo Handling: 100+ stands, cargo handling anywhere on ramp. Warehouse Space: 55,000 s.m. Occupied: 95 per cent.

Customs: Yes Avg. Customs Clearance Time: within minutes.

Agriculture Inspector: Yes Freight Forwarders: 100+

Traffic: Total '05 Tonnage: 150,649 m.t., -2.2 per cent. Total '05 Aircraft Movements: 215,247, +4.6 per cent.

Distance to Connecting Transport (miles): Rail Terminal: On Site, Ocean Port: 35, Highway: On Site, Truck Terminal: On Site, Inland Waterway Port: 10, Intermodal Ctr: several.

Comments: Recently released master plan to be completed in 2030. Facilities will be expanded to handle 500,000 tonnes of cargo.

Nottingham East Midlands Airport

NEMA HQ, Bldg 34, Ambassador Road, Nottingham EMA, Castle Donington, Derby, United Kingdom, DE74 2SA.

Identifier: EMA.

Contact: Bill Blanchard.

Phone: +44 1332 852 894.

Fax: +44 1332 853 202.

E-Mail: cargo@nottinghamema.com

WWW.NEMAcargo.com

Air Service: Total Carriers: 50+, All-Cargo: 10, Non-Scheduled Charter: 20+

Cargo Space: Total Ramp/Tarmac Surface for Cargo Handling: 220,000 s.m./2,367 million s.f. Warehouse Space: 85,225 s.m./917,000 s.f. Occupied: 95 per cent.

FTZ: No

Special Services/Facilities: Handling for large animals and equine (all exports and EU imports only) HazMat, bonded and secure storage, EU approved Border Inspection Post.

Customs: Yes Avg. Customs Clearance Time: immediate to 2 hrs.

Agriculture Inspector: Off-site but available at short notice.

Traffic: Total '05 Tonnage: 292,993 m.t., +5 per cent. Total '05 Aircraft Movements: 19,185 (cargo only), +2.5 per cent.

Distance to Connecting Transport (miles): Rail Terminal: 7, Highway: 1, Truck Terminal: 6, Ocean Port: 66.

Comments: Airport operates 24/7 and runs all-cargo flight five nights a week to the U.S. and Hong Kong. Cargo Terminal 5 (40,000 s.f.) opens fall 2006.

Robin Hood Airport/Doncaster Sheffield

Heyford House, First Avenue, Doncaster, United Kingdom, DN9 3RH.

Identifier: DSA
Contact: Stuart Sinclair, Airfreight Dev Mgr.
Phone: +44 1302 801056.
Fax: +44 1302 801011.
E-Mail: ssinclair@robinhoodairport.com
WWW.robinhoodairport.com
Air Service: Total Carriers: 8.

Cargo Space: Total Ramp/Tarmac Surface for Cargo Handling: 100,000 s.f., Warehouse Space: 47,000 s.f. Occupied: 90 per cent.

FTZ: No.

Special Services/Facilities: Handling for large animals, equine; quarantine, HazMat, bonded and secure storage. Planned refrigeration for perishable food.

Customs: Yes. Avg. Customs Clearance Time: 1 hr.
Agriculture Inspector: 8 miles away.
Traffic: Total '05 Aircraft Movements: 8,000 (new airport opened April 2005.
Comments: Numerous ad hoc freighters handled.

YUGOSLAVIA

Airport Belgrad

Beograd 59, 11180 Belgrad, Belgrade, Serbia, Yugoslavia

Identifier: BEG.
Contact: Slobodan Jaredic, Head of Cargo Dept.
Phone: +381 11 2097 692.
Fax: +381 11 2286 191.
E-Mail: cargo@beg.aero
WWW.beg.aero
Air Service: Total Carriers: 15, All-Cargo: 20, Non-Scheduled Charter: 4

Cargo Space: Total Ramp/Tarmac Surface for Cargo Handling: 2,500 s.m. Warehouse Space: 4,300 s.m. Occupied: 50 per cent.

FTZ: No

Special Services/Facilities: Handling for equine; refrigeration for cut flowers, perishables, frozen goods; HazMat, bonded and secure storage. Planned handling for large animals; quarantine facilities under construction.

Customs: Yes Avg. Customs Clearance Time: 24 hrs
Agriculture Inspector: Yes Freight Forwarders: more than 80.

Traffic: Total '05 Tonnage: 8,015 tons, -8 per cent. Total '05 Aircraft Movements: 37,614, +3 per cent.

Distance to Connecting Transport (kms): Rail Terminal: 15, Hwy: 1, Truck Terminal: 5, Inland Waterway Port: 20, Intermodal Centre: 20.

Comments: Working with strategic partner to develop logistics center with new facility (6,000 s.m.), logistics zone (min. 20,000 s.m.) and business centre; completion date was March 2007.

INTERNATIONAL AIR CARRIER LIABILITY: THE MONTREAL CONVENTION

January 20, 2006

The 1999 Montreal Convention came into force on 4 November 2003 and is in force for 66 States among them almost all States of major importance in international air transport. In this new treatise, Professors Paul Stephen Dempsey and Michael Milde of McGill's Institute of Air and Space Law present to the reader a compact analytical guide to the 1999 Montreal Convention addressing air carrier passenger and cargo liability in international aviation.

4

Marine Cargo Ships and Ocean Shipping

CARGO SHIP

A *cargo ship* or *freighter* is any sort of ship or vessel that carries cargo, goods and materials from one port to another. Thousands of cargo carriers ply the world's seas and oceans each year; they handle the bulk of international trade. Cargo ships are usually specially designed for the task, being equipped with cranes and other mechanisms to load and unload, and come in all sizes.

Specialized types of cargo vessels include container ships and bulk carriers (technically tankers and supertankers are cargo ships, although they are routinely thought of as a separate category).

History

The earliest records of waterborne activity mention the carriage of items for trade; the evidence of history and archaeology shows the practice to be widespread by the beginning of the first millennium BC. The desire to operate trade routes over longer distances and at more seasons of the year motivated improvements in ship design during the Middle Ages.

Before the middle of the 19th century, the incidence of piracy resulted in most cargo ships being armed, sometimes quite heavily, as in the case of the Manila galleons and East Indiamen.

Piracy

Piracy is still quite common in some waters, particularly around Asia, most notably in the Malacca Straits, a narrow channel between Indonesia and Singapore/Malaysia. In 2004, the governments of those three nations agreed to provide better protection for the ships passing through the Straits. Also piracy prone are the waters off Somalia and Nigeria, while smaller vessels are also in danger along parts of the South American coasts.

Definitions

While the definitions have become "cross-pollinated" over the years, "cargo" technically refers to the goods carried aboard the ship for hire, while "freight" refers to the compensation the ship or charterer receives for carrying the cargo.

Generally, the modern ocean shipping business is divided into two classes:

1. *Liner business*: typically (but not exclusively) container vessels (wherein "general cargo" is carried in 20 or 40-foot "boxes"), operating as "common carriers", calling a regularly-published schedule of ports. A common carrier refers to a regulated service where any member of the public may book cargo for shipment, according to long-established and internationally agreed rules.
2. *Tramp-tanker business*: generally this is private business arranged between the shipper and receiver and facilitated by the vessel owners or operators, who offer their vessels for hire to carry bulk (dry or liquid) or break bulk (cargoes with individually handled pieces) to any suitable port(s) in the world, according to a specifically drawn contract, called a charter party.

Larger cargo ships are generally operated by shipping lines: companies that specialize in the handling of cargo in general. Smaller vessels, such as coasters, are often owned by their operators.

Merchant vessels usually carry the designation *M/V* for "Motor Vessel" (oil/Diesel). It is used as part of a ship's name, such as "M/V *Independence*", similarly to how "SS" (now seldom used) stands for "Steam Ship" (coal) in names such as SS *Uganda*.

Famous cargo ships would include the Liberty ships of World War II, which were prefabricated all over the USA and then assembled by the coast in an average of six weeks and as little as four days. These ships allowed the allies to replace older cargo vessels with ones that were faster then the Kriegsmarine's U-boats could sink and contributed significantly to the ability of the Allies to keep Britain in the war and build up troops and equipment for the D-Day landings.

Lake freighters built for the Great Lakes in North America differ in design from "salties" because of the difference in wave size and frequency in the lakes. A number of these boats are so large that they cannot leave the lakes because they do not fit into the locks on the Saint Lawrence Seaway.

Sizes of Cargo Ships

Cargo ships are categorized partly by their capacity, partly by their weight, and partly by their dimensions (often with reference to the various canals and canal locks through which they can travel). Some common categories include:

- Small handy size, carriers of 20,000-28,000 deadweight tonnage.
- Handy size, carriers of 28,000-40,000 deadweight tonnage.
- Handymax, carriers of 40,000-50,000 dwt.

- Seawaymax, the largest size which can traverse the St. Lawrence Seaway.
- Aframax, oil tankers between 75,000 and 115,000 dwt. This is the largest size defined by the average freight rate assessment (AFRA) scheme.
- Suezmax, the largest size which can traverse the Suez Canal.
- Panamax, the largest size which can traverse the Panama Canal (generally: vessels with a width smaller than 32.2 meter).
- Capesize, vessels larger than Panamax and Suezmax, which must traverse the Cape of Good Hope and Cape Horn in order to travel between oceans.
- VLCC (Very Large Crude Carrier), supertankers between 150,000 and 320,000 dwt.
- ULCC (Ultra Large Crude Carrier), enormous supertankers between 320,000 and 550,000 dwt.

USHIP

uShip, Inc. (founded in 2003) is based in Austin, TX. uShip is an online auction marketplace for shipping. It uses a reverse auction system where users typically list large or awkward items (furniture, freight, cars, boats, etc.). uShip claims to have 25,000 registered service providers (as of August 2006), most of whom appear to be small movers, goods transporters, freight carriers, auto/boat haulers, etc.

uShip says that their reverse auction model helps to reduce shipping costs (uShip claims 60% savings) because movers competitively bid against each other and are often filling empty space in their trucks. uShip also claims that their feedback rating system, which is similar to that of eBay, builds trust and credibility between service providers and their customers.

- General
- Household Moving
- Vehicles
- Freight (Less-than-Truckload (LTL) Shipping)
- Special Care
- Agricultural
- Livestock
- Ridesharing/Carpooling (People).

IMPORT/EXPORT CONSOLIDATION

FedEx Trade Networks customizes cargo management service programmes that provide visibility of cargo and the most cost-effective usage of ocean container space.

Features of our consolidation programmes:

- Vendor coordination and management
- Bookings/on-hand notices
- Container load plans
- Inspection and sorting of cargo

- Positioning of samples
- Document collection and distribution
- Cargo insurance.

In addition, FedEx Trade Networks consolidation programmes offer reduced LCL rates, improved transit times, and allow your import and export transactions to be handled by one provider managing all related services.

Fuel Surcharges

Effective January 1, 2007, FedEx Express adjusted the fuel price at which surcharges begin, resulting in a 2 per cent overall fuel surcharge reduction. A fuel surcharge will be triggered only when the price of a gallon of kerosene-type jet fuel rises above $0.98. See the FedEx Express Fuel Surcharge Table Effective January 1, 2007.

Table 4.1: Surcharge Effective from January 1, 2007

FedEX Express		*FedEX Ground*	
Surcharge	*Effective Date*	*Surcharge*	*Effective Date*
8.50%	March 5, 2007-April 1, 2007	3.50%	March 5, 2007-April 1, 2007
10.00%	April 2, 2007-May 6, 2007	3.50%	April 2, 2007-May 6, 2007

The FedEx Express fuel surcharge for U.S., U.S. outbound and Puerto Rico express services is based on the spot price for jet fuel. This fuel surcharge does not apply to FedEx International Express Freight® (IXF) and FedEx International Airport-to-Airport℠ (ATA) services. The FedEx Express fuel surcharge for IXF and ATA services is based on chargeable weight. The fuel surcharge rate for FedEx Ground services applies to both U.S. and international shipments.

The surcharge percentage for FedEx Express services is subject to monthly adjustment based on a rounded average of the U.S. Gulf Coast (USGC) spot price for a gallon of kerosene-type jet fuel. The surcharge percentage for FedEx Ground services is subject to monthly adjustment based on a rounded average of the national U.S. on-highway average price for a gallon of diesel fuel.

Table 4.2: FedEx Express Fuel Surcharge (price per gallon)

At Least	*But Less Than*	*Surcharge*
	$0.98	0.00%
$0.98	$1.02	0.50%
$1.02	$1.06	1.00%
$1.06	$1.10	1.50%
$1.10	$1.14	2.00%
$1.14	$1.18	2.50%
$1.18	$1.22	3.00%
$1.22	$1.26	3.50%
$1.26	$1.30	4.00%
$1.30	$1.34	4.50%

(*Contd.*)

At Least	*But Less Than*	*Surcharge*
$1.34	$1.38	5.00%
$1.38	$1.42	5.50%
$1.42	$1.46	6.00%
$1.46	$1.50	6.50%
$1.50	$1.54	7.00%
$1.54	$1.58	7.50%
$1.58	$1.62	8.00%
$1.62	$1.66	8.50%
$1.66	$1.70	9.00%
$1.70	$1.74	10.00%
$1.74		10.50%

Fuel surcharge percentages and associated trigger points are subject to change without notice. If the fuel surcharge rises above 10.50 per cent or there are changes to the trigger points, the Table 4.2 will be updated.

Table 4.3: FedEx Ground Fuel Surcharge (prices per gallon)

Least	*But Less Than*	*Surcharge*
	$1.50	0.00%
$1.50	$1.58	0.50%
$1.58	$1.66	0.75%
$1.66	$1.74	1.00%
$1.74	$1.82	1.25%
$1.82	$1.90	1.50%
$1.90	$1.98	1.75%
$1.98	$2.06	2.00%
$2.06	$2.14	2.25%
$2.14	$2.22	2.50%
$2.22	$2.30	2.75%
$2.30	$2.38	3.00%
$2.38	$2.46	3.25%
$2.46	$2.54	3.50%
$2.54		3.75%

Fuel surcharge percentages and associated trigger points are subject to change without notice. See the FedEx Ground Tariff for more details. If the fuel surcharge rises above 3.75 per cent or there are changes to the trigger points, the above table will be updated.

Effective January 1, 2007 (FedEX Express)

For FedEx Express shipments, the related fuel surcharge is assessed on the net package rate plus applicable transportation-related surcharges.

For shipments within the U.S., this applies to the following transportation-related surcharges: courier pickup, delivery area surcharge, freight delivery reattempt, freight extended service area delivery, freight extended service area pickup, freight residential delivery, freight residential pickup, freight Saturday delivery, oversize residential delivery, return on-call pickup (FedEx ExpressTag®), Saturday delivery and Saturday pickup.

For FedEx Express U.S. export shipments, this applies to the following transportation-related surcharges: broker routing fee, courier pickup, extended service area delivery, extended service area pickup, FedEx International Premium® pickup, FedEx International Premium residential delivery, FedEx International Premium residential pickup, Saturday delivery and Saturday pickup.

Effective January 1, 2007 (FedEX Ground)

For FedEx Ground shipments, the related fuel surcharge is assessed on the net package rate plus applicable transportation-related surcharges.

For FedEx Ground shipments this applies to the following transportation-related surcharges: electronic call tag, manual call tag, oversize and unauthorized oversize packages, delivery area surcharge, residential delivery, and rural delivery.

Fuel Surcharge Updates

Changes to the FedEx Express and FedEx Ground fuel surcharges will be applied effective the first Monday of each month. The surcharge percentage will be reflected on your FedEx invoice. Information on the fuel surcharge for each month will be available approximately two weeks before the surcharge is applicable.

- For FedEx Express, see the USGC index for the spot price per gallon of kerosene-type jet fuel.
- For FedEx Ground, see the on-highway index for the price of a gallon of diesel fuel.
- The prices in these indexes are published by the U.S. Department of Energy and FedEx is not responsible for the information provided.

Table 4.4: Historical Fuel Surcharge Rates

FedEx Express		*FedEX Ground*	
Surcharge	*Effective Date*	*Surcharge*	*Effective Date*
10.50%	Feb. 5, 2007–March 4, 2007	3.75%	Feb. 5, 2007–March 4, 2007
9.50%	Jan. 1, 2007–Feb. 4, 2007	3.75%	Jan. 1, 2007–Feb. 4, 2007
11.50%	Dec. 4, 2006–Dec. 31, 2006	3.50%	Dec. 4, 2006–Dec. 31, 2006

INTERNATIONAL MARINE INSURANCE MANAGERS

International Marine Insurance Managers has a Binding Authority contracted to underwrite various marine risks on behalf of Lloyd's of London, the world's leading insurance market providing specialist insurance services to businesses in over 120 countries.

Lloyd's is the world's second largest commercial insurer and sixth largest reinsurance group. Approximately 5 per cent of world reinsurance is placed at Lloyd's, which also accounts for 50 per cent of the London market's international insurance premiums.

The strength of International Marine Insurance Managers is its solid relationship with Lloyd's of London since 1996. The manner in which Lloyd's do business, their credibility and what they stand for are unsurpassed in the insurance industry. Lloyd's is totally committed to IMIM and has met all obligations in terms of settling claims since the relationship was incepted.

Lloyd's trusts IMIM's local knowledge and experience. With the changing times in South Africa involving mergers, acquisitions and job losses, Lloyd's has been a significant and consistent player with the capacity required to underwrite big risks.

IMIM's Strengths

- IMIM has the reputation of being a solid Underwriting Manager/ Lloyd's Coverholder.
- IMIM has good market relationships countrywide which have assisted us in the writing of new business.
- IMIM has a core of good technical skills.
- IMIM is focused on teamwork.
- IMIM has a solid relationship with Lloyd's and access to their capacity.

The History of IMIM

International Marine was registered in November 1996 as Marine Underwriters SA (Pty) Ltd and was tribunalized at Lloyd's to conduct Marine business on behalf of various Lloyd's syndicates. Due to a change in legislation Marine Underwriters SA (Pty) Ltd name changed to International Marine Insurance Managers SA (Pty) Ltd. From November 1996 to the end of December 1998 International Marine acted solely as Underwriting Managers on behalf of Lloyd's.

Despite having also had full underwriting management agreements with local insurer's such as Fedsure General later acquired by Hollard, International Marine Insurance Managers have always maintained strong ties with Lloyd's of London via our London Broker Butcher Robinson and Staples (BRS).

Currently International Marine Insurance Managers has two full binding authorities with Lloyd's Syndicates, underwritten 100 per cent by Kiln (UK) (mainly Commercial Fishing Vessels and cargo) and the other lead by AMLIN which is mainly a general Cargo and stock throughout facility.

International Marine Insurance Managers also writes small craft, yachts, Marine Liability and Goods in transit business.

IMIM is a founder member of the Cape Town Regional Chamber of Commerce.

Kiln acquired a 25 per cent stake in International Marine Insurance Managers in 2004.

Some Background on Marine Insurance

The first marine insurance company was established in 1668 in Paris. This was followed by the famous "London Assurance" and "Royal Exchange Assurance", both established in 1720 and protected by royal charter against corporate competition for their first 100 years of operation.

An important factor for the dominant role played by the "London Market" was the establishment by one Edward T. Lloyd of a base where the shipping and trading intelligentsia of the time met and exchanged information, gossip, capital and risks. These wealthy individuals became known as "members" when Lloyds became incorporated in 1871. Members agreed to accept the various risks associated with the transportation of goods and the running of vessels against a proper remuneration, or insurance premium, payable in advance.

In addition, Lloyd's provided a number of additional services such as cargo and vessel surveys, vessel classification, vessel registration, shipping intelligence, shipping publications and claims settling etc. Lloyd's was also instrumental in developing its own marine policy, the so called SG-form released in 1779. This policy remained in active use almost worldwide for over 200 years until a revision in 1982.

CONVENTION FOR THE UNIFICATION OF CERTAIN RULES RELATING TO INTERNATIONAL CARRIAGE BY AIR

Chapter I: Scope—Definitions

Article 1

1. This Convention applies to all international carriage of persons, luggage or goods performed by aircraft for reward. It applies equally to gratuitous carriage by aircraft performed by an air transport undertaking.
2. For the purposes of this Convention the expression "international carriage" means any carriage in which, according to the contract made by the parties, the place of departure and the place of destination, whether or not there be a break in the carriage or a transhipment, are situated either within the territories of two High Contracting Parties, or within the territory of a single High Contracting Party, if there is an agreed stopping place within a territory subject to the sovereignty, suzerainty, mandate or authority of another Power, even though that Power is not a party to this Convention. A carriage without such an agreed stopping place between territories subject to the sovereignty, suzerainty, mandate or authority of the same High Contracting Party is not deemed to be international for the purposes of this Convention.
3. A carriage to be performed by several successive air carriers is deemed, for the purposes of this Convention, to be one undivided carriage, if it has been regarded

by the parties as a single operation, whether it had been agreed upon under the form of a single contract or of a series of contracts, and it does not lose its international character merely because one contract or a series of contracts is to be performed entirely within a territory subject to the sovereignty, suzerainty, mandate or authority of the same High Contracting Party.

Article 2

1. This Convention applies to carriage performed by the State or by legally constituted public bodies provided it falls within the conditions laid down in Article 1.
2. This Convention does not apply to carriage performed under the terms of any international postal Convention.

Chapter II: Documents of Carriage

Section I—Passenger Ticket

Article 3

1. For the carriage of passengers the carrier must deliver a passenger ticket which shall contain the following particulars:
   - (*a*) the place and date of issue;
   - (*b*) the place of departure and of destination;
   - (*c*) the agreed stopping places, provided that the carrier may reserve the right to alter the stopping places in case of necessity, and that if he exercises that right, the alteration shall not have the effect of depriving the carriage of its international character;
   - (*d*) the name and address of the carrier or carriers; and
   - (*e*) a statement that the carriage is subject to the rules relating to liability established by this Convention.
2. The absence, irregularity or loss of the passenger ticket does not affect the existence or the validity of the contract of carriage, which shall nonetheless be subject to the rules of this Convention. Nevertheless, if the carrier accepts a passenger without a passenger ticket having been delivered he shall not be entitled to avail himself of those provisions of this Convention which exclude or limit his liability.

Section II—Luggage Ticket

Article 4

1. For the carriage of luggage, other than small personal objects of which the passenger takes charge himself, the carrier must deliver a luggage ticket.
2. The luggage ticket shall be made out in duplicate, one part for the passenger and the other part for the carrier.

3. The luggage ticket shall contain the following particulars:

   (*a*) the place and date of issue;
   (*b*) the place of departure and of destination;
   (*c*) the name and address of the carrier or carriers;
   (*d*) the number of the passenger ticket;
   (*e*) a statement that delivery of the luggage will be made to the bearer of the luggage ticket;
   (*f*) the number and weight of the packages;
   (*g*) the amount of the value declared in accordance with Article 22(2); and
   (*h*) a statement that the carriage is subject to the rules relating to liability established by this Convention.

4. The absence, irregularity or loss of the luggage ticket does not affect the existence or the validity of the contract of carriage, which shall none the less be subject to the rules of this Convention. Nevertheless, if the carrier accepts luggage without a luggage ticket having been delivered, or if the luggage ticket does not contain the particulars set out at (*d*), (*f*) and (*h*) above, the carrier shall not be entitled to avail himself of those provisions of the Convention which exclude or limit his liability.

Section III—Air Consignment Note

Article 5

1. Every carrier of goods has the right to require the consignor to make out and hand over to him a document called an "air consignment note"; every consignor has the right to require the carrier to accept this document.
2. The absence, irregularity or loss of this document does not affect the existence or the validity of the contract of carriage which shall, subject to the provisions of Article 9, be none the less governed by the rules of this Convention.

Article 6

1. The air consignment note shall be made out by the consignor in three original parts and be handed over with the goods.
2. The first part shall be marked "for the carrier," and shall be signed by the consignor. The second part shall be marked "for the consignee"; it shall be signed by the consignor and by the carrier and shall accompany the goods. The third part shall be signed by the carrier and handed by him to the consignor after the goods have been accepted.
3. The carrier shall sign on acceptance of the goods.
4. The signature of the carrier may be stamped; that of the consignor may be printed or stamped.
5. If, at the request of the consignor, the carrier makes out the air consignment

note, he shall be deemed, subject to proof to the contrary, to have done so on behalf of the consignor.

Article 7

The carrier of goods has the right to require the consignor to make out separate consignment notes when there is more than one package.

Article 8

The air consignment note shall contain the following particulars:

(*a*) the place and date of its execution;
(*b*) the place of departure and of destination;
(*c*) the agreed stopping places, provided that the carrier may reserve the right to alter the stopping places in case of necessity, and that if he exercises that right the alteration shall not have the effect of depriving the carriage of its international character;
(*d*) the name and address of the consignor;
(*e*) the name and address of the first carrier;
(*f*) the name and address of the consignee, if the case so requires;
(*g*) the nature of the goods;
(*h*) the number of the packages, the method of packing and the particular marks or numbers upon them;
(*i*) the weight, the quantity and the volume or dimensions of the goods;
(*j*) the apparent condition of the goods and of the packing;
(*k*) the freight, if it has been agreed upon, the date and place of payment, and the person who is to pay it;
(*l*) if the goods are sent for payment on delivery, the price of the goods, and, if the case so requires, the amount of the expenses incurred;
(*m*) the amount of the value declared in accordance with Article 22 (2);
(*n*) the number of parts of the air consignment note;
(*o*) the documents handed to the carrier to accompany the air consignment note;
(*p*) the time fixed for the completion of the carriage and a brief note of the route to be followed, if these matters have been agreed upon; and
(*q*) a statement that the carriage is subject to the rules relating to liability established by this Convention.

Article 9

If the carrier accepts goods without an air consignment note having been made out, or if the air consignment note does not contain all the particulars set out in Article 8 (*a*) to (*i*) inclusive and (*q*), the carrier shall not be entitled to avail himself of the provisions of this Convention which exclude or limit his liability.

Article 10

1. The consignor is responsible for the correctness of the particulars and statements relating to the goods which he inserts in the air consignment note.
2. The consignor will be liable for all damage suffered by the carrier or any other person by reason of the irregularity, incorrectness or incompleteness of the said particulars and statements.

Article 11

1. The air consignment note is prima facie evidence of the conclusion of the contract, of the receipt of the goods and of the conditions of carriage.
2. The statements in the air consignment note relating to the weight, dimensions and packing of the goods, as well as those relating to the number of packages, are prima facie evidence of the facts stated; those relating to the quantity, volume and condition of the goods do not constitute evidence against the carrier except so far as they both have been, and are stated in the air consignment note to have been, checked by him in the presence of the consignor, or relate to the apparent condition of the goods.

Article 12

1. Subject to his liability to carry out all his obligations under the contract of carriage, the consignor has the right to dispose of the goods by withdrawing them at the aerodrome of departure or destination, or by stopping them in the course of the journey on any landing, or by calling for them to be delivered at the place of destination or in the course of the journey to a person other than the consignee named in the air consignment note, or by requiring them to be returned to the aerodrome of departure. He must not exercise this right of disposition in such a way as to prejudice the carrier or other consignors and he must repay any expenses occasioned by the exercise of this right.
2. If it is impossible to carry out the orders of the consignor the carrier must so inform him forthwith.
3. If the carrier obeys the orders of the consignor for the disposition of the goods without requiring the production of the part of the air consignment note delivered to the latter, he will be liable, without prejudice to his right of recovery from the consignor, for any damage which may be caused thereby to any person who is lawfully in possession of that part of the air consignment note.
4. The right conferred on the consignor ceases at the moment when that of the consignee begins in accordance with Article 13. Nevertheless, if the consignee declines to accept the consignment note or the goods, or if he cannot be communicated with, the consignor resumes his right of disposition.

Article 13

1. Except in the circumstances set out in the preceding Article, the consignee is entitled, on arrival of the goods at the place of destination, to require the carrier to hand over to him the air consignment note and to deliver the goods to him, on payment of the charges due and on complying with the conditions of carriage set out in the air consignment note.
2. Unless it is otherwise agreed, it is the duty of the carrier to give notice to the consignee as soon as the goods arrive.
3. If the carrier admits the loss of the goods, or if the goods have not arrived at the expiration of seven days after the date on which they ought to have arrived, the consignee is entitled to put into force against the carrier the rights which flow from the contract of carriage.

Article 14

The consignor and the consignee can respectively enforce all the rights given them by Articles 12 and 13, each in his own name, whether he is acting in his own interest or in the interest of another, provided that he carries out the obligations imposed by the contract.

Article 15

1. Articles 12, 13 and 14 do not affect either the relations of the consignor or the consignee with each other or the mutual relations of third parties whose rights are derived either from the consignor or from the consignee.
2. The provisions of Articles 12, 13 and 14 can only be varied by express provision in the air consignment note.

Article 16

1. The consignor must furnish such information and attach to the air consignment note such documents as are necessary to meet the formalities of customs, octroi or police before the goods can be delivered to the consignee. The consignor is liable to the carrier for any damage occasioned by the absence, insufficiency or irregularity of any such information or documents, unless the damage is due to the fault of the carrier or his agents.
2. The carrier is under no obligation to enquire into the correctness or sufficiency of such information or documents.

Chapter III: Liability of the Carrier

Article 17

The carrier is liable for damage sustained in the event of the death or wounding of a passenger or any other bodily injury suffered by a passenger, if the accident which caused the damage so sustained took place on board the aircraft or in the course of any of the operations of embarking or disembarking.

Article 18

1. The carrier is liable for damage sustained in the event of the destruction or loss of, or of damage to, any registered luggage or any goods, if the occurrence which caused the damage so sustained took place during the carriage by air.
2. The carriage by air within the meaning of the preceding paragraph comprises the period during which the luggage or goods are in charge of the carrier, whether in an aerodrome or on board an aircraft, or, in the case of a landing outside an aerodrome, in any place whatsoever.
3. The period of the carriage by air does not extend to any carriage by land, by sea or by river performed outside an aerodrome. If, however, such a carriage takes place in the performance of a contract for carriage by air, for the purpose of loading, delivery or transshipment, any damage is presumed, subject to proof to the contrary, to have been the result of an event which took place during the carriage by air.

Article 19

The carrier is liable for damage occasioned by delay in the carriage by air of passengers, luggage or goods.

Article 20

1. The carrier is not liable if he proves that he and his agents have taken all necessary measures to avoid the damage or that it was impossible for him or them to take such measures.
2. In the carriage of goods and luggage the carrier is not liable if he proves that the damage was occasioned by negligent pilotage or negligence in the handling of the aircraft or in navigation and that, in all other respects, he and his agents have taken all necessary measures to avoid the damage.

Article 21

If the carrier proves that the damage was caused by or contributed to by the negligence of the injured person the Court may, in accordance with the provisions of its own law, exonerate the carrier wholly or partly from his liability.

Article 22

1. In the carriage of passengers the liability of the carrier for each passenger is

limited to the sum of 125,000 francs. Where, in accordance with the law of the Court seized of the case, damages may be awarded in the form of periodical payments, the equivalent capital value of the said payments shall not exceed 125,000 francs. Nevertheless, by special contract, the carrier and the passenger may agree to a higher limit of liability.

2. In the carriage of registered luggage and of goods, the liability of the carrier is limited to a sum of 250 francs per kilogram, unless the consignor has made, at the time when the package was handed over to the carrier, a special declaration of the value at delivery and has paid a supplementary sum if the case so requires. In that case the carrier will be liable to pay a sum not exceeding the declared sum, unless he proves that that sum is greater than the actual value to the consignor at delivery.
3. As regards objects of which the passenger takes charge himself the liability of the carrier is limited to 5,000 francs per passenger.
4. The sums mentioned above shall be deemed to refer to the French franc consisting of 65 milligrams gold of millesimal fineness 900. These sums may be converted into any national currency in round figures.

Article 23

Any provision tending to relieve the carrier of liability or to fix a lower limit than that which is laid down in this Convention shall be null and void, but the nullity of any such provision does not involve the nullity of the whole contract, which shall remain subject to the provisions of this Convention.

Article 24

1. In the cases covered by Articles 18 and 19 any action for damages, however founded, can only be brought subject to the conditions and limits set out in this Convention.
2. In the cases covered by Article 17 the provisions of the preceding paragraph also apply, without prejudice to the questions as to who are the persons who have the right to bring suit and what are their respective rights.

Article 25

1. The carrier shall not be entitled to avail himself of the provisions of this Convention which exclude or limit his liability, if the damage is caused by his wilful misconduct or by such default on his part as, in accordance with the law of the Court seized of the case, is considered to be equivalent to wilful misconduct.
2. Similarly the carrier shall not be entitled to avail himself of the said provisions, if the damage is caused as aforesaid by any agent of the carrier acting within the scope of his employment.

Article 26

1. Receipt by the person entitled to delivery of luggage or goods without complaint is prima facie evidence that the same have been delivered in good condition and in accordance with the document of carriage.
2. In the case of damage, the person entitled to delivery must complain to the carrier forthwith after the discovery of the damage, and, at the latest, within three days from the date of receipt in the case of luggage and seven days from the date of receipt in the case of goods. In the case of delay the complaint must be made at the latest within fourteen days from the date on which the luggage or goods have been placed at his disposal.
3. Every complaint must be made in writing upon the document of carriage or by separate notice in writing despatched within the times aforesaid.
4. Failing complaint within the times aforesaid, no action shall lie against the carrier, save in the case of fraud on his part.

Article 27

In the case of the death of the person liable, an action for damages lies in accordance with the terms of this Convention against those legally representing his estate.

Article 28

1. An action for damages must be brought, at the option of the plaintiff, in the territory of one of the High Contracting Parties, either before the Court having jurisdiction where the carrier is ordinarily resident, or has his principal place of business, or has an establishment by which the contract has been made or before the Court having jurisdiction at the place of destination.
2. Questions of procedure shall be governed by the law of the Court seized of the case.

Article 29

1. The right to damages shall be extinguished if an action is not brought within two years, reckoned from the date of arrival at the destination, or from the date on which the aircraft ought to have arrived, or from the date on which the carriage stopped.
2. The method of calculating the period of limitation shall be determined by the law of the Court seized of the case.

Article 30

1. In the case of carriage to be performed by various successive carriers and falling within the definition set out in the third paragraph of Article 1, each carrier

who accepts passengers, luggage or goods is subjected to the rules set out in this Convention, and is deemed to be one of the contracting parties to the contract of carriage insofar as the contract deals with that part of the carriage which is performed under his supervision.

2. In the case of carriage of this nature, the passenger or his representative can take action only against the carrier who performed the carriage during which the accident or the delay occurred, save in the case where, by express agreement, the first carrier has assumed liability for the whole journey.
3. As regards luggage or goods, the passenger or consignor will have a right of action against the first carrier, and the passenger or consignee who is entitled to delivery will have a right of action against the last carrier, and further, each may take action against the carrier who performed the carriage during which the destruction, loss, damage or delay took place. These carriers will be jointly and severally liable to the passenger or to the consignor or consignee.

Chapter IV: Provisions Relating to Combined Carriage

Article 31

1. In the case of combined carriage performed partly by air and partly by any other mode of carriage, the provisions of this Convention apply only to the carriage by air, provided that the carriage by air falls within the terms of Article 1.
2. Nothing in this Convention shall prevent the parties in the case of combined carriage from inserting in the document of air carriage conditions relating to other modes of carriage, provided that the provisions of this Convention are observed as regards the carriage by air.

Chapter V: General and Final Provisions

Article 32

Any clause contained in the contract and all special agreements entered into before the damage occurred by which the parties purport to infringe the rules laid down by this Convention, whether by deciding the law to be applied, or by altering the rules as to jurisdiction, shall be null and void. Nevertheless for the carriage of goods arbitration clauses are allowed, subject to this Convention, if the arbitration is to take place within one of the jurisdictions referred to in the first paragraph of Article 28.

Article 33

Nothing contained in this Convention shall prevent the carrier either from refusing to enter into any contract of carriage, or from making regulations which do not conflict with the provisions of this Convention.

Article 34

This Convention does not apply to international carriage by air performed by way of experimental trial by air navigation undertakings with the view to the establishment of a regular line of air navigation, nor does it apply to carriage performed in extraordinary circumstances outside the normal scope of an air carrier's business.

Article 35

The expression "days" when used in this Convention means current days not working days.

Article 36

The Convention is drawn up in French in a single copy which shall remain deposited in the archives of the Ministry for Foreign Affairs of Poland and of which one duly certified copy shall be sent by the Polish Government to the Government of each of the High Contracting Parties.

Article 37

1. This Convention shall be ratified. The instruments of ratification shall be deposited in the archives of the Ministry for Foreign Affairs of Poland, which will notify the deposit to the Government of each of the High Contracting Parties.
2. As soon as this Convention shall have been ratified by five of the High Contracting Parties it shall come into force as between them on the ninetieth day after the deposit of the fifth ratification. Thereafter it shall come into force between the High Contracting Parties who shall have ratified and the High Contracting Party who deposits his instrument of ratification on the ninetieth day after the deposit.
3. It shall be the duty of the Government of the Republic of Poland to notify to the Government of each of the High Contracting Parties the date on which this Convention comes into force as well as the date of the deposit of each ratification.

Article 38

1. This Convention shall, after it has come into force, remain open for accession by any State.
2. The accession shall be effected by a notification addressed to the Government of the Republic of Poland, which will inform the Government of each of the High Contracting Parties thereof.
3. The accession shall take effect as from the ninetieth day after the notification made to the Government of the Republic of Poland.

Article 39

1. Any one of the High Contracting Parties may denounce this Convention by a notification addressed to the Government of the Republic of Poland, which will at once inform the Government of each of the High Contracting Parties.
2. Denunciation shall take effect six months after the notification of denunciation, and shall operate only as regards the Party who shall have proceeded to denunciation.

Article 40

1. Any High Contracting Party may, at the time of signature or of deposit of ratification or of accession declare that the acceptance which he gives to this Convention does not apply to all or any of his colonies, protectorates, territories under mandate, or any other territory subject to his sovereignty or his authority, or any territory under his suzerainty.
2. Accordingly any High Contracting Party may subsequently accede separately in the name of all or any of his colonies, protectorates, territories under mandate or any other territory subject to his sovereignty or to his authority or any territory under his suzerainty which has been thus excluded by his original declaration.
3. Any High Contracting Party may denounce this Convention, in accordance with its provisions, separately or for all or any of his colonies, protectorates, territories under mandate or any other territory subject to his sovereignty or to his authority, or any other territory under his suzerainty.

Article 41

Any High Contracting Party shall be entitled not earlier than two years after the coming into force of this Convention to call for the assembling of a new international conference in order to consider any improvements which may be made in this Convention. To this end he will communicate with the Government of the French Republic which will take the necessary measures to make preparations for such conference.

This Convention done at Warsaw on the 12th October, 1929, shall remain open for signature until the 31st January, 1930.

Additional Protocol

(With reference to Article 2) The High Contracting Parties reserve to themselves the right to declare at the time of ratification or of accession that the first paragraph of Article 2 of this Convention shall not apply to international carriage by air performed directly by the State, its colonies, protectorates or mandated territories or by any other territory under its sovereignty, suzerainty or authority.

MONTREAL PROTOCOL

To amend the convention for the unification of certain rules relating to international carriage by air signed at Warsaw on 12 October, 1929. As amended by the protocol done at The Hague on 28 September, 1955 signed at Montreal on 25 September, 1975.

The Governments Undersigned

CONSIDERING that it is desirable to amend the Convention for the Unification of Certain Rules Relating to International Carriage by Air signed at Warsaw on 12 October, 1929 as amended by the Protocol done at The Hague on 28 September, 1955,

Have agreed as follows:

Chapter I: Amendments to the Convention

Article I

The Convention which the provisions of the present Chapter modify is the Warsaw Convention as amended at The Hague in 1955.

Article II

In Article 2 of the Convention—paragraph 2 shall be deleted and replaced by the following:

"2. In the carriage of postal items the carrier shall be liable only to the relevant postal administration in accordance with the rules applicable to the relationship between the carriers and the postal administrations.

3. Except as provided in paragraph 2 of this Article, the provisions of this Convention shall not apply to the carriage of postal items."

Article III

In Chapter II of the Convention, Section III (Articles 5 to 16) shall be deleted and replaced by the following:

"Section III—Documentation Relating to Cargo"

Article 5

1. In respect of the carriage of cargo an air waybill shall be delivered.
2. Any other means which would preserve a record of the carriage to be performed may, with the consent of the consignor, be substituted for the delivery of an air waybill. If such other means are used, the carrie shall, if so requested by the consignor, deliver to the consignor a receipt for the cargo permitting

identification of the consignment and access to the information contained in the record preserved by such other means.

3. The impossibility of using, at points of transit and destination, the other means which would preserve the record of the carriage referred to in paragraph 2 of this Article does not entitle the carrier to refuse to accept the cargo for carriage.

Article 6

1. The air waybill shall be made out by the consignor in three original parts.
2. The first part shall be marked "for the carrier"; it shall be signed by the consignor. The second part shall be marked "for the consignee"; it shall be signed by the consignor and by the carrier. The third part shall be signed by the carrier and handed by him to the consignor after the cargo has been accepted.
3. The signature of the carrier and that of the consignor may be printed or stamped.
4. If, at the request of the consignor, the carrier makes out the air waybill, he shall be deemed, subject to proof to the contrary, to have done so on behalf of the consignor.

Article 7

When there is more than one package:

(*a*) the carrier of cargo has the right to require the consignor to make out separate air waybills;
(*b*) the consignor has the right to require the carrier to deliver separate receipts when the other means referred to in paragraph 2 of Article 5 are used.

Article 8

The air waybill and the receipt for the cargo shall contain:

(*a*) an indication of the places of departure and destination;
(*b*) if the places of departure and destination are within the territory of a single High Contracting Party, one or more agreed stopping places being within the territory of another State, an indication of at least one such stopping place; and
(*c*) an indication of the weight of the consignment.

Article 9

Non-compliance with the provisions of Articles 5 to 8 shall not affect the existence or the validity of the contract of carriage, which shall, none the less, be subject to the rules of this Convention including those relating to limitation of liability.

Article 10

1. The consignor is responsible for the correctness of the particulars and statements relating to the cargo inserted by him or on his behalf in the air waybill or furnished by him or on his behalf to the carrier for insertion in the receipt for the cargo or for insertion in the record preserved by the other means referred to in paragraph 2 of Article 5.
2. The consignor shall indemnify the carrier against all damage suffered by him, or by any other person to whom the carrier is liable, by reason of the irregularity, incorrectness or incompleteness of the particulars and statements furnished by the consignor or on his behalf.
3. Subject to the provisions of paragraphs 1 and 2 of this Article, the carrier shall indemnify the consignor against all damage suffered by him, or by any other person to whom the consignor is liable, by reason of the irregularity, incorrectness or incompleteness of the particulars and statements inserted by the carrier or on his behalf in the receipt for the cargo or in the record preserved by the other means referred to in paragraph 2 of Article 5.

Article 11

1. The air waybill or the receipt for the cargo is prima facie evidence of the conclusion of the contract, of the acceptance of the cargo and of the conditions of carriage mentioned therein.
2. Any statements in the air waybill or the receipt for the cargo relating to the weight, dimensions and packing of the cargo, as well as those relating to the number of packages, are prima facie evidence of the facts stated; those relating to the quantity, volume and condition of the cargo do not constitute evidence against the carrier except so far as they both have been, and are stated in the air waybill to have been, checked by him in the presence of the consignor, or relate to the apparent condition of the cargo.

Article 12

1. Subject to his liability to carry out all his obligations under the contract of carriage, the consignor has the right to dispose of the cargo by withdrawing it at the airport of departure or destination, or by stopping it in the course of the journey on any landing, or by calling for it to be delivered at the place of destination or in the course of the journey to a person other than the consignee originally designated, or by requiring it to be returned to the airport of departure. He must not exercise this right of disposition in such a way as to prejudice the carrier or other consignors and he must repay any expenses occasioned by the exercise of this right.
2. If it is impossible to carry out the orders of the consignor the carrier must so inform him forthwith.

3. If the carrier obeys the orders of the consignor for the disposition of the cargo without requiring the production of the part of the air waybill or the receipt for the cargo delivered to the latter, he will be liable, without prejudice to his right of recovery from the consignor, for any damage which may be caused thereby to any person who is lawfully in possession of that part of the air waybill or the receipt for the cargo.
4. The right conferred on the consignor ceases at the moment when that of the consignee begins in accordance with Article 13. Nevertheless, if the consignee declines to accept the cargo, or if he cannot be communicated with, the consignor resumes his right of disposition.

Article 13

1. Except when the consignor has exercised his right under Article 12, the consignee is entitled, on arrival of the cargo at the place of destination, to require the carrier to deliver the cargo to him, on payment of the charges due and on complying with the conditions of carriage.
2. Unless it is otherwise agreed, it is the duty of the carrier to give notice to the consignee as soon as the cargo arrives.
3. If the carrier admits the loss of the cargo, or if the cargo has not arrived at the expiration of seven days after the date on which it ought to have arrived, the consignee is entitled to enforce against the carrier the rights which flow from the contract of carriage.

Article 14

The consignor and the consignee can respectively enforce all the rights given them by Articles 12 and 13, each in his own name, whether he is acting in his own interest or in the interest of another, provided that he carries out the obligations imposed by the contract of carriage.

Article 15

1. Articles 12, 13 and 14 do not affect either the relations of the consignor and the consignee with each other or the mutual relations of third parties whose rights are derived either from the consignor or from the consignee.
2. The provisions of Articles 12, 13 and 14 can only be varied by express provision in the air waybill or the receipt for the cargo.

Article 16

1. The consignor must furnish such information and such documents as are necessary to meet the formalities of customs, octroi or police before the cargo can be delivered to the consignee. The consignor is liable to the carrier for any

damage occasioned by the absence, insufficiency or irregularity of any such information or documents, unless the damage is due to the fault of the carrier, his servants or agents.

2. The carrier is under no obligation to enquire into the correctness or sufficiency of such information or documents."

Article IV

Article 18 of the Convention shall be deleted and replaced by the following:

"Article 18

1. The carrier is liable for damage sustained in the event of the destruction or loss of, or damage to, any registered baggage, if the occurrence which caused the damage so sustained took place during the carriage by air.
2. The carrier is liable for damage sustained in the event of the destruction or loss of, or damage to, cargo upon condition only that the occurrence which caused the damage so sustained took place during the carriage by air.
3. However, the carrier is not liable if he proves that the destruction, loss of, or damage to, the cargo resulted solely from one or more of the following:
   (*a*) inherent defect, quality or vice of that cargo;
   (*b*) defective packing of that cargo performed by a person other than the carrier or his servants or agents;
   (*c*) an act of war or an armed conflict;
   (*d*) an act of public authority carried out in connexion with the entry, exit or transit of the cargo.
4. The carriage by air within the meaning of the preceding paragraphs of this Article comprises the period during which the baggage or cargo is in the charge of the carrier, whether in an airport or on board an aircraft, or, in the case of a landing outside an airport, in any place whatsoever.
5. The period of the carriage by air does not extend to any carriage by land, by sea or by river performed outside an airport. If, however, such carriage takes place in the performance of a contract for carriage by air, for the purpose of loading, delivery or transhipment, any damage is presumed, subject to proof to the contrary, to have been the result of an event which took place during the carriage by air."

Article V

Article 20 of the Convention shall be deleted and replaced by the following:

"Article 20

In the carriage of passengers and baggage, and in the case of damage occasioned by delay in the carriage of cargo, the carrier shall not be liable if he proves that he and his servants and agents have taken all necessary measures to avoid the damage or that it was impossible for them to take such measures."

Article VI

Article 21 of the Convention shall be deleted and replaced by the following:

"Article 21

1. In the carriage of passengers and baggage, if the carrier proves that the damage was caused by or contributed to by the negligence of the person suffering the damage the Court may, in accordance with the provisions of its own law, exonerate the carrier wholly or partly from his liability.
2. In the carriage of cargo, if the carrier proves that the damage was caused by or contributed to by the negligence or other wrongful act or omission of the person claiming compensation, or the person from whom he derives his rights, the carrier shall be wholly or partly exonerated from his liability to the claimant to the extent that such negligence or wrongful act or omission caused or contributed to the damage."

Article VII

In Article 22 of the Convention:

(*a*) in paragraph 2 (*a*) the words "and of cargo" shall be deleted.
(*b*) after paragraph 2 (*a*) the following paragraph shall be inserted:

"(*b*) In the carriage of cargo, the liability of the carrier is limited to a sum of 17 Special Drawing Rights per kilogramme, unless the consignor has made, at the time when the package was handed over to the carrier, a special declaration of interest in delivery at destination and has paid a supplementary sum if the case so requires. In that case the carrier will be liable to pay a sum not exceeding the declared sum, unless he proves that the sum is greater than the consignor's actual interest in delivery at destination."

(*c*) paragraph 2 (*b*) shall be designated as paragraph 2 (*c*).
(*d*) after paragraph 5 the following paragraph shall be inserted:

"6. The sums mentioned in terms of the Special Drawing Right in this Article shall be deemed to refer to the Special Drawing Right as defined by the International Monetary Fund. Conversion of the sums into national currencies shall, in case of judicial proceedings, be made according to the value of such currencies in terms of the Special Drawing Right at the date of the judgement. The value of a national currency, in terms of the Special Drawing Right, of a High Contracting Party which is a Member of the International Monetary Fund, shall be calculated in accordance with the method of valuation applied by the International Monetary Fund, in effect at the date of the judgement, for its operations and transactions. The value of a national currency, in terms of the Special Drawing Right, of a High Contracting Party which is not a Member of the International Monetary Fund, shall be calculated in a manner determined by that High Contracting Party. Nevertheless, those States which are not Members of the International Monetary Fund and whose law does not permit the application of the provisions of paragraph 2 (*b*) of Article 22 may, at the time of ratification or accession or at any time thereafter, declare that the limit of liability of the carrier in judicial proceedings in their territories is fixed at a sum of two hundred and fifty monetary units per kilogramme. This monetary unit corresponds to sixty-five and a half milligrammes of gold of millesimal fineness nine hundred. This sum may be converted into the national currency concerned in round figures. The conversion of this sum into the national currency shall be made according to the law of the State concerned."

Article VIII

Article 24 of the Convention shall be deleted and replaced by the following:

"Article 24

1. In the carriage of passengers and baggage, any action for damages, however founded, can only be brought subject to the conditions and limits set out in this Convention, without prejudice to the question as to who are the persons who have the right to bring suit and what are their respective rights.
2. In the carriage of cargo, any action for damages, however founded, whether under this Convention or in contract or in tort or otherwise, can only be brought subject to the conditions and limits of liability set out in this Convention without prejudice to the question as to who are the persons who have the right to bring suit and what are their respective rights. Such limits of liability constitute maximum limits and may not be exceeded whatever the circumstances which gave rise to the liability."

Article IX

Article 25 of the Convention shall be deleted and replaced by the following:

"Article 25

In the carriage of passengers and baggage, the limits of liability specified in Article 22 shall not apply if it is proved that the damage resulted from an act or omission of the carrier, his servants or agents, done with intent to cause damage or recklessly and with knowledge that damage would probably result; provided that, in the case of such act or omission of a servant or agent, it is also proved that he was acting within the scope of his employment."

Article X

In Article 25 A of the Convention paragraph 3 shall be deleted and replaced by the following:

> "3. In the carriage of passengers and baggage, the provisions of paragraphs 1 and 2 of this Article shall not apply if it is proved that the damage resulted from an act or omission of the servant or agent done with intent to cause damage or recklessly and with knowledge that damage would probably result."

Article XI

After Article 30 of the Convention, the following Article shall be inserted:

> "Article 30 A
> Nothing in this Convention shall prejudice the question whether a person liable for damage in accordance with its provisions has a right of recourse against any other person."

Article XII

Article 33 of the Convention shall be deleted and replaced by the following:

> "Article 33
> Except as provided in paragraph 3 of Article 5, nothing in this Convention shall prevent the carrier either from refusing to enter into any contract of carriage or from making regulations which do not conflict with the provisions of this Convention."

Article XIII

Article 34 of the Convention shall be deleted and replaced by the following:

> "Article 34
> The provisions of Articles 3 to 8 inclusive relating to documents of carriage shall not apply in the case of carriage performed in extraordinary circumstances outside the normal scope of an air carrier's business."

Chapter II: Scope of Application of the Convention as Amended

Article XIV

The Warsaw Convention as amended at The Hague in 1955 and by this Protocol shall apply to international carriage as defined in Article 1 of the Convention, provided that the places of departure and destination referred to in that Article are situated either in the territories of two Parties to this Protocol or within the territory of a single Party to this Protocol with an agreed stopping place in the territory of another State.

Chapter V: Final Clauses

Article XV

As between the Parties to this Protocol, the Warsaw Convention as amended at The Hague in 1955 and this Protocol shall be read and interpreted together as one single instrument and shall be known as the Warsaw Convention as amended at The Hague, 1955, and by Protocol No. 4 of Montreal, 1975.

Article XVI

Until the date on which this Protocol comes into force in accordance with the provisions of Article XVIII, it shall remain open for signature by any State.

Article XVII

1. This Protocol shall be subject to ratification by the signatory States.
2. Ratification of this Protocol by any State which is not a Party to the Warsaw Convention or by any State which is not a Party to the Warsaw Convention as amended at The Hague, 1955, shall have the effect of accession to the Warsaw Convention as amended at The Hague, 1955, and by Protocol No. 4 of Montreal, 1975.
3. The instruments of ratification shall be deposited with the Government of the Polish People's Republic.

Article XVIII

1. As soon as thirty signatory States have deposited their instruments of ratification of this Protocol, it shall come into force between them on the ninetieth day after the deposit of the thirtieth instrument of ratification. It shall come into force for each State ratifying thereafter on the ninetieth day after the deposit of its instrument of ratification.
2. As soon as this Protocol comes into force it shall be registered with the United Nations by the Government of the Polish People's Republic.

Article XIX

1. This Protocol, after it has come into force, shall be open for accession by any non-signatory State.
2. Accession to this Protocol by any State which is not a Party to the Warsaw Convention or by any State which is not a Party to the Warsaw Convention as

amended at The Hague, 1955, shall have the effect of accession to the Warsaw Convention as amended at The Hague, 1955, and by Protocol No. 4 of Montreal, 1975.

3. Accession shall be effected by the deposit of an instrument of accession with the Government of the Polish People's Republic and shall take effect on the ninetieth day after the deposit.

Article XX

1. Any Party to this Protocol may denounce the Protocol by notification addressed to the Government of the Polish People's Republic.
2. Denunciation shall take effect six months after the date of receipt by the Government of the Polish People's Republic of the notification of denunciation.
3. As between the Parties to this Protocol, denunciation by any of them of the Warsaw Convention in accordance with Article 39 thereof or of The Hague Protocol in accordance with Article XXIV thereof shall not be construed in any way as a denunciation of the Warsaw Convention as amended at The Hague, 1955, and by Protocol No. 4 of Montreal, 1975.

Article XXI

1. Only the following reservations may be made to this Protocol:

   (*a*) A State may at any time declare by a notification addressed to the Government of the Polish People's Republic that the Warsaw Convention as amended at The Hague, 1955, and by Protocol No. 4 of Montreal, 1975, shall not apply to the carriage of persons, baggage and cargo for its military authorities on aircraft, registered in that State, the whole capacity of which has been reserved by or on behalf of such authorities; and

   (*b*) Any State may declare at the time of ratification of or accession to the Additional Protocol No. 3 of Montreal, 1975, or at any time thereafter, that it is not bound by the provisions of the Warsaw Convention as amended at The Hague, 1955, and by Protocol No. 4 of Montreal, 1975, insofar as they relate to the carriage of passengers and baggage. Such declaration shall have effect ninety days after the date of receipt of the declaration by the Government of the Polish People's Republic.

2. Any State having made a reservation in accordance with the preceding paragraph may at any time withdraw such reservation by notification to the Government of the Polish People's Republic.

Article XXII

The Government of the Polish People's Republic shall promptly inform all States

Parties to the Warsaw Convention or to that Convention as amended, all signatory or acceding States to the present Protocol, as well as the International Civil Aviation Organization, of the date of each signature, the date of deposit of each instrument of ratification or accession, the date of coming into force of this Protocol, and other relevant information.

Article XXIII

As between the Parties to this Protocol which are also Parties to the Convention, Supplementary to the Warsaw Convention, for the Unification of Certain Rules Relating to International Carriage by Air Performed by a Person Other than the Contracting Carrier, signed at Guadalajara on 18 September, 1961 (hereinafter referred to as the "Guadalajara Convention") any reference to the "Warsaw Convention" contained in the Guadalajara Convention shall include reference to the Warsaw Convention as amended at The Hague, 1955, and by Protocol No. 4 of Montreal, 1975, in cases where the carriage under the agreement referred to in Article 1, paragraph (b) of the Guadalajara Convention is governed by this Protocol.

Article XXIV

If two or more States are Parties both to this Protocol and to the Guatemala City Protocol, 1971, or to the Additional Protocol No. 3 of Montreal, 1975, the following rules shall apply between them:

(*a*) The provisions resulting from the system established by this Protocol, concerning cargo and postal items, shall prevail over the provisions resulting from the system established by the Guatemala City Protocol, 1971, or by the Additional Protocol No. 3 of Montreal, 1975; and
(*b*) The provisions resulting from the system established by the Guatemala City Protocol, 1971, or by the Additional Protocol No. 3 of Montreal, 1975, concerning passengers and baggage, shall prevail over the provisions resulting from the system established by this Protocol.

Article XXV

This Protocol shall remain open for signature until 1 January 1976 at the Headquarters of the International Civil Aviation Organization and thereafter until it comes into force in accordance with Article XVIII at the Ministry for Foreign Affairs of the Polish People's Republic. The International Civil Aviation Organization shall promptly inform the Government of the Polish People's Republic of any signature and the date thereof during the time that the Protocol shall be open for signature at the Headquarters of the International Civil Aviation Organization.

IN WITNESS WHEREOF the undersigned Plenipotentiaries, having been duly authorized, have signed this Protocol.

DONE at Montreal on the twenty-fifth day of September of the year One Thousand Nine Hundred and Seventy-five in four authentic texts in the English, French, Russian and Spanish languages. In the case of any inconsistency, the text in the French language, in which language the Warsaw Convention of 12 October, 1929 was drawn up, shall prevail.

5

Cargo Management Policy and Law: Select Case Studies

EVERGREEN SEAL MANAGEMENT POLICY

Seal Management Policy

The use of EMC high security seals (including two types of LOCKTAINER 2000 and new type of GREENSEAL 2005), which is to meet with the criteria of ISO PAS 17712, as an integral part of supply and transportation chain security.

EMC High security seals will be used also for Italia Marittima S.P.A and HATSU Marine LTD containers movements.

The policy of Seal Management is to minimize the risk of unauthorized access to the seal thereby reducing the risk of seal pilferage and the introduction of contraband person or material into the sealed container, so as to comply with all applicable domestic and international laws and regulations which including but not limited to the followings:

- ISO PAS 17712-HSBS (Global Minimum Standards);
- International Ship and Port Facility Security Code (ISPS);
- Customs-Trade Partnership Against Terrorism (C-TPAT) Programme;
- U.S. Customs and Border Protection (CBP); and
- Super Carriers Initiative Programme (SCIP).

This is the common interest of the shipper, carrier, and recipient of the container.

Scope

These security measures should apply to all the seal been used for EVERGREEN business model and risk involved for the screening of our agents or service provider which is contracted to provide the transportation service.

EVERGREEN fleet shall also acknowledge of their responsibilities on Seal Management and monitoring requirements of ISPS CODE, C-TPAT, CBP & SCIP for the aims of vessel's security, smuggling and stowaway prevention.

Liability in Seal Management

The liability of maintaining the seal safety is following the seal distribution flow, i.e. wherever the seal is, so is the responsibility rested on the custodian.

When the seal is under EMC TPE/COD-OPD custody, EMC TPE/COD-OPD will assume the whole responsibility of the seal safety. When EMC TPE/COD-OPD distributed the seal to DCC, but have not reached LCC, the seal will be the responsibility of the DCC. When the LCC received the seal from the DCC, but not released to her Business Partner, the LCC will assume the whole responsibility of the seal.

The whole responsibility of Control and Accountability (hereinafter C/A) means any loss caused thereby regarding the seal C/A safety issues will be payable by the management who had the custody of the stock or under his direct control or within his business territory which he should act as an external auditor.

Management is responsible for establishing Seal Security Procedures in their departments/agencies. This means that management is responsible for identifying the risks that could prevent them from achieving the seal control and making sure that appropriate internal controls (procedures and auditing) are in place to mitigate those risks.

Management is also responsible for ongoing monitoring of internal controls to make sure that controls are still working and whether risks have changed requiring new controls or procedures.

EMC TPE/COD-OPD will be in charge of the:

- Drafting the global seal management policy.
- Identifying the DCC distribution area.
- Auditing the security procedure been setup in each DCC/LCC.
- Summarizing the annual seal consumption and placing the purchasing order.
- Seal purchasing ordered by the specific number range.
- Seal Manufacturer security evaluation.
- Auditing security procedures in manufacturer factory is properly established.
- Ensuring the safety enroute from manufacturer factory to EVERGREEN seal.
- Distribution/storage centre in Kaohsiung.
- Recording all the seal number range been distributed to each DCC custody.
- Dispatching the required seal quantity to DCC.
- Maintaining proper on-line system to monitor all seal safety globally.
- Setting up the auto filtering function for any seal discrepancy is found on system.

DCC follow the seal management policy will be in charge of:

- Applying the required quantity in his distribution area to EMC TPE/COD-OPD.
- Dispatching the required seal quantity to LCC and inform GCC of the suitable dispatch route and contact window.
- Ensuring the security procedure been setup in each LCC and his own DCC.

- External auditing the security procedures in each LCC.
- Internal auditing to make sure the security procedures are still working and whether.risks have changed requiring new controls or procedures.
- Recording all the seal number range been distributed from his custody to each LCC.
- Enforcing the relevant regulations of C-TPAT.
- Clarifying any related regulations and requirements from competent authorities.
- Governing seal management issues and disputes between each LCC and find the best way to improve it, if the case is severe, circulating the event and reporting to EMC TPE.

LCC follow the seal Management policy will be in charge of:

- Filing the quantity required annually to DCC.
- Keeping the received seal in a safe storage from unauthorized accessing.
- Establishing an applicable security procedures to comply with EVERGREEN Seal Management policy.
- Ensuring the proper security procedure been established in EVERGREEN business partner including but not limited to ocean terminal, inland terminal, trucking company and railway company.
- Acting as owner's REP to execute external audit of the Business Partner security procedures of the seal management, whereas the safety cannot be achieved, the practice of the seal releasing to the Business Partner should be carefully reviewed and revised accordingly.
- Evoking the internal audit periodically to make sure that controls are still working and whether risks have changed requiring new controls or procedures.
- Informing the LCC contact window and suitable dispatch route to DCC/GCC.
- Maintaining the on-line system seal management status and correct seal number.

Consigner under US CBP seal requirements will be in charge of:

- All laden containers destined to the Jurisdiction of US CBP are to be affixed with Seals in compliance with ISO/PAS 17712 Sealed container/trailer until such a time as the carrier assumes control.
- Affixing a seal at point of origin.
- Establishing verifiable security systems for cargo storage and handling facilities and container yards in order to prevent the improper manipulation and transportation or handling of cargo and/or containers/trailers.
- Ensuring a system is in place to verify seal numbers, weights and quantity of cargo received, when practical. Safeguard the use of seals and maintain a log of seal numbers issued and used. Ensuring that all manifests and/or bills of lading or other documentation (including electronic data transmissions) submitted for cargo to be shipped are complete and includes all pertinent seal information. Seals are to be affixed by a responsible, designated representative of the consigner entity at random in order to avoid seals being affixed in sequential order.

The seal is under constant risk of been:

- Stolen from storage
- Forgery as new one
- Duplicated the same number for switching
- Re-shaped to be as another one
- Broken and fixed as original one
- Locking un-sufficient so as to involve the unauthorized introduction.

Terms and Definitions

- *GCC:* is the Global Control Centre of the Seal Management.
- *DCC:* is the District Control Centre requesting the annual seal quantity and distributing the same to the LCC.
- *LCC:* is Local Control Centre who render the service to book the container for carrier. By the service contract signed by CBD-BCD, this usual refer to Local Office or Agent.
- *High security seal:* High security seals consist of a metal rod, threaded or unthreaded, flexible or rigid, with a formed head, secured with separate locking mechanism, which is of the intent to delay intrusion.
- *Consigner* means cargo producer, shipper, cargoes forwarder, etc who render his cargo in the sealed container for ocean transportation.
- *Carrier* means Evergreen Group Company provide the vessels for container transportation.
- *Distributor* means the designated representative in charge of seals' distribution.
- *Importer* means consignee and all related parties receiving the sealed container.
- *Manufacturer* means the vender supply the EVERGREEN specified seal type for ocean transportation.
- *PIC:* Responsible and designated person in-charge for security seals is defined as an employee who maintains a position of trust (i.e. security personnel) within the business and has received appropriate instruction and training in the proper use and distribution of high security seals each day.
- *SCO* means Seal Control Officer in internal audit team which job is to check the Seal monthly and review the security procedures every three months.
- *ISO PAS* 17712, Freight Containers-Mechanical Seals adopted May 2003, which seal shall be the high security type as per ISO guidelines.
- *C-TPAT* (Customs-Trade Partnership Against Terrorism) is the U.S. joint initiative among Customs, importers, terminal operators, carriers and others in the supply chain to make a self-assessment of their security, which including Foreign Manufacturers Eligibility Requirements and Application Instruction, the Security Recommendations for Manufacturers and Agreement to Voluntarily Participate for Foreign Manufacturers.
- *ISPS CODE,* the provisions of SOLAS Chapter Xl-2 and the International Ship and Port Facility Security Code into the existing port State control structured processes.

- *CBP, U.S. Customs and Border Protection* (U.S. Department of Homeland Security) requires that C-TPAT importers, carriers and manufacturers who wish to qualify for expedited processing and other related benefits under the U.S./Mexico FAST initiative will be required to adhere to the procedures, protocols and standards with regards to the use of high security seals.
- *Super Carriers Initiative Programme* (SCIP), the United States Customs Service. This cooperative Agreement is made between the *Carrier* having its principal place of business and the U.S. Customs, which indicates that this Agreement cannot, by law, exempt the Carrier from statutory sanctions in the event illegal drugs are discovered by Customs on board the Carrier's vessel.

Reference

- ISO PAS 17712-HSBS (Global Minimum Standards);
- International Ship and Port Facility Security Code (ISPS);
- Customs-Trade Partnership Against Terrorism (C-TPAT) Programme;
- U.S. Customs and Border Protection (CBP); and
- Super Carriers Initiative Programme (SCIP).

Evergreen Seal Management Policy

EVERGREEN Seal Management Policy which affords EVERGREEN to set forth guidelines for the proper management of seals life span including the factory manufacturing stage to effectively cut off by authorized parties and seek to ensure that pertinent security measures are in place and adhere to exercise prudent oversight for supply and transportation chain security.

Security Procedures in Place of Each Stage

EMC TPE/COD-OPD should verify the security procedures in the manufacturer comply with acceptable standard and the safety requirement in receiving and dispatching the new seal to the DCC.

DCC should verify the security procedures in each LCC is pertinent to the local practice and suitable to meet this Seal Management policy.

LCC should establish security procedures in accordance with this Seal Management policy with particularly regard to the ISO standard including the planning, doing, checking and action plan to ensure all the vulnerable parts in the procedure will be properly identified and coped with.

Correct Usage of the Seal

The first responsibility for the consigner/business partner, and seal(s) distributors and controllers of the Agents and Carrier are to ensure that all personnel involved with the procurement and use of the security seals are fully aware of the type of seal, the correct method of application, and the way in which the seal should be checked prior to removal.

The agent or the PIC shall also correctly instruct the receiving party about the handling of the seals with particular regard to the possible seal lost or theft or damage that shall be prevented and reported to the carrier for the follow up actions.

Distribution

All seal been received and distributed should be in written and properly signed by receiving party.

Only 1 (one) seal shall be distributed for each empty container been released to the consigner and the number shall be duly recorded by PIC with entry of the seal and container number.

The seal in stock should be distributed to each consigner in the First-in-First out order to consume the stock in timely manner.

Seal shall be issued at random in order to avoid seals being affixed in sequential order.

Safety in Warehouse

The seal should be stocked in a secure and locked place with adequate lighting for easy patrolling by the security guard at night time or the infrared sensor should mounted to trigger the lighting and proper TV surveillance equipment whenever any intruder is sensed.

Access to such secure locations must be restricted to those parties responsible for the inventory and distributing of seals.

Verification of Seal been Used

Upon receipt of container/trailer, ensure that all seal information is true and correct as reflected on manifests, bills of lading or other documentation related to the movement of cargo

The correct seal number shall be used in all EDI data with 10 characters including the digits. For example: EMCWU99999, EMCLDS9999, EMCD999999, HMLAD99999 or ITSCX99999.

The consumed seal number should be cross checked either by the CODECO/depot booking data, ALDS/TMNL sailing data, EL/EQC status, Baplie/TMNL sailing data or shipper's Paper data to verify the actual consumption, pertinent to local practice.

All seals that are removed from a cargo container/trailer for legitimate intermediate examinations (customs inspection, conveyance damage surveys, law enforcement activity, etc.) must be placed in the container just inside the doors, in plain view, before a new seal is affixed to the container.

The seal number changed during his transportation chain out of any reason should be updated on all documents and system's EDI data by LCC, including but not limit to local B/L system, Shipment online, Container Movement Status, ALDS.

Reporting Requirement

All seals that are removed from a cargo container/trailer for legitimate intermediate examinations (customs inspection, conveyance damage surveys, law enforcement activity, etc.) must annotate and report any changes due to legitimate intermediate examination purposes as described above.

Any seal discrepancies or anomalies from a cargo container/trailer by any cause must annotate and report the changes in seal management system by LCC, seal missing case should bring out to relevant parties attention and correcting action must be taken.

For the seal discrepancies or anomalies communication purpose, all relevant parties involved shall setup a designated mail box "seal@local_mail_server" for concern parties to exchange the seal issues. In EMC TPE, the mail box is seal@evergreen-marine.com.

Record Keeping

All seal interchange records should be duplicated by another copy in sound place and keep not less than 5 years period.

The record keeping procedure should have the error detecting mechanics to alarm the abnormal consumption.

All seal records must keep in a secure place and ready to produce whenever be requested by authorized parties.

Audit System

Internal Audit Team Should be Set up by Management Level:

1. To ensure the seal security procedure is properly followed and reviewed every three months by SCO.
2. To check the Seal inventory at least once per month to identify the possible missing source.
3. To have a designated PIC to registry the seal daily consumption and the number been used.
4. SCO and PIC should not be the same person and the SCO assigned by management level should be arranged in turn to avoid any possible internal conspiracy.
5. Internal audit systems need to be monitored to assess whether audit are still working and whether risks have changed requiring new procedures. This is accomplished through ongoing management monitoring activities and include external auditing.

External Audit Process

The external audit process should include—planning, examination, reporting, and follow-up.

1. During the planning phase, audit issues are identified, the audit objectives are established and criteria are developed. Before beginning the audit work, the scope of the audit is communicated to the LCC through both a written notice of intent to conduct the audit and an introductory meeting.
2. The DCC should communicate regularly with the LCC throughout the examination. The audit is conducted in an objective, independent, professional, and courteous manner, and is sensitive to the added workload it imposes on the LCC. As soon as possible after the examination has been completed, the DCC audit unit discusses results and possible recommendations with the LCC managers involved. The commitments made or action plan put forward by the LCC managers in response to these recommendations are included in the final report to GCC.
3. The DCC audit unit should have a quality-control process to ensure that audit reports are complete and accurate. The DCC audit unit also ensures that the draft report is made available to LCC representatives of the organization being audited, so that they have the opportunity to raise any questions or concerns related to the completeness and accuracy of the report.
4. If a DCC audit report contains recommendations, the managers of the audited LCC must draw up an action plan within a mutually agreed-upon time. This plan must describe the stages and schedules of the measures that will be taken to solve the problems raised, and must be included in the final report.

Follow-up Process

A follow-up action will be conducted on all audits within 1 to 3 months of the final report. This follow-up may focus on all of the recommendations in the report, or only on those considered by the DCC/GCC to be more urgent. The LCC involved will be notified in advance of the objectives and planned activities of the follow-up. The follow-up report will be submitted to the DCC/GCC for approval.

When the job function is switching, the relieving procedure should accompany by a designated SCO.

Action Plan Authority

1. LCC management should take action plan to counter the deficiency found by PIC or SCO in the Seal Management procedure.
2. SCO should correctly verify the discrepancy found in monthly inventory check and locate the possible leakage source.
3. SCO should report the suspect missing seal number range to the LCC

management and make proper announcement/legal action to local/external authorities to prevent the possible illegal usage by other party.

4. LCC management will have to inform the DCC/GCC to update the missing seal range in Shipment online system to filter out once any attempt try to use it on loaded container.
5. Beside the missing case, any other incident regarding the seal leakage should report to LCC/DCC/GCC, LCC should take proper announcement/legal action to proper authorities and management level.
6. Any doubt of the seal number been used on the loaded container should refer to SCO to verify the place of origin and take proper action to protect line's interest.
7. If the cause of the seal discrepancy cannot identified in LCC district, the mail exchanged with other LCC or DCC should always refer to management level to stress the cause of the case and the possible expense thereafter.
8. DCC should verify the seal discrepancies or anomalies in his jurisdiction and report to GCC for possible security measures been taken to cope with.
9. GCC will have the final jurisdiction over the Seal management issues between each DCC and/or LCC.

EMC Seal and its Proper Locking Way

Two types of EMC High Security Bolt Seal are utilized currently:

1. LOCKTAINER 2000 (Old type of EMC Seal)

(*a*) Manufacturer: Universeal International
[Seal No.: EMC (carrier code)-AA (two letters)- 00001 (five numbers)]

(*b*) Manufacturer: Abric Worldwide SDN BHD
[Seal No.: EMC (carrier code)- A (one letter)- 00001 (six numbers)]

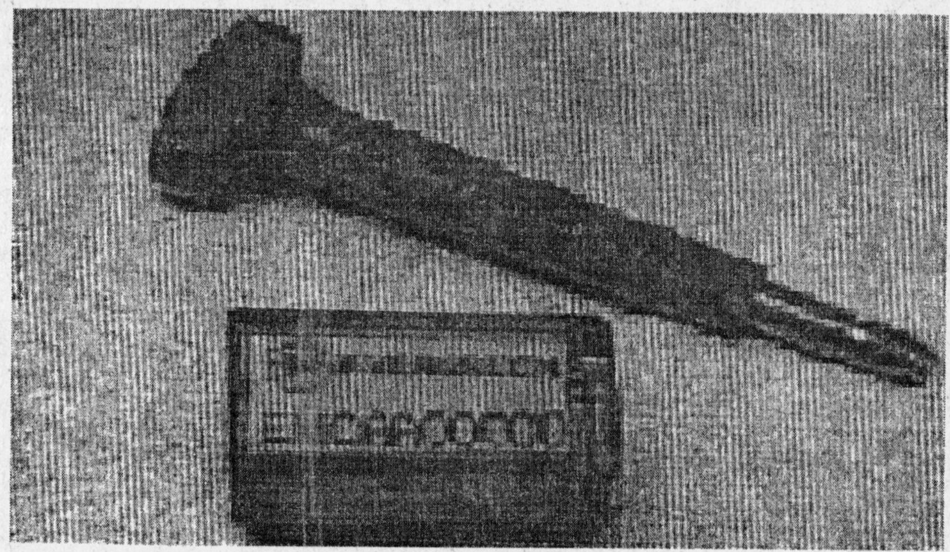

This type was supplied by the manufacturer:
UNIVERSAL INTERNATIONAL in the year of 2000.

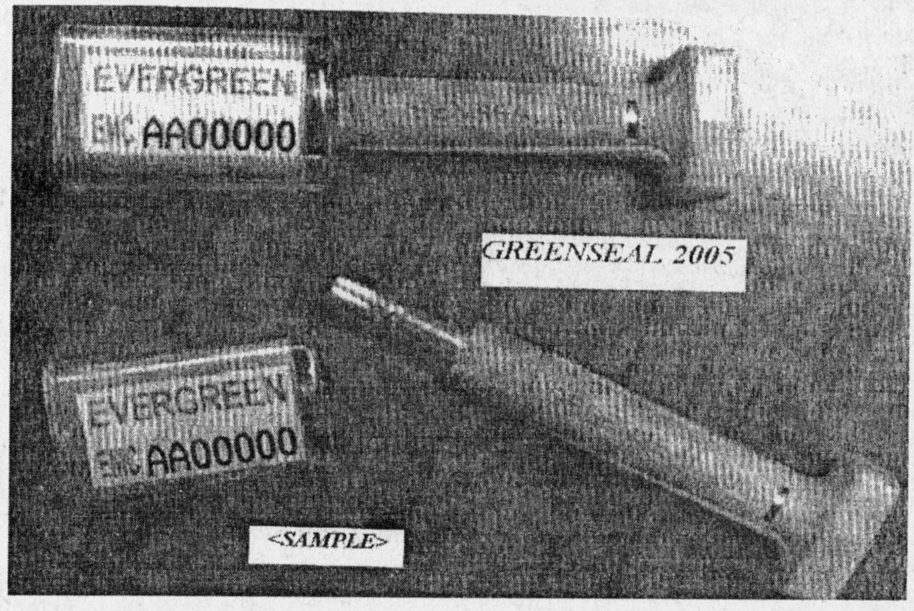

2. GREENSEAL 2005 (Newly designed EMC Seal)
EMC High Security Bolt Seal modified (GREENSEAL 2005)
which was supplied by two makers.

Container Sealing Procedure

All containers must be sealed with a EMC high security bolt seal. When possible, the seal should always be placed in the SecuraCam position.

Examples are depicted below:

This design of SecuraCam and keeper has been applied for all new constructed dry and reefer containers in 2004 due to the need to ensure container sealing security.

Correct sealing way for new constructed dry and reefer containers.

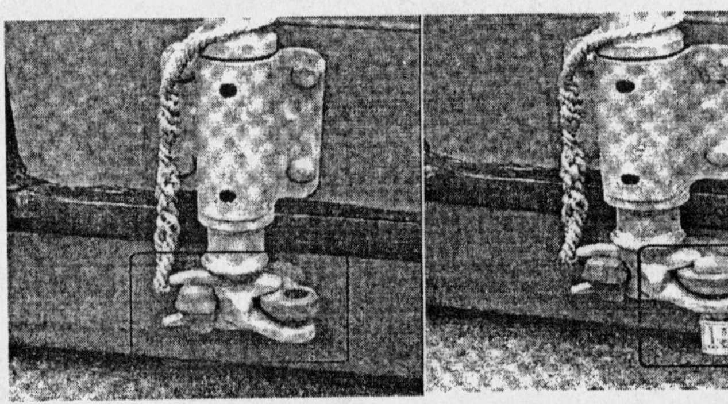

SecuraCam Position for Sealing Security

Accurate Sealing Way at Secura-Cam Position

Both of Alternate 1 & Alternate 2 for Seal Locking

Correct Sealing Way at Either Alternate 1 or Alternate 2 Position or the both

**No SecuraCam Position Designed for Containers
Constructed before the Year of 2004**

GATI INTERNATIONAL: AN OVERVIEW

Gati pioneered the cargo management movement in India. And then spread its wings over the sub-continent. The logistics leader is now making its presence felt in the SAARC countries and the Asia Pacific region.

Gati International, the global operations wing, provides us with a strategic USP—an international reach, along with a highly focused expertize in India centric operations. This ensures that Gati remains the undisputed leader not just in Indian operations, but also in India—focused operations.

We now have offices in Singapore, Hong Kong, China and Sri Lanka which offer a range of distribution solutions to and from India.

Bringing India and the World Closer

Easy Connections between India and the Asia Pacific

Gati takes care of the hassles of pick-up, customs clearance and delivery of freight and cargo. Services offered include inbound air/sea movement and outbound air/sea movement, along with:

- Strategic tie-ups with global players
- Same day connection
- Online track and trace facility
- Consignee and consignor nominated freight terms
- Door to door service
- Door to airport/port service
- Airport/port to airport/port service
- Airport/port to door service
- Customs clearance service
- Bonded storage service
- Assured space for air shipments
- Break-bulk and container services.

Company Profile

Gati is a leader in express cargo delivery and a pioneer in distribution and supply chain management solutions in India since 1989.

We at Gati Limited take immense pride in our status as pioneers in the Indian cargo and logistics management industry. Headquartered in Secunderabad, Andhra Pradesh, our network extends across the Asia Pacific and we also have an office in Singapore—Gati International.

We provide customers with quality service through speedy and efficient movement of cargo. We also offer top-of-the-line supply chain management services across India, the SAARC countries and Asia Pacific markets.

Having started out in 1989 as a cargo management company, we have grown into an organization with 6400 dedicated professionals and a turnover of Rs 4577 million. Our business philosophy is to integrate the latest and best technological innovations into our service and support network.

Reach is key: Currently, Gati has the largest fleet of vehicles on the road-over 2000 vehicles. The network reaches out to 594 districts (out of 602) in India. A tie up with Indian Airlines offers our customers access to India's largest air network, thus ensuring speedy delivery of goods.

Our endeavour is to create unique and lasting solutions for our customers. In 2001, for instance, we were the first to launch an exclusive cargo train between Mumbai and Kolkata. We also offer a wide range of solutions. Our network goes out to countries across the globe and right down to the smallest district in India.

At Gati, we strongly believe that technology drives innovation. Web-based tracking systems enable our customers monitor their cargo online. Our technological solutions provide customers with state-of-the-art cargo management tools. We use mechanized racking systems at our 600,000 sq.ft automated warehouse at Panvel in Maharashtra.

Time implies money: We were the first to offer a money-back guarantee on our express cargo services. Keeping customer satisfaction in mind, we launched the cash-on-delivery scheme and were also the first to announce a toll-free number to look into complaints and requests.

Customer knows best: All services and solutions are custom-designed for our clients. Our clients range from large corporates, small and medium enterprises, units in cluster markets, wholesalers and individuals. Our services are backed by a strong, structured, multi-modal network.

From a global multinational corporate to the small chikankari trader in Lucknow, our customers know they will always come first. Gati stands for commitment, integrity and efficiency and enjoys immense goodwill among its clients.

From inception till today, Gati stands for a commitment to integrity and goodwill towards customers and the industry.

Group Companies

Continuous progress is our mantra. Our unmatched infrastructure, quality-conscious personnel and technological capabilities are all focused on one goal—to move your cargo to its destination on time. To this end, we have enhanced our services with a greater focus on cargo management and customer satisfaction, and have improved our operations by superior strategic planning.

We have an alliance with Jubilee Commercial, an IATA accredited freight forwarder that started operations in 1998 as Air Cargo Agent. Today Jubilee Commercial is a member of the Federation of Freight Forwarders Associations of India, Federation of

Indian Chamber of Commerce and Industry and International Federation of Freight Forwarders. Jubilee is now set to become a one-stop solution provider for all freight forwarding services including customs clearance for International cargo.

Service in India

Value Added Services

Gati's bouquet of value added services are designed to take care of your business needs:

- FOD (Freight-on-delivery): Option of paying at the time of delivery.
- COD (Cash-on-delivery): Collection of cash against delivery from your customer and remitting it to you online through e-banking.
- DOD (Draft/Cheque-on-delivery): Collection of draft/cheque on your behalf at the time of delivery.
- Inbound Rate Agreement: Ensures hassle-free, convenient supplies from your vendors. Also gives you the advantage of dealing with one company at agreed rates.
- Documentation Assistance: Information on forms, permits, legal/statutory requirements including clearance of check posts.
- Holiday and Sunday Pick-up/Delivery: At Gati, we are sensitive to your urgent delivery commitments which is why we provide the option for pick-up and deliveries on Sundays/holidays.
- Octroi Clearing Facility: Octroi clearance on behalf of customers.
- Tamper-proof packing: Special bags for safe handling of high value cargo.
- Fragile goods packaging: Gati offers packaging solutions for fragile goods like marble statues and glassware.

Gati Priority—Flying High, Touching the Sky

Speed, Reliability and Reach

Every operation at Gati Priority follows this principle. Our large fleet of surface vehicles and a strategic alliance with Indian Airlines, the largest airline network in India, helps us meet every possible business need. Customers come to Gati for quality at an affordable price.

With Gati, customers are assured of:

- Reserved space in 34 designated air movement sectors
- 24X7 service counters at major air transit centres
- Multi-modal connectivity for easy and quick transit at non-airport locations
- Flexi—pricing options based on urgency and load factor

- Door pick-up and door delivery
- Online track and trace
- Option of same day delivery
- Expertize in handling high value/perishable goods.

Zipp

Zipp Makes the Difference

We go beyond the normal courier service with Zipp and provide you with unique price and transit time options.

- Express courier service
- 48-96 hours delivery for most locations in India
- Online track and trace facility
- Holiday and Sunday pick-up and delivery option
- A pre-paid payment option in the form of Zipp envelopes and boxes
- Cash-on-delivery facility
- Customized delivery options for mass mailing
- An invoicing facility for regular repeat booking needs, with options for centralized billing to suit your business.

Warehousing

Gati Warehousing—Logistics Solutions Made to Order

Logistics and supply chain management are an integral part of our businesses. A sharp and steady focus on these key functions has helped Gati gain a competitive edge over the rest of the market. In recent times Indian industry has begun to acknowledge the strategic importance of logistics and warehousing functions to their businesses. And Gati's expertize and experience in this area is being harnessed by many companies.

Gati offers its services as a 3PL or a third party logistics provider. A 3PL provider allows a company to:

- Concentrate on core competencies
- Create greater competitive flexibility and release working capital
- Get lean and agile
- Exploit the better know-how and scale efficiencies of logistics companies.

Maximum Space, Minimum Investment

Gati's warehousing facilities consist of completely modern storage systems and material handling equipment. Thus, Gati is able to offer customers very high levels of operational efficiency.

With branches in all metros and mini metros, Gati has more than 200 storage locations across India.

With over 600,000 sq. ft. of warehousing space spread all over the country and serving multiple clients, Gati is able to offer many more customer friendly solutions:

- Flexible hiring options
- Modern racking and handling equipment
- Reduction in material breakage, damage etc
- Engineering solutions to design and build warehouses as per requirements
- Warehouse management system.

Warehouse Management System

Manage inventory in real-time. Gati's web-based warehouse management system provides both functionality and flexibility for customers to manage warehouse operations. The web-based WMS can be updated online thus allowing customers a real-time picture of their inventory. The WMS gives precise, detailed, real-time information about every aspect of customer operations.

The WMS application has the functionality to take care of multi-company/multi-location capabilities. And, the multi-warehouse system has been designed so that every warehouse can write its own rules.

The central focus is the powerful inventory control and management system-making the management of diverse inventory holdings less complex and more organized.

The web-based WMS has resulted in:

- Improved inventory accuracy
- Decrease in order processing time
- Improved customer service levels
- Elimination of put away and picking errors
- Less returns
- Reduced shipping errors
- Capacity utilization.

Milestones

From inception, we at Gati have been obsessed with providing the best possible service. This obsession has not only led to dramatic changes in our business, but has also resulted in setting new benchmarks for the industry. Here are some snapshots of our story:

1989

Cargo industry gets a shake up Gati is born as Gati Cargo Management Services.

1989–1995

Revolutionary Ideas

Gati offers a money back guarantee on cargo services. On time and intact. Else you get your money back. Gati offers cash-on-delivery for convenience of customers. A toll-free number for customers is introduced for the first time in India.

1996

Alliance in the Air

Gati, already having the largest surface network, ties-up with Indian Airlines, India's largest air network to facilitate faster delivery of shipments.

1997

Logistics is the Name of the Game

Gati introduces the concept of third party logistics (3PL). Subsequently it offers complete logistics and supply chain management solutions.

1998

Extending Our Range

Gati extends its service range by launching Suvidha—a courier service. Since then, Suvidha has been relaunched as Zipp.

1999

Improving Our Reach

Gati expands into SAARC countries, ties up with Bhutan and Maldives postal department.

Training and Development Needs

The P.D. Agarwal Development Centre is set up in Pune exclsuively for employee training and development.

2001

Millenium Parcel Express

Gati launches the first exclusive cargo train between Mumbai and Kolkata in association with Indian Railway.

Gati Nagar is Reborn

After the Gujarat earthquake, Gati adopted Maye, a village in Bhuj and has rehabilitated the entire earthquake affected village. The villagers have renamed the village Gati Nagar.

2003

The Customer Votes

Gati bags the Voice of Customer Award for "The Best Logistics Company 2003" in a survey conducted by Frost and Sullivan. **Gati@web.**

A Smarter Way to Work

Gati simplifies internal work processes for faster and better communication. *India-centric global reach* Gati sets up base in Singapore, the international business hub, in order to reach out to the world faster.

2004

Automation Rules

Gati introduces mechanized racking systems in the automated warehouse at Panvel, Maharashtra.

2005

State-of-the-art Mechantronic warehouses with APL racking and modern handling equipment in major cities across India. Gati was given the Champion CIO award for less than Rs. 1000 crore category of the Enterprise Connect Award- 2005 Gati was awarded the Amity HR-excellence award in 2005.

2006

Awarded the 'Best Logistics Partner' by HCL Infosystems. Awarded Consumer SuperBrand status in the logistics category for 2006-2007. Nominated for NDTV 'Business leadership Awards' 2006 in logistics category. 10th October, 2006 Gati rolls outs its corporate transformation exercise *social Responsibility Initiatives.*

Gati is a socially responsible company. Through a number of initiatives, we have tried to make a difference to the lives of people around us. Here is an account of the work we have done so far.

Maye Village, Bhuj District, Gujarat

26 January, 2001: Gujarat is hit by a massive earthquake. Bhuj district is the worst affected.

Gati personnel sprang into action and reached Maye village the same day to provide food, clothing, medication and water to the earthquake-affected community. A team of doctors was also brought in to provide medical aid to the 400 families in Maye. Gati was the first to build makeshift houses for these families-houses that were scientifically designed to resist earthquakes. Even today, though the villagers have managed to rebuild their homes, they still retain these structures.

Gati Government School, Hyderabad, Andhra Pradesh

In 2003, Gati agreed to develop a government school located at Banjara Hills. As a contribution to the government's Janmabhoomi programme, Gati built a school building with all necessary facilities—spacious classrooms, toilets and staff rooms. The building has 27 rooms and a playground. Gati also provided the furniture for school students and staff. Today the school strength stands at 1100 students. The housekeeping and security of the school is still under our purview.

Tsunami Relief Fund

The Tsunami that struck South-East, Asia on December 2004 was one of nature's worst disasters ever. It left in its wake more than 10 lakh people dead and over four million displaced. The tsunami relief operations have been hailed as one of the fastest and most massive operations ever. Gati was one of the first to reach the rescue scenes at Nagapattnam and Cuddalore. Gati brought in food, water, clothing, medication and a team of doctors.The team took special care of children, who were the most affected. Gati also provided the affected community with essential utensils like plates, glasses etc.

MC High School, Nagore, Tamil Nadu

After rehabilitating tsunami-affected people at Nagapattnam and Cuddalore, Gati undertook a related project—the development of the MC High School at Nagore. This school includes about 500 students who belong to tsunami-affected families. Gati has already started work on constructing a building with 18 rooms, a kitchen and toilets. More development work is in the process.Gati has also actively participated in the Kargil contributions, as well as rescue and rehabilitation works for other natural disasters in India. We are proud to be a socially responsible corporate citizen of India.

India is Destination Future for Logistics Services: CII

The industry in India, particularly the manufacturing sector can sustain a 10-15 per cent growth if supply chain development keeps pace with the desire and the developments in the manufacturing sector.

This was the view expressed by Jamshyd Godrej, chairman and managing director, Godrej and Boyce Manufacturing Company, and echoed by other industry leaders who participated at the logistics 2005 being organized by CII in Mumbai from October 27-29, 2005.

A resurgent Indian manufacturing sector is today, constrained by the supply chain bottlenecks and cost escalations owing to it, he said.

According to Cyrus Guzder, chairman, CII National Council on Transportation and Logistics, weak transport infrastructure is holding back the development of the logistics industry, and thereby acting as a roadblock to the nation's progress.

Stressing the role of proper infrastructure, H R Srinivasan, chairman, logistics summit 2005 and vision holder, take Solutions Ltd pointed out that with logistics costs being substantial part of product cost in India, the role of infrastructure and optimization of its use with existing systems is key to logistics effectiveness.

Responding to the concerns of industry on the lack of proper infrastructure, the advisor to the deputy chairman, planning commission, said that the government is actively trying to bring all the infrastructure sectors authorities together, for greater synergy and sharing of knowledge.

He went on to say that this was a very large and complex exercise, but hopefully, it would yield results soon.

Almost to supplement this point, Ravi Budhiraja, chairman, JNPT mentioned that in the near future there would be 30 per cent spare capacity in the Port infrastructure of the country, which would be in keeping with international practices of creating capacity before demand.

Speaking at the summit, Cedric Foo, deputy president, NOL group, Singapore, said that land side evacuation of Indian ports were very poor resulting in inadequate utilisation of the country's Port infrastructure. He said that there is urgent need for the road and rail network to align with the port infrastructure.

Putting a context to the deliberations on "logistics effectiveness: role of infrastructure and supply chain innovations," Guzder mentioned that Indian is today being promoted as the "destination future" by logistics service providers all over the world.

He added that Indian players are also getting into position in different ways by providing a wide spectrum of logistics services, though it is being held back owing to congestion, over regulation, fragmentation, and weak transport infrastructure.

Gati Corporation Looking to Raise $43 Million

Gati Corporation has approved an issue of 15.71 lakh shares at Rs 423 per share to AMP Cap investors. The company is looking to raise almost $43 million. The company, according to its Managing Director, Mr Mahendra Agarwal, has a plan of putting in $100 million in the next three years.

Excerpts from CNBC-TV18'S Exclusive Interview

How much money are you looking to raise? Are you going to be using this for expansion?

We are looking at raising almost $43 million. We have also raised some money through rights issue, which was done about six months ago. In the next three years, we are going to put in $100 million in the company, in addition to $25- 30 million that we have already put in the last couple of years.

Half of this money will come through equity. The balance would come through internal accruals. We are putting all this money to enhance the capability of the company. What are the plans to use the route of equity to raise this cash?

About $15 million has already come from AMP investment. Another $3 million is going to come through the convertible warrants and $20 million through FCCBs. In the EGM, we have already passed the resolution. By next month, this $20 million should come through FCCB. Another $5 million will come from the promoters. We have already raised the balance through the rights issue.

What are your plans to ease your debt interest?

With AMP investment we have already become a debt-free company. This year, we are going to close almost at Rs. 400 crore without looking at our fuel station, which brings in about Rs. 80 crore. We have already passed a resolution in the EGM that fuel stations will be hived off into its own subsidiary. This Rs 400 crore will go up to Rs. 1,000 crore in the next three years. In June 2009, Gati will be a 20-year-old company.

What will be the total equity dilution? What kind of EPS can we expect from Gati in June FY06?

The EPS will be almost Rs. 18. Last year, it was Rs. 17. So we are looking at an EPS more than that, despite the dilution. When the FCCB gets converted in the future, the total dilution would be almost about 20-22 per cent and the promoters' holding at that time would come down to almost 45 per cent. But we don't expect the EPS to go down. Further, we are expecting the bottomline to almost double than the topline growth.

There was a talk of foreign partnership with TNT. How open are you to that? Are you in conversation with companies?

We were and are not in conversation with any company. Gati is a truly Indian multinational. It is on a very strong footing. It is a leader in express distribution and supply chain solution. With the infusion of this fund, we are going to enhance our capability and are going to create a world-class facility in terms of warehousing.

How soon does the fuel station get hived off into a separate entity?

That will happen in the next two-three months.

THE LAW OFFICES OF COUNTRYMAN AND MCDANIEL

The firm was established in 1978 to serve the specific claims, business, corporate, estate planning and trade needs of *Air and Ocean Freight Forwarders, Indirect Air Carriers, NVOCCs, Consolidators, Customs Brokers, Domestic Motor Carriers, Ramp Service Providers, Warehouses, Cold Store Operators* and their *Insurance Underwriters* in the United States and to supervise disputes abroad.

Offering a wide variety of legal, business and customs services, *The Law Offices of Countryman & McDaniel* actively serves client needs throughout the United States and coordinates a network of qualified correspondent legal counsel, surveyors and other consultants in the U.S. and most major trading nations.

Our firm brings focus upon the current industry need to enhance cargo loss prevention techniques and rapid response cargo recovery programmes. They are not all listed here, but our firm currently supervises litigation in over 85 nations.

Legal, Logistics and Claim Services Index

Attorneys and Law Firm Profile
Logistics and Claims details below:

- Customs Broker Legal Practice
- Freight Forwarder and General Logistics Legal Practice
- Litigation Services for Customs and Logistics Providers
- Services on behalf of Liability and Marine Insurance Underwriters
- Regulatory Law Practice before Federal Agencies
- Interception of Counterfeit and Grey Market Goods
- Alternative Dispute Resolution Services.

Business, Corporate, Estate Planning and Special Service

- Business and Corporate Services
- Personal Legal Services, including Estate Planning, for Logistics Executives, Employees and Families
- Accomplished Consultants for Special Legal Needs.

Logistics and Claims

- Customs Broker Legal Practice
- Practice before U.S. Customs
- C-TPAT (Customs-Trade Partnership against Terrorism)—Application and Certification
- Broker Compliance
- Broker Professional Liability Claims
- Duty Drawback
- Interception of Counterfeit and Grey Market Goods
- U.S. Court of International Trade
- Licensed U.S. Customs Broker on Staff.

Freight Forwarder and General Logistics Legal Practice—Air-Ocean-Inland-Motor Truck-Warehouse

- Third Party Liability Claims Representation and Defense—Air-Ocean-Inland-Motor Truck-Warehouse
- Bill of Lading and Transport Document Analysis—Do Your Documents ReflectCurrent Law and Protect The Company?
- Overseas Agent Contracts and Services—Are You Protected?
- Staff Training and Claims Seminars in All Modes
- Supply Chain Risk Analysis.

Litigation Services for Customs and Logistics Providers—State-Federal-Administrative

- Business Litigation on behalf of Logistics Providers
- Cargo Claims Analysis and Disposition
- Coordination of Foreign Lawsuits
- Employee Claims and Disputes
- Litigation Defense on behalf of Logistics Providers
- NVOCC and air forwarder Bill of Lading Liability Claims
- Customs Broker Liability and E & O Claims
- Motor Truck Cargo Claims
- Professional Transport Errors and Omissions Liability Claims
- Warehouse and Cold Store Liability Claims
- Litigation Defense on behalf of Logistics Insurance Underwriters—Air-Ocean-Inland-Marine-Motor Truck-Warehouse.

Services on behalf of Liability and Marine Insurance Underwriters

- Policy analysis and programme Consultation
- Coordinating Counsel Network Programme Services
- The Cargo Law Network—Correspondent Lawyers in the U.S. and Most Major Trading Nations
- Marine Insurance Claims Analysis & Defense
- NVOCC and Air Forwarder Bill of Lading Liability Claims
- Customs Broker Liability and E & O Claims
- Motor Truck Cargo Claims
- Professional Transport Errors and Omissions Liability Claims
- The Cargo Law Network—Correspondent Lawyers in the U.S. and Most Major Trading Nations
- Warehouse and Cold Store Liability Claims.

Regulatory Law Practice

- U.S. Customs
- Federal Aviation Administration
- Federal Maritime Commission
- Department of Transportation—DoT.
- U.S. Coast Guard
- Combating Counterfeit and Grey Market Goods.

Alternative Dispute Resolution Services

- Arbitrations
    - Qualified Arbitrators to Decide Disputes

- Mediations
  - Qualified Mediators to Resolve Disputes
- The Cargo Law Network—Correspondent Lawyers in the U.S. and Most Major Trading Nations

Business, Corporate, Estate Planning and Special Service

- Business and Corporate Services for Companies
  - Logistics Agency Agreements—Domestic and Foreign
  - Business Agreements and Contracts
  - Business Restructuring
  - C-TPAT Applications and Certification
  - Interception of Counterfeit and Grey Market Goods
  - Commercial Lease Review
  - Commercial Real Estate Purchase Transaction Review
  - Corporate Formations
  - Corporate Employee Handbooks
  - Mergers and Buy-outs
  - Maintenance of Corporate Minutes
  - Tax Consultations.

Personal Legal Services for Logistics Executives, Employees and Families

- Estate Planning: Trusts, Wills and Probate Services
- Personal Finance Restructure
- Real Estate Practice and Transactional Services
- Personal Injury
- Tax Consultation.

Accomplished Consultants for Special Legal Needs

- Bankruptcy
- Copyright and Trademark
- Practice before U.S. Customs
- C-TPAT Certification
- Interception of Counterfeit and Grey Market Goods
- International Trade Consultants
- Foreign Attorneys
- Special Security
- Specialized International Investigation
- The Cargo Law Network—Correspondent Lawyers in the U.S. and Most Major Trading Nations
- Transport, Operations and Marine Insurance
- Transportation Project Consultants
- White Collar Crime.

A Firm Designed to Serve the Special Needs of U.S. Domestic and International

Logistics Service Providers and Customs Professionals

- Index to Countryman and McDaniel General Services
- Contact Countryman and McDaniel
- Legal Services of the Firm
- Our Staff Attorneys and Law Firm Profile
- The Cargo Law Network—Lawyers in the U.S. and Most Major Trading Nations
- Library and Search Engine of the Cargo Letter
- Search Engine for this Internet Portal—Find Everything You Need
- Transport Reference Desk—Virtual Transport Library
- 24 Hour International Vessel Casualties and Pirates Database
- The Photo Gallery of Cargo Loss—Photos and Lessons Learned
- Transport Law Navigator—all air, ocean, motor and customs laws
- Library and Search Engine of the Cargo Letter
- Mega Portal of Trade and Transport References and Services
- General Reference Desk—virtual public library.

THE CARGO LAW NETWORK OF LEGAL SERVICES

Since 1978 *The Law Offices of Countryman and McDaniel* has actively served client needs throughout the United States and Abroad—in the coordination of a network of correspondent legal counsel, surveyors and other consultants—to all six continents, utilizing *The Cargo Law Network*. Accordingly, we are able to administrate International liability programmes for both insurance underwriters and private logistics companies—without the increased expense of contacting one of the multinational law firms operating today.

We currently provide these International services for a wide variety of client and underwriter interests with active cases in some 40 nations.

We are told by both private and institutional clients that the *Cargo Law Network* programme is both economical to operate and also reduces indemnity payments. We believe that the reasons for these conclusions are obvisous.

Reaching the goal of serving whatever overseas legal challenge might suddenly arise around the globe for our clients was not easy, nor achieved overnight. *The Cargo Law Network* is a product of trust, built upon years of process. The assignment of overseas cases for the defense our clients protection is part of an ongoing process—not just some instant reaction to the receipt of a case to be handled. Client interests must be served by assignment of the partiular legal case to a fully qualified logistics lawyer who is loyal to the concept of a long term relationship with *Cargo Law Network* representation.

We take great pride in this accomplishment—the esablishment of a functioning legal system for logistics providers, developed over the past twenty years. This system is now available to serve our client interests through *The Law Offices of Countryman and McDaniel.*

The Cargo Law Network works "both ways." Cases are accepted from client interests in the United States for the administration of overseas cases. Likewise, cases are accepted from our clients overseas for the handling of claims within the 50 U.S. states and Canada.

The Cargo Law Network: The need arrives all too often. You receive some mysterious document from overseas which *"looks like"* a lawsuit. Many times we find that your company is only being harassed. There is no lawsuit, just an *"interesting"* document designed to panic you into paying money which is not owed. Other times, the lawsuit is quite real and your company must file papers in Bangkok or Mumbai or Shanghai within the next several days. *What will you do?* You can either grab the Mumbai phone book or retain a huge multinational law firm which will likely charge three times the claim amount to obtain the services of a disinterested junior legal associate. We are quite proud that *The Cargo Law Network* has functioned for many years as a viable alternative. The goal is for efficient disposition of the claim.

We are far too busy here to have any claim last any longer that it needs to be. Rapid closure is the common goal.

In such diverse areas as Argentina, Brazil, Chile, Korea, Peru, The People's Republic of China, Hong Kong, Taiwan, Singapore, Thailand, Taiwan, Australia, New Zealand, Israel, Kuwait, the Emirates, India, the European Union, the United Kingdom, Uruguay, the Dominican Republic, Puerto Rico, Canada, Mexico—and all the others listed below—*The Cargo Law Network* has directed a steady flow of hundreds of International logistics and customs related legal cases for many years since 1978.

The Law Offices of Countryman and McDaniel services are provided on behalf of private logistics companies and to support the International insurance programmes which have been placed in our charge. Whether by private assignment or through an insurance underwriter, there is no reason why any so-called "International Case" should exist beyond our ability to dispose of the matter by letter—if that result is at all possible.

The Law Offices of Countryman and McDaniel brings focus upon current industry needs to enhance cargo loss prevention techniques and rapid response cargo recovery programmes. They are not all listed here, but our firm currently supervises litigation in 40 nations. This *Cargo Law Network* system has been years in the making and of great benefit to companies and underwriters facing liability risks overseas and throughout the 50 United States.

We will continue to expand this area of our practice and find that it holds various advantages for our transport and insurance company clients.

Use of The Cargo Law Network Advantages Include:

1. The ability of clients to instantly locate logistics attorneys in overseas locations is an asset that does not generally exist.
2. Once, or if, an overseas lawyer is located by a client, use of "*Local Counsel*" is as problematic and risky as selecting a good plumber at random from the phone book. Who have your hired?
3. If the client is viewed by the overseas attorney as a "*one time*" case opportunity, billing will not be efficient. Unfair exploitation may be the result. In *The Cargo Law Network*, our local counsel receive assignments for many clients—all dependent upon *The Cargo Law Network* for future work. We have established uniformity in most venues.
4. The client may be called upon to post a substantial case retainer which is not in proportion to the task at hand. *This important issue is a common obsticale to overseas representation.* But once credit is established by the client with our firm—*The Cargo Law Network* "*Local Counsel*" do not require payment of an initial retainer. "*Local Counsel*" relies upon *The Cargo Law Network*—and will take immediate action as required. Many quite impressive examples of such responses for *The Cargo Law Network* are available on request.
5. The absence of loyalty to a "*one time client*" limits the availability of rapid response and positive outcome from any overseas attorney. But as often happens—*immediate response* is often required to protect client interests. *The Cargo Law Network* is able to protect client interests by arranging, say, for the filing of a response to a lawsuit at Bangkok or Shanghai or Caracas, or Ahmadabad—*often within hours*, by means of our *The Cargo Law Network* request.
6. Reliance on the established *Cargo Law Network* removes the risk of unpaid billings for local counsel. Not once in 24 years have we experienced unresolved billing problems when working with "*Local Counsel.*"
7. Use of the *Cargo Law Network* does not limit the client to the single option of retaining a very expensive multinational law firm, which may assign an inexperienced junior associate to the case and thereby accomplish little to benefit the case outcome.
8. While more important for some cases than others, *Countryman and McDaniel* involvement as coordinating counsel is a cost efficient method of enhancing the case result. Our familiarity with the air and ocean logistics and customs

brokerage industry (forwarders and licensed customs brokers being on our own staff) allows for an "*attorney to attorney*" dialogue which can help speed the case to a conclusion at reduced cost. We work in all the transport modes and trade environments.

9. All "*Cargo Law Network Local Counsel*" are required to abide by a strict set of "*Billing Guidelines*" when joining the *Cargo Law Network*. Contrary to the practice in most nations, our "Local Counsel" are required to itemize billings and follow other curbs on "over billing", such as assigning only one lawyer to attend proceedings unless prior permission has been obtained. Our "*Billing Guidelines*" follow those required by many US and UK insurance companies.
10. Bearing in mind that most logistics disputes feature many potential locations in which a lawsuit might be filed, use of *The Cargo Law Network* frequently allows us to promote final resolution in the nation whose laws most favour our client cause or where the cause will be handled most fairly. As only one example, we recently obtained dismissal for a case pending in the U.S. District Court for The Southern District of New York, in favour of continued proceedings in the Maritime Court of Shanghai, People's Republic of China. Our client would likely lose the case in New York, but will likely prevail under Chinese law, using the services of our very dedicated local counsel at Shanghai.
11. Of greatest importance over the years has been our ability to avoid the cost and uncertainty of litigation overseas by using the insights of *Cargo Law Network Local Counsel* to obtain prompt analysis and "tips" which allow for dispute resolution *by letter from our offices* in the United States. Examples of this process are numerous. Many of our cases involve shipments which have no connection with the United States, except a U.S. client. In these "three corner" cases a *Cargo Law Network Local Counsel* instant e-mail chat has often allowed us to choose the correct case direction for case handling. To simply regard the case as a local matter in the country where the legal case was filed, without consuting *Cargo Law Network Local Counsel* at origin would have been a disaster to the client cause.

We would be pleased to discuss your International experiences.

Partial List of the Countries Currently Served by the Cargo Law Network

- Argentina
- Australia
- Belgium
- Brazil
- Canada—All Provinces
- Caribbean Basin
- Chile
- Columbia
- Costa Rica

- Czech Republic
- Dominican Republic
- Ecuador
- Finland
- France
- Germany
- Guatemala
- Greece
- Honduras
- Hong Kong
- India and Provinces
- Israel and Palentine Interests
- Italy
- Japan
- Kuwait
- Mexico
- Netherlands (Holland)
- New Zealand
- Norway
- Panama
- People's Republic of China—All Provinces
- Peru
- Philippines
- Puerto Rico
- Romania
- Russia and Former Soviet Interests
- Saudi Arabia
- Singapore
- South Korea
- Spain
- St. Maarten
- Taiwan—Republic of China
- Thailand
- Turkey
- United Kingdom
- Uruguay
- United States—Currently in 43 Jurisdictions
- Vietnam
- Virgin Islands
- Venezuela

Required Legal Notice: The Law Offices of Countryman and McDaniel are quite proud of the years of work which have been spent in building *The Cargo Law Network*, but it must be understood that our firm does not purport to practice law overseas, nor are we able to represent ourselves as expert in the laws of all the nations in which we coordinate cases. *"Local Counsel"* firms are retained by our clients, under *"Powers of Attorney"* which are required by most courts of the world, but not in the United States. A great many of the *"Local Counsel"* in *The Cargo Law Network* have demonstrated their talent and dedication continuously over the years. Case frequency in other areas of the world limits our contact and thus our familiarity with performance in given situations.

Appendix

Basic Guide to Leadership and Supervision

This guide is basic, yet comprehensive, in nature to be useful to new managers and supervisors. Note that many organizations struggle, not from lack of advanced information—rather, they never really master the basics. This guide will help you master the basics.

Each topic includes references to Web addresses that provide additional, advanced, free information. These Web addresses are spelled out in the text of the guide. Therefore, the reader might best benefit from this guide by printing it out for continued reference.

INTRODUCTION TO MANAGEMENT AND SUPERVISION

What is "Management"?

Traditional Interpretation

There are a variety of views about this term. Traditionally, the term "management" refers to the set of activities, and often the group of people, involved in four general functions, including planning, organizing, leading and coordinating activities. (Note that the four functions recur throughout the organization and are highly integrated.)

Another Interpretation

Some writers, teachers and practitioners assert that the above view is rather outmoded and that management needs to focus more on leadership skills, e.g., establishing vision and goals, communicating the vision and goals, and guiding others to accomplish them. They also assert that leadership must be more facilitative, participative and empowering in how visions and goals are established and carried out. Some people assert that this really is not a change in the management functions, rather it is re-emphasizing certain aspects of management.

What do Managers do?

Both of the above interpretations acknowledge the major functions of planning, organizing, leading and coordinating activities—they put different emphasis and suggest different natures of activities in the following four major functions. They still agree that what managers do is the following:

1. *Planning* : Including identifying goals, objectives, methods, resources needed to carry out methods, responsibilities and dates for completion of tasks. Examples of planning are strategic planning, business planning, project planning, staffing planning, advertising and promotions planning, etc.
2. *Organizing Resources*: To achieve the goals in an optimum fashion. Examples are organizing new departments, human resources, office and file systems, re-organizing businesses, etc.
3. *Leading*: Including to set direction for the organization, groups and individuals and also influence people to follow that direction. Examples are establishing strategic direction (vision, values, mission and/or goals) and championing methods of organizational performance management to pursue that direction.
4. *Controlling, or Coordinating*: This occurs with the organization's systems, processes and structures to effectively and efficiently reach goals and objectives. This includes ongoing collection of feedback, and monitoring and adjustment of systems, processes and structures accordingly. Examples include use of financial controls, policies and procedures, performance management processes, measures to avoid risks etc.

   Another common view is that "management" is getting things done through others. Yet another view, quite apart from the traditional view, asserts that the job of management is to support employee's efforts to be fully productive members of the organizations and citizens of the community.

   To most employees, the term "management" probably means the group of people (executives and other managers) who are primarily responsible for making decisions in the organization. In a nonprofit, the term "management" might refer to all or any of the activities of the board, executive director and/or programme directors.

- For additional and advanced information, see Management (Introduction) at http://www.manage-menthelp.org/mng_thry/mng_thry.htm
- For additional and advanced information, see Planning (many kinds) at http://www.managementhelp.org/plan_dec/plan_dec.htm
- For additional and advanced information, see Leadership at http://www.managementhelp.org/ldrship/ldrship.htm
- For additional and advanced information, see Coordinating Activities at http://www.manage-menthelp.org/cntrllng/cntrllng.htm
- For additional and advanced information, see Management Developmentat http://www.manage-menthelp.org/mgmt_dev/mgmt_dev.htm

What is "Supervision"?

There are several interpretations of the term "supervision", but typically supervision is the activity carried out by supervisors to oversee the productivity and progress of employees who report directly to the supervisors. For example, first-level supervisors supervise entry-level employees. Depending on the size of the organization, middle-managers supervise first-level supervisors, chief executives supervise middle-managers, etc. Supervision is a management activity and supervisors have a management role in the organization.

What do Supervisors do?

Supervision of a group of employees often includes :

1. Conducting basic management skills (decision making, problem solving, planning, delegation and meeting management)
2. Organizing their department and teams
3. Noticing the need for and designing new job roles in the group
4. Hiring new employees
5. Training new employees
6. Employee performance management (setting goals, observing and giving feedback, addressing performance issues, firing employees, etc.)
7. Conforming to personnel policies and other internal regulations
    - For additional and advanced information, see Basic Overview of Supervision at http://www.management-help.org/suprvise/suprvise.htm
    - For additional and advanced information, see Supervisory Developmentat http://www.manage-menthelp.org/supr_dev/supr_dev.htm

Core Skills in Management and Supervision Problem Solving and Decision Making

Much of what managers and supervisors do is solve problems and make decisions. New managers and supervisors, in particular, often solve problems and decisions by reacting to them. They are "under the gun", stressed and very short for time. Consequently, when they encounter a new problem or decision they must make, they react with a decision that seemed to work before. It is easy with this approach to get stuck in a circle of solving the same problem over and over again. Therefore, as a new manager or supervisor, get used to an organized approach to problem solving and decision making. Not all problems can be solved and decisions made by the following, rather rational approach. However, the following basic guidelines will get you started. Do not be intimidated by the length of the list of guidelines. After you have practiced them a few times, they will become second nature to you—enough that you can deepen and enrich them to suit your own needs and nature.

(Note that it might be more your nature to view a "problem" as an "opportunity". Therefore, you might substitute "opportunity" for "problem" in the following guidelines.)

Define the Problem

This is often where people struggle. They react to what they think the problem is. Instead, seek to understand more about why you think there is a problem.

Defining the Problem: (with input from yourself and others) Ask yourself and others, the following questions:

(*a*) What can you see that causes you to think there is a problem?
(*b*) Where is it happening?
(*c*) How is it happening?
(*d*) When is it happening?
(*e*) With whom is it happening?

(*Hint*: Don't jump to "Who is causing the problem?" When we're stressed, blaming is often one of our first reactions. To be an effective manager, you need to address issues more than people.)

(*f*) Why is it happening?
(*g*) Write down a five-sentence description of the problem in terms of "The following should be happening, but isn't ..." or "The following is happening and should be: ..." As much as possible, be specific in your description, including what is happening, where, how, with whom and why. (It may be helpful at this point to use a variety of research methods.

Defining Complex Problems

If the problem still seems overwhelming, break it down by repeating steps a-f until you have descriptions of several related problems.

Verifying Your Understanding of the Problems

It helps a great deal to verify your problem analysis for conferring with a peer or someone else.

Prioritize the Problems

(*a*) If you discover that you are looking at several related problems, then prioritize which ones you should address first.
(*b*) Note the difference between "important" and "urgent" problems. Often, what we consider to be important problems to consider are really just urgent problems. Important problems deserve more attention. For example, if you're continually answering "urgent" phone calls, then you've probably got a more "important" problem and that's to design a system that screens and prioritizes your phone calls.

Understand Your Role in the Problem

Your role in the problem can greatly influence how you perceive the role of others. For example, if you're very stressed out, it'll probably look like others are, too, or, you may resort too quickly to blaming and reprimanding others. Or, you are feel very guilty about your role in the problem, you may ignore the accountabilities of others.

Look at Potential Causes for the Problem

(*a*) It is amazing how much you don't know about what you don't know. Therefore, in this phase, it is critical to get input from other people who notice the problem and who are effected by it.
(*b*) It is often useful to collect input from other individuals one at a time (at least at first). Otherwise, people tend to be inhibited about offering their impressions of the real causes of problems.
(*c*) Write down what your opinions and what you have heard from others.
(*d*) Regarding what you think might be performance problems associated with an employee, it is often useful to seek advice from a peer or your supervisor in order to verify your impression of the problem.
(*e*) Write down a description of the cause of the problem and in terms of what is happening, where, when, how, with whom and why.

Identify Alternatives for Approaches to Resolve the Problem

At this point, it is useful to keep others involved (unless you're facing a personal and/or employee performance problem). Brainstorm for solutions to the problem. Very simply put, brainstorming is collecting as many ideas as possible, then screening them to find the best idea. It is critical when collecting the ideas to not pass any judgement on the ideas—just write them down as you hear them. (A wonderful set of skills used to identify the underlying cause of issues is Systems Thinking.)

Select an Approach to Resolve the Problem

When selecting the best approach, consider the following points:

(*a*) Which approach is the most likely to solve the problem for the long-term?
(*b*) Which approach is the most realistic to accomplish for now? Do you have the resources? Are they affordable? Do you have enough time to implement the approach?
(*c*) What is the extent of risk associated with each alternative? (The nature of this step, in particular, in the problem solving process is why problem solving and decision making are highly integrated.)

Plan the Implementation of the Best Alternative (This is Your Action Plan)

(*a*) Carefully consider "What will the situation look like when the problem is solved?"

(*b*) What steps should be taken to implement the best alternative to solving the problem? What systems or processes should be changed in your organization, for example, a new policy or procedure? Don't resort to solutions where someone is "just going to try harder."
(*c*) How will you know if the steps are being followed or not? (these are your indicators of the success of your plan).
(*d*) What resources will you need in terms of people, money and facilities?
(*e*) How much time will you need to implement the solution? Write a schedule that includes the start and stop times, and when you expect to see certain indicators of success.
(*f*) Who will primarily be responsible for ensuring implementation of the plan?
(*g*) Write down the answers to the above questions and consider this as your action plan.
(*h*) Communicate the plan to those who will involved in implementing it and, at least, to your immediate supervisor. (An important aspect of this step in the problem-solving process is continually observation and feedback.)

Monitor Implementation of the Plan

Monitor the indicators of success:

(*a*) Are you seeing what you would expect from the indicators?
(*b*) Will the plan be done according to schedule?
(*c*) If the plan is not being followed as expected, then consider: Was the plan realistic? Are there sufficient resources to accomplish the plan on schedule? Should more priority be placed on various aspects of the plan? Should the plan be changed?

Verify if the Problem has been Resolved or not

One of the best ways to verify if a problem has been solved or not is to resume normal operations in the organization. Still, you should consider:

(*a*) What changes should be made to avoid this type of problem in the future? Consider changes to policies and procedures, training, etc.
(*b*) Lastly, consider "What did you learn from this problem solving?" Consider new knowledge, understanding and/or skills.
(*c*) Consider writing a brief memo that highlights the success of the problem solving effort, and what you learned as a result. Share it with your supervisor, peers and subordinates.

For additional and advanced information, see:

- Research Methods at http://www.managementhelp.org/research/research.htm

- Systems Thinking at http://www.managementhelp.org/systems/systems.htm
- Collecting and Sharing Feedback at http://www.managementhelp.org/commskls/feedback/feedback.htm
- Making Decisions at http://www.managementhelp.org/prsn_prd/decision.htm
- Problem Solving at http://www.managementhelp.org/prsn_prd/prob_slv.htm
- Planning (Basics) at http://www.managementhelp.org/plan_dec/gen_plan/gen_plan.htm
- Group-Based Problem Solving and Decision Making at http://www.managementhelp.org/grp_skll/grp_dec/grp_dec.htm

Planning

Quick Look at Some Basic Terms

Planning typically includes use of the following basic terms:

Note: It is not critical to grasp completely accurate definitions of each of the following terms. It is more important for planners to have a basic sense for the difference between goals/objectives (results) and strategies/tasks (methods to achieve the results).

1. *Goals*: Goals are specific accomplishments that must be accomplished in total, or in some combination, in order to achieve some larger, overall result preferred from the system, for example, the mission of an organization. (Going back to our reference to systems, goals are outputs from the system.)
2. *Strategies or Activities*: These are the methods or processes required in total, or in some combination, to achieve the goals. (Going back to our reference to systems, strategies are processes in the system.)
3. *Objectives*: Objectives are specific accomplishments that must be accomplished in total, or in some combination, to achieve the goals in the plan. Objectives are usually "milestones" along the way when implementing the strategies.
4. *Tasks*: Particularly in small organizations, people are assigned various tasks required to implement the plan. If the scope of the plan is very small, tasks and activities are often essentially the same.
5. *Resources (and Budgets)*: Resources include the people, materials, technologies, money, etc., required to implement the strategies or processes. The costs of these resources are often depicted in the form of a budget. (Going back to our reference to systems, resources are input to the system.)

Basic Overview of Typical Phases in Planning

Whether the system is an organization, department, business, project, etc., the basic planning process typically includes similar nature of activities carried out in similar sequence. The phases are carried out carefully or—in some cases—intuitively, for example, when planning a very small, straightforward effort. The complexity of the various phases (and their duplication throughout the system) depend on the scope of the system. For example, in a large corporation, the following phases would be carried out in the corporate offices, in each division, in each department, in each group, etc.

Notes

1. Different groups of planners might have different names for the following activities and groups them differently. However, the nature of the activities and their general sequence remains the same.

2. The following are typical phases in planning. They do not comprise the complete, ideal planning process.

1. *Reference Overall Singular Purpose ("Mission")/Desired Result from System*: During planning, planners have in mind (consciously or unconsciously) some overall purpose or result that the plan is to achieve. For example, during strategic planning, it is critical to reference the mission, or overall purpose, of the organization.
2. *Take Stock Outside and Inside the System*: This "taking stock" is always done to some extent, whether consciously or unconsciously. For example, during strategic planning, it is important to conduct an environmental scan. This scan usually involves considering various driving forces, or major influences, that might effect the organization.
3. *Analyze the Situation*: For example, during strategic planning, planners often conduct a "SWOT analysis". (SWOT is an acronym for considering the organization's strengths and weaknesses, and the opportunities and threats faced by the organization.) During this analysis, planners also can use a variety of assessments, or methods to "measure" the health of systems.
4. *Establish Goals*: Based on the analysis and alignment to the overall mission of the system, planners establish a set of goals that build on strengths to take advantage of opportunities, while building up weaknesses and warding off threats.
5. *Establish Strategies to Reach Goals*: The particular strategies (or methods to reach the goals) chosen depend on matters of affordability, practicality and efficiency.
6. *Establish Objectives along the Way to Achieving Goals*: Objectives are selected to be timely and indicative of progress toward goals.
7. *Associate Responsibilities and Time Lines with Each Objective*: Responsibilities are assigned, including for implementation of the plan, and for achieving various goals and objectives. Ideally, deadlines are set for meeting each responsibility.
8. *Write and Communicate a Plan Document*: The above information is organized and written in a document which is distributed around the system.
9. *Acknowledge and Celebrate Accomplishment of the Plan*: This step is frequently forgotten, which can lead to increasing frustration and skepticism on the part of those people who are responsible to carry out the plan.

Guidelines to Ensure Successful Planning and Implementation

A common failure in many kinds of planning is that the plan is never really implemented. Instead, all focus is on writing a plan document. Too often, the plan sits collecting dust on a shelf. Therefore, most of the following guidelines help to ensure that the planning process is carried out completely and is implemented completely—or, deviations from the intended plan are recognized and managed accordingly.

1. Involve the Right People in the Planning Process

Going back to the reference to systems, it is critical that all parts of the system continue to exchange feedback in order to function effectively. This is true no matter what type of system. When planning, get input from everyone who will responsible to carry out parts of the plan, along with representative from groups who will be effected by the plan. Of course, people also should be involved if they will be responsible to review and authorize the plan.

2. Write Down the Planning Information and Communicate it Widely

New managers, in particular, often forget that others don't know what these managers know. Even if managers do communicate their intentions and plans verbally, chances are great that others won't completely hear or understand what the manager wants done. Also, as plans change, it's extremely difficult to remember who is supposed to be doing what and according to which version of the plan. Key stakeholders (employees, management, board members, funders, investor, customers, clients, etc.) may request copies of various types of plans. Therefore, it's critical to write plans down and communicate them widely.

3. Goals and Objectives Should Be SMARTER

SMARTER is an acronym, that is, a word composed by joining letters from different words in a phrase or set of words. In this case, a SMARTER goal or objective is:

Specific: For example, it is difficult to know what someone should be doing if they are to pursue the goal to "work harder." It is easier to recognize "Write a paper."

Measurable: It is difficult to know what the scope of "Writing a paper" really is. It is easier to appreciate that effort if the goal is "Write a 30-page paper."

Acceptable: If I am to take responsibility for pursuit of a goal, the goal should be acceptable to me. For example, I am not likely to follow the directions of someone telling me to write a 30-page paper when I also have to five other papers to write. However, if you involve me in setting the goal so I can change my other commitments or modify the goal, I am much more likely to accept pursuit of the goal as well.

Realistic: Even if I do accept responsibility to pursue a goal that is specific and measurable, the goal won't be useful to me or others if, for example, the goal is to "Write a 30-page paper in the next 10 seconds."

Time frame: It may mean more to others if I commit to a realistic goal to "Write a 30-page paper in one week." However, it will mean more to others (particularly if they are planning to help me or guide me to reach the goal) if I specify that I will write one page a day for 30 days, rather than including the possibility that I will write all 30 pages in last day of the 30-day period.

Extending: The goal should stretch the performer's capabilities. For example, I might be more interested in writing a 30-page paper if the topic of the paper or the way that I write it will extend my capabilities.

Rewarding: I am more inclined to write the paper if the paper will contribute to an effort in such a way that I might be rewarded for my effort.

4. Build in Accountability (Regularly Review Who's Doing What and By When?)

Plans should specify who is responsible for achieving each result, including goals and objectives. Dates should be set for completion of each result, as well. Responsible parties should regularly review status of the plan. Be sure to have someone of authority "sign off" on the plan, including putting their signature on the plan to indicate they agree with and support its contents. Include responsibilities in policies, procedures, job descriptions, performance review processes, etc.

5. Note Deviations from the Plan and Replan Accordingly

It is OK to deviate from the plan. The plan is not a set of rules. It is an overall guideline. As important as following the plan is noticing deviations and adjusting the plan accordingly.

6. Evaluate Planning Process and the Plan

During the planning process, regularly collect feedback from participants. Do they agree with the planning process? If not, what don't they like and how could it be done better? In large, ongoing planning processes (such as strategic planning, business planning, project planning, etc.), it is critical to collect this kind of feedback regularly.

During regular reviews of implementation of the plan, assess if goals are being achieved or not. If not, were goals realistic? Do responsible parties have the resources necessary to achieve the goals and objectives? Should goals be changed? Should more priority be placed on achieving the goals? What needs to be done?

Finally, take 10 minutes to write down how the planning process could have been done better. File it away and read it the next time you conduct the planning process.

7. Recurring Planning Process is at Least as Important as Plan Document

Far too often, primary emphasis is placed on the plan document. This is extremely unfortunate because the real treasure of planning is the planning process itself. During planning, planners learn a great deal from ongoing analysis, reflection, discussion, debates and dialogue around issues and goals in the system. Perhaps there is no better example of misplaced priorities in planning than in business ethics. Far too often, people put emphasis on written codes of ethics and codes of conduct. While these documents certainly are important, at least as important is conducting ongoing communications around these documents. The ongoing communications are what sensitize people to understanding and following the values and behaviours suggested in the codes.

8. Nature of the Process Should be Compatible to Nature of Planners

A prominent example of this type of potential problem is when planners don't prefer the "top down" or "bottom up", "linear" type of planning (for example, going from general to specific along the process of an environmental scan, SWOT analysis, mission/vision/values, issues and goals, strategies, objectives, timelines, etc.). There are other ways to conduct planning.

9. Critical—But Frequently Missing Step—Acknowledgement and Celebration of Results

It is easy for planners to become tired and even cynical about the planning process. One of the reasons for this problem is very likely that far too often, emphasis is placed on achieving the results. Once the desired results are achieved, new ones are quickly established. The process can seem like having to solve one problem after another, with no real end in sight. Yet when one really thinks about it, it is a major accomplishment to carefully analyze a situation, involve others in a plan to do something about it, work together to carry out the plan and actually see some results. So acknowledge this—celebrate your accomplishment!

> For additional and advanced information, see Planning (many kinds) at http://www.managementhelp.org/plan_dec/plan_dec.htm

Effective Delegation

The hallmark of good supervision is effective delegation. Delegation is when supervisors give responsibility and authority to subordinates to complete a task, and let the subordinates figure out how the task can be accomplished. Effective delegation develops people who are ultimately more fulfilled and productive. Managers become more fulfilled and productive themselves as they learn to count on their staffs and are freed up to attend to more strategic issues.

Delegation is often very difficult for new supervisors, particularly if they have had to scramble to start the organization or start a major new product or service themselves. Many managers want to remain comfortable, making the same decisions they have always made. They believe they can do a better job themselves. They don't want to risk losing any of their power and stature (ironically, they do lose these if they don't learn to delegate effectively). Often, they don't want to risk giving authority to subordinates in case they fail and impair the organization.

However, there are basic approaches to delegation that, with practice, become the backbone of effective supervision and development. Thomas R. Horton, in *Delegation and Team Building: No Solo Acts Please* (Management Review, September 1992, pp. 58-61) suggests the following general steps to accomplish delegation:

1. *Delegate the whole task to one person*: This gives the person the responsibility and increases their motivation.
2. *Select the right person*: Assess the skills and capabilities of subordinates and assign the task to the most appropriate one.
3. Clearly specify your preferred results. Give information on what, why, when, who and where. You might leave the "how" to them. Write this information down.
4. Delegate responsibility and authority—assign the task, not the method to accomplish it
   Let the subordinate complete the task in the manner they choose, as long as the results are what the supervisor specifies. Let the employee have strong input as to the completion date of the project. Note that you may not even know how to complete the task yourself—this is often the case with higher levels of management.
5. Ask the employee to summarize back to you, their impressions of the project and the results you prefer.
6. *Get ongoing non-intrusive feedback about progress on the project*: This is a good reason to continue to get weekly, written status reports from all direct reports. Reports should cover what they did last week, plan to do next week and any potential issues. Regular employee meetings provide this ongoing feedback, as well.
7. Maintain open lines of communication: *Don't hover over the subordinate, but sense what they're doing and support their checking in with you along the way.*
8. *If you're not satisfied with the progress, don't take the project back*: Continue to work with the employee and ensure they perceive the project as their responsibility.
9. *Evaluate and reward performance*: Evaluate results more than methods. Address insufficient performance and reward successes. See the next major section, "Employee Performance Management."

- For additional and advanced information, see Delegation at http://www.managementhelp.org/guiding/delegate/delegate.htm

Basics of Internal Communications

Effective communications is the "life's blood" of an organization. Organizations that are highly successful have strong communications. One of the first signs that an organization is struggling is that communications have broken down. The following guidelines are very basic in nature, but comprise the basics for ensuring strong ongoing, internal communications.

1. *Have all employees provide weekly written status reports to their supervisors:* Include what tasks were done last week, what tasks are planned next week, any pending

issues and date the report. These reports may seem a tedious task, but they're precious in ensuring that the employee and their supervisor have mutual understanding of what is going on, and the reports come in very handy for planning purposes. They also make otherwise harried employees stand back and reflect on what they're doing.

2. *Hold monthly meetings with all employees together*: Review the overall condition of the organization and review recent successes. Consider conducting "in service" training where employees take turns describing their roles to the rest of the staff. For clarity, focus and morale, be sure to use agendas and ensure follow-up minutes. Consider bringing in a customer to tell their story of how the organization helped them. These meetings go a long way toward building a feeling of teamwork among staff.
3. Hold weekly or biweekly meetings with all employees together if the organization is small (e.g., under 10 people); otherwise, with all managers together.
   Have these meetings even if there is not a specific problem to solve—just make them shorter. (Holding meetings only when there are problems to solve cultivates a crisis-oriented environment where managers believe their only job is to solve problems.) Use these meetings for each person to briefly give an overview of what they are doing that week. Facilitate the meetings to support exchange of ideas and questions. Again, for clarity, focus and morale, be sure to use agendas, take minutes and ensure follow-up minutes. Have each person bring their calendar to ensure scheduling of future meetings accommodates each person's calendar.
4. *Have supervisors meet with their direct reports in one-on-one meetings every month*: This ultimately produces more efficient time management and supervision. Review overall status of work activities, hear how it is going with both the supervisor and the employee, exchange feedback and questions about current products and services, and discuss career planning, etc. Consider these meetings as interim meetings between the more formal, yearly performance review meetings.

For additional and advanced resources about face-to-face communications, see:

- Internal Communications at http://www.management help.org/org_comm/org_comm.htm#anchor919248
- Feedback at http://www.managementhelp.org/commskls/feedback/feedback.htm
- Listening at http://www.managementhelp.org/commskls/listen/listen.htm
- Presenting at http://www.managementhelp.org/commskls/presntng/presntng.htm
- Non-Verbal Communications at http://www.management help.org/commskls/non_vrbl/non_vrbl.htm

For additional and advanced resources about interpersonal communications, see:

- Building Trust at http://www.managementhelp.org/intrpsnl/trust.htm

- Conflict (Interpersonal) at http://www.managementhelp .org/intrpsnl/conflict.htm
- Etiquette (Manners) at http://www.managementhelp.org/intrpsnl/etiqette.htm
- Handling Difficult People at http://www.managementhelp .org/intrpsnl/diffcult.htm
- Valuing Diversity at http://www.managementhelp.org/intrpsnl/divrsity.htm
- Negotiating at http://www.managementhelp.org/intrpsnl/negotate.htm
- Office Politics at http://www.managementhelp.org/intrpsnl/off_pltc.htm

For additional and advanced resources about written communications, see:

- Communications (Writing) at http://www.management help.org/commskls/cmm_writ.htm

Meeting Management

Meeting management tends to be a set of skills often overlooked by leaders and managers. The following information is a rather "Cadillac" version of meeting management suggestions. The reader might pick which suggestions best fits the particular culture of their own organization. Keep in mind that meetings are very expensive activities when one considers the cost of labour for the meeting and how much can or cannot get done in them. So take meeting management very seriously.

The process used in a meeting depends on the kind of meeting you plan to have, e.g., staff meeting, planning meeting, problem solving meeting, etc. However, there are certain basics that are common to various types of meetings. These basics are described below.

(Note that there may seem to be a lot of suggestions listed below for something as apparently simple as having a meeting. However, any important activity would include a long list of suggestions. The list seems to become much smaller once you master how to conduct the activity.)

Selecting Participants

1. The decision about who is to attend depends on what you want to accomplish in the meeting. This may seem too obvious to state, but it is surprising how many meetings occur without the right people there.
2. Don't depend on your own judgement about who should come. Ask several other people for their opinion as well.
3. If possible, call each person to tell them about the meeting, it is overall purpose and why their attendance is important.
4. Follow-up your call with a meeting notice, including the purpose of the meeting, where it will be held and when, the list of participants and whom to contact if they have questions.

5. Send out a copy of the proposed agenda along with the meeting notice.
6. Have someone designated to record important actions, assignments and due dates during the meeting. This person should ensure that this information is distributed to all participants shortly after the meeting.

Developing Agendas

1. Develop the agenda together with key participants in the meeting. Think of what overall outcome you want from the meeting and what activities need to occur to reach that outcome. The agenda should be organized so that these activities are conducted during the meeting. In the agenda, state the overall outcome that you want from the meeting.
2. Design the agenda so that participants get involved early by having something for them to do right away and so they come on time.
3. Next to each major topic, include the type of action needed, the type of output expected (decision, vote, action assigned to someone), and time estimates for addressing each topic
4. Ask participants if they'll commit to the agenda.
5. Keep the agenda posted at all times.
6. Don't overly design meetings; be willing to adapt the meeting agenda if members are making progress in the planning process.
7. Think about how you label an event, so people come in with that mindset; it may pay to have a short dialogue around the label to develop a common mindset among attendees, particularly if they include representatives from various cultures.

Opening Meetings

1. Always start on time; this respects those who showed up on time and reminds late-comers that the scheduling is serious.
2. Welcome attendees and thank them for their time.
3. Review the agenda at the beginning of each meeting, giving participants a chance to understand all proposed major topics, change them and accept them.
4. Note that a meeting recorder if used will take minutes and provide them back to each participant shortly after the meeting.
5. Model the kind of energy and participant needed by meeting participants.
6. Clarify your role(s) in the meeting.

Establishing Ground Rules for Meetings

You don't need to develop new ground rules each time you have a meeting, surely. However, it pays to have a few basic ground rules that can be used for most of your meetings. These ground rules cultivate the basic ingredients needed for a successful meeting.

1. Four powerful ground rules are: participate, get focus, maintain momentum and reach closure. (You may want a ground rule about confidentiality.)
2. List your primary ground rules on the agenda.
3. If you have new attendees who are not used to your meetings, you might review *each* ground rule.
4. Keep the ground rules posted at all times.

Time Management

1. One of the most difficult facilitation tasks is time management—time seems to run out before tasks are completed. Therefore, the biggest challenge is keeping momentum to keep the process moving.
2. You might ask attendees to help you keep track of the time.
3. If the planned time on the agenda is getting out of hand, present it to the group and ask for their input as to a resolution.

Evaluations of Meeting Process

It is amazing how often people will complain about a meeting being a complete waste of time—but they only say so after the meeting. Get their feedback during the meeting when you can improve the meeting process right away. Evaluating a meeting only at the end of the meeting is usually too late to do anything about participants' feedback.

1. Every couple of hours, conduct 5-10 minutes "satisfaction checks."
2. In a round-table approach, quickly have each participant indicate how they think the meeting is going.

Evaluating the Overall Meeting

1. Leave 5-10 minutes at the end of the meeting to evaluate the meeting; don't skip this portion of the meeting.
2. Have each member rank the meeting from 1-5, with 5 as the highest, and have each member explain their ranking.
3. Have the chief executive rank the meeting last.

Closing Meetings

1. Always end meetings on time and attempt to end on a positive note.
2. At the end of a meeting, review actions and assignments, and set the time for the next meeting and ask each person if they can make it or not (to get their commitment).
3. Clarify that meeting minutes and/or actions will be reported back to members in at most a week (this helps to keep momentum going).

For additional and advanced information, see

Meeting Management at http://www.management help.org/grp_skll/meetings/meetings.htm

Managing Yourself

There are many sources of additional information and advice referenced at the end of this section.

Role of New Manager or Supervisor of Often Very Stressful

The experience of a first-time supervisor or manager is often one of the most trying in their career. They rarely have adequate training for the new management role—they were promoted because of their technical expertise, not because of their managerial expertise. They suddenly have a wide range of policies and other regulations to apply to their subordinates. Work is never "done". They must represent upper management to their subordinates, and their subordinates to upper management. They're stuck in the middle. They can feel very alone.

Guidelines to Manage Yourself

Everyone in management has gone through the transition from individual contributor to manager. Each person finds their own way to "survive". The following guidelines will help you keep your perspective and your health.

1. *Monitor your work hours*: The first visible, undeniable sign that things are out of hand is that you're working too many hours. Note how many hours you are working per week. Set a limit and stick to that limit. Ask your peers or boss for help.
2. *Recognize your own signs of stress*: Different people show their stress in different ways. Some people have "blow ups." Some people get very forgetful. Some people lose concentration. For many people, they excel at their jobs, but their home life falls apart. Know your signs of stress. Tell someone else what they are. Ask them to check in with you every two weeks to see how you are doing. Every two weeks, write down how you are doing—if only for a minute. Stick in it a file marked "%*#)%&!!#$".
3. *Get a mentor or a coach*: Ideally, your supervisors is a very good mentor and coach. Many people have "been there, done that" and can serve as great mentors to you.
4. *Learn to delegate*: Delegating is giving others the responsibility and authority to carry out tasks. You maintain the accountability to get them done, but you let others decide how they will carry out the tasks themselves. Delegation is a skill to learn. Start learning it.
5. *Communicate as much as you can*: Have at least one person in your life with whom you are completely honest. Hold regular meetings with staff—all of them in one meeting at least once a month, and meet at least once every two weeks with each of your direct reports. A common problem among new managers and supervisors (or among experienced, but ineffective ones) is not meeting unless there is something to say. There

is always something to communicate, even if to say that things are going well and then share the health of your pets. New managers and supervisors often assume that their employees know as much as they do. One of the first signs of an organization in trouble is that communications break down. Err on the side of too much communication, rather than not enough.

6. *Recognize what's important from what's urgent—fix the system, not the problem*: One of the major points that experienced manages make is that they have learned to respond to what's important, rather than what's urgent. Phone calls, sick employees, lost paperwork, disagreements between employees all seem to suddenly crop up and demand immediate attention. It can seem like your day is responding to one crises after another. As you gain experience, you quit responding to the crisis and instead respond to the problem that causes the crises. You get an answering machine or someone else to answer the phone. You plan for employees being gone for the day—and you accept that people get sick. You develop a filing system to keep track of your paperwork. You learn basic skills in conflict management. Most important, you recognize that management is a process—you never really "finish" your to-do list—your list is there to help you keep track of details. Over time, you learn to relax.

7. *Recognize accomplishments*: Our society promotes problem solvers. We solve one problem and quickly move on to the next. The culture of many organizations rewards problem solvers. Once a problem is solved, we quickly move on to the next to solve that one, too. Pretty soon we feel empty. We feel as if we're not making a difference. Our subordinates do, too. So in all your plans, include time to acknowledge accomplishments—if only by having a good laugh by the coffee machine, do take time to note that something useful was done.

For additional sources of information to manage your productivity, see:

- Delegation at http://www.managementhelp.org/guiding/delegate/delegate.htm
- Decision Making
- Organizing Yourself at http://www.managementhelp.org/prsn_prd/off_org.htm
- Problem Solving at http://www.managementhelp.org/prsn_prd/prob_slv.htm
- Time Management at http://www.managementhelp.org/prsn_prd/time_mng.htm
- Getting Coached at http://www.managementhelp.org/guiding/coaching/coaching.htm#anchor4294655486
- Getting a Mentor at http://www.managementhelp.org/guiding/mentrng/mentrng.htm#anchor4294745062

For additional sources of information to manage your well-being, see:

- Assertiveness at http://www.managementhelp.org/prsn_wll/assrtvns.htm
- Attitude at http://www.managementhelp.org/prsn_wll/attitude.htm
- Burnout at http://www.managementhelp.org/prsn_wll/burnout.htm

- Cynicism at http://www.managementhelp.org/prsn_wll/cynicism.htm
- Emotional Intelligence at http://www.managementhelp .org/prsn_wll/emotions.htm
- Financial Fitness at http://www.managementhelp.org/prsn_wll/finance.htm
- Job Satisfaction
- Motivating and Inspiring Yourself at http://www. managementhelp.org/prsn_wll/motivate.htm
- Physical Fitness at http://www.managementhelp.org/prsn_wll/fitness.htm
- Self-Confidence at http://www.managementhelp.org/prsn_wll/confdenc.htm
- Stress Management at http://www.managementhelp.org/prsn_wll/stress.htm
- Work-Life Balance at http://www.managementhelp.org/prsn_wll/wrk_life.htm

Designing Organization and Staff

Overall, the organization and its various groups should be organized in the configuration that reaches business goals in the most effective and efficient fashion. Guidelines in this section will help you ensure your organization and its various groups are organized in the best configuration possible.

Note: Sources for additional and advanced information are included at the end of this section.

If you are in an already established organizations, then organizing will be easier if you have been (1) Conducting strategic planning to regularly review the purpose of your organization, its overall goals and who should be doing what to meet those goals. (2) Using sound principles of employee performance management to regularly review what employees should be doing to produce results, how they're doing toward their results, and what must be done to help them do a better job of achieving results

If you are in an already established organizations, then typical problems that suggest need for organizing (or Re-organizing). There are several problems that seem to keep coming up in small businesses, whether for-profit or nonprofit. These problems include:

1. An employee keeps complaining (and you agree) that he or she is overloaded with work.
2. Employees complain that their activities overlap.
3. An employee indicates (and you agree) that he or she does not have enough work to do during a work day.
4. Employees complain that they're reporting to more than one boss, or supervisor.
5. An employee complains that their work includes very different tasks. For example, they may have a highly complex and demanding project (e.g., leading strategic planning) and a large routine, recurring task (sorting a great deal of the organization's daily mail).
6. Management notices a large amount of employee turnover, that is, employees don't stay long enough with the organization.
7. A department, or major function in the organization, has recurring problems.

Note: It is not always problems that provoke the need for organizing. For example, if the organization has been conducting strategic planning and produced new goals, these goals may require the organization to reorganize. For example, if the business wants to expand marketshare in a certain region, then the organization may need a new office in that region, more sales people, etc.

General Principles to Remember: Whether you are in an already established or a new organization, the activity of organizing and re-organizing can be a major undertaking that has substantial effect on everyone in the organization. Therefore, before we visit some specific guidelines for carrying out change, it is important to keep the following general principles in mind:

1. Don't get wrapped up in doing change for the sake of change. Know why you are making the change. Know what overall goal(s) do you hope to accomplish.
2. Successful change must involve the strong, ongoing, visible participation of top management.
3. Usually there is a champion who initially instigates the change by being visionary, persuasive and consistent.
4. A change agent role is usually responsible to translate the vision to a realistic plan and carry out the plan.
5. Take care of yourself first. Organization-wide change can be highly stressful.
6. The process won't be an "aha!" It will likely not be as bad as you might expect, but won't be as good as you'd prefer either.
7. Keep perspective. Keep focused on meeting the needs of your customers.
8. Don't seek to control change, but rather to expect it, understand it and manage it.
9. Change is usually best carried out as a team-wide effort.
10. Communications about the change should be frequent and with all organization members.
11. To sustain change, the structures of the organization itself should be modified, including strategic plans, policies and procedures.

General Guidelines for Planning the Organizing: Recurring problems often seem to have little to do with the business's overall purpose and goals. However, any attempts at reorganizing may be just fine tuning, or tweaking, if not done with the long-term in mind. In fact, the recurring problems may be a symptom of the organization's not having clearly thought out what its overall purpose and goals are. Without visiting the overall purpose and goals, redesign is usually a highly reactive and very short-term fix. Therefore:

1. Carefully consider conducting a strategic planning process to guide you through reviewing your organization's purpose.
2. Consider using a consultant. Ensure the consultant is highly experienced in organization-wide change. Ask to see references and check the references.

3. Plan the change. How do you plan to reach the goals, what will you need to reach the goals, how long might it take and how will you know when you have reached your goals or not? What will you need in resources and how much will they probably cost? Focus on the coordination of the departments/programmes in your organization, not on each part by itself. Have someone in charge of the plan.
4. Document a plan. Forums should be held for organization members to express their ideas for the plan. They should be able to express their concerns and frustrations as well. Note that plans do change. That is fine, but communicate that the plan has changed and why.
5. Include closure in the plan to acknowledge and celebrate your accomplishments.
6. Get as much feedback as practical from employees during planning and implementation of the change, including what they think are the problems and what should be done to resolve them. If possible, work with a team of employees to manage the change.
7. Widely communicate the plan, including the need for change. The best approaches to address resistance to change is through increased and sustained communications and education.

Guidelines During Organizational Design: One of the most frequent and straightforward means to guide decisions about organizational design is to examine similar businesses, including similar design and nature of services and products. However, management should still undertake careful examination of the design of their business. The following guidelines will help you in this activity.

Lewis, Lewis and Souflee, in *Management of Human Service Organizations* (Books/Cole, 1991, p. 80) list several key questions developing an organizational design. These questions apply, whether for profit or nonprofit organization. [Items in brackets "[!!]" were inserted by Carter McNamara.!!].

1. What are the primary goals and objectives that the organization should be designed to meet? (Strategic planning will help you determine what these goals are.)
2. What continuing activities need to be performed in order to implement the strategies that have been selected as part of the planning process? (Strategic planning will help you determine the answer to this question, too.)
3. How can the necessary activities to be divided so that individuals or groups can be assigned responsibility for performing them [that is, organized into separate roles and jobs!!]? [Activities should be grouped into related and similar activities as much as possible so that individuals are working on tasks that are related and similar.!!]
4. Once activities have been grouped into specific jobs, what kind of authority and responsibility should be assigned?
5. How and by whom should decisions be made? [Attempt to always and ultimately have one person who is singularly responsible for decisions!!].

6. How specialized should roles be?
7. Who should control the work being performed?
8. How can communication and coordination among members of the organization be facilitated?
9. How can job and role descriptions be developed to take into account both functions and accountabilities?
10. How can coordination and communication with the external social environment be facilitated?
    [Also strive to have:
11. Every employee ultimately reporting to one person, if possible, and they should know who that person is. Job descriptions are often complained about, but they are useful in specifying who reports to whom.
12. Carefully consider the span of control, that is, how many people are reporting to whom. Can each manager really supervise that many people in an effective fashion?
13. When done designing the group, always build structure into the new design through the use of organizational charts, job descriptions, policies and procedures that document the design and who is doing what in it.

- For additional and advanced information, see Strategic Planning at http://www.managementhelp.org/plan_dec/str_plan/str_plan.htm
- For additional and advanced information, see Specifying Jobs and Roles at http://www.management help.org/staffing/specify/specify.htm
- For additional and advanced information, see Common Dimensions in Organizations (features to consider about organizations) at http://www.management help.org/org_thry/dimensns.htm
- For additional and advanced information, see Key Concepts in the Design of an Organization at http://www.managementhelp.org/org_thry/concepts.htm
- For additional and advanced information, see Organizing (many kinds) at http://www.management help.org/orgnzing/orgnzing.htm
- For additional and advanced information, see Organizational Change at http://www.management help.org/org_chng/org_chng.htm

STAFFING

Defining a New Job Role

1. *Recognizing the need for the new role*: Often, managers realize the need for a new organizational role when employees continue to report being short-handed and mention the same tasks are not being done. Ideally, planning for a new role is done during strategic planning or when a new product or service is added to the organization.

- For additional information, see Workforce Planning at http://www.managementhelp.org/staffing/planning/planning.htm

2. *Draft a job description:* Management should draft a job description which specifies the general responsibilities of the position along with some of the specific duties to be conducted by the role, the title for the position, and any special skills, training or credentials required. (Do not seek job descriptions from other organizations and merely adopt those. Your open position is unique and job descriptions are very important so you should develop your own—the process of completing the job description is usually enlightening.) Note which job activities are essential and which are non-essential. Add whom the position reports to and note if the position is full-time or part-time. Consider if the position requires any special physical skills (this may be important when considering accommodations to candidates with physical disabilities and effects from the Americans with Disabilities Act). If the position must be filled by a paid employee (see the next paragraph to consider if a volunteer or consultant is more appropriate), consider if the position is exempt or non-exempt (exempt from being paid overtime). Usually, highly skilled and/or professional roles are exempt, while entry-level positions are non-exempt and will be paid for over-time. Invite employees to review and edit the drafted job description. Consider including a six-month probationary period for the new position and if you do so, be sure to update your personnel policies to describe your organization's use of the probationary conditions. A probationary period allows you to fire an employee during the six months if you have concerns and greatly decreases the chances you will be sued for wrongful termination.

- For additional and advanced information, see Conducting Job and Task Analyses at http://www.management help.org/staffing/specify/job_nlyz/job_nlyz.htm
- For additional information, see Job Descriptions at http://www.management-help.org/staffing/specify/job_desc/job_desc.htm

3. *Would a volunteer (in the case of nonprofits) or consultant be appropriate?* At this point, consider if the new position might be filled by a volunteer or consultant. If the activities associated with the role are highly critical for an extended duration, e.g., over six months, and require both critical and general skills, you may be better off to count on hiring an employee. On the other hand, if the role's activities are entry-level and if you are not sure that the position is really needed for the long-term, consider getting volunteers to fill the role. If the role requires highly skilled personnel for a fixed duration, consider hiring a consultant.

- For additional and advanced information, see Hiring a Consultant at http://www.managementhelp.org/staffing/outsrcng/consult/consult.htm
- For additional and advanced information, see Volunteer Programmes at http://www.managementhelp.org/staffing/outsrcng/volnteer/volnteer.htm

4. *Determine the approximate cost of the new role*: Estimate the salary range for the new position. Set this range by talking to other organizations with similar product or services, or by scanning classified sections of newspapers with ads for similar roles. Finalize how much the position will cost the organization by adding "fringe" to the

salary. For planning purposes, fringe might be estimated at 40 per cent of the salary. Fringe includes costs of benefits planned for the new role, including health and dental and life insurance, and retirement benefits, along with required unemployment taxes, worker's compensation and any pension plans. Note that, depending on the state in which you live, you may be required to required to pay certain employment taxes for part-time people, often if they are at or over half-time. Additional costs of the position result from training, equipment, rental of space, postage, copying, etc. (You should develop a compensation programme, with policies that outline the procedure for determination of salary and benefits.

- For additional and advanced information, see Benefits and Compensation at http://www.managementhelp.org/pay_ben/pay_ben.htm

5. *Get feedback and authorization from the board (in the case of corporations)*: You may want to work with the board chair to prepare for communication of the new job to the board. Propose the new position to the board by attaching a proposal letter to the drafted job description along with description of how the position will be funded and sending it to all board members for their review before the next board meeting. At the board meeting, invite open discussion and questions about the new role. Seek their authorization for the new position.

6. *Finalize the job description*: Update the job description with relevant feedback from the board (in the case of corporations). It is important that the job description be as accurate as possible because it is the basis for determining initial compensation, conveying the role to the new employee and conducting regular performance appraisals. Be sure to note the version of the job description by including the date on the bottom. The job description should be reviewed and updated annually, usually by the employee and supervisor during the performance review cycle.

- For additional and advanced information, see Job Descriptions at http://www.managementhelp.org/staffing/specify/job_desc/job_desc.htm

Hiring (Advertising, Screening and Selecting)

1. *Advertise the position*: Post advertisements in classified sections of local major and neighbourhood newspapers. In the ads, include the job title, general responsibilities, minimum skills and/or education required, whom they should send a resume to if they are interested and by when. Consider having a closing date after which you won't accept resumes. Mention the role to customers. Send cover letters and job descriptions to professional organizations. Be sure to mention the role to all employees to see if they have any favourite candidates.

- For additional and advanced information, see Advertising for Employees at http://www.managementhelp.org/staffing/recruit/advrtzng/advrtzng.htm

2. *Current employees should be able to apply for the job*: Considerations in hiring them for the new role will have to include the impact on the organization if the employee leaves behind a critical and unfilled role in the organization. Some organizations may elect to give internal candidates the first shot at the job.

3. *Screen resumes*: When screening resumes, note the candidate's career objective—or the lack of it. If not specified, the candidate may not have considered what they want to do in the future, which may impact their commitment to your new role. Note if they stayed at jobs long or left quickly. Are there holes in their work history? Note their education and training. Is it appropriate for the new role? Consider what capabilities and skills might be evidenced in their past and current work activities. If you have lots of resumes, it helps greatly to enter in a word processor, the "highlights" and "concerns" information about each candidate; otherwise, after about 10 resumes, they all look the same. Having information online helps you keep perspective and you can go back later and have a strong overview of the candidates. Consider routing resumes past key employees to collect their rankings. Interview all candidates that meet the minimum qualifications. (At this point, be sure that you arc not excluding candidates because of unfair biases.)

- For additional and advanced information, see Screening Applicants at http://www.managementhelp.org/staffing/screeng/screeng.htm

4. *Interview candidates*: Send the job description to candidates before they come to the interview meeting. While interviewing candidates, always apply the same questions to all candidates to ensure fairness. All questions should be in regard to performing the duties of the job. Ask about their compensation needs and expected or needed benefits. Attempt to ask open-ended questions, i.e., avoid "yes-no" questions. Talk for at most 25 per cent of the time—for the rest, listen. Don't rely on your memory—ask permission from the interviewee to take notes. Find out when they can start if offered the job. Consider having multiple people at the interview; although this can be intimidating to the interviewee, this practice can ensure them a much more objective and fair presentation. Have the same interviewers in all of the interviews if possible. Consider asking some challenging, open-ended questions, such as "What skills do you bring to this job?", "What concerns do you have about filling this role?", "What was your biggest challenge in a past job and how did you meet it?" Don't ask questions about race, nationality, age, gender, disabilities (current or previous), marital status, spouses, children and their care, criminal records or credit records. Have all interviewers share/record their impressions of the candidate soon after the interview meeting. Explain to the candidate that you will be getting back to them soon, and always do this. Ask if you can get and check any references. Always check references and share them with the interviewers. Be sure to tell candidates of any relevant personnel policies terms, such as probationary periods. (The best way to deal with a poor performer is not to hire him or her in the first place. It is often wise to have a probationary period of, e.g., six months, wherein if the employee does not meet the responsibilities of the position, you can terminate the employee.) If practical, look into the applicant's background to ascertain if they have a criminal record.

- For additional and advanced information, see Interviewing Job Candidates at http://www.managementhelp.org/staffing/screeng/intrvwng/intrvwng.htm
- For additional and advanced information, see Background Checks at http://www.managementhelp.org/staffing/screeng/bck_grnd/bck_grnd.htm

5. *Select the candidate*: Usually, this is not as easy as one would like because two or three candidates come in close. Have a highly focused meeting with all interviewers. Have each suggest their favourite candidate. If there is disagreement, focus discussion to identify the one or two areas in which interviewers disagree about the candidates. Then have each interviewer explain their impressions. At this point, interviewers usually come to consensus and agree on one candidate.

- For additional and advanced information, see Selecting (Hiring) New Employees at http://www.management help.org/staffing/selectng/selectng.htm

6. *If there does not seem to be suitable candidate*: Consider if the job requirements are too stringent or are an odd mix. For example, you might not find someone who's highly interested in a certain technical skill or service and who also shows strong interest in general skills. Reconfigure the job so that required skills and training are somewhat similar and the role becomes more standard. Or, consider hiring the candidate who came in closest and plan for dedicated training to bring their skills to the needed levels. Or, re-advertise the position. Consider getting advice from a human resources professional (at this point, your need for them is quite specific, so they might provide services on a pro bono basis). Or, consider hiring a consultant on a short-term basis, but only as a last resort as this may be quite expensive.

- For additional and advanced information, see Workforce Planning at http://www.managementhelp.org/staffing/planning/planning.htm
- For additional and advanced information, see Hiring a Consultant at http://www.managementhelp.org/staffing/outsrcng/consult/consult.htm

7. *If everyone turns down the job*: The best strategy is to ask the candidates why they turned the job down. Usually, you will hear the same concerns, e.g., the pay is too low or the benefits incomplete, the organization seems confused about what it wants from the role, the interview process seemed hostile or contentious, etc. Reconvene the interviewers and consider what you heard from the candidates. Recognize what went wrong and correct the problem. Call back your favourite candidates, admit the mistake and what you did, and why you'd like to make an offer to them again.

8. *Offer letter*: If they accept an offer, always follow-up with an offer letter, specifying the compensation, benefits, and starting date and reference an attached job description. Ask them to sign a copy of the offer letter and return it to you.

- For additional and advanced information, see Job Offers at http://www.managementhelp.org/staffing/selectng/job_offr/job_offr.htm

9. *Start a personnel file*: Include in the file, the signed offer letter, tax withholding forms, the job description and any benefits forms.

- For additional and advanced information, see Personnel Records at http://www.managementhelp.org/policies/prsn_rec/prsn_rec.htm

Building Teams

Management experts assert that most work (and most learning) occurs in teams. Therefore, it is important to know how to design, build and support highly effective teams.

Note: There are several major "breakthroughs" in how teams are designed and carried out. These activities can be done. These breakthroughs are in regard to the extent of independence of the teams, producing, for example, self-organized teams, self-directed teams and self-managed teams.

Major Types of Teams (or Groups)

There are many types of teams. The type used depends very much on the nature of the results the team is to accomplish.

Fomal and informal teams are "official" parts of the overall organization, assigned to a major, ongoing function, for example, quality management, patient care, etc. Management appoints formal teams. Informal teams are usually loosely organized groups of people who volunteer to come together to address a non-critical, short-term purpose.

Committees are organized to address, major ongoing tasks in an organization and membership is based on position, for example, committees in boards of directors, grievance committees, etc.

Problem solving teams: These teams are formed to address a particular, major problem currently faced by the organization. Often, their overall goal is to provide a written report that includes recommendations for solving the problem. Membership is comprised of people who perceive and experience the problem, as well as those who can do something about it.

Self-directed and self-managed teams: These increasingly used types of teams afford members great latitude in how they achieve the overall results preferred from the team. For example, they may select their leader who serves for a limited time and purpose, depending on the particular point in the group's process. This type of team is used especially when the team is working in a complex, rapidly changing environment.

Stages of Team Development

It helps a great deal to have some basic sense for the life of a team. Teams go through several major phases including the following:

Forming: Members first get together. Individually, they consider "What am I here for?", "Who else is here", "Who am I comfortable with?", etc. During this stage, it is important to get members involved, including to introduce themselves to each other. The team may require clear leadership to facilitate clarity and comfort for involvement of members.

Storming: During this stage, members are beginning to voice their individual differences, trying for join with others who share the same beliefs, trying to jockey for position in the group. Therefore, it is important for members to continue to be highly involved, including voicing their concerns in order to feel represented and understood. The team leader should focus on clarity of views, achieving consensus (or commonality of views) and recording decisions.

Norming: In this stage, members begin to share common commitment to the purpose of the group, including its overall goals and how it will reach those goals. The team leader should focus on achieving clarity of roles, structure and process of the group.

Performing: In this stage, the team is "humming." Members are actively participating in the team process in order to achieve the goals of the group and its organization. During this stage, the style of leadership becomes more indirect as members take on stronger participation and involvement in the group process.

Closing and celebration: At this stage, it is clear to members and their organization that the team has achieved its overall purpose (or a major milestone along the way). It is critical to acknowledge this point in the life of the team, lest members feel unfulfilled and skeptical about future team efforts.

Guidelines for Designing Teams

1. *Set clear goals for the results to be produced by the team*: The goals should be designed to be "SMARTER", that is, be specific, measurable, acceptable to members, realistic, and have a time frame to be started and stopped, extend the capabilities of members and provide reward for their accomplishment. As much as possible, include input from other members of the organization when designing and wording these goals. Goals might be, for example, "produce a project report that specifies project plan, schedule and budget to develop and test a complete employee performance management system within the next year". Write these goals down for eventual communication to and discussion with all team members.
2. *Set clear goals for the effectiveness of the team process*: The goals should also be designed to be "SMARTER". Goals might be, for example, attain 90 per cent participation of all members during the first 6 weeks of weekly attendance, achieve 90 per cent satisfaction ratings among members, each person takes at least one turn at facilitating the group, meetings start and stop on time, etc. Write these goals down for eventual communication to all team members. Write these goals down for eventual communication to and discussion with all team members.
3. *Determine time frames for commencing and terminating the team, if applicable*: Write these times down for eventual communication to and discussion with all team members.

4. *Determine the type of team*: Various types of teams have various purposes. Consider use of permanent teams, committees, self-directed teams, problem solving teams, etc.
5. *Determine the membership of the group*: Consider the extent of expertise needed to achieve the goals, including areas of knowledge and skills. Include at least one person who has skills in facilitation and meeting management. Attempt to include sufficient diversity of values and perspectives to ensure robust ideas and discussion. A critical consideration is availability—members should have the time to attend every meeting.
6. *Determine the structure of the group*: Structure includes the number of people in the group, how often they will meet and when and who will be the leader of the group.
7. *Determine the process of the group*: Depending on the nature of the results to be produced by the group, the process might be focused on open discussion, action planning, problem solving and decision making, generating recommendations, etc.
8. *Identify any needs for training and materials*: For example, members might benefit from brief overview of the stages of development of a team, receive training and packets of materials in regard to their goals and the structure and process of their team, etc.
9. *Identify the costs to provide necessary resources for the team*: Consider the cost of paying employees to attend the meeting, trainers and/or consultants, room rental, office supplies, etc.
10. *Plan the first meeting*: In the first meeting, communicate the goals of the team, why each member was selected, the overall benefit of the goals to the organization, the time frame for the team effort, who will lead the team (at least, initially), when the team might meet and where, etc. Have this information written down to hand out to each member.
11. *Early on, plan team building activities to support trust and strong working relationships among members*: Team building activities can include, for example, a retreat in which members introduce themselves, exercises in which members help each other solve a short problem or meet a specific and achievable goal, extended period in which members can voice their concerns and frustrations about their team assignments, etc.
12. *Support team meetings and processes*: At this point, it is critical that supervisors remain available to provide support and resources as needed. Monitor that team goals are being met. Provide ongoing encouragement and visibility to members. One of the most important forms of support a supervisor can provide is coordination with other supervisors to ensure that team members are freed up enough to attend team meetings.

- For additional and advanced information, see Goals and Objectives Should Be SMARTER at http://www.managementhelp.org/policies/prsn_rec/prsn_rec.htm

- For additional and advanced information, see Committees at http://www.managementhelp.org/policies/prsn_rec/prsn_rec.htm
- For additional and advanced information, see Conflict Management in Groups at http://www.management help.org/policies/prsn_rec/prsn_rec.htm
- For additional and advanced information, see Facilitating in Face-to-Face Groups at http://www.management help.org/policies/prsn_rec/prsn_rec.htm
- For additional and advanced information, see Group Dynamics (about nature of groups, stages of group development, etc) at http://www.managementhelp.org/policies/prsn_rec/prsn_rec.htm
- For additional and advanced information, see Group-Based Problem Solving and Decision Making at http://www.managementhelp.org/policies/prsn_rec/prsn_rec.htm
- For additional and advanced information, see Meeting Management at http://www.managementhelp.org/policies/prsn_rec/prsn_rec.htm
- For additional and advanced information, see Self-Directed and Self-Managed Work Teams at http://www. managementhelp.org/policies/prsn_rec/prsn_rec.htm
- For additional and advanced information, see Team Building at http://www.managementhelp.org/policies/prsn_rec/prsn_rec.htm

Training

Orienting New Employees

Develop an employee orientation checklist and consider the following activities for inclusion on the list. The following activities should be conducted by the employee's supervisor.

1. *Before the employee begins employment, send them a letter welcoming them*: to the organization, verifying their starting date and providing them a copy of the employee policies and procedures manual. Note that you will dedicate time for them to discuss with manual with you later.
2. *When the employee begins employment, meet with them*: to explain how they will be trained, introduce them to staff, give them keys, get them to sign any needed benefit and tax forms, explain the time-recording system (if applicable), and provide them copies of important documents (an organization chart, last year's final report, the strategic plan, this year's budget, and the employee's policies and procedure manual if they did not get one already).
3. *Show them the facilities*: including layout of offices, bathrooms, storage areas, kitchen use, copy and fax systems, computer configuration and procedures, telephone usage, and any special billing procedures for use of office systems.
4. *Schedule any needed computer training*: including use of passwords, overview of software and documentation, location and use of peripherals, and where to go to get questions answered.

5. Review any policies and/or procedures about use of facilities.
6. *Assign an employee to them as their "buddy"*: who remains available to answer any questions.
7. *Take them to lunch on the first day*: and invite other employees along.
8. *Meet with them at the end of the day*: to hear any questions or comments.
9. *Meet with the new employee during the first few days*: of employment to review the job description again. Remind them to review the employee manual and sign a form indicating they have reviewed the manual and will comply with its contents. Review any specific goals for the position, e.g., goals from the strategic plan. In the same meeting, explain the performance review procedure and provide them a copy of the performance review document.
10. *Have one-on-one meetings with the new employee on a weekly basis for the first six weeks*: to discuss the new employee's transition into the organization, get status on work activities, hear any pending issues or needs, and establish a working relationship with their supervisor.

- For additional and advanced information, see Employee Orientation at http://www.managementhelp.org/trng_dev/orientng/orientng.htm

Job Training

Some Basics to Know about Training

Variety of Reasons for Training

Employee job training can be initiated for a variety of reasons for an employee or group of employees, e.g.:

(*a*) When a performance appraisal indicates performance improvement is needed.
(*b*) To "benchmark" the status of improvement so far in a performance improvement effort.
(*c*) As part of an overall professional development programme.
(*d*) As part of succession planning to help an employee be eligible for a planned change in role in the organization.
(*e*) To "pilot", or test, the operation of a new performance management system
(*f*) To train about a specific topic.

Very Basic Types of Training

When planning training for your employees, it helps to understand some basics about training. Let us look at four types of training:

- *Self-directed learning*: Self-directed learning is where the learner decides what he or she will learn and how.

- *Other-directed learning*: Other-directed learning is where other people decide what the learner will learn and how.
- *Informal training*: Informal training has no predetermined form. Examples are reading books to learn about a subject, talking to friends about the subject, attending a presentation, etc.
- *Formal training*: Formal training has a predetermined form. The form usually includes specification of learning results, learning objectives and activities that will achieve the results, and how the training will be evaluated. Examples might be college courses, workshops, seminars, etc.
- *Informal means of training*: This is probably the most common type of training and includes, for example, on-the-job training, coaching from supervisors, using manuals and procedures, advice from peers, etc.
- *Coaching*: Probably the most common form of informal training is job coaching.

— The supervisor, or some other expert at the subject matter or skill, tells the employee how to do something.
— The employee tries it.
— The expert watches and gives feedback.
— The employee tries it until he or she gets it right.

The above approach works best in tasks or jobs that include straightforward procedures or routines. As jobs and roles become more complex, employees often require more formal training.

Common Pitfalls in Employee Training

1. New managers and supervisors often underestimate the value of training.
2. Or, they perceive it as occurring only in classrooms.
3. Or, they assume that because an employee has attended a course, workshop or seminar, than he or she must have learned what they needed to know.
4. Or, they believe that good training can only occur from highly trained professionals.

Learn How to Plan Your Training

Supervisors and employees can accomplish highly effective training by following certain guidelines.

The following guidelines (along with additional advice and resources to fill out your training plan) are included in the complete guidelines to design your training plan at http://www.managementhelp.org/trng_dev/gen_plan.htm

Determining Your Overall Goals in Training

1. Are there any time lines that you should consider in your plan?

2. Are you pursuing training and development in order to address a performance gap?
3. Or, is your plan to address a growth gap?
4. Or, is your plan to address an opportunity gap?
5. Get feedback from others.
6. Should you conduct a self-assessment?
7. Is a list of competencies, job descriptions or job analysis available to help you identify your training and development goals?
8. Begin thinking about how much money you will need to fund your plan.
9. Write down your training goals.

Identifying Your Learning Objectives and Activities

1. What new areas of knowledge or skills are needed to reach the training goals. Each of these new areas is a learning objectives. Write down the learning objectives.
2. In what sequence should the learning objectives be attained?
   — Carefully consider—When you have achieved all of your learning objectives, will you indeed have achieved all of your overall training goals?
   — What are the best learning activities (methods) for you to achieve your learning objectives? Do your learning activities include your ongoing reflections about your learning?
   — What observable results, or evidence of learning, will you produce from your learning activities that can be reviewed for verification of learning?
   — Who will verify that each of your learning objectives were reached?
3. Now that you know what activities that will be conducted, think again about any costs that will be needed, e.g., for materials, facilities, etc.
4. How will you handle any ongoing time and stress management issues while implementing your plan?

Developing any Materials You May Need

Consider if you need to obtain, or start: (*a*) Enrolling in courses, (*b*) Buying books, (*c*) Scheduling time with experts, (*d*) Getting a mentor, (*e*) Scheduling time with your supervisor, etc.

Planning Implementation of Your Training Plan

1. During your training, how will you be sure that you understand the new information and materials?
2. Will your learning be engaging and enjoyable?
3. Are you sure that you will receive the necessary ongoing feedback, coaching, mentoring, etc., during your training and development activities?

4. Where will you get necessary administrative support and materials?

Planning Evaluation of Your Training Plan and Experiences

1. Who's in charge of implementing and tracking your overall plan?
2. Consider having a local training expert review the plan.
3. Are approaches to evaluation included in all phases of your plan?

For example, are your methods being pretested before being applied? Do you understand the methods as they are being applied? Are regularly providing feedback about how well you understand the materials? How will you (and your supervisor, if applicable) know if implementation of the plan achieves the training goals identified in the plan? Are there any plans for follow-up evaluation, including assessing your results several months after you have completed your plan?

Budget Necessary Resources for Training

Consider costs of trainers, consultants, room rental, books, tuition, labour to pay the employee while attending training, etc.

Additional general resources about training and development:

- For additional and advanced information, see Employee Training Programmes at http://www.management help.org/trng_dev/trn_prog/trn_prog.htm
- For additional and advanced information, see Self-Directed Learning in the Workplace at http://www.management help.org/trng_dev/methods/slf_drct.htm
- For additional and advanced information, see Basic Terms in Training and Development at http://www.managementhelp.org/trng_dev/basics/terms.htm
- For additional and advanced information, see Reasons and benefits for training and development at http://www.managementhelp.org/trng_dev/basics/reasons.htm
- For additional and advanced information, see Basics to know about adult learning at http://www.management help.org/trng_dev/trng_dev/basics/adlt_lrn.htm
- For additional and advanced information, see Basic Requirements of Learners in Training and Development at http://www.managementhelp.org/trng_dev/basics/learner.htm
- For additional and advanced information, see Basic Requirements of Supervisors with Employees in Training and Development >at http://www.managementhelp.org/trng_dev/basics/suprvsr.htm
- For additional and advanced information, see Suggestions to Enrich Any Training and Development Plan at http://www.managementhelp.org/trng_dev/gdlns.htm

- For additional and advanced information, see Some Typical Ways of Learning at http://www.managementhelp.org/trng_dev/methods methods.htm#anchor 931247
- For additional and advanced information, see Some New Ways of Learning in the Workplace at http://www. managementhelp.org/trng_dev/methods/methods.htm#anchor789424

Additional resources about designing training Plans

- For additional and advanced information, see Complete guidelines to design your training plan at http://www.managementhelp.org/trng_dev/gen_plan.htm
- For additional and advanced information, see Management development at http://www.managementhelp.org/mgmt_dev/mgmt_dev.htm
- For additional and advanced information, see Leadership development at http://www.managementhelp.org/ldr_dev/ldr_dev.htm
- For additional and advanced information, see Supervisoral development at http://www.managementhelp.org/supr_dev/supr_dev.htm

Employee Performance Management Setting Goals

New Managers and Supervisors often Lack Perspective on Performance of Employees

One of the common problems that new managers and supervisors experience is no clear, strong sense whether their employees are really being effective or not. The first step toward solving this problem is to establish clear performance goals.

Some people have a strong negative reaction toward setting goals because they fear goals as "the law" that must be maintained and never broken. Some people fear they will not achieve the goals. Others have disdain for goals because goals seem to take the "heart" out their work.

Advantages of Goals

Despite the negative views that one can have about goals, they hold certain strong advantages in the workplace. They:

1. provide clear direction to both supervisor and employee
2. form a common frame of reference around which the supervisor and employee can effectively communicate
3. clearly indicate success, and can facilitate strong sense of fulfillment for employee and supervisor
4. help clarify the roles of the supervisor and employee.

Goals for Performance Gaps, Growth Gaps, Opportunity Gaps and Training Gaps

Goals can be established for a variety of reasons, for example, to overcome performance problems, qualitfy for future jobs and roles, take advantage of sudden opportunities that arise and/or give direction to training plans.

Performance gaps are identified during the employee performance management process. Ideally, performance gaps are addressed by performance improvement plans. In these plans, goals are established to improve performance, and may include, for example, increased effort on the part of the employee, support from the supervisor, and certain training and resources to assist the employee in their development. Dedicated employees can greatly appreciate having specific performance goals for them to achieve in order to keep their jobs, verify their competence to their supervisor and accomplish overall professional development.

Growth gaps are identified during career planning. Employees perceive certain areas of knowledge and skills that they would like to accomplish in order to qualify for certain future roles and positions. Employees often appreciate having clear-cut goals that mark what they need to do to advance in their careers.

Opportunity gaps are identified when a sudden opportunity arises for the employee. If the employee is highly interested in taking advantage of the opportunity, then he or she will appreciate knowing exactly what they need to accomplish (what goals they need to achieve) to grab the opportunity.

Training gaps are identified when hiring a new employee, during employee performance management or career planning. Gaps are usually in terms of areas of knowledge, skills or abilities. Training plans can be designed with clear-cut training goals to give direction to the employee and trainer.

Whatever the type of goal, it is critical that the employee have strong ownership and commitment to achieving the goal.

Goals can be Agreeable to Supervisors and Employees

These views can be addressed, largely by:

(*a*) ensuring that employees are strongly involved in identifying them,
(*b*) goals are conveyed as guidelines and that they can be missed as long as there is clear explanation for missing the goals before they are missed, and
(*c*) the goals are "SMARTER" (more on this below).

When setting goals with employees, strive to design and describe them to be "SMARTER." This acronym is described in this guide, in a sub-section listed above, and stands for:

1. Specific
2. Measurable
3. Acceptable
4. Realistic
5. Timely
6. Extending capabilities
7. Rewarding

If goals seem insurmountable to the employee, then break goals down into smaller goals, or sub-goals or objectives. Each of these should be SMARTER, as well.

(For further explanation, see the above subsection " Goals and Objectives Should Be SMARTER" included in the above topic "Planning".)

- For additional and advanced information, see Goal Setting with Employees at http://www.managementhelp.org/emp_perf/goal_set/goal_set.htm

Supporting Employee Motivation

Clearing Up Common Myths about Employee Motivation

The topic of motivating employees is extremely important to managers and supervisors. Despite the important of the topic, several myths persist—especially among new managers and supervisors. Before looking at what management can do to support the motivation of employees, it is important first to clear up these common myths.

Myth #1—"I can motivate people"

Not really—they have to motivate themselves. You cannot motivate people anymore than you can empower them. Employees have to motivate and empower themselves. However, you can set up an environment where they best motivate and empower themselves. The key is knowing how to set up the environment for each of your employees.

Myth #2—"Money is a good motivator"

Not really. Certain things like money, a nice office and job security can help people from becoming less motivated, but they usually don't help people to become more motivated. A key goal is to understand the motivations of each of your employees.

Myth #3—"Fear is a damn good motivator"

Fear is a great motivator—for a very short time. That is why a lot of yelling from the boss won't seem to "light a spark under employees" for a very long time.

Myth #4—"I know what motivates me, so I know what motivates my employees"

Not really. Different people are motivated by different things. I may be greatly motivated by earning time away from my job to spend more time my family. You might be motivated much more by recognition of a job well done. People are motivated by the same things. Again, a key goal is to understand what motivates each of your employees.

Myth #5—"Increased job satisfaction means increased job performance"

Research shows this is not necessarily true at all. Increased job satisfaction does not necessarily mean increased job performance. If the goals of the organization are not aligned with the goals of employees, then employees are not effectively working toward the mission of the organization.

Myth #6—"I cannot comprehend employee motivation—it is a science"

Nah. Not true. There are some very basic steps you can take that will go a long way toward supporting your employees to motivate themselves toward increased performance in their jobs.

Basic Principles to Remember

1. Motivating employees starts with motivating yourself: It is amazing how, if you hate your job, it seems like everyone else does, too. If you are very stressed out, it seems like everyone else is, too. Enthusiasm is contagious. If you are enthusiastic about your job, it is much easier for others to be, too. Also, if you are doing a good job of taking care of yourself and your own job, you will have much clearer perspective on how others are doing in theirs.
   A great place to start learning about motivation is to start understanding your own motivations. The key to helping to motivate your employees is to understand what motivates them. So what motivates you? Consider, for example, time with family, recognition, a job well done, service, learning, etc. How is your job configured to support your own motivations? What can you do to better motivate yourself?
2. *Always work to align goals of the organization with goals of employees*: As mentioned above, employees can be all fired up about their work and be working very hard. However, if the results of their work don't contribute to the goals of the organization, then the organization is not any better off than if the employees were sitting on their hands—maybe worse off! Therefore, it is critical that managers and supervisors know what they want from their employees. These preferences should be worded in terms of goals for the organization. Identifying the goals for the organization is usually done during strategic planning. Whatever steps you take to support the motivation of your employees (various steps are suggested below), ensure that employees have strong input to identifying their goals and that these goals are aligned with goals of the organization. (Goals should be worded to be "SMARTER").
3. *Key to supporting the motivation of your employees is understanding what motivates each of them*: Each person is motivated by different things. Whatever steps you take to support the motivation of your employees, they should first include finding out what it is that really motivates each of your employees. You can find this out by asking them, listening to them and observing them.

4. *Recognize that supporting employee motivation is a process, not a task*: Organizations change all the time, as do people. Indeed, it is an ongoing process to sustain an environment where each employee can strongly motivate themselves. If you look at sustaining employee motivation as an ongoing process, then you will be much more fulfilled and motivated yourself.
5. *Support employee motivation by using organizational systems (for example, policies and procedures)—don't just count on good intentions*: Don't just count on cultivating strong interpersonal relationships with employees to help motivate them. The nature of these relationships can change greatly, for example, during times of stress. Instead, use reliable and comprehensive systems in the workplace to help motivate employees. For example, establish compensation systems, employee performance systems, organizational policies and procedures, etc., to support employee motivation. Also, establishing various systems and structures helps ensure clear understanding and equitable treatment of employees.

Steps You Can Take

The following specific steps can help you go a long way toward supporting your employees to motivate themselves in your organization.`

1. *Do more than read this article—apply what you are reading here*: This maxim is true when reading any management publication.
2. *Briefly write down the motivational factors that sustain you and what you can do to sustain them*: This little bit of "motivation planning" can give you strong perspective on how to think about supporting the motivations of your employees.
3. *Make of list of three to five things that motivate each of your employees*: Read the article How to Motivate Today's Worker (at http: / /edge.lowe.org/resource/ document/htmldocs/6440.HTM). Notice the list of motivating factors in the section "Assessing Your Approach." Fill out the list yourself for each of your employees and then have each of your employees fill out the list for themselves. Compare your answers to theirs. Recognize the differences between your impression of what you think is important to them and what they think is important to them. Then meet with each of your employees to discuss what they think are the most important motivational factors to them. Lastly, take some time alone to write down how you will modify your approaches with each employee to ensure their motivational factors are being met. (NOTE: This may seem like a "soft, touchy-feely exercise" to you. If it does, then talk to a peer or your boss about it. Much of what is important in management is based very much on "soft, touchy-feely exercises." Learn to become more comfortable with them. The place to start is to recognize their importance.)
4. *Work with each employee to ensure their motivational factors are taken into consideration in your reward systems*: For example, their jobs might be redesigned to be more

fulfilling. You might find more means to provide recognition, if that is important to them. You might develop a personnel policy that rewards employees with more family time, etc.

5. *Have one-on-one meetings with each employee*: Employees are motivated more by your care and concern for them than by your attention to them. Get to know your employees, their families, their favourite foods, names of their children, etc. This can sound manipulative—and it will be if not done sincerely. However, even if you sincerely want to get to know each of your employees, it may not happen unless you intentionally set aside time to be with each of them.
6. *Cultivate strong skills in delegation*: Delegation includes conveying responsibility and authority to your employees so they can carry out certain tasks. However, you leave it up to your employees to decide how they will carry out the tasks. Skills in delegation can free up a great deal of time for managers and supervisors. It also allows employees to take a stronger role in their jobs, which usually means more fulfillment and motivation in their jobs, as well.
7. *Reward it when you see it*: A critical lesson for new managers and supervisors is to learn to focus on employee behaviours, not on employee personalities. Performance in the workplace should be based on behaviours toward goals, not on popularity of employees. You can get in a great deal of trouble (legally, morally and interpersonally) for focusing only on how you feel about your employees rather than on what you are seeing with your eyeballs.
8. *Reward it soon after you see it*: This helps to reinforce the notion that you highly prefer the behaviours that you are currently seeing from your employees. Often, the shorter the time between an employee's action and your reward for the action, the clearer it is to the employee that you highly prefer that action.
9. *Implement at least the basic principles of performance management*: Good performance management includes identifying goals, measures to indicate if the goals are being met or not, ongoing attention and feedback about measures toward the goals, and corrective actions to redirect activities back toward achieving the goals when necessary. Performance management can focus on organizations, groups, processes in the organization and employees.
10. *Establish goals that are SMARTER:* SMARTER goals are: specific, measurable, acceptable, realistic, timely, extending of capabilities, and rewarding to those involved.
11. *Clearly convey how employee results contribute to organizational results*: Employees often feel strong fulfillment from realizing that they are actually making a difference. This realization often requires clear communication about organizational goals, employee progress toward those goals and celebration when the goals are met.
12. *Celebrate achievements*: This critical step is often forgotten. New managers and supervisors are often focused on a getting "a lot done." This usually means identifying and solving problems. Experienced managers come to understand that acknowledging and celebrating a solution to a problem can be every bit as

important as the solution itself. Without ongoing acknowledgement of success, employees become frustrated, skeptical and even cynical about efforts in the organization.

13. *Let employees hear from their customers (internal or external)*: Let employees hear customers proclaim the benefits of the efforts of the employee. For example, if the employee is working to keep internal computer systems running for other employees (internal customers) in the organization, then have other employees express their gratitude to the employee. If an employee is providing a product or service to external customers, then bring in a customer to express their appreciation to the employee.
14. *Admit to yourself (and to an appropriate someone else) if you don't like an employee*: Managers and supervisors are people. It is not unusual to just not like someone who works for you. That someone could, for example, look like an uncle you don't like. In this case, admit to yourself that you don't like the employee. Then talk to someone else who is appropriate to hear about your distaste for the employee, for example, a peer, your boss, your spouse, etc. Indicate to the appropriate person that you want to explore what it is that you don't like about the employee and would like to come to a clearer perception of how you can accomplish a positive working relationship with the employee. It often helps a great deal just to talk out loud about how you feel and get someone else's opinion about the situation. As noted above, if you continue to focus on what you see about employee performance, you will go a long way toward ensuring that your treatment of employees remains fair and equitable.

For additional and advanced information, see:

- Benefits and Compensation at http://www.management help.org/pay_ben/pay_ben.htm
- Coaching at http://www.managementhelp.org/guiding/coaching/coaching.htm
- Counseling (addressing performance problems) at http://www.managementhelp.org/guiding/counslng/counslng .htm
- Delegating at http://www.managementhelp.org/guiding/delegate/delegate.htm
- Employee Performance Management at http://www. managementhelp.org/emp_perf/emp_perf.htm
- Employee Wellness Programmes at http://www.manage menthelp.org/emp_well/emp_well.htm
- Establishing Employee Performance Goals at http://www.managementhelp.org/emp_perf/emp_perf.htm# anchor1972621
- Goals and Objectives should be SMARTER at http://www.managementhelp.org/plan_dec/gen_plan/gen_plan.htm#anchor1384873
- Mentoring at http://www.managementhelp.org/guiding/mentrng/mentrng.htm

- Morale (Boosting) at http://www.managementhelp.org/guiding/morale/morale.htm
- Motivating (additional articles about supporting employee motivation) at http://www.managementhelp.org/guiding/motivate/motivate.htm
- Performance Management (basic concepts) at http://www.management help.org/perf_mng/perf_mng.htm
- Policies (Personnel) at http://www.managementhelp.org/policies/policies/policies.
- Power and Influence at http://www.managementhelp.org/guiding/influenc/influenc.htm
- Rewarding Performance at http://www.management help.org/emp_perf/rewards/rewards.htm

Observing and Giving Feedback

McGill and Beatty (in "Action learning: A practitioner's guide", London: Kogan Page, 1994, p. 159-163) provide useful suggestions about sharing effective feedback:

1. Clarity—Be clear about what you want to say.
2. Emphasize the positive—This is not being collusive in the person's dilemma.
3. Be specific—Avoid general comments and clarify pronouns such as "it," "that," etc.
4. Focus on behaviour rather than the person.
5. Refer to behaviour that can be changed.
6. Be descriptive rather than evaluative.
7. Own the feedback—Use 'I' statements.
8. Generalizations—Notice "all," "never," "always," etc., and ask to get more specificity—often these words are arbitrary limits on behaviour.
9. Be very careful with advice—People rarely struggle with an issue because of the lack of some specific piece of information; often, the best help is helping the person to come to a better understanding of their issue, how it developed, and how they can identify actions to address the issue more effectively.

- For additional and advanced information, see Giving and Receiving Feedback at http://www.managementhelp.org/commskls/feedback/feedback.htm

Addressing Performance Issues

(Note that if your organization's policies about performance management indicate a specific procedure for handling performance issues, that procedure should be followed very carefully. Otherwise, a court may interpret your official policies to be modified by how you actually handled a performance issue and you may lose protection from your related policies in court.)

1. Note that performance issues should always be based on behaviours that you see, not on characteristics of the employee's personality.

2. Convey performance issues to employees when you see first see the issues! Don't wait until the performance review! Worse yet, don't ignore the behaviours in case they "go away."
3. *When you first convey a performance issue to an employee, say what you noticed and would like to see instead*: Be specific about what you saw that you consider to be a performance problem. Ask the employee for feedback. Ask the employee if there is any special training or more resources they need to do their job. Explore if the job is configured so that most people would probably fail, and so the job needs to be redesigned. Tell them that you want the behaviour to improve. If they react strongly and claim they will quit, give them a day to think it over. In any case, remind them that you support them in their role.
4. *Consider special circumstances*: You can usually fire someone if they committed certain gross acts, such as theft, blatant insubordination, a major impropriety, e.g., telling information to competitors or spreading confidential information about customers, etc. However, if there is poor performance or chronic absenteeism because of potential verified alcoholism or depression, it is best to consult an expert to deal with this situation.
5. *Make notes about the first meeting and its results, and keep it in a file for yourself*: This note may come in handy later on if the performance problem persists. (In the case of a corporation, you might mention the situation to your board. The board will likely be a precious and objective asset to dealing with this situation, especially if things with the employee get worse.)
6. *If the problem occurs again over the next month or two, immediately issue them a written warning*: In the memo, clearly specify what you saw, mention the previous meeting and its date, say the behaviours have not improved, warn them that if this occurs again over some period (e.g., the next month), they will be promptly terminated. Meet with them to provide them the memo. If you are convinced that the employee is trying hard, but can't improve, consider placing him or her elsewhere in the organization. Attempt to have this meeting on other than on a Friday. Otherwise, employees are left to ruminate about the situation without ready access to you for at least three days. (In the case of corporations, update the board.)
7. *On the third occurrence, consider firing the employee*:

- For additional and advanced information, see Addressing Performance Problems at http://www.management help.org/emp_perf/prf_issu/prf_issu.htm

Conducting Performance Appraisals/Reviews

Yearly performance reviews are critical. Organization's are hard pressed to find good reasons why they can't dedicate an hour-long meeting at least once a year to ensure the mutual needs of the employee and organization are being met. Performance reviews help supervisors feel more honest in their relationships with their subordinates and feel better about themselves in their supervisoral roles. Subordinates are assured clear understanding of what's expected from them, their own personal strengths and areas for development and a solid sense of their relationship with their supervisor. Avoiding performance issues ultimately decreases morale, decreases credibility of management, decreases the organization's overall effectiveness and wastes more of management's time. Conduct the following activities.

1. *Design a legally valid performance review process; consider these legal requirements of the performance review process*: Patricia King, in her book, *Performance Planning and Appraisal,* states that the law requires that performance appraisals be: job-related and valid; based on a thorough analysis of the job; standardized for all employees; not biased against any race, colour, sex, religion, or nationality; and performed by people who have adequate knowledge of the person or job. Be sure to build in the process, a route for recourse if an employee feels he or she has been dealt with unfairly in an appraisal process, e.g., that the employee can go to his or her supervisor's supervisor. The process should be clearly described in a personnel policy.
2. *Design a standard form for performance appraisals* and include the name of the employee, date, the performance form was completed, dates specifying the time interval over which the employee is being evaluated, performance dimensions (include responsibilities from the job description, any assigned goals from the strategic plan, along with needed skills, such as communications, administration, etc.), a rating system (e.g., poor, average, good, excellent), space for commentary for each dimension, a final section for overall commentary, a final section for action plans to address improvements, and lines for signatures of the supervisor and employee. Signatures may either specify that the employee accepts the appraisal or has seen it, depending on wording on the form.
3. *Schedule the first performance review for six months after the employee starts employment*: Schedule another six months later, and then every year on the employee's anniversary date.
4. *Initiate the performance review*: Tell the employee that you are initiating a scheduled performance review. Remind them of what is involved in the process. Schedule a meeting about two weeks out.
5. *Have the employee suggest any updates to the job description and provide written input to the appraisal*: (Note that by now, employees should have received the job descriptions and goals well in advance of the review, i.e., a year before. The employee should also be familiar with the performance appraisal procedure and form.) Have them record their input to the appraisal concurrent to the your recording yours. Have them record their input on their own sheets (their feedback will be combined on the official form later on in the process). You and the employee can exchange each of your written feedback in the upcoming review meeting.
6. *Record your input to the appraisal*—always reference the job description and associated formal goals for basis of review. Be sure you are familiar with the job requirements and have sufficient contact with the employee to be making valid

judgements. Don't comment on the employee's race, sex, religion, nationality, or a handicap or veteran status. Record major accomplishments, exhibited strengths and weaknesses according to the dimensions on the appraisal form, and suggest actions and training or development to improve performance. Use examples of behaviours wherever you can in the appraisal to help avoid counting on hearsay. Always address behaviours, not characteristics of personalities. The best way to follow this guideline is to consider what you saw with your eyes. Be sure to address only the behaviours of that employee, rather than behaviours of other employees.

7. *Hold the performance appraisal meeting*: State the meeting's goals of exchanging feedback and coming to action plans, where necessary. In the meeting, let the employee speak first and give their input. Respond with your own input. Then discuss areas where you disagree. Attempt to avoid defensiveness; admitting how you feel at the present time, helps a great deal. Discuss behaviours, not personalities. Avoid final terms such as "always," "never," etc. Encourage participation and be supportive. Come to terms on actions, where possible. Try to end the meeting on a positive note.
8. *Update and finalize the performance appraisal form*: Add agreed-to commentary on to the form. Note that if the employee wants to add attach written input to the final form, he or she should be able to do so. The supervisor signs the form and asks the employee to sign it. The form and its action plans are reviewed every few months, usually during one-on-one meetings with the employee.
9. *Note that if the supervisor has been doing a good job supervising, then nothing should be surprising to the employee during the appraisal*: Any performance issues should have been conveyed when they occurred, so nothing should be a surprise in the review meeting.

- For additional and advanced information, see Employee Performance Appraisals/Reviews at http://www.managementhelp.org/emp_perf/emp_perf.htm #anchor1974259

Firing Employees

1. *You should consider firing the employee only if*: you have: (*a*) given the employee clear indication of what you originally expected from him or her (via a written job description previously provided to him or her); (*b*) have clearly written personnel policies which specify conditions and directions about firing employees and the employee initialized a copy of the policy handbook to verify that he or she had read the policies; (*c*) warned the employee in successive and dated memos which clearly described degrading performance over a specified time despite your specific and recorded offers of assistance and any training (the number of memos depends on the nature of the problem, but should be no more than three or four); and (*d*) you clearly observe the employee still having the performance problem.

(Note that if the employee is being fired within a probationary period specified in your personnel policies, you may not have to meet all of the above conditions.)

2. *Take a day or so to consider what you are about to do*: Consult with members of your board (in the case of corporations).
3. *If you still decide to fire the employee, do so promptly*: Both for your credibility with other employees and so as not begin procrastinating about this rather painful, upcoming event.
4. *Write a letter of termination to the employee*: As with the previous letters of warning, be clear about the observed behaviours, when you saw them, earlier warnings and their consequences, what you did in response, and the consequence that must now be enacted according to your policies.
5. *Tell the computer system administrator to change the employee's password*: And assert that this action should be done promptly and in complete confidence.
6. *Meet with the employee. Provide them the letter. Explain how the termination will occur*: Including when, what they must do, what you request from them and when. Ask for any keys. Give them a half hour or so to remove personal items (you may choose to monitor them during this removal, depending on the nature of the grounds for dismissal). Consider changing the door locks to the facilities. Change the passwords on phone systems, if applicable.
7. *As with other meetings, make notes of what was said and exchanged*: Keep them in your records.

- For additional and advanced information, see Firing Employees at http://www.managementhelp.org/emp_perf/prf_issu/firing/firing.htm

Personnel Policies

Need for Personnel Policies

From review of the above personnel management information, it is clear that there are numerous considerations and potential areas for litigation when dealing with personnel issues. There are numerous rules and regulations which regulate the nature of the relationship between an employee and his or her organization, e.g., about affirmative action, managing personnel files, employee retirement, rights of privacy, discrimination and harassment, wrongful termination, etc. Consequently, it is better to have thought out these potentially controversial situations before they occur and establish guidelines by which they might or will be addressed. These general guidelines are called policies. Specific activities resulting from the guidelines are often called procedures.

Developing Personnel Policies

Each organization should carefully consider what policies it requires and how they should worded. Many organizations begin developing their personnel policies by reviewing policies from other organizations. This is fine as long the organization carefully reviews each policy, modifies them according to the nature and needs of the organization and has all policies approved by the board (in the case of corporations).

When developing policies, always consult a lawyer who is well versed in federal, state and local laws regarding employment practices, e.g., the Employee Law—Civil Rights Act of 1964, Americans with Disabilities Act of 1992, and Occupational Safety and Health Acts. Personnel policies may need to be governed to by union rules or other contractual agreements.

Note that the online information referenced from these Web pages and the associated examples should be considered as guidance, rather than as policies to be adopted as is for any organization.

Training on Policies

Note that if management's behaviours do not conform to the personnel policies, courts will consider the related policies to be superseded by the behaviours. Therefore, it is critical that management have basic understanding of the major points made in each personnel policy.

Consider setting aside a half day per year for employees to review the policies and procedures to ensure they are up-to-date. Any recommended changes should be discussed with and approved by the board (in the case of corporations).

In addition, each employee should have a manual that includes all personnel policies.

Developing an Employee Manual

Document all intended policies and procedures and collect them in a policies and procedures manual. Having all policies and procedures in a manual facilitates training about them to all employees. All employees should have read the manual to understand and accept its contents. They should sign a form indicating so, and provide the signed form to the organization's administrator.

All supervisors should be trained about the policies and procedures. A large number of suits brought against organizations is because, although the organizations had clear policies, supervisors did not enact the policies because they did not understand them. Note that courts may consider policies and procedures as superseded by the actual behaviours displayed by supervisors.

The board (in the case of corporations) should authorize all policies in the manual and every employee should receive a copy of the manual.

Each policy should include wording to the effect that the policies are for general guidance in the relationships between employees and the organization, the board (in the case of corporations) has authorized the policy, that policies can be changed at any time and that the policies do not constitute a contract between the organization and the employee. Consider the following wording on the cover of your policies manual:

"Nothing contained in or implied by this manual creates or shall be deemed to create or constitute a contractual obligation to employees on the part (of the organization). The policies, procedures and guidelines contained in this manual are subject to change at any time, do not

confer any obligation (on the part of the organization) and do not create any right to employment on the part (of the organization)."

- For additional and advanced information, see Employee Manuals/Handbooks at http://www.management help.org/policies/handbook/handbook.htm

Sample List of Personnel Policies

The following list is an example of policies included in a personnel policies manual (or an "Employee Handbook"). The contents of your manual will depend on the nature and needs of your organization.

Work Schedule

- Work day hours
- Lunch periods
- Holidays
- Vacation
- Sick Time
- Personal Leave
- Leave of Absence
- Severe Weather
- Jury Duty.

Hiring Procedures

- Americans with Disabilities Act
- Interviewing job candidates
- Checking references
- Offering employment
- New employee and internal orientation
- New employee orientation—general information
- Agency-wide new employee orientation
- Intern orientation
- New employee and internal orientation checklist.

Compensation

- Paydays
- Overtime and compensation time
- Classifying employees as exempt or non-exempt
- Salary ranges
- Positioning pay within a salary range
- Maintaining competitive salary information

- Reclassifying positions
- Salary review policy
- Promotional increases
- Withholding salary increase due to performance
- Withholding salary increase due to leave of absence.

Payroll Information and Timekeeping Procedures

- Payroll information—General
- Payroll information—Direct deposit procedures
- Payroll information—Required and voluntary payroll deductions
- Timekeeping—General discussion of non-exempt and exempt employee classifications
- Supervisor's signature.

Benefits

- Eligibility and general information
- Types of available benefits
- Medical insurance
- Dental insurance
- Disability insurance
- Supervisory communication
- Life insurance
- Confidentiality note
- Retirement plan
- Social security
- Employee advisory resource.

Workers' Compensation Information and Procedures

- When there is an injury or accident on the job
- What is covered under Workers' Compensation
- Type of injury covered by Worker's Compensation Insurance
- Medical expenses resulting from a work-related injury
- Resources available.

Performance Assessment Procedures

- Performance assessment cycle
- Performance assessment process
- Dealing with performance issues
- Discipline: when the positive approach does not work
- Separation from employment checklist

- Communications by the supervisor regarding personnel issues
- COBRA
- Leave-taking procedures.

Financial Management

- Budget management
- Capital expenditures
- Supervisor's responsibilities in maintaining the budget
- Operating management
- Financial reporting.

Data Practices

- Policy
- Procedures
- Definitions
- Security of Records
- External releases
- Internal releases
- Use of data
- Legal procedures
- Destruction of records
- Employee access.

For Additional and advance information, see Personnel, Policies and Records Management at http://www.mapnp.org/library/policies/policies.htm

Additional Free Resources

Closely Related Library Links

Benefits at http://www.mapnp.org/library/pay_ben/benefits/benefits.htm
Compensation at http://www.mapnp.org/library/pay_ben/cmpnstn/cmpnstn.htm
Communications (face-to-face) at http://www.mapnp.org/library/commskls/cmin_face.htm
Communications (written at) at http://www.mapnp.org/library/commskls/cmm_wril.him
Employee Performance Management at http://www mapnp.org/library/grp_perf/grp_perf.htm
Group Performance Management at http://www.mapnp.or/library/grp_perf/grp_perf.htm
Leading People at http://www.mapnp.org/library/ldr_dev/cmptncy/cmptncy.htm
Leading Yourself at http://www.mapnp.org/library/ldr_dev/cmptncy/cmpmcy.htm#anchor551899

Personnel Polices and Records at http://www.mapnp.org/library/policies/policies.htm
Suptervision (an Intoroduction) at http://www.mapnp.org/library/supervise/suprevise.htm
Staffing at http://www.mapnp.org/library/staffing/staffing.htm
Training Basics at http://www.mapnp.org/library/trng_dev/trng_dev.htm

Generally Related Links in this Library

Introduction to Organizations at http://www.mapnp.org/library/org_thry/org_thry.htm
Introduction to Management at http://www.mapnp.org/library/mng_thry/mng_thry.htm
Management Development Planning at http://www.mapnp.org/library/mgmt_dev/mgmt_dev.htm
Overview of Leadership at http://www.mapnp.org/library/ldrship/ldrship.htm
Leadership Development Planning at http://www.mapnp.org/library/ldr_dev/ldr_dev.htm
Supervision (an Introduction) at http://www.mapnp.org/library/supfvise/suprvise.htm
Supervisoral Development Planning at http://www.mapnp.org/library/supr_dev/supr_dev.htm

Glossary of Terms

Abandonment: Giving up the proprietary rights in insured property to the Underwriter in exchange for payment of a constructive total loss.

Absolute Liability: Liability for damages even though fault or negligence cannot be proven.

Absorption: Acceptance by the carrier of a portion of a joint rate or charge which is less than the amount which it would receive for the service in the absence of such joint rate or charge.

Acceptance of Goods: The process of receiving a consignment from a consignor, usually against the issue of a receipt. As from this moment and on this place the carrier's responsibility for the consignment begins.

Accident: An event or occurrence which is unforeseen and unintended.

Accident and Health Insurance: A type of coverage that pays benefits, sometimes including reimbursement for loss of income, in case of sickness, accidental injury, or accidental death.

Accident Insurance: A form of health insurance against loss by accidental bodily injury.

Accidental Bodily Injury: Injury to the body as the result of an accident.

Accidental Death Benefit: A benefit in addition to the face amount of a life insurance policy, payable if the insured dies as the result of an accident. Sometimes referred to as double indemnity.

Accounting: The process of recording, summarizing, and allocating all items of income and expense of the company and analyzing, verifying and reporting the results.

Accredited Person: A person employed or contracted by the Other Party who has successfully completed the AQIS training course for the relevant Scheme along with any subsequent training and meets all of the pre-requisites detailed in the Scheme for which the accreditation applies.

Accumulation Period: (1) The time between the first premium payment and the first benefit payout under a deferred annuity. (2) A specified period of time, such as 90 days, during which the insured person must incur eligible medical expenses at least equal to the deductible amount in order to establish a benefit period under a major medical expense or comprehensive medical expense policy.

Accumulation Units: The mechanism used to account for the insured's deposits in a variable annuity contract during the premium paying period. The number of units purchased depends upon the current valuation of a unit in dollars.

Acknowledgement of Receipt: A notification relating to the receipt of e.g., goods, messages and documents.

Acquisition Costs: The insurer's cost of putting new business in force, including the agent's commission, the cost of clerical work, fees for medical examinations and inspection reports, sales promotion expense, etc.

ACS: The Australian Customs Service.

Active Inventory: Covers raw material, work in progress, finished products that will be used or sold within a given period without extra cost or loss. This term does not cover the so-called reserve inventory.

Activities of Daily Living: A list of activities, normally including mobility, dressing, bathing, toileting, transferring, and eating which are used to assess degree of impairment and determine eligibility for some types of insurance benefits.

Acts of War, Confiscation, Detainment, Revolution (Free of Capture, Seizure Clause): Exclusion in most marine cargo policies, which states that coverage is not provided when due to capture, seizure, arrest, detainment, confiscation, preemption, requisition or nationalization, whether in time of peace or war. This clause also excludes from coverage loss due to hostilities or warlike operations (including atom bombs), embargoes or other interferences with the free flow of trade. Coverage for these hazards can be obtained through the Cargo War Risk Policy.

Actual Cash Value (ACV): The replacement cost of property damaged or destroyed at the time of loss, with deduction for depreciation. Actual cash value cannot exceed the applicable limit of liability shown in the declarations of the policy, nor the amount it would cost to repair or replace such property with material of like kind and quality within a reasonable amount of time after a loss.

Actual Demand: Customers' orders and often also the allocation of items, ingredients and/or raw materials to production or distribution.

Actual Total Loss: An actual total loss occurs when (1) the insured property is completely destroyed or (2) the Assured is irretrievably deprived of the insured property or (3) cargo changes in character so that it is no longer the thing that was insured or (4) a ship is posted "missing" at Lloyd's, in which case both the ship and its cargo are deemed to be an actual total loss.

Actual Voyage Number: A code for identification purposes of the voyage and vessel which actually transports the container/cargo.

Actuarial Cost Method: One of several systems for determining either the contributions to be made under a retirement plan, or level of benefits when the contributions are fixed. In addition to forecasts of mortality, interest and expenses, some of the methods involve estimates of future labour turnover, salary scales and retirement rates.

Actuarial Equivalent: If the present values of two series of payments are equal, taking into account a given interest rate and mortality according to a given table, the two series are said to be actuarially equivalent on this basis. For example, a lifetime monthly benefit of $ 67.60 beginning at age 60 (on a given set of actuarial assumptions) can be said to be the actuarial equivalent of $100 a month beginning at age 65. The actual benefit amounts are different but the present value of the two benefits, considering mortality and interest, is the same.

Actuarially Fair: The price for insurance which exactly represents the expected losses.

Actuary: A person professionally trained in the technical aspects of pensions, insurance and related fields. The actuary estimates how much money must be contributed to an insurance or pension fund in order to provide future benefits.

Added Value: The value attributed to products, and services as the result of a particular process (e.g.), production process, storage, transport).

Additional Insured: An assured party specifically named under an insurance policy that is not automatically included as an insured under the policy of another, but for whom the named insured's policy provides a certain degree of protection. An endorsement is typically required to effect additional insured status. The named insured's impetus for providing additional insured status to others may be a desire to protect the other party because of a close relationship with that party (e.g., employees or members of an insured club) or to comply with a contractual agreement requiring the named insured to do so (e.g., customers or owners of property leased by the named insured).

Additional Named Insured: (1) An individual or entity, other than the first named insured, identified as an insured in the policy declarations or an addendum to the policy declarations. (2) An individual or entity who is added to a policy with the status of named insured after the policy is written. Such an individual or entity would have the same rights and responsibilities as an individual or entity named as an insured in the policy declarations (other than those rights and responsibilities reserved to the first named insured). In this sense the term can be contrasted with additional insured, an individual or entity added to a policy as an *insured* but not as a *named* insured. The term additional named insured has not acquired a uniformly agreed-upon meaning within the insurance industry, and use of the term in the two different senses defined above often produces confusion in requests for additional insured status between contracting parties.

Adhesion, Contract of: A contract that is drafted by one party and accepted or rejected by the other, with no opportunity to bargain with respect to its terms.

Adjustable Life Insurance: A type of insurance that allows the policy-holder to change the plan of insurance, raise or lower the face amount of the policy, increase or decrease the premium and lengthen or shorten the protection period.

Adjusted Gross Estate: Approximately the net worth of a deceased's estate—the beginning point for the computation of estate taxes. In addition to the deceased's assets while alive, the value will also generally include the proceeds of life insurance.

Adjuster: A person who investigates and settles losses for an insurance carrier.

Adjusting: The process of investigating and settling losses with or by an insurance carrier.

Adjustment Bureau: Organization for adjusting insurance claims that is supported by insurers using the bureau's services.

Administrative Services Only (ASO) Plan: An arrangement under which an insurance carrier or an independent organization will, for a fee, handle the administration of claims, benefits and other administrative functions for a self-insured group.

Advance Arrangement: An agreement between the shipper and the carrier, concerning contacts between those parties prior to tendering the consignmentlhcolumn.html.

Advance Funding: Pension-funding method in which the employer systematically and periodically sets aside funds prior to the employee's retirement.

Advance Premium Mutual: Mutual insurance company owned by the policy owners that does not issue assessable policies but charges premiums expected to be sufficient to pay all claims and expenses.

Advanced Amount: lhcolumn.htmlfooter.htmlfooter.htmlf cash or cash equivalents expressed in a monetary amount given to a driver to cover expenses during a trip.

Advanced Charge: A charge paid by a carrier to an agent or to another carrier, which the delivering carrier then collects from the consignee. Such charges are usually for agents' forwarding fees and incidental expenses paid out of pocket for account of the shipment by an agent or other carrier (aircargo).

Advanced Interline: An interline carrier that picks up cargo from the shipper and delivers it to another carrier for shipment to the consignee.

Adverse Selection: The tendency of persons who present a poorer-than-average risk to apply for, or continue, insurance to a greater extent than do persons with average or better-than-average expectations of loss.

Advertising Injury: Injury rising out of an offense committed in the course of your advertising activities, if such injury rises out of libel, slander, defamation, violation of right of privacy, piracy, unfair competition or infringement of copyright, title or slogan.

Advice Note: A written piece of information e.g. about the status of the goods.

Advisory Committee for Innovation and Technology Transfer: See Strategic Programme for Innovation and Technology Transfer.

AEP for FCL: Automatic Entry Processing for Full Container Loads.

AEP System: Automatic Entry Processing system. The system that processes the electronic import entries lodged by Accredited Persons.

Aft: At, near or towards the stern or rear of a vessel or an aircraft.

Age Limits: Stipulated minimum and maximum ages below and above which the company will not accept applications or may not renew policies.

Agency Fee: Fee payable by a ship owner or ship operator to a port agent.

Agent: An insurance company representative licensed by the state who solicits, negotiates or effects contracts of insurance, and provides service to the policy-holder for the insurer.

Agents: Intelligent software that can be used in an exchange or auction to monitor prices and conditions on behalf of buyer and supplier, and in some cases to automatically execute trades.

Aggregate Deductible: Deductible in some property and health insurance contracts in which all covered losses during a year are added together and the insurer pays only when the aggregate deductible amount is exceeded.

Aggregate Indemnity: The maximum dollar amount that may be collected for any disability or period of disability under the policy.

Aggregate Inventory: The inventory for any group of items or products, involving multiple stock-keeping units. Synonym: Aggregate Stock.

Aggregate Limit: (1) A limit in an insurance policy stipulating the most it will pay for all covered losses sustained during a specified period of time, usually one year. Aggregate limits are commonly included in liability policies. While not often used in property insurance, aggregates are sometimes included with respect to certain catastrophic exposures, e.g., earthquake and flood. (2) The dollar amount of reinsurance coverage during one specified period, usually 12 months, for all reinsurance losses sustained under a treaty during such period.

Agreed Amount Endorsement: An endorsement to a policy made by the insurance company wherein it waives the coinsurance clause on the specified property. As long as this endorsement is in effect, there would be no coinsurance penalty at the time of a claim. By combining an Agreed Amount Endorsement with a Replacement Cost Endorsement you can obtain an unusually high quality of insurance coverage.

AIDS: Acquired immune deficiency syndrome. A fatal, incurable disease caused by a virus that can damage the brain and destroy the body's ability to fight off illness.

AIM: See Automatic Identification Manufacturers.

AIMS: AQIS Import Management System. The electronic system that enables lodgement and processing of imported consignments based on data entered via ICS.

AIN: AQIS Identification Number. A unique number used to identify AQIS treatment providers.

Alien Insurer: An insurance company domiciled in another country. Contrast Foreign Insurer.

Alienated Premises Exclusion: An exclusion that eliminates coverage for property damage liability to premises sold by an entity. For example, a person owns a lot and builds a house on it. After the house is completed and sold, a subcontractor's faulty wiring causes the house to burn. The buyer, or his/her insurance company, sues for the cost of repairing or rebuilding the house. There is no coverage for this exposure under standard liability policies.

Allied Lines: A term for forms of property insurance allied with fire insurance, covering such perils as windstorm, hail, explosion and riot.

Allocated Benefits: Benefits for which the maximum amount payable for specific services is itemized in the contract.

Allocation: The process of assigning activities, costs or facilities e.g., space to a certain organizational units.

Allotment: A share of the capacity of a means of transport assigned to a certain party, e.g., a carrier or an agent, for the purpose of the booking of cargo for a specific voyage.

All-Risks Policy: Coverage by an insurance contract that promises to cover all losses except those losses specifically excluded in the policy. To be covered for damage or loss under a "basic" contract, the damage or loss must be caused by a peril that is "named" or listed in the contract. Consequently, if damage or loss is caused by a peril that is not named, there is no coverage. In an all-risk policy, coverage is provided unless specifically excluded. The contract's exclusions must be considered in determining coverage.

Alternate Delivery System: Health services provided in other than an impatient acute-care hospital. Examples include skilled and intermediary nursing facilities, hospice programmes and home health care. Alternate delivery systems are designed to provide needed service in a more cost effective manner.

Ambulatory Care: Medical services that are provided on an outpatient (non-hospitalized) basis. Services may include diagnosis, treatment and rehabilitation.

Amendment: A formal document changing the provisions of an insurance policy signed jointly by the insurance company officer and the policy holder or his authorized representative.

Amidships: At or in the middle of a vessel.

Amortization: Paying an interest-bearing liability by gradual reduction through a series of installments, as opposed to one lump-sum payment.

Announced Audit: Audits scheduled by AQIS. A Quarantine Officer makes contact with the Other Party and arranges a convenient date for the audit. Announced audits occur in line with the prescribed audit rate for the Other Party.

Annual Statement: The annual report, as of December 31, of an insurer to a state insurance department, showing assets and liabilities, receipts and disbursements, and other financial data, presented according to Statutory Accounting Principles.

Annuitant: The person during whose life an annuity is payable, usually the person to receive the annuity.

Annuity: A contract that provides an income for a specified period of time, such as a number of years or for life.

Annuity Certain: A contract that provides an income for a specified number of years, regardless of life or death.

Annuity Consideration: The payment, or one of the regular periodic payments, an annuitant makes for an annuity.

Antiselection: The tendency of persons who present a poorer-than-average risk to apply for, or continue, insurance to a greater extent than do persons with average or better-than-average expectations of loss.

Apparel: A vessel's outfit, such as rigging, anchor and life boats. The term used in distribution/transport of clothing for a single piece of clothing, a garment.

Application: A signed statement of facts made by a person applying for life insurance and then used by the insurance company to decide whether or not to issue a policy. The application becomes part of the insurance contract when the policy is issued.

Apron: See Platform.

APRYCLEE: A network of national information centres of information technologies.

AQIS: The Australian Quarantine and Inspection Service.

AQIS Premises ID: The field in ICS where the Accredited Person enters the Activity Code (e.g. NPNT) that will determine what activity will occur, *i.e.*, inspection by AQIS.

AQIS Processing Types: The code added to the AEP Code field on the entry by the Accredited Person. This code indicates to AQIS what documents the Accredited Person has accepted and what activity should be performed. AQIS Processing Types determine what Quarantine directions will be added to the Import Declaration by the AEP system.

Arbitration: A form of alternative dispute resolution where an unbiased person or panel renders an opinion as to reponsibility for or extent of a loss.

Area Code: A code for the area where a container is situated.

Area of Repair: Geographical area where a container is under repair.

Area Off Hire Lease: Geographical area where a leased container becomes off hire.

Area Off Hire Sublease: Geographical area where a subleased container becomes off hire.

Area on Hire Lease: Geographical area where a leased container becomes on hire.

Area on Hire Sublease: Geographical area where a subleased container becomes on hire.

Arrival Notice: A notice sent by a carrier to a nominated notify party advising of the arrival of a certain shipment.

Arson: The willful and malicious burning of, or attempt to burn, any structure or other property, often with criminal or fraudulent intent.

Articles Dangereux de Route: Abbreviation: ADR—An European agreement concerning the international carriage of dangerous goods by road.

Assailing Thieves: Hazard generally covered under a marine cargo policy, which includes loss due to thievery when accompanied by violence, but does not include petty thievery.

Assembly: The stage of production in which components are put together into an end product appropriate to the process concerned.

Assessment Association: An insurer that does not charge a fixed premium for insurance, but rather assesses its members periodically to pay its losses. Assessment insurers usually collect an advance premium which is estimated to cover losses and expenses, but reserve the right to make additional assessments whenever the premium collected is insufficient.

Assessment Mutual: Mutual insurance company that has the right to assess policy-owners for losses and expenses.

Assets: All funds, property, goods, securities, rights of action, or resources of any kind owned by an insurance company. Statutory accounting, however, excludes non-admitted assets, such as deferred or overdue premiums, that would be considered assets under Generally Accepted Accounting Principles (GAAP).

Assigned Risk: See Automobile Insurance Plan.

Assignment: (1) The legal transfer of one person's interest in an insurance policy to another person.
(2) The transfer of certain rights from one party to another.
(3) The passing of beneficial rights from one party to another.

Association Captive: Type of captive insurer owned by members of a sponsoring organization or group, such as a trade association.

Association Group: A group formed from members of a trade or a professional association for group insurance under one master health insurance contract.

Association Group Plan: Health insurance plans designed for members of a professional association or trade association. Members may be protected under a group health insurance policy or by individual franchise policies.

Assumption of Risk Doctrine: Defense against a negligence claim that bars recovery for damages if a person understands and recognizes the danger inherent in a particular activity or occupation.

Assumptions: Conditions and rules underlying the calculation of a pension benefit, including expected interest, mortality and turnover.

Assurance: See Insurance.

Auctions: Let multiple buyers bid competitively for products from individual suppliers. Suitable for hard-to-move goods such as used capital equipment (forklifts) and surplus or excess inventory. Prices only move up, but buyers can buy below list prices while sellers sell for more than a liquidator pays. Auctions are becoming a feature of many Net markets, but some use auctions as their primary market mechanism. Examples: AdAuction, TradeOut.com (used equipment).

Audit: (1) A methodical examination and review of a situation or condition (as within a business enterprise) concluding with a detailed report of findings.
(2) A systematic examination of the Other Party and the systems it has in place to determine whether procedures, activities and arrangements have been implemented effectively, and are suitable to achieve the requirements of the Compliance Agreement and meet the outcomes of the Scheme.

Audit, Insurance: Sometimes factors that enter into determining appropriate premiums for insurance coverage can't be known in advance; therefore, accurate premiums for the coverage provided can't be billed by the insurance carrier. This often is true in the case of Worker's Compensation and Product Liability insurance, where such things as payroll and sales can't be determined ahead of time. An audit serves as an examination of the insured's records after the fact to adjust the initial premium billed to reflect the actual coverage.

Audit Rate: The number of formal audits performed within the review period. The review level at which the Other Party is prescribed to operate under determines the audit rate applied to the Other Party.

Authentication: Proof by means of a signature or otherwise that a certain document or certain data is of undisputed origin and genuine.

Authorization: The commission to a certain person or body to act on behalf of another person or body. The person or body can be authorized e.g., to issue Bills of Lading or to collect freight.

Auto Container: Container equipped for the transportation of vehicles.

Automatic Identification: A means of identifying an item e.g. a product, parcel or transport unit by a machine (device) entering the data automatically into a computer. The most widely used technology at present is bar code; others include radio frequency, magnetic stripes and optical character recognition.

Automatic Identification Manufacturers: *Abbreviation: AIM*— International organization of companies and/or associations involved or interested in automatic identification.

Automatic Premium Loan: Cash borrowed from a life insurance policy's cash value to pay an overdue premium after the grace period for paying the premium has expired.

Automatic Reinsurance: An agreement that the insurer must cede and the reinsurer must accept all risks within certain explicitly defined limits. The reinsurer undertakes in advance to grant reinsurance to the extent specified in the agreement in every case where the ceding company accepts the application and retains its own limit.

Automobile Insurance Plan: One of several types of shared market mechanisms where persons who are unable to obtain such insurance in the voluntary market are assigned to a particular company, usually at a higher rate than the voluntary market. Formerly called **Assigned Risk.** Compare Automobile Reinsurance Facility, Residual Market.

Automobile Liability Insurance: Coverage designed to provide protection for the insured against financial loss because of legal liability for car-related injuries to others or damage to their property.

Automobile Physical Damage Insurance: Coverage to pay for damage to or loss of an insured automobile resulting from collision, fire, theft, or other perils.

Automobile Reinsurance Facility: One of several types of shared market mechanisms used to make automobile insurance available to persons who are unable to obtain such insurance in the regular market.

Automobile Shared Market: A programme in which all automobile insurers in each state and the District of Columbia participate to make coverage available to car owners who are unable to obtain auto insurance in the voluntary market. Except in Maryland, which operates a state-funded mechanism whose losses are subsidized by private insurers, each state uses one of three systems (an automobile insurance plan, a joint underwriting association, or a reinsurance facility) to guarantee the availability of automobile insurance.

Average: (1) In marine insurance: a loss or damage to or in respect of goods or equipment. The numerical result obtained by dividing the sum of two or more quantities by the number of quantities.
(2) A marine partial loss. This can be particular average or general average (which see).

Average Adjusters: In general average affairs average adjusters are entrusted with the task of apportioning the loss and expenditure over the parties interested in the maritime venture and to determine which expenses are to be regarded as average or general average.

Average Clause: A clause in a marine insurance policy, whereby partial losses are subject to special conditions (e.g. a franchise or deductible is to be applied to claims).

Average Indexed Monthly Earnings (AIME): Under the OASDI programme, the person's actual earnings are indexed to determine his or her Primary Insurance Amount (PIA).

Aviation Insurance: Aircraft insurance including coverage of aircraft or their contents, the owner's liability, and accident insurance on the passengers.

Avoidance: See Loss Avoidance.

Backbone: A central high speed network that connects smaller, independent networks, the NSFnet is an example.

Back-end Systems: Legacy enterprise systems that handle order processing, inventory, and receivables management for both buyers and suppliers. To deploy a digital trading platform, companies must often integrate new technologies with these older systems, which can include mainframe or ERP applications.

Back Haul: The return movement of a means of transport which has provided a transport service in one direction.

Back Letter: Back letters are drawn up in addition to a contract in order to lay down rights and/or obligations between both contracting parties, which, for some reason cannot be included in the original contract. This expression is sometimes used for letters of indemnity which are drawn up if the condition of the goods loaded gives rise to remarks and, nevertheless, the shipper insists upon receiving clean Bills of Lading. Letters of indemnity are only allowed in very exceptional circumstances.

Back Order: A customer's order or commitment that is unfilled due to insufficient stock.

Back Scheduling: A method of obtaining a production schedule by working backwards from the required due date, in order to predict the latest start date in consistent with meeting that due date.

Backlog: The quantity of goods still to be delivered, received, produced, issued, etc., for which the planned or agreed date has expired. The total number of customer orders which have been received but not yet been shipped. *Synonym*: Open Order.

BAF: See Bunker Adjustment Factor.

Bailee: An individual or entity who holds property of another. Examples are dry cleaners, jewellers, repairers.

Bailee Insurance: Coverage designed to protect for loss or damage to property of customers regardless of a bailee's legal liability. Bailee Insurance is Inland Marine Coverage on property entrusted to the Insured for storage, repair, or servicing. It is typically purchased by businesses such as dry cleaners, jewellers, repairers, furriers, etc.

Balespace: The balespace of a vessel is the capacity of cargo spaces under deck (including hatchways but excluding void spaces behind cargo battens and beams) expressed in cubic metres or cubic feet.

Ballast: Materials, solely carried to improve the trim and the stability of the vessel. In vessels usually water is carried as ballast in tanks, specially designed for that purpose.

Banking System: For marine purposes the practice of always keeping more than one piece of cargo on the quay or in the vessel ready for loading or discharging in order to avoid delays and to obtain optimal use of the loading gear.

Bar Coding: A method of encoding data for fast and accurate electronic readability. Bar codes are a series of alternating bars and spaces printed or stamped on products, labels, or other media, representing encoded information which can be read by electronic readers, used to facilitate timely and accurate input of data to a computer system. Bar codes represent letters and/or numbers and special characters like +, / , –, ., etc.

Bare Boat Charter: A charter whereby the charterer leases the bare ship and appoints the master and crew himself.

Barge: Flat bottomed inland cargo vessel for canals and rivers with or without own propulsion for the purpose of transporting goods. *Synonym:* Lighter.

Bark: The external natural layer covering trees and branches. This material is distinct and separable from processed timber.

Barratry of the Master: An action of the master of a ship which violates the trust given to him, provided such action is not taken in connivance with the ship owner. Hazard covered in the Marine Cargo Policy.

Barrier: The point at which imported goods, passengers, crews, ships etc., are subject to quarantine intervention, e.g., airports, seaports and mail centres.

Bars: Special devices mounted on container doors to provide a watertight locking. *Synonym:* Door lock bars.

Base: Home depot of container or trailer.

Basic Form: See Dwelling Property 1.

Basic Principles of Marine Insurance (a) ***Insurable interest***: In legal terminology, the shipment of a consignment of goods is called an adventure or venture. A person may only buy insurance in a marine venture if there is an insurable interest— i.e., that the person stands to benefit, or expects to benefit from the safe and due arrival of the insured goods and will be adversely affected by its loss or any damage caused to it. Different persons may have an insurable interest in the goods at risk at any one time, e.g., the exporter, or confirming house or bank which is advancing funds to the exporter under, say, a letter of credit.

Unlike other branches of insurance, the assured need not have an insurable interest at the time of effecting the insurance, but in order to recover under the policy, the person must be 'interested' at the time of the loss. However, there must at least be an expectation of acquiring an interest when entering a contract with the insurers.

In an export transaction, it is either the buyer's or the seller's responsibility to arrange insurance cover for the goods in transit. The arrangements made will vary with the agreed trade terms (Incoterms) and will reflect the passing of the insurable interest from one party to another. It is not necessary, however, for each party to take out separate insurance cover—one party should always take out the cover on a warehouse-to-warehouse basis, and, in certain circumstances, will cede or assign the policy to the next party.

The interest of an exporter who is selling on an f.o.b. basis, for example, is transferred when the goods pass the ship's rail; the risk moves from the seller to the buyer, and the buyer becomes the person who acquires an insurable interest and should therefore arrange marine insurance for the voyage.

(b) *Utmost good faith*: In the formation of a contract of marine insurance, the principle of utmost good faith ('uberrima fides' in Latin) must be observed by both the assured and the insurer. Before a contract is concluded, the assured must disclose to the insurer all material circumstances of which s/he is aware which could affect the risk s/he is asking the insurer to bear. A material circumstance is something that will influence the judgement of an underwriter in fixing a particular premium, or in deciding whether or not he will accept the risk in the first place or on what terms. For example, the dangerous nature of a particular export product must be declared. A marine underwriter does not normally inspect the goods or the conveyance(s) which will be used to transport an exporter's goods, and so s/he must rely on the integrity of the assured to disclose all relevant facts. An exporter, for example, must pack his merchandise in a manner suitable to withstand the risks of transit. If s/he misleads an insurer into believing that the packing of the goods is adequate when, in fact, it is inferior, and subsequent breakages occur, the insurer may refuse a claim from the assured. Any non-disclosure of a material fact entitles the insurer to avoid the contract, irrespective of whether the non-disclosure was intentional or inadvertent.

(c) *Indemnity*: The contract of marine insurance is a contract of indemnity, i.e. in the event of the assured experiencing financial loss or having to incur certain expenses arising from loss of, or damage to, the goods caused by any of the perils stated in the insurance contract, the insurer undertakes to compensate the assured for the financial loss s/he has suffered. A corollary of the principle of indemnity is that of subrogation, i.e. underwriters acquire, in terms of common law, any rights which the assured may have against third parties such as carriers. The assured, therefore, may only recover from one source, e.g. the insurer, in respect of loss or damage. The standard marine insurance policy contains the following information:

- An agreement by the insurer to provide insurance cover in return for the payment of the premium.
- Name(s) of the insurer(s).
- Policy number.
- Name of the assured.
- Subject-matter insured.
- Value to be covered. This should also include, for example, freight charges, import duty, anticipated profit on the consignment, etc.
- Premium amount.
- Description of the voyage.
- Name or description of the vessel or other conveyance.
- Scope of insurance cover, e.g. 'all risks including war and strikes'.
- Claims procedure including details of where claims will be paid and in which currency.
- Reference to the clauses which are to apply.

Basic Stock: Items of an inventory intended for issue against demand during the resupply lead-time.

Basis: An amount attributed to an asset for income tax purposes; used to determine gain or loss on sale or transfer; used to determine the value of a gift (except donations to charities, which generally are recorded at the current value of the asset at the time the gift is made).

Batch: A collection of products or data which is treated as one entity with respect to certain operations e.g., processing and production.

Batch Lot: A definite quantity of some product manufactured or produced under conditions that are presumed uniform and for production control purposes passing as a unit through the same series of operations.

Batch Production: The production process whereby products/components are produced in batches and where each separate batch consists of a number of the same products/components.

Battens: Members protruding from the inside walls of a vessel's hold or a (thermal) container to keep away the cargo from the walls to provide an air passage. They may be integral with the walls, fastened to the walls or added during cargo handling.

Bay: A vertical division of a vessel from stem to stern, used as a part of the indication of a stowage place for containers. The numbers run from stem to stern; odd numbers indicate a 20 foot position, even numbers indicate a 40 foot position.

Bay Plan: A stowage plan that shows the locations of all the containers on the vessel.

BC Code: Safe working practice code for solid bulk cargo.

Bending-moment: It is the result of vertical forces acting on a ship as a result of local differences between weight and buoyancy. The total of these forces should be zero, otherwise change of draft will occur. At sea the bending moment will change as a result of wave impact which than periodically changes the buoyancy distribution. *Note*: The maximum allowed bending moment of a vessel is restricted by the class bureau to certain limits which are different under port and sea conditions.

Beneficiary: The person or entity designated or provided for by an insurance policy's terms to receive any benefits provided by the policy or plan upon the death of the Insured.

Benefit of Insurance Clause: A clause by which the bailee of goods claims the benefit of any insurance policy effected by the cargo owner on the goods in care of the bailee. Such a clause in a contract of carriage, issued in accordance with the Carriage of Goods by Sea Act, is void at law.

Benefit Period: A period of time, typically one to three years, during which major medical benefits are paid after the deductible is satisfied. When the benefit period ends, the Insured must then satisfy a new deductible in order to establish a new benefit period.

Benefits: The amount payable by the insurance company to a claimant, assignee or beneficiary under each coverage.

Berth: A location in a port where a vessel can be moored, often indicated by a code or name.

Bilateral Transport Agreement: Agreement between two nations concerning their transport relation.

Bill of Health: The Bill of Health is the certificate issued by local medical authorities indicating the general health conditions in the port of departure or in the ports of call. The Bill of Health must have visa before departure by the Consul of the country of destination.

When a vessel has free pratique, this means that the vessel has a clean Bill of Health certifying that there are no questions of contagious disease and that all quarantine regulations have been compiled with, so that people may embark and disembark.

Bill of Lading: Contract of carriage and receipt for goods, issued by carrier. *Abbreviation:* B/L, plural Bs/L. A document which evidences a contract of carriage by sea. The document has the following functions:

- A receipt for goods, signed duly by a authorized person on behalf of the carriers.
- A document of title to the goods described therein.
- Edidence of the terms and conditions of carriage agreed upon between the two parties;

B/L R 302: A modern document for either combined Transport or Port to Port shipments depending whether the relevant spaces for place of receipt and/or place of delivery are indicated on the face of the document. Synonyms: Combined Transport Bill of Lading or Multimodal Transport document.

B/L R 300: A classic marine Bill of Lading in which the carrier is also responsible for the part of the transport actually performed by himself. Sea Waybill: A non-negotiable document, which can only be made out to a named consignee. No Surrender of the document by the consignee is required.

Bill of Lading Clause: A particular article, stipulation or single proviso in a Bill of Lading. A clause can be standard and can be preprinted on the B/L.

Bill of Material: A list of all parts, sub-assemblies and raw materials that constitute a particular assembly, showing the quantity of each required item.

Bill of Materials Function: Ability to present predefined lists of items routinely required by buyers for a specific purpose. Can greatly reduce the planning process. In vertical markets, the challenge is developing a complete list of items that need to be purchased for specific products or projects. PartMiner (electronic components) uses this function to create a complete view of buyer activity, both purchases that go to contract suppliers and purchases made on its anonymous spot market. Enables a market to combine a channel enabler approach with an exchange.

Bimodal Trailer: A road semi-trailer with retractable running gear to allow mounting on a pair of rail boogies. *Synonym*: Road-Rail trailer A trailer which is able to carry different types of standardized unit loads, (e.g. a chassis which is appropriate for the carriage of one FEU or two TEU's).

Binder: A written or oral contract issued temporarily to place insurance in force when it is not possible to issue a new policy or endorse the existing policy immediately. A binder is subject to receipt of the premium and all the terms of the policy to be issued. It is a legal agreement that serves to effect insurance coverage for a specified period of time until the actual insurance policy can be issued.

Binding Receipt: A receipt given for a premium payment accompanying the application for insurance. If the policy is approved, this binds the company to make the policy effective from the date of the receipt.

Blackout Period: The period during which Social Security benefits are not paid to a surviving spouse—between the time the youngest child reaches age sixteen and the widow's sixtieth birthday.

Blanket Contract: A contract of health insurance affording benefits, such as accidental death and dismemberment, for all of a class of persons not individually identified. It is used for such groups as athletic teams, campers, travel policy for employees, etc.

Blanket Insurance: A policy designed to provide coverage under a single limit for two or more items (e.g., building and/or contents), two or more locations, or a combination of items and/or locations.

Blanket Medical Expense: A provision which entitles the insured person to collect up to a maximum established in the policy for all hospital and medical expenses incurred, without any limitations on individual types of medical expenses.

Block Policy: A form of Inland Marine Insurance designed to cover loss to the property of a merchant, wholesaler, or manufacturer including: property of others in the Insured's care, custody, or control, property on consignment, and property sold but not delivered. Common block policies are jeweller's block and furrier's block policies.

Blue Cross: An independent, non-profit membership corporation providing protection on a service basis against the cost of hospital care in a limited geographical area.

Blue Shield: An independent, non-profit membership corporation providing protection on a service basis against the cost of surgical and medical care in a limited geographical area.

Boatman: Person who attends to the mooring and unmooring of vessels.

Boat Owners Package Policy: A special package policy for boat owners that combines physical damage insurance, medical expense insurance, liability insurance, and other coverages in one contract.

Boiler and Machinery Insurance: Coverage for loss arising out of the operation of pressure, mechanical, and electrical equipment. It covers loss of the boiler and machinery itself, damage to other property, and business interruption losses.

Bollard: Post, fixed to a quay or a vessel, for securing mooring ropes.

Bolster: See Container Bolster.

Bona Fide: In good faith; without dishonesty, fraud or deceit.

Bond: (1) A certificate issued by a government or corporation as evidence of a debt. The issuer of the bond promises to pay the bondholder a specified amount of interest for a specified period and to repay the loan on the expiration (maturity) date. (2) A certificate or policy issued by an insurance company guaranteeing performance, fidelity or surety.

Bonded: The storage of certain goods under charge of customs viz., customs seal until the import duties are paid or until the goods are taken out of the country. *Bonded warehouse* (place where goods can be placed under bond). *Bonded store* (place on a vessel where goods are placed behind seal until the time that the vessel leaves the port/country again). *Bonded goods* (dutiable goods upon which duties have not been paid, i.e. goods in transit or warehoused pending customs clearance).

Bond Register: List of consignees with details, produced by a High Volume Specialist Operator (HVSO).

Booking: The offering by a shipper of cargo for transport and the acceptance of the offering by the carrier or his agent.

Book of Business: The number, size and type of accounts (policy-holders) that an agent services, and upon which he earns commissions.

Booking Reference Number: The number assigned to a certain booking by the carrier or his agent.

Border: The geographical areas of Australia subject to the *Quarantine Act 1908 (Cth).* (Pre-border refers to the area beyond the border of Australia).

Bottleneck: A stage in a process that limits performance.

Note: Generally this is interpreted as a facility, function, department etc., that impedes performance, for example, a warehouse or distribution centre where goods arrive at a faster rate than they can be transported or stored, thus causing stock-piling at improper moments or in unwanted areas.

Bottom Fittings: Special conical shaped devices inserted between a container and the permanent floor on the deck of a vessel in order to avoid shifting of the container during the voyage of this vessel.

Bottom Lift: Handling of containers with equipment attached to the four bottom corner fittings (castings).

Box Pallet: Pallet with at least three fixed, removable or collapsible vertical sides.

Branch Office System: Type of marketing system under which branch offices are established in various areas. Salaried branch managers, who are employees of the company, are responsible for hiring and training new agents.

Breach: Is defined as: (*a*) Where a pest or disease is detected within the national quarantine barrier, but has not spread beyond the original host shipment with which it was imported; or (*b*) A failure to comply with quarantine legislation and policies and the requirements of the Compliance Agreement.

Break Bulk: To commence discharge.

Break Bulk Cargo: General cargo conventionally stowed as opposed to unitized, containerized and Roll On-Roll Off cargo. *Synonym*: Conventional Cargo.

Break in Service: A calendar year, plan year or other consecutive 12-month period designated by the plan during which a plan participant does not complete more than 500 hours of service.

Broadcasters Liability Insurance: The legal liabilities of a broadcaster are numerous and vary from the use of incorrect news stories, libel and slander, invasion of privacy, copyright infringement, and unauthorized use of plot, characters, or music. Broadcasters' Liability Insurance covers these exposures, as well as defense costs in contesting suits or claims. Employees are covered as Insureds while acting within the scope of their duties as such.

Broadened Named Insured: Regarding liability coverages, these coverages will automatically apply to "... any affiliated, associated, allied or subsidiary company or entity (including subsidiaries thereof), now held or hereinafter acquired or constituted ..."

Broad Form Property Coverage Including Completed Operations: A coverage extension that is of great value to the general contractor as respects "completed operations" property damage liability claims. Without it, the normal Comprehensive General Liability policy will not respond for "completed operations" claims (i.e., claims rising out of work performed on behalf of the Insured by subcontractors). With this coverage extension, this exposure is covered. Additional broadening coverage features are also included, but none as important as the above to the general contractor.

Broken Stowage: The cargo space which is unavoidably lost when stowing cargo. The percentage of wasted space depends upon e.g., the kind of cargo, the packing and the used spaces.

Broker: (1) A marketing specialist who represents buyers of Property and Liability Insurance and who deals with either agents or companies in arranging for the coverage required by the customer. (2) A person authorised/licensed by ACS, generally employed by a Brokerage, to clear goods through Customs and Quarantine. (3) Person who acts as an agent or intermediary in negotiating contracts.

Broker Accreditation Course: A course for training Accredited Persons in assessing barrier documentation on behalf of AQIS, in order to facilitate the quarantine clearance of freight.

Brokerage: A company that employs Brokers licensed by ACS to clear goods through Customs and Quarantine.

Brussels Tariff Nomenclature: *Abbreviation*: BTN—The old Customs Cooperation Council Nomenclature for the classification of goods. Now replaced by the Harmonized System.

BSI Specification: British Standards Institution Specification for freight containers.

BTN: See Brussels Tariff Nomenclature.

B2b (business-to-business): Describes online transactions between one business, institution, or government agency and another. Differentiated from *b2c* (business-to-consumer) plays such as Amazon.com, eBay and Yahoo.

Buffer Stock: A quantity of goods or articles kept in store to safeguard against unforeseen shortages or demands.

Builders Risk Insurance: Indemnifies for loss of or damage to a building under construction. Insurance is normally written for a specified amount on the building and applies only in the course of construction. Coverage customarily includes fire and extended coverage and vandalism and malicious mischief. Builders Risk Coverage can be extended to a "special" form as well. The Builders Risk Policy also may include coverage for items in transit to the construction site (up to a certain percentage of value) and items stored at the site.

Bulk Bags: A large polythene liner that can be fitted to a 20'GP as an alternative to bulk containers.

Bulk Cargo: Unpacked homogeneous cargo poured loose in a certain space of a vessel or container e.g. oil and grain.

Bulk Carrier: Single deck vessel designed to carry homogeneous unpacked dry cargoes such as grain, iron ore and coal.

Bulk Container: Shipping container designed for the carriage of free-flowing dry cargoes, which are loaded through hatchways in the roof of the container and discharged through hatchways at one end of the container.

Bulkhead: Upright partition dividing compartments on board a vessel. The functions of bulkheads are:

- To increase the safety of a vessel by dividing it into watertight compartments.

- To separate the engine room from the cargo holds.
- To increase the transverse strength of a vessel.
- To reduce the risk of spreading fire to other compartments A vertically mounted board to provide front wall protection against shifting cargo and commonly seen on platform trailers (road cargo).

Synonym: Header Board.

Bull Rings: Rings for lashing the cargo in containers.

Bunker: (Tank) spaces on board a vessel to store fuel.

Bunker Adjustment Factor: *Abbreviation*: BAF— Adjustment applied by shipping lines or liner conferences to offset the effect of fluctuations in the cost of bunkers.

Bunkers: Quantity of fuel on board a vessel.

Bureau Veritas: French classification society.

Burglary: Breaking and entering into another person's property with felonious intent.

Burglary and Theft Insurance: Coverage against property losses due to burglary, robbery, or larceny.

Business Insurance: A policy which primarily provides coverage of benefits to a business as contrasted to an individual. It is issued to indemnify a business for the loss of services of a key employee or a partner who becomes disabled.

Business Interruption Insurance: Coverage designed to provide protection for a business owner against losses resulting from a temporary shutdown because of fire or other insured peril. The insurance provides reimbursement for lost net profits and necessary continuing expenses. This form of insurance provides loss of income coverage (i.e., disability income) for your business by replacing your operating income during the period when damage to the premises or other property prevents income from being earned.

Business Life Insurance: Life insurance purchased by a business enterprise on the life of a member of the firm. It is often bought by partnerships to protect the surviving partners against loss caused by the death of a partner, or by a corporation to reimburse it for loss caused by the death of a key employee.

Business Logistics: Logistics within a business system. The coordinating function of material management and physical distribution, which executes the integral control of the goods flow.

Business Process Re-engineering: The fundamental analysis and radical redesign of everything: business processes and management systems, job definitions, organizational structures and beliefs and behaviours to achieve dramatic performance improvements to meet contemporary requirements. Information Technology (IT) is a key enabler in this process. *Acronym*: BPR.

Buyer's Market: A 'buyer's market' is considered to exist when goods can easily be secured and when the economic forces of business tend to cause goods to be priced at the purchaser's estimate of value. In other words, a state of trade favourable to the buyer, with relatively large supply and low prices.

Buy-sell Agreement: An agreement made by the owners of a business to purchase the share of a disabled or deceased owner. The value of each owner's share of the business and the exact terms of the buying-and-selling process are established before death or the beginning of disability.

CAD: See Cash Against Documents.

CAF: See Currency Adjustment Factor.

Cafeteria Plan: Generic term for an employee benefit plan that allows employees to select among the various group life, medical expense, disability, dental and other plans that best meet their specific needs. Also called flexible benefit plans.

Calendar-year Deductible: Amount payable by an Insured during a calendar year before a group or individual Health Insurance Policy begins to pay for medical expenses.

Call: The visit of a vessel to a port.

Call Sign: A code published by the International Telecommunication Union in its annual List of Ships' Stations to be used for the information interchange between vessels, port authorities and other relevant participants in international trade.

CALS Test Network: The CALS Test Network (CTN) is a confederation of hundreds of industry and government organizations that have agreed to evaluate and demonstrate the interchange and functional use of digital technical information using CALS standards. This is accomplished through a collaborative multi-service effort. *Acronym*: CTN.

Cancelable: A contract of Health Insurance that may be canceled during the policy term by the insurer or Insured.

Cancellation: The discontinuance of an insurance policy before its normal expiration date, either by the Insured or the company.

Capacity: (1) The amount of capital available to an insurance company or to the industry as a whole for underwriting general insurance coverage or coverage for specific perils. (2) The amount of insurance a company or the industry are able to write, due to limitations on or availability of capital. (3) The ability, in a given time, of a resource measured in quality and quantity. The quantity of goods which can be stored in or loaded into a warehouse, store and/or loaded into a means of transport at a particular time.

Capacity Control: Process of registering and steering of capacity.

Capital Gain: Profit realized on the sale of securities. An unrealized capital gain is an increase in the value of securities that have not been sold.

Capital Retention Approach: A method used to estimate the amount of life insurance to own. Under this method, the insurance proceeds are retained and are not liquidated.

Capitation: A method of payment for health services in which a physician or hospital is paid a fixed, per capita amount for each person served regardless of the actual number of services provided to each person.

Captive Insurance Company: A company owned solely or in large part by one or more non-insurance entities for the primary purpose of providing insurance coverage to the owner or owners. The company's stock is controlled by one interest or a group of related interests so as to provide coverage for their business operations. A captive insurance company may be a non-admitted, non-resident, or foreign insurer. Sometimes it may provide reinsurance to a self-insured or a domestic company.

Captive Insurer: Insurance company established and owned by a parent firm in order to insure its loss exposures while reducing premium costs, providing easier access to a reinsurer, and perhaps easing tax burdens. See also Association captive.

Care, Skill and Diligence: It is defined as the standard of care which a reasonable person in a like position would exercise taking into account all circumstances.

Career Average Formula: A pension plan formula that bases retirement benefits on earnings during all years of service to the employer.

Cargo: Cargo is basically defined as anything that is loaded onto any type or form of vehicle for the purpose of being transported from A to B, always provided that the "thing" doesn't happen to be a human being.

Risk Factors: An infinitely variable combination of risk factors such as mode of transportation, type of goods, packing, size/weight/value, trip route, trip duration, season and socio-economic environment, would make up the risk covered by a marine policy in terms of cargo.

Cargo Conditions: Although the policy form is an important part of the contract of insurance, it would be useless taken on its own, i.e., without the special conditions provided by the clauses attached to it. There are a bundle of different clauses in use today. For example, there are special trade clauses for shipments of coal, oil, rubber, timber, frozen food and meat, as well as a variety of special extension clauses.

The (UK) Marine Insurance Act of 1906 provides the basis for marine insurance contracts and, within the legal parameters laid down in this Act, the Institute of London Underwriters have approved numerous 'clauses' defining the risks covered, circumstances excluded, etc., to be incorporated into insurance policies. Some of these have broad application and are therefore in everyday use. Others are specific to certain trades and classes of goods. The tenets of the Marine Insurance Act, and the Institute Clauses, have been widely adopted amongst trading nations, including South Africa.

The standard policy document represents only the skeleton of a marine insurance contract. It is the clauses, which are incorporated by attachment to the policy, that are the essence of the contract, but the policy may contain, by agreement, specific wordings which extend or restrict the basic cover by imposing, for example, warranties, special conditions, a franchise or an excess.

The main clauses are:

- Institute Cargo Clauses which consist of:
- Institute Cargo Clauses (A)
- Institute Cargo Clauses (B)
- Institute Cargo Clauses (C)
- Institute Cargo Clauses (Air)
- Institute War Clauses
- Institute Strikes Clauses
- Institute Trade Clauses
- Additional Clauses
- Additional Terms.

Cargo: Goods transported or to be transported, all goods carried on a ship covered by a B/L.

Any goods, wares, merchandise, and articles of every kind whatsoever carried on a ship, other than mail, ship's stores, ship's spare parts, ship's equipment, stowage material, crew's effects and passengers' accompanied baggage (IMO). Any property carried on an aircraft, other than mail, stores and accompanied or mishandled baggage. Also referred to as 'goods' (ICAO).

Cargo Handling: All procedures necessary to enable the physical handling of goods.

Cargo Insurance: Type of Ocean Marine Insurance designed to protect the shipper of the goods against financial loss if the goods are damaged or lost.

Cargo Restriction Code: A code indicating that the use of a certain container is restricted to particular cargo.

Cargo Tracer: A document sent by the agent to all relevant parties, stating that certain cargo is either missing or overlanded.

Cargo Unit: A vehicle, container, pallet, flat, portable tank or any other entity or any part thereof which belongs to the ship but is not permanently attached to that ship.

Carriage: The process of transporting (conveying) cargo, from one point to another. *Synonym*: Transport.

Carriage and Insurance Paid To (...named place of destination) *"Carriage and insurance paid to..."* means that the seller has the same obligations as under CPT but with the addition that the seller has to procure cargo insurance against the buyer's risk of loss of or damage to the goods during the carriage. The seller contracts for insurance and pays the insurance premium.

The buyer should note that under the CIP term the seller is only required to obtain insurance on minimum coverage. The CIP term requires the seller to clear the goods for export. This term may be used for any mode of transport including multimodal transport.

Carriage Paid To (...named place of destination) *"Carriage paid to... "* means that the seller pays the freight for the carriage of the goods to the named destination. The risk of loss of or damage to the goods, as well as any additional costs due to events occurring after the time the goods have been delivered to the carrier, is transferred from the seller to the buyer when the goods have been delivered into the custody of the carrier.

Carrier: (1) The party undertaking transport of goods from one point to another. (2) 'Carrier' means any person who, in a contract of carriage, undertakes to perform or to procure the performance of carriage, by rail, road, se, air, inland waterway or by a combination of such modes. If subsequent carriers are used for the carriage to the agreed destination, the risk passes when the goods have been delivered to the first carrier.

CPT term requires the seller to clear the goods for export.

This term may be used for any mode of transport including multimodal transport.

Carrier Haulage: The inland transport service which is performed by the sea-carrier under the terms and conditions of the tariff and of the relevant transport document.

Carriers Bill of Lading Ports: Terminal, Pre-terminal port or Post-terminal Port as per tariff, indicated on the Bill of Lading and which is not the port physically called at by Carriers' ocean vessels. *Note*: Under normal circumstances in the B/L only ports should be mentioned which are actually called at.

Carriers' Lien: When the shipper ships goods 'collect', the carrier has a possessory claim on these goods, which means that the carrier can retain possession of the goods as security for the charges due.

Carrying Temperature: Required cargo temperature during transport and storage. See also Setting/Air Delivery Temperature.

Cartage: See Haulage.

Cash Against Documents": *Abbreviation*: CAD—Terms of payment: if the buyer of goods pays for the goods against transfer of the documents, entitling him to obtain delivery of the goods from the carrier.

Cash on Delivery: *Abbreviation:* COD—Terms of payment: if the carrier collects a payment from the consignee and remits the amount to the shipper.

Cash Surrender Value: The amount available in cash upon voluntary termination of a policy by its owner before it becomes payable by death or maturity.

Casualty Insurance: Insurance concerned with the Insured's legal liability for injuries to others or damage to other persons' property; also encompasses such forms of insurance as plate glass, burglary, robbery and workers' compensation.

Catalog Aggregation: Normalizing product data from multiple vendors so it can be easily compared. Virtual distributors and content aggregators often provide this service to buyers. Most valuable when products are complex and have many attributes. Prices are set, sometimes on contract.

Catastrophe: Event which causes a loss of extraordinary magnitude, such as a hurricane or tornado.

Causes-of-loss Form: Form added to Commercial Property Insurance policy that indicates the causes of loss that are covered. There are four causes-of-loss forms: basic, broad, special and earthquake.

CCD: Containerised Cargo Clearance.

Cede: To transfer all or part of a risk written by an insurer (the ceding, or primary company) to a reinsurer.

Cell: Location on board of a container vessel where one container can be stowed.

Cell-guide: Steel bars and rails used to steer containers during loading and discharging whilst sliding in the ship.

Cell Position: The location of a cell on board of a container vessel identified by a code for successively the bay, the row and the tier, indicating the position of a container on that vessel.

Cellular Vessel: A vessel, specially designed and equipped for the carriage of containers.

Central Warehouse: A warehouse which performs central functions for a number of warehouses (e.g. keeping capacity stock).

Centre of Gravity: Point at which the entire weight of a body may be considered as concentrated so that if supported at this point the body would remain in equilibrium in any position.

Certificate: A document by which a fact is formally or officially attested and in which special requirements and conditions can be stated.

Certificate of Analysis: A document, often required by an importer or governmental authorities, attesting to the quality or purity of commodities.

The origin of the certification may be a chemist or any other authorized body such as an inspection firm retained by the exporter or importer. In some cases, the document may be drawn up by the manufacturer certifying that the merchandise shipped has been tested in his facility and found conform to the specifications.

Certificate of Classification: A certificate, issued by the classification society and stating the class under which a vessel is registered.

Certificate of Delivery: A certificate indicating the condition of a vessel upon delivery for a charter including ballast, available bunkers and fresh water.

Certificate of Free Sale: A certificate, required by some countries as evidence that the goods are normally sold on the open market and approved by the regulatory authorities in the country of origin.

Certificate of Insurance: A statement of coverage issued to an individual insured under a group insurance contract, outlining the insurance benefits and principal provisions applicable to the member.

Certificate of Origin: A certificate, showing the country of original production of goods. Frequently used by customs in ascertaining duties under preferential tariff programmes or in connection with regulating imports from specific sources.

Certificate of Redelivery: A certificate, indicating the condition of a vessel upon redelivery from a charter including ballast, available bunkers and fresh water.

Certified Financial Planner (CFP): Professional who has attained a high degree of technical competency in financial planning and has passed a series of professional examinations by the College of Financial Planning.

Certified Insurance Counsellor (CIC): Professional in Property and Liability Insurance who has passed a series of examinations by the Society of Certified Insurance Counsellors.

Cession: Amount of the insurance ceded to a reinsurer by the original insuring company in a reinsurance operation.

CFR: See Cost and Freight.

CFS: See Container Freight Station.

Chain Conveyor: A conveyor consisting of two or more strands of chain running in parallel tracks with the loads carried directly on the chains.

Change of Occupation Clause: Provision in a Health Insurance policy stipulating that if the Insured changes to a more hazardous occupation, the benefits are reduced based on the amount of benefits the premium would have purchased for the more hazardous occupation.

Channel Enablers: Marketplaces friendly to existing distribution channels rather than trying to create a new channel. Maintain relationships for the traders rather than in the Net market itself. Examples: IMXchange.com (market for mortgage lenders and brokers), Channelpoint (market between insurance brokers and carriers).

Charge: An amount to be paid for carriage of goods based on the applicable rate of such carriage, or an amount to be paid for a special or incidental service in connection with the carriage of goods.

Charge Type: A separate, identifiable element of charges to be used in the pricing/rating of common services rendered to customers.

Charter Contract: See Charter Party.

Charter Party: A contract in which the ship owner agrees to place his vessel or a part of it at the disposal of a third party, the charterer, for the carriage of goods for which he receives a freight per ton cargo, or to let his vessel for a definite period or trip for which a hire is paid.

Chartered Financial Consultant (ChFC): An individual who has attained a high degree of technical competency in the fields of financial planning, investments, and Life and Health Insurance and has passed ten professional examinations administered by the American College.

Chartered Life Underwriter (CLU): An individual who has attained a high degree of technical competency in the fields of Life and Health Insurance and who is expected to abide by a code of ethics. Must have minimum of three years of experience in

Life or Health Insurance sales and have passed ten professional examinations administered by the American College.

Chartered Property and Casualty Underwriter (CPCU): Professional who has attained a high degree of technical competency in Property and Liability Insurance and has passed ten professional examinations administered by the American Institute for Property and Liability Underwriters.

Charterer: The legal person who has signed a charter party with the owner of a vessel or an aircraft and thus hires or leases a vessel or an aircraft or a part of the capacity thereof.

Chassis: (1) A wheeled carriage onto which an ocean container is mounted for inland conveyance.

(2) The part of a motor vehicle that includes the engine, the frame, suspension system, wheels, steering mechanism etc., but not the body.

Choice No-Fault: Allows auto insureds the choice of remaining under the tort system or choosing no-fault at a reduced premium.

Churn: The relentless cycle of acquiring new customers and losing others that characterizes consumer e-commerce and reduces lifetime customer value because switching is so easy. (See switching costs, lifetime value of the customer.)

CIF: "Cost, Insurance and Freight" means that the seller has the same obligations as under CFR but with the addition that he has to procure marine insurance against the buyer's risk of loss of or damage to the goods during the carriage. The seller contracts for insurance and pays the insurance premium. The buyer should note that under the CIF term the seller is only required to obtain insurance on minimum coverage. The CIF term requires the seller to clear the goods for export. This term can only be used for sea and inland waterway transport. When the ship's rail serves no practical purposes such as in the case of roll-on/ roll-off or container traffic, the CIP term is more appropriate to use.

CIM: Computer Integrated Manufacturing, an ESPRIT project on the use of information technology in industrial environments.
Acronym: CIM.

CIP: See Carriage and Insurance Paid To (...named place of destination).

Claim: (1) A charge made against a carrier for loss, damage or delay.

(2) A request for payment of a loss which may come under the terms of an insurance contract.

Claim-Made Policy: A Liability Insurance Policy under which coverage applies to claims filed during the policy period.

Claims Adjustor: Person who settles claims: an agent, company adjustor, independent adjustor, adjustment bureau, or public adjustor.

Class Rating: Rate-making method in which similar Insureds are placed in the same underwriting class and each is charged the same rate. Also called manual rating.

Classification: Arrangement according to a systematic division of a number of objects into groups, based on some likenesses or some common traits.

Classification Clause (Cargo): A clause in a cargo insurance open cover which details the minimum classification for an overseas carrying vessel that is acceptable to the insurers for carriage of the insured goods at the premium rate/s agreed in the contract. Goods carried by lower class vessels are accepted under the open cover, subject to payment of an additional premium.

Classification Society: An organization, whose main function is to carry out surveys of vessels, its purpose being to set and maintain standards of construction and upkeep for vessels, their engines and their safety equipment. A classification society also inspects and approves the construction of shipping containers.

Clean Bill of Lading: A Bill of Lading which does not contain any qualification about the apparent order and condition of the goods to be transported (it bears no stamped clauses on the front of the B/L).

It bears no superimposed clauses expressly declaring a defective condition of the goods or packaging (resolution of the ICS 1951).

Clean, Cleared, Cleaning: Removal of all quarantine risk material including soil, dirt, faeces, leaves, twigs, grass and any other plant or animal material.

Clean on Board: When goods are loaded on board and the document issued in respect to these goods is clean.

Note: Through the usage of the UCP 500 rules the term has now become superfluous.

Clearance Terminal: Terminal where Customs facilities for the clearance of goods are available.

Cleared Without Examination: *Abbreviation*: CWE—Cleared by customs without inspection.

Client: A party with which a company has a commercial relationship concerning the transport of e.g., cargo or concerning certain services of the company concerned, either directly or through an agent. *Synonym*: Customer.

Clip on Unit: *Abbreviation*: COU—Detachable aggregate for a temperature controlled container (Conair).

Closed Ventilated Container: A container of a closed type, similar to a general purpose container, but specially designed for carriage of cargo where ventilation, either natural or mechanical (forced), is necessary.

CLP: See Container Load Plan.

CLU: See Chartered Life Underwriter.

CNC: See Compagneurs Nationales des Conteneurs.

Coalition: Coalitions are either buy-side or sell-side and are generally groups of buyers or sellers who agree to channel procurement through a single marketplace. They operate a marketplace without having a third party, neutral Net market as the hub. Many claim to be neutral—that anyone can join—but, by the nature of their partnership their first audience is either buyers or sellers. The advantage of coalitions, particularly buy-side coalitions, is they can do a lot of transactions, which creates marketplace liquidity. However, the problem with coalitions is they have several challenges to overcome—political challenges, both from regulators and relationships between powerful companies, as well as technology challenges of integrating legacy systems. Due to the complexity of these issues, none are operational yet. If they do in fact successfully overcome these obstacles and operationalize, we expect they will conduct a large number of transactions because they can force their suppliers to go through this marketplace to conduct the transactions.

COC: Carrier Owned Container.

COD: See Cash On Delivery.

Cofferdam: An empty space on board of a vessel between two bulkheads or two decks separating oil tanks from each other and/or the engine room or other compartments.

C. and F.: A sale term relating to goods. Cost and Freight. The consignee makes his own insurance arrangements for the goods throughout the period of transit.

Coinsurance: (1) A provision under which an Insured who carries less than the stipulated percentage of insurance to value, will receive a loss payment that is limited to the same ratio which the amount of insurance bears to the amount required; (2) a policy provision frequently found in Medical Insurance, by which the Insured person and the insurer share the covered losses under a policy in a specified ratio, i.e., 80 per cent by the insurer and 20 per cent by the insured. (3) Where two or more parties share the same insured risk. A reinsurer is not a co-insurer with the original insurer.

Collapsible Container: Container which can be easily folded, disassembled and reassembled.

Collateral Source Rule: A legal rule, which states that the defendant cannot introduce any evidence that shows the injured party has received compensation from other collateral sources.

Collision Insurance: Protection against loss resulting from any damage to the policy-holder's car caused by collision with another vehicle or object, or by upset of the insured car, whether it was the Insured's fault or not.

Co-loading: The loading, on the way, of cargo from another shipper, having the same final destination as the cargo loaded earlier.

Co-makership: The long-term relationship between e.g., a supplier or a carrier and a customer, on the basis of mutual confidence. *Synonym*: Co-shippership.

Combination Charge: An amount which is obtained by combining two or more charges.

Combination Chassis: A chassis which can carry either one forty foot or thirty foot container or a combination of shorter containers e.g. 2 × 20 foot.

Combined Ratio: Basically, a measure of the relationship between dollars spent for claims and expenses and premium dollars taken in; more specifically, the sum of the ratio of losses incurred to premiums earned and the ratio of commissions and expenses incurred to premiums written. A ratio above 100 means that for every premium dollar taken in, more than a dollar went for losses expenses and commissions.

Combined Transport: Intermodal transport where the major part of the journey is by one mode such as rail, inland waterway or sea and any initial and/or final leg carried out by another mode such as road. *Synonym:* Multimodal Transport.

Combined Transport Bill of Lading: See: Bill of Lading R302.

Combined Transport Document: *Abbreviation:* CTD—Negotiable or non-negotiable document evidencing a contract for the performance and/or procurement of performance of combined transport of goods. *Synonym:* Multi modal transport document.

Combined Transport Operator: *Abbreviation:* CTO—A party who undertakes to carry goods with different modes of transport. *Synonym:* Multimodal Transport Operator.

Commercial General Liability Policy (CGLP): Commercial Liability Policy drafted by the Insurance Services Office containing two coverage forms—an occurrence form and a claims-made form.

Commercial Invoice: A document showing commercial values of the transaction between the buyer and seller.

Commercial Lines: Insurance for businesses, organizations, institutions, governmental agencies, and other commercial establishments.

Commercial Multiple Peril Policy: A package of insurance that includes a wide range of essential coverages for the commercial establishment.

Commercial Package Policy (CPP): A commercial policy that can be designed to meet the specific insurance needs of business firms. Property and Liability Coverage forms are combined to form a single policy.

Commission: The part of an insurance premium paid by the insurer to an agent or broker for his services in procuring and servicing the insurance.

Commissioner: A state officer who administers the state's insurance laws and regulations. In some states, this regulator is called the director or superintendent of insurance.

Commodity Box Rate: A rate classified by commodity and quoted per container.

Commodity Code: Code used in the Harmonized System for the classification of goods which are most commonly produced and traded.

Commodity: As per Goods.

Common Access Reference: A key to relate all subsequent transfers of data to the same business case or file.

Common Stock: Securities that represent an ownership interest in a corporation.

Community Property: A special ownership form requiring that one-half of all property earned by a husband or wife during marriage belongs to each. Community property laws do not generally apply to property acquired by gift, by will, or by descent.

Compagneurs Nationals des Containers: *Abbreviation:* CNC—affiliate of the French National Railways for container traffic.

Company Adjustor: Claims adjustor who is a salaried employee representing only one company.

Company Stamp or Seal: A stamp or seal that is used by an incorporated business entity to make an impression on a document that certifies that document as being correct, and assigns the document with an identifier or direct link to that business entity.

Comparative Negligence: Under this concept a plaintiff (the person bringing suit) may recover damages even though guilty of some negligence. His or her recovery, however, is reduced by the amount or percent of that negligence.

Completed Operations: Liability arising out of faulty work performed away from the premises after the work or operations are completed. Applicable to contractors, plumbers, electricians, repair shops and similar firms. This form of liability insurance provides coverage for bodily injury and property damage rising from completed or abandoned operations, provided the incident occurs away from premises owned or rented by the insured. Operations are deemed completed at the earliest of: (1) when all operations to be performed by or on behalf of the Insured under contract have been completed; (2) when all operations to be performed by or on behalf of the Insured at the site of the operations have been completed; (3) when the portion of work out of which injury or damage rises has been put to its intended use by a party other than the contractor or sub-contractor.

Compliance Agreement: A legally binding agreement between AQIS/the Commonwealth and an Other Party, which requires the Other Party to meet specific requirements in respect of goods in an agreed manner.

Component: A uniquely identifiable product that is considered indivisible for a particular planning or control purpose, and/or which cannot be decomposed without destroying it. *Note*: A component for one organizational group may be the final assembly of another group (e.g., electric motor).

Compradore: A local advisor or agent employed by a foreign party or company who acts as an intermediary in transactions with local inhabitants.

Comprehensive Automobile Insurance: Coverage designed to provide protection against loss resulting from damage to the insured auto, other than loss by collision or upset.

Comprehensive General Liability Insurance: Under this form of insurance and regarding a covered occurrence, the company will pay all sums the Insured becomes legally obligated to pay as damages due to bodily injury (Coverage A) or property damage (Coverage B).

Comprehensive Major Medical Insurance: A policy designed to give the protection offered by both a basic and a major medical Health Insurance Policy. It is characterized by a low deductible amount, a coinsurance feature, and high maximum benefits.

Comprehensive Medical Expense Insurance: A form of Health Insurance which provides, in one policy, protection for both basic hospital expense and major medical expense coverages. The major medical part of a comprehensive policy is characterized by a deductible amount, coinsurance, and high maximum benefits.

Comprehensive Personal Liability Insurance: Protection against loss arising out of legal liability to pay money for damage or injury to others for which the Insured is responsible. It does not include automobile or business operation liabilities.

Compulsory Auto Liability Insurance: Insurance laws in some states require motorists to carry at least certain minimum auto coverages. This is called compulsory insurance.

Compulsory Insurance: Any form of insurance which is required by law.

Compulsory Insurance Law: Law protecting accident victims against irresponsible motorists by requiring owners and operators of automobiles to carry certain amounts of liability insurance in order to license the vehicle and drive legally within the state.

Computer Extra Expense Insurance: Coverage designed to provide protection if computer or EDP equipment is damaged or destroyed by fire or any other insured peril. In such an event it would probably be necessary to incur certain extra expenses to continue business operations.

Computer Virus: A programme that can infect other programmes by modifying them to include a possibly evolved copy of itself.

Conair Container: Thermal container served by an external cooling system (e.g., a vessel's or Clip On Unit), which regulates the temperature of cargo. *Note*: Conair is a brand name.

Concealment: Deliberate failure of an applicant for insurance to reveal a material fact to the insurer.

Concurrent Causation: Legal doctrine that states when a property loss is due to two causes, one that is excluded and one that is covered, the policy provides coverage.

Conditional Receipt: A receipt given for premium payments accompanying an application for insurance. If the application is approved as applied for, the coverage is effective as of the date of the prepayment or the date on which the last of the underwriting requirements, such as a medical examination, has been fulfilled.

Conditionally Renewable: Continuance provision of a Health Insurance Policy under which the company cannot cancel the policy during its term but can refuse to renew under certain conditions stated in the contract.

Conditions: Provisions inserted in an insurance contract that qualify or place limitations on the Insurer's promise to perform.

Cones: Devices for facilitating the loading, positioning and lashing of containers. The cones insert into the bottom castings of the container. *Synonym*: Locating pin.

Confining Sickness: An illness that confines an Insured person to his home or to a hospital.

Congestion: Accumulation of vessels at a port to the extent that vessels arriving to load or discharge are obliged to wait for a vacant berth.

Connecting Road Haulage: See Drayage.

Consequential Loss: Financial loss occurring as the consequence of some other loss, often called an indirect loss. Consequential loss or damage is indirect loss or damage resulting from loss or damage caused by a covered peril, such as fire or windstorm. In the case of loss caused where windstorm is a covered peril, if a tree is blown down and cuts electricity used to power a freezer and the food in the freezer spoils, if the insurance policy extends coverage for consequential loss or damage then the food spoilage would be a covered loss. Business Interruption Insurance, extends consequential loss or damage coverage for such items as extra expenses, rental value, profits and commissions, etc.

Conservation: The attempt by the insurer to prevent the lapse of a policy.

Consideration Clause: The clause that stipulates the basis on which the company issues the insurance contract. In Health Policies, the consideration is usually the statements in the application and the payment of premium.

Consideration: One of the elements for a binding contract. Consideration for an insurance policy is acceptance by the insurance company of the payment of the premium and the statement made by the prospective policy-holder in the application, balanced by the insurance company's promise to provide benefits in the case of loss.

Consignee: The party such as mentioned in the transport document by whom the goods, cargo or containers are to be received.

Consignment: A separate identifiable number of goods (available to be) transported from one consignor to one consignee via one or more than one modes of transport and specified in one single transport document. Synonym for the USA: Shipment.

Consignment Instructions: Instructions from either the seller/consignor or the buyer/consignee to a freight forwarder, carrier or his agent, or other provider of a service, enabling the movement of goods and associated activities. The following functions can be covered: Movement and handling of goods (shipping, forwarding and stowage) Customs formalities; Distribution of documents; Allocation of documents (freight and charges for the connected operations); Special instructions (insurance, dangerous goods, goods release, additional documents required).

Consignment Note: A document prepared by the shipper and comprising a transport contract. It contains details of the consignment to be carried to the port of loading and it is signed by the inland carrier as proof of receipt.

Consignment Stock: The stock of goods with an external party (customer) which is still the property of the supplier. Payment for these goods is made to the supplier at the moment when they are sold (used) by this party.

Consignor: See Shipper.

Consolidate: To group and stuff several shipments together in one container.

Consolidated Container: Container stuffed with several shipments (consignments) from different shippers for delivery to one or more consignees.

Consolidation: The grouping together of smaller consignments of goods into a large consignment for carriage as a larger unit in order to obtain a reduced rate.

Consolidation Point: Location where consolidation of consignments takes place.

Consolidator: A firm or company which consolidates cargo.

Consortium: Consortium is a form of cooperation between two or more carriers to operate in a particular trade.

Consular Invoice: An invoice covering shipment of goods certified by a consular official of the destination country, and used normally by customs or officials concerned with foreign exchange availability to ascertain the correctness of commercial invoice values.

Container: (1) An article of transport equipment (lift-van, movable tank or other similar structure): (*a*) fully or partially enclosed to constitute a compartment intended for containing goods; (*b*) of a permanent character and accordingly strong enough to be suitable for repeated use; (*c*) specially designed to facilitate the carriage of goods, by one or more modes of transport, without intermediate reloading; (*d*) designed for ready handling, particularly when being transferred from one mode of transport to another; (*e*) designed to be easy to fill and to empty; and (*f*) having an internal volume of one cubic metre or more.

(2) An item of equipment as defined by the International Organization for Standardization (ISO) for transport purposes. It must be of:

- a permanent character and accordingly strong enough to be suitable for repeated use
- specially designed to facilitate the carriage of goods, by one or more modes of transport without intermediate reloading
- fitted with devices permitting its ready handling, particularly from one mode of transport to another
- so designed as to be easy to fill and empty
- having an internal volume of 1 m3 or more

The term container includes neither vehicles nor conventional packing synonym: Freight.

Container Bolster: A container floor without sides or end walls which does not have the ISO corner fittings and is generally used for Ro/Ro operations. *Synonym*: Bolster. *Note*: A bolster cannot be handled either full or empty by a container spreader without special gear.

Container Chassis: A vehicle specially built for the purpose of transporting a container so that, when container and chassis are assembled, the produced unit serves as a road trailer.

Container Check Digit: The 7th digit of the serial number of a container used to check whether prefix and serial number are correct.

Container Depot: Storage area for empty containers.

Container Freight Station: *Abbreviation*: CFS—A facility at which (export) LCL cargo is received from merchants for loading (stuffing) into containers or at which (import) LCL cargo is unloaded (stripped) from containers and delivered to merchants.

Container Inspection Area: That portion within the QAP designated for performing inspections of containers.

Container Lease: The contract by which the owner of containers (lessor) gives the use of containers to a lessee for a specified period of time and for fixed payments.

Container Load Plan: A list of items loaded in a specific container and where appropriate their sequence of loading.

Container Logistics: The controlling and positioning of containers and other equipment.

Container Manifest: The document specifying the contents of particular freight containers or other transport units, prepared by the party responsible for their loading into the container or unit. *Synonym*: Unit packing list, Container Load Plan.

Container Moves: The number of actions performed by one container crane during a certain period.

Container Number: Identification number of a container consisting of prefix and serial number and check digit (e.g. KNLU 123456-7).

Container Owner: A party who has a container at his disposal and who is entitled to lease or sell the container.

Container Platform: A container floor without sides or end walls which can be loaded by spreader directly and is generally used for Lo-Lo operations.

Container Pool: A certain stock of containers which is jointly used by several container carriers and/or leasing companies.

Container Prefix: A four letter code that forms the first part of a container identification number indicating the owner of a container. *Synonym*: Owner's Container Code.

Container Safety Convention: *Abbreviation*: CSC—International convention for safe containers.

Container Serial Number: A seven digit serial number (6 plus 1 Check Digit) that forms the second part of a container identification number.

Container Service Charges: Charges to be paid by cargo interests as per tariff.

Container Size Code: An indication of 2 digits of the nominal length and nominal height.

Container Size/Type: Description of the size and type of a freight container or similar unit load device as specified in ISO6346.

Container Stack: Two or more containers, one placed above the other forming a vertical column.

Container Sublease: Contract by which a carrier gives the use of containers to another carrier for a specified period of time and for fixed payments.

Container Terminal: Place where loaded and/or empty containers are loaded or discharged into or from a means of transport.

Container Type Code: Two digits, the first of which indicates the category and the second of which indicates certain physical characteristics or other attributes.

Container Yard: *Abbreviation*: CY—A facility at which FCL traffic and empty containers are received from or delivered to the Merchant by or on behalf of the Carrier. *Note*: Often this yard is used to receive goods on behalf of the merchant and pack these in containers for FCL traffic. *Synonym*: Marshalling Yard.

Containerised Cargo Clearance: Clean, Cleaned, Cleaning: Removal of all quarantine risk material including soil, dirt, faeces, leaves, twigs, grass and any other plant or animal material.

Containerised Cargo Clearance for FCL/X Scheme: This scheme requires persons accredited under it to assess non-commodity documentation in respect to FCL/X cargo against AQIS requirements.

Containerized: Indication that goods have been stowed in a container.

Contamination: Quarantine risk material including, but not limited to, soil, insects, dirt, faeces, leaves, twigs, grass and any other plant or animal material adhering to goods, included with goods or associated with packaging accompanying goods.

Contents Broad Form: *See* Homeowners policy.

Contingent Annuity Option: An option under which an employee may elect to receive, under certain conditions, a reduced amount of annuity with the same income, or a specified fraction, to be paid after his death to another person designated as his contingent annuitant, for that person's lifetime. The contingent annuitant is usually the husband or the wife (see Joint and Survivor Annuity).

Contingent Beneficiary: The person or persons designated to receive the benefits of a policy or plan if the primary beneficiary dies while the Insured is living.

Contingent Liability: Liability arising out of work done by independent contractors for a firm. A firm may be liable for the work done by an independent contractor if the activity is illegal, the situation does not permit delegation of authority, or the work is inherently dangerous.

Contingent Owner: The person to succeed as owner of a Life Insurance Policy if the original owner dies.

Contraband: Goods forbidden by national law to be imported or exported.

Contract: (1) An agreement enforceable by law between two or more parties stipulating their rights and obligations which are required by one or both parties to acts or forbearance by the other or both. (2) A binding agreement between two or more parties for the doing or not doing certain things. A contract of insurance is imbodied in a written document called the Policy.

Contract Holder: The group, entity or person to whom a group annuity contract is issued.

Contract Logistics: The contracting out of all the warehousing, transport and distribution activities or a part thereof by manufacturing companies.

Contract of Affreightment: An agreement whereby the ship owner agrees to carry goods by water, or furnishes a vessel for the purpose of carrying goods by water, in return for a sum of money called freight. There are two forms: the charter party and the contract contained in the Bill of Lading.

Contractor Integrated Technical Information Service: A technical information service based on the integration of databases (contractor, sub-contractor and government) contractually established and managed by the defense contractor to receive, maintain, and provide access to technical and support information on a defense system.

Contractors Liability Insurance: Coverage designed to provide protection for: (1) Premises/Operations. The premises portion provides for payment on the Insured's behalf of all sums he or she becomes liable to pay, resulting from bodily injury and/or property damage caused by an insured peril and rising out of the ownership, maintenance, or use of premises and operations in progress. The operations portion covers operations in progress and is intended for situations where your principal business operations are performed away from your premises. (2) Completed Operations. This portion of liability insurance provides for possible liability for bodily injury and/or property damage after work is complete and the insured has left the job site.

Contractual Liability: Legal liability of another party that the business firm agrees to assume by a written or oral contract. It is common in construction and other agreements (written or oral) for one party to assume the liability of another. This is sometimes referred to as a hold harmless agreement. The extent to which one holds another harmless varies from contract to contract, job to job, etc.

Contractual Port of Loading: A port at which an ocean vessel does not call, but which is equalized with the actual port of call and upon which inland haulage services and inland tariffs are based. *Synonym*: Commercial POL/POD. *Note*: Generally speaking it is seen as the port to be mentioned on the B/L from which cargo is accepted (e.g., delivered by the consignee for sea transport).

Contribution: The term relates to circumstances where more than one party covers the risk. Each party is deemed to be liable for his proportion of the loss. If the assured recovers in full from one insurer, that insurer is entitled to recover from the other insurer for that part of the loss which should have been paid by the latter. The term is used in marine insurance, also, in relation to contributions paid by the assured in connection with salvage and/or general average.

Contribution by Equal Shares: Type of other-insurance provision often found in liability insurance contracts that requires each company to share equally in the loss until the share of each insurer equals the lowest limit of liability under any policy or until the full amount of loss is paid.

Contributory: A Group Insurance plan issued to an employer under which both the employer and employee contribute to the cost of the plan. Seventy-five per cent of the eligible employees must be insured (See Non-contributory).

Contributory Negligence: Negligence of the damaged person that helped to cause the accident. Some states bar recovery to the plaintiff if the plaintiff was contributorily negligent to any extent. Others apply comparative negligence.

Contributory Value: The value on which a contribution to a general average loss or salvage award is calculated.

Control: The registration and check on data and activities as well as determining supervising procedures and changes related to procedures.

Conventional Cargo: See Break Bulk Cargo.

Conversion Privilege: The right given to an insured person to change insurance without evidence of medical insurability, usually to an individual policy upon termination of coverage under a group contract.

Convertible Bond: A bond that offers the holder the privilege of converting the bond into a specified number of shares of stock.

Convertible Term Insurance: Term insurance which can be exchanged, at the option of the policy-holder and without evidence of insurability, for another plan of insurance.

Convertor Dolly: An auxiliary undercarriage assembly consisting of a chassis, fifth wheel and towbar used to convert a semitrailer or a container chassis to a full trailer.

Conveyance: Transport of goods from one place to another.

Conveyor: A mechanical device in the form of a continuous belt for transporting cargo.

Coordination of Benefits (COB): The mechanism used in group health insurance to designate the order in which the multiple carriers are to pay benefits and to prevent duplicate payments.

Core Competence: The combination of individual skills and use of technologies that underlay the various products and or services of a business.

Corner Fittings: Fittings located at the corners of containers providing means of supporting, stacking, handling and securing the container. *Synonym*: Corner casting.

Corner Post: Vertical structural member at either side of an 'end frame' of a container joining a top and a bottom corner fitting (and thereby forming a 'corner structure').

Correction Message: A substitution for what has been wrong in a prior data interchange between computers in accordance with interchange agreements.

Corrective Action Request (CAR): A formal AQIS document which records and details non-conformities detected during an inspection or audit of an Other Party's performance under a Compliance Agreement or as a QAP, and the proposed corrective action and the date for rectification.

Corridor Deductible: Major medical plan deductible that excludes benefits provided by a basic plan if both a basic and a supplemental group major Medical Expense Policy are in force.

Co-shippership: See Co-makership.

Cost and Freight: "Cost and Freight" means that the seller must pay the costs and freight necessary to bring the goods to the named port of destination but the risk of loss of or damage to the goods, as well as any additional costs due to events occurring after the time the goods have been delivered on board the vessel, is transferred from the seller to the buyer when the goods pass the ship's rail in the port of shipment. The CFR term requires the seller to clear the goods for export. This term can only be used for sea and inland waterway transport. When the ship's rail serves no practical purpose, such as in the case of roll-on/roll-off or container traffic, the CPT term is more appropriate to use.

Cost Basis: An amount attributed to an asset for income tax purposes; used to determine gain or loss on sale or transfer; used to determine the value of a gift.

Cost Containment: The controller reduction of inefficiencies in the consumption, allocation, or production of health care services that contribute to higher than necessary costs.

Cost, Insurance and Freight: *Abbreviation*: CIF.

Cost-of-Living Rider: Benefit that can be added to a life insurance policy under which the policy owner can purchase one-year term insurance equal to the percentage change in the consumer price index with no evidence of insurability.

COT: The customer arranges his own transport of the container to and from the terminal or depot but agrees to restitute the container back to the terminal or depot.

COU: See Clip On Unit.

Council of European and Japanese National Shipowner's Associations: *Abbreviation*: CENSA—The main objectives of this organization are to promote and protect sound shipping policies in all sectors of shipping, to coordinate and present the views of its members and to exchange views with other shipowner groups.

Country Damage: Damage to baled or bagged goods (e.g., cotton) caused by excessive moisture from damp ground or exposure to weather, or by grit, dust or sand forced into the insured property by windstorm or inclement weather.

Country of Departure: Country from which a certain means of transport is scheduled to depart or has departed.

Country of Despatch: Country from which the goods are shipped.

Country of Origin: Country in which the goods have been produced or manufactured, according to criteria laid down for the purpose of application of the customs tariff, of quantitative restrictions, or of any other measure related to trade.

Country of Provenance: The country from which goods or cargo are sent to the importing country.

Country (Rural) Tailgate Inspection: A tailgate inspection that is performed by Quarantine Officers on containers that are going to be delivered to a rural destination for unpacking. The actual tailgate involves an external inspection (as per the External Container Inspection Regime Work Instruction) of the container and a visual verification of the container and goods at the opened container doors. The primary purpose of this inspection is to ensure that the container and its contents are free of

QRM. The tailgate must occur without any unpack of the commodities and without the Quarantine Officer entering the container.

Coverage: The scope of protection provided under a contract of insurance; any of several risks covered by a policy.

Coverage for Damage to Your Auto: That part of the personal auto policy insuring payment for damage or theft of the insured automobile. This optional coverage can be used to insure both collision and other-than-collision losses.

Covered: A person covered by a pension plan is one who has fulfilled the eligibility requirements in the plan, for whom benefits have accrued, or are accruing, or who is receiving benefits under the plan.

Covered Expenses: Hospital, medical, and miscellaneous health care expenses incurred by the insured that entitle him/her to a payment of benefits under a health insurance policy. Found most often in connection with major medical plans, the term defines, by either description, reasonableness, or necessity to specify the type and amount of expense which will be considered in the calculation of benefits.

Covered Participant: A person covered by a pension plan is one who has fulfilled the eligibility requirements in the plan, for whom benefits have accrued, or are accruing, or who is receiving benefits under the plan.

CPCU: *See* Chartered Property and Casualty Underwriter.

CPT: See Carriage Paid To (...named place of destination).

Crane: A machine designed for moving and lifting weight by means of a movable projecting arm or a horizontal beam which is able to travel over a certain distance.

Credibility: A statistical measure of the degree to which past results make good forecasts of future results.

Credibility Factor: The weight given to an individual insured's past experience in computing premiums for future coverage.

Credit Health Insurance: A form of health insurance on a borrower, usually under an installment purchase agreement. The benefits cover the obligations of the borrower and are payable to the creditor.

Credit Insurance: A guarantee to manufacturers, wholesalers, and service organizations that they will be paid for goods shipped or services rendered. Applies to that part of working capital which is represented by accounts receivable.

Credit Life Insurance. Term life insurance issued through a lender or lending agency to cover payment of a loan, installment purchase, or other obligation, in case of death.

Crew Member: Any person actually employed for duties on board during a voyage in the working or service of a ship and included in the crew list (IMO).

Critical Mass: When enough buyers and sellers participate in a Net market so goods or services change hands efficiently. Also, the time when a market gains momentum, achieves liquidity, and becomes a more efficient way to buy or sell than the traditional physical market or channel.

Critical Non-Conformity: A major breach of the Schedule and/or Processes and Outcomes Document resulting in the immediate suspension of the Schedule.

Critical Path Method: A network planning technique used for planning and controlling the activities in a project. By showing each of these activities and their associated times, the 'critical path' can be determined. The critical path is the series of successive activities which takes up most time and is therefore decisive for the total lead time of the project.

Crop Hail Insurance: Coverage designed to provide financial protection against damage to growing crops as a result of hail or certain other named perils.

Cross Liability Endorsement: In the event of claim by one insured for which another insured covered by the same policy may be held liable, this endorsement covers the insured against whom the claim is made in the same manner as if separate policies had been issued. However, it does not operate to increase the insurance company's overall limit of liability.

Cross Purchase Agreement: Specifies the terms for the surviving partners or shareholders to buy a deceased's share of the business's ownership.

Cross Trades: Term used in shipping for the services of a vessel between nations other than the nation in which the vessel is registered (UNCTAD).

Cruise Ship: A ship on an international voyage carrying passengers participating in a group programme and accommodated on board, for the purpose of making scheduled temporary tourist visits at one or more different ports, and which during the voyage does not normally: (*a*) embark or disembark any other passengers; (*b*) load or discharge any cargo.

CSC: See Container Safety Convention.

CSR: Customer Service Representatives support the work of insurance agents with a variety of tasks that must be done within a company or agency to deliver services to and handle requests from clients.

CTD: See Combined Transport Document.

CTO: See Combined Transport Operator.

Currency: A medium of exchange of value, defined by reference to the geographical location of the authorities responsible for it ISO4217. In general, the monetary unit, involved in a transaction and represented by a name or a symbol.

Currency Adjustment Factor: *Abbreviation*: CAF—Adjustment applied by shipping lines or liner conferences on freight rates to offset losses or gains for carriers resulting from fluctuations in exchange rates of tariff currencies.

Current Assumption Whole Life Insurance: Non-participating whole life policy in which the cash values are based on the Insurer's current mortality, investment, and expense experience. An accumulation account is credited with a current interest rate that changes over time. Also called interest-sensitive whole life insurance.

Currently Insured: Status of a covered person under the Old-age, Survivors, and Disability Insurance (OASDI) programme who has at least six quarters of coverage out of the last thirteen quarters, ending with the quarter of death, disability, or entitlement to retirement benefits.

Customer: See Client.

Customer Pick Up: Cargo picked up by a customer at a warehouse.

Customer Service: The way in which during a commercial relationship the wishes and demands of the (prospective) client are catered for supporting activities at the customer interface adding value to a product (CEN273).

Customer Service Level: A performance measure of customer service. *Note*: generally this is seen as the degree with which customer orders can be executed, in accordance with the terms which are generally accepted in the market.

Customs: The department of the Civil Service that deals with the levying of duties and taxes on imported goods from foreign countries and the control over the export and import of goods e.g. allowed quota, prohibited goods.

Customs Broker: An authorized agent specialized in customs clearance procedures on account of importers/exporters. *Customs Clearance Agent*.

Customs Invoice: Document required by the customs in an importing country in which an exporter states the invoice or other price (e.g., selling price, price of identical goods), and specifies costs for freight, insurance and packing etc., terms of delivery and payment, for the purpose of determining the customs value in the importing country of goods consigned to that country.

Customs Value: The worth of an item or group of items expressed in a monetary amount, within a consignment declared to Customs for duty and statistical reasons.

CWE: See Cleared Without Examination.

CY: See Container Yard.

Cybernetics: The study of control processes in mechanical, biological, electrical and information systems.

CYC: Container Yard Charges—Charges at destination.

Cycle Stock: That portion of stock available or planned to be available in a give period for normal demand, excluding excess stock and safety stock. Form on which physical damage is recorded (e.g., containers).

Damaged Cargo Report: Written statement concerning established damages to cargo and/or equipment.

Damage to Property of Others: Coverage for an insured who damages another's property. Payment is made despite the lack of legal liability. Coverage is included in Section II of the Homeowners Policy.

Dangerous Goods: Goods are to be considered dangerous if the transport of such goods might cause harm, risk, peril, or other evil to people, environment, equipment or any property whatsoever.

Dangerous Goods Declaration: Document issued by a consignor in accordance with applicable conventions or regulations, describing hazardous goods or materials for transport purposes, and stating that the latter have been packed and labelled in accordance with the provisions of the relevant conventions or regulations.

Dangerous Goods Packing Certificate: A document as part of the dangerous goods declaration in which the responsible party declares that the cargo has been stowed in accordance with the rules in a clean container in compliance with the IMDG regulations and properly secured.

Data Plate: A metal identification plate affixed to a container which displays among others the gross and tare weights and external dimensions.

DDP (Delivered Duty Paid): The seller fulfils his obligation to deliver when the goods have been made available at the named place in the country of importation. The seller has to bear the risks and costs, including duties, taxes and other charges of delivering the goods thereto, cleared for importation. If the parties wish to exclude from the seller's obligations some of the costs payable upon importation of the goods (such as value added tax (VAT)), this should be made clear by adding words to this effect: "Delivered duty paid, VAT unpaid (...named place of destination)." This term may be used irrespective of the mode of transport.

DDU: See Delivered Duty Unpaid (...named place of destination).

Deadload: The difference between the actual and calculated ship's draft.

Deadweight: *Abbreviation*: DWT—The total weight of cargo, cargo equipment, bunkers, provisions, water, stores and spare parts which a vessel can lift when loaded to her maximum draught as applicable under the circumstances. The deadweight is expressed in tons.

Death Benefit: A payment made to a designated beneficiary upon the death of the employee annuitant.

Debenture: A bond that is backed only by the general credit of the issuing corporation. No specific property is pledged as security behind the loan.

Debit Insurance: See Industrial Life Insurance.

Debris Removal Clause: This clause extends insurance coverage to include the cost of debris removal resulting from damage caused by a covered loss up to a specified limit of loss. The clause is an additional Property Insurance coverage.

Decision Support System: *Abbreviation*: DSS—An interactive computer-based system which generates a number of alternatives to solve an unstructured problem. These alternatives are being interpreted by the manager (decision-maker), whereafter he decides which alternative is to be used to solve the problem.

Deck: Any extended horizontal structure in a vessel or an aircraft, serving as a floor and structural support, covering, partially or fully, a portion of the vessel or aircraft.

Declaration of Origin: Appropriate statement as to the origin of the goods, made in connection with their exportation by the manufacturer, producer, supplier, exporter or other competent person on the commercial invoice or any document relating to goods.

Declarations: Statements in an insurance contract that provide information about the property or life to be insured and used for underwriting and rating purposes and identification of the property or life to be insured.

Declared Value for Carriage: The value of the goods declared to the carrier by the shipper for the purpose of determining charges or of establishing the limit of the carrier's liability for loss, damage or delay. It is also the basis for possible applicable valuation charges.

Declination: The insurer's refusal to insure an individual after evaluation of the application for insurance and any other pertinent factors.

Deconsolidation: The process of unpacking a container for the purposes of inspection.

Decoupling Inventory: A stock retained to make the independent control of two successive operations possible.

Decoupling Point: The point in the supply chain which provides a buffer between differing input and output rates.

Deductible: An amount which a policyholder agrees to pay, per claim or per accident, toward the total amount of an insured loss.

Deep Tank: Tank fitted and equipped for the carriage of vegetable oil (e.g., palm oil and coconut oil) and other liquids in bulk. By means of oil-tight bulkheads and/or decks it is possible to carry different kinds of liquid in adjacent tanks. Deep tanks may be equipped with heating facilities in order to carry and discharge oil at the required temperature (shipping).

Default Charge: A (standard) charge applicable for a trade, stretch or location. In the absence of specifics (not otherwise specified/enumerated) a general amount has been set.

Deferred Annuity: An annuity providing for the income payments to begin at some specified future date.

Deferred Compensation: Arrangements by which compensation to employees for past or current services is postponed until some future date.

Deferred Group Annuity: A type of group annuity providing for the purchase each year of a paid-up deferred annuity for each member of the group, the total amount received by the member at retirement being the sum of these deferred annuities.

Defined Benefit Plan: A pension plan stating either (1) the benefits to be received by employees after retirement or (2) the method of determining such benefits. The employer's contributions under such a plan are actuarially determined.

Defined Contribution Plan: A plan under which the contribution rate is fixed and benefits to be received by employees after retirement depend to some extent upon the contributions and their earnings.

Degroupage: Splitting up shipments into small consignments.

Delivered At Frontier (...named place): *Abbreviation*: DAF.

Delivered Duty Paid (...named place of destination): *Abbreviation*: DDP.

Delivered Duty Unpaid (...named place of destination): *Abbreviation*: DDU.

Delivered Ex Quay (...named port of destination): *Abbreviation*: DEQ.

Delivered Ex Ship (...named port of destination): Abbreviation: DES

Delivering Carrier: The carrier who delivers the consignment to the consignee or his agent (aircargo).

Delivery: The process of delivering the consignment to the consignee at the agreed place.

Delivery Instruction: Document issued by a buyer giving instructions regarding the details of the delivery of goods ordered.

Delivery Note: A document recording the delivery of products to a consignee (customer).

Delivery Order: A document issued by or on behalf of the carrier authorizing the release of import cargo identified thereon and manifested under a single Bill of Lading (shipping).

Delivery Party: The party to which goods arc to be delivered.

Delivery Reliability: The proportion of total delivery occasions in which the time, place, quality and quantity of products delivered accords with the order.

Delivery Schedule: The required and/or agreed time of delivery of goods or services, purchased for a future period.

Delivery Time: The time between order and delivery.

Demand: The quantity of goods required by the market to be delivered in a particular period or at a specific date.

Demise Charter: A contract whereby the ship owner leases his vessel to the charterer for a period of time during which the whole use and management of the vessel passes to the charterer, which involves that the charterer is to pay all expenses for the operation and maintenance of the vessel. Officers and crew will become servants of the charterer. A demise charter whereby the charterer has the right to place his own master and crew on board of the vessel is also called 'bareboat charter'.

Density of Commodity: The mass of a commodity to its volume.

Dependency Period: Period of time following the readjustment period during which the surviving spouse's children are under eighteen and therefore dependent of the parent.

Dependent Benefits: Social Security benefits available to the spouse or children of a Social Security beneficiary.

Dependent Demand: A demand directly related to or derived from the demand for other items or end products. Dependent demands are therefore calculated, and need not and should not be forecast.

Deposit Administration Group Annuity: A type of group annuity providing for the accumulation of contributions in an undivided fund out of which annuities are purchased as the individual members of the group retire.

Deposit Premium: The money paid by a prospective policy holder when an application is made for an insurance policy. It is usually equal, at least, to the first month's estimate premium and is applied toward the actual premium when billed.

Deposit Term Insurance: A form of Term Insurance, not really involving a "deposit," in which the first-year premium is larger than subsequent premiums. Typically, a partial endowment is paid at the end of the term period. In many cases, the partial endowment can be applied toward the purchase of a new term policy, or, perhaps, a whole life policy.

Depot: The place designated by the carrier where empty containers are kept in stock and received from or delivered to the container operators or merchants.

Depreciation: A decrease in the value of property over a period of time due to wear and tear or obsolescence. Depreciation is used to determine the actual cash value of property at time of loss (See Actual Cash Value).

DEQ: See Delivered Ex Quay (...named port of destination).

Derrick: Lifting equipment on board a conventional vessel for loading and discharging cargo, consisting of a post attached to the deck and an inclined spar.

DES: See Delivered Ex Ship (...named port of destination).

Designated Port: (*a*) A first port of entry, landing place or a port where imported animals, plants or other goods may be landed as declared by the *Quarantine Proclamations 2000;* and (*b*) A port where there are sufficient Quarantine Officers available to allow for staff to respond to any possible contamination within a reasonable amount of time.

Despatch: The process of sending goods. *Synonym*: Dispatch.

Despatch Advice: Information send by shippers to the recipient of goods informing that specified goods are sent or ready to be sent advising the detailed contents of the consignment. *Synonym*: Despatch note.

Despatch Days: The days gained if the free time included in the rate and allowed for the use of certain equipment is not fully used.

Destination: Place for which goods or a vehicle is bound. The ultimate stopping place according to the contract of carriage.

Detection: The detection of goods, vectors or receptacles of quarantine interest at the barrier.

Det Norske Veritas: Norwegian classification society.

Detention: Keeping equipment beyond the time allowed. See demurrage.

Detention Charge: Charges levied on usage of equipment exceeding free time period as stipulated in the pertinent inland rules and conditions.

Deterioration: The downgrading of a product due to long storage, damage to packing or other external influences.

Devanning: See Stripping, Unpacking.

Deviation from a Route: A divergence from the agreed or customary route.

Diagnosis-Related Groups (DRGs): System that reimburses health care providers fixed amounts for all care given in connection with standard diagnostic categories.

Difference in Conditions Insurance (DIC): All-Risks Policy that covers other perils not insured by basic Property Insurance contracts, supplemental to and excluding the coverage provided by underlying contracts. DIC insurance provides coverage designed to close specific gaps in standard insurance policies and is usually available only for larger industrial or commercial risks. It allows coverage to be customized to extend to such exposures as water damage, flood, collapse, earthquake, landslide, etc., according to the Insured's needs. DIC coverage may be provided by means of a separate insurance policy or it may be added by endorsement to the basic policy.

Dimensions: Measurements in length, width and height, regarding cargo.

Direct Delivery: The conveyance of goods directly from the vendor to the buyer. Frequently used if a third party acts as intermediary agent between vendor and buyer. Direct discharge from vessel onto railroad car, road vehicle or barge with the purpose of immediate transport from the port area (usually occurs when ports lack adequate storage space or when ports are not equipped to handle a specific cargo).

Direct Interchange: Transfer of leased equipment from one lessee to another (container).

Direct Loss: Financial loss that results directly from an insured peril.

Direct or Held Covered: A condition requiring that the insured voyage be direct from one place to another. If the voyage is delayed en route or there is a deviation from the direct route the insurance cover continues subject to payment of an additional premium, but only if the Assured gives prompt notice of such delay or deviation immediately on receipt of advices, unless the policy provides otherwise.

Direct Placement: Sale of an entire issue of bonds or stock by the issuer to one or a few large institutional customers such as an insurance company without trying to market the issue publicly.

Direct Premiums Written: Property and casualty insurance premiums written (less return premiums) without any allowance for premiums for assumed or ceded reinsurance.

Direct Response System: A marketing method where insurance is sold without the services of an agent. Potential customers are solicited by advertising in the mail, newspapers, magazines, television, radio and other media.

Direct Route: The shortest operated route between two points.

Direct Writer: The industry term for a company which uses its own sales employees to write its policies. Sometimes refers to companies which contract with exclusive agents.

Directors' and Officers' Liability: The exposure of corporate managers to claims from shareholders, government agencies, and employees, and others alleging mismanagement.

Disability: A physical or a mental impairment that substantially limits one or more major life activities of an individual. It may be partial or total. (See Partial Disability; Total Disability.)

Disability Benefit: (1) A feature added to some life insurance policies providing for waiver of premium, and sometimes payment of monthly income, if the policy holder becomes totally and permanently disabled. (2) Periodic payments, usually monthly, payable to participants under some retirement plans, if such participants are eligible for the benefits and become totally and permanently disabled prior to the normal retirement date.

Disability Income Insurance: A form of health insurance that provides periodic payments to replace income when an insured person is unable to work as a result of illness, injury, or disease.

Disability Insured: Status of an individual who is insured for disability benefits under the Old-Age, Survivors, and Disability Insurance (OASDI) programme. The covered person must be fully insured and have at least twenty quarters of coverage out of the last forty, ending with the quarter in which the disability occurs. Fewer quarters are required for persons under age thirty.

Disappearing Deductible: Deductible in an insurance contract that provides for a decreasing deductible amount as the size of the loss increases, so that small claims are not paid but large losses are paid in full.

Disbursement: Sums paid out by a ship's agent at a port and recovered from the carrier.

Discharge: The unloading of a vehicle, a vessel or an aircraft. The landing of cargo.

Disclosure: The duty of the Assured and his broker to tell the Underwriter every material circumstance before acceptance of the risk.

Discrepancy: Difference between the particulars given and the particulars found.

Discrete Code: A bar code in which the spaces between characters (intercharacter gaps) are not part of the code as each character begins and ends with a bar. The spaces can therefore vary in width, specified tolerances. An example is Code 39.

Disease: Includes a micro-organism, a disease agent, an infectious agent or a parasite.

Disintermediation: When a Net market bypasses a traditional channel, more directly linking buyers with suppliers.

Dismemberment: Loss of body members (limbs), or use thereof, or loss of sight due to injury.

Dismemberment Insurance: A form of health insurance that provides payment in case of loss by bodily injury of one or more body members (such as hands or feet) or the sight of one or both eyes.

Dispatch: See Despatch.

Displacement: The weight of the quantity of water displaced by the vessel. The displacement of the vessel on her light draft represents the weight of the vessel ready for use including stores etc.

Disposable Pallet: Pallet intended to be discarded after a single cycle of use. *Synonym:*

One-way pallet, Expendable pallet.

Disposable Personal Income: Personal income less personal tax and basic non-tax payments. It is the income available to people for discretionary spending and saving.

Disposal Chain: A sequence of events in a goods-flow which gets rid of a specific good. This may include removal, recycling, waste dumping etc.

Disposal of Goods: The act of getting rid of goods.

Dispositioning: All activities relating to the inland movement of empty and or full containers.

Distribution: The set of activities which ensure the availability of goods in the desired quality, quantity, place and time for the customer.

Distribution Centre: A warehouse for the receipt, the storage and the dispersal of goods among customers. *Synonym*: Branch Warehouse.

Distribution Channel: The route by which a company distributes goods.

Distribution Requirements Planning: *Abbreviation*: **DRP-I**—The function of determining the need to replenish stock at branch warehouses. Distribution Resource Planning Abbreviation: **DRP-II**—The set of concepts, procedures and techniques, being an extension of DRP-I, for the effective planning and control of the physical distribution.

Dividend: (1) A return of part of the premium on participating insurance to reflect he difference between the premium charged and the combination of actual mortality, expense and investment experience. Such premiums are calculated to provide some margin over the anticipated cost of the insurance protection. (2) In capital stock companies, a share of the profits distributed to stockholders.

Dividend Addition: An amount of paid-up insurance purchased with a policy dividend and added to the face amount of the policy.

Divider: A vertically mounted partition in a compartment on board. *Synonym*: Partition.

Dock Receipt: Document issued by a shipping line acknowledging that goods are received for shipment.

Document: Anything printed, written, relied upon to record or prove something.

Document Holder: Usually fastened to the door on the front of a container. May contain e.g., a certificate of approval of the container.

Document of Title: A term to mean that possession of the specified document entitles the holder to control of the goods listed in that document.

Documentary Credit: The basis of international trade by means of which payment is made against surrender of the specified documents.

Dollar Threshold: In no-fault auto insurance states with the dollar threshold, it prevents individuals from suing in tort to recover for pain and suffering unless their medical expenses exceed a certain dollar amount.

Domestic Insurer: An insurance company is a domestic company in the state in which it is incorporated.

Donor: The person making a gift.

Door Lock Bars: See Bars.

Double Banking: Two vessels moored alongside each other on a certain berth.

Double-deck Pallet: Flat pallet with a top and bottom deck.

Double Indemnity: A policy provision usually associated with death, which doubles payment of a designated benefit when certain kinds of accidents occur.

Down Time: The period of time when a machine is not available for production due to a functional failure or maintenance.

Draft: The draft of a vessel is the vertical distance between the waterline and the underside of the keel of the vessel. During the construction of a vessel the marks showing the draft are welded on each side of the vessel near the stem, the stern and amidships. *Synonym*: Draught.

Dramshop Law: Law that imputes negligence to the owner of a business that sells liquor in the case that an intoxicated customer causes injury or property damage to another person. Usually excluded from general liability policies.

Draught: See Draft.

Drawback: Repayment of any part of customs or excise duties previously collected on imported goods, when those goods are exported again.

Drayage: The hauling of a load by a cart with detachable sides (dray). Road transportation between the nearest railway terminal and the stuffing place. *Synonym*: Connecting Road Haulage.

Dread Disease Insurance: Insurance providing an unallocated benefit, subject to a maximum amount, for expenses incurred in connection with the treatment of specified diseases, such as cancer, poliomyelitis, encephalitis and spinal meningitis.

Drilling Rig: A structure, which drills wells in the bottom in order to search for oil.

DRIVE: Dedicated Road Infrastructure for Vehicle safety in Europe, a major initiative begun in 1988 to apply information technology to the improvement of road safety and the reduction of environmental pollution by road traffic. *Acronym*: DRIVE.

Driver Education Credit: Student discount or reduction in premium amount for which young drivers become eligible on completion of a driver education course.

Drop Off Charge: Charge made by container owner and/or terminal operators for delivery of a leased, or pool container into depot stock. The drop off charge may be a combination of actual handling and storage charges with surcharges.

DRP-I: See Distribution Requirements Planning.

DRP-II: See Distribution Resource Planning.

Dry Bulk Container: Container consisting of a cargo-carrying structure, firmly secured within a framework, for the carriage of dry solids in bulk without packaging. Containers of this type have type codes 80 and 81.

Dry Cargo Container: Shipping container which is designed for the carriage of goods other than liquids.

DSS: See Decision Support System.

Dunnage: (1) Materials used for supporting or protecting consignments during transportation. Dunnage is not intrinsically associated with the cargo. (2) Stowage material, mainly timber or board, used to prevent damage to cargo during carriage.

Duplication of Benefits: Overlapping or identical coverage of the same insured under two or more health plans, usually the result of contracts of different insurance companies, service organizations, or pre-payment plans; also known as multiple coverage.

Duty Free Zone: An area where goods or cargo can be stored without paying import customs duties awaiting further transport or manufacturing.

Duty of Assured Clause (Cargo): This appears in the institute Cargo Clauses published for use with the MAR form of policy. It directs the attention of the Assured, his agents, etc., to the duty (as required by the MIA, 1906) to take reasonable measures to avert or minimise any loss which is recoverable under the policy; also to ensure that all rights against carriers and others are properly preserved and exercised. Underwriters agree to reimburse the Assured for any reasonable expenditure incurred by his compliance with the clause; in practice, these expenses are termed "sue and labour" charges (which see).

Dwelling Property: (1) Property insurance policy that insures the dwelling at actual cash value, other structures, personal property, fair rental value, and certain other coverages. Covers a limited number of perils. (2) Property insurance policy that insures the dwelling and other structures at replacement cost. It adds additional coverages and has a greater list of covered perils than the Dwelling Property 1 policy. (3) Property insurance policy that covers the dwelling and other structures against direct physical loss from any peril except for those perils otherwise excluded. However, personal property is covered on a named-perils basis.

DWT: See Deadweight.

Early Retirement: Retirement of a participant prior to the normal retirement date, usually with a reduced amount of annuity. Early retirement is generally allowed at any time during a period of 5 to 10 years preceding the normal retirement date.

Earned Income: Employment income derived from salary, wages, commissions, or fees.

Earned Premium: The portion of a premium which is the property of an insurance company, based on the expired portion of the policy period. For example, an insurance company is considered to have earned 75 per cent of an annual premium after a period of nine months of an annual policy has elapsed.

Earnings Test (Retirement Test): Determination of the amount of Social Security benefits payable to a beneficiary after adjusting for earnings.

Econometric Models: A system of simultaneous equations for forecasting, based on mutual dependency among the variables used.

Economic Loss: The estimated total cost, both insured and uninsured, of mishaps (such as motor vehicle accidents, work accidents, and fires); includes such factors as property damage, funeral expenses, wage loss, insurance administration costs, and medical, hospital and legal costs.

Economic Policy: Special type of participating whole life insurance in which the dividends are used to buy Term Insurance or paid-up additions equal to the difference between the face amount of the policy and some guaranteed amount.

Economic Speed: That speed of a means of transport which produces the best possible financial result for the owner. Such speed should not be in excess of the maximum or minimum output allowed for the engine(s).

Economy of Scale: A phenomenon which encourages the production of larger volumes of a commodity to reduce its unit cost by distributing fixed costs over a greater quantity.

ECSI : Export Cargo Shipping Instruction/Preadvice—Instructions from shipper with details of all parties involved and description of goods.

EDI: See Eletronic Data Interchange.

EDI for Administration, Commerce and Transport: United Nations rules for Electronic Data Interchange for Administration, Commerce and Transport. They comprise a set of internationally agreed upon standards, directories and guidelines for the electronic interchange of structured data related to trade in goods and services between independent computerized information systems.

EDIFACT: See Electronic Data Interchange for Administration, Commerce and Transport.

EDP: See Electronic Data Processing.

EDR: See Equipment Damage Report.

Effective Date: The date on which the insurance under a policy begins.

EFTA: European Free Trade Association—Comprising Iceland, Norway and Switzerland.

EHA (Equipment Handover Agreement): Interchange (Fr)—An agreement àcknowledging the condition of the carrier's equipment when handedover and returned, which includes the terms of contract under which the equipment was taken over.

EIR: See Equipment Interchange Receipt.

Electronic Commerce: The end-to-end digital exchange of all information needed to conduct business. Examples include EDI transactions, electronic mail, archives, audit trails, and all forms of records, including graphical images.

Electronic Data Interchange for Administration, Commerce and Transport: *Abbreviation*: EDIFACT. The ISO application level syntax rules for the structuring of user data and of the associated service data in the interchange of messages in an open environment.

Electronic Data Interchange: *Abbreviation*: EDI—The transfer of structured data, by agreed standards from applications on the computer of one party to the applications on the computer of another party by electronic means.

Electronic Data Processing: *Abbreviation*: EDP—The computerized handling of information (e.g. business data).

Elements of a Negligent Act: Four elements an injured person must show to prove negligence: existence of a legal duty to use reasonable care, failure to perform that duty, damages or injury to the claimant, and proximate cause relationship between the negligent act and the infliction of damages.

Elevator: Equipment used to discharge some bulk cargoes such as grain which is removed from the hold by a continuous line of buckets or by suction and carried on a conveyor belt to store.

Eligibility Date: The date on which an individual member of a specified group becomes eligible to apply for insurance under an (group Life or Health) insurance plan.

Eligibility Period: A specified length of time, such as one month, following the eligibility date during which an individual member of a particular group will remain eligible to apply for insurance under a group life or health insurance policy without evidence of insurability.

Eligibility Requirements: For retirement plans, (1) The conditions which an employee must satisfy to participate in a retirement plan, for instance completion of 1 to 3 years of service with the employer, the attainment of a specified age, such as 25, or (2) Conditions which an employee must satisfy to obtain a retirement benefit, such as the completion of 15 years of service and the attainment of age 65.

Eligible Employees: Those members of a group who have met the eligibility requirements under a group life or health insurance plan.

Elimination Period: A period of time between the period of disability and the start of disability income insurance benefits, during which no benefits are payable. The elimination period may be as short as a few days or as long as one year or more. (See Waiting Period.)

Embargo: A government order prohibiting the entry or departure of commercial vessels or goods at its ports. The refusal by a carrier, for a limited period, to accept for transport over any route or segment thereof, and to or from any area or point, of a connecting carrier, any commodity, type of class of cargo duly tendered.

Embezzlement: Fraudulent use or taking of another's property or money which has been entrusted to one's care.

Emergency Medical Service: *Abbreviation*: EMS—Medical procedures in case of emergencies on board of vessels.

Employee Benefit Plan Insurance: Coverage designed to protect the employer against claims by employees or former employees resulting from negligent acts or omissions in the administration of the insured's employee benefits programmes. Coverage is intended to extend to the administration of these plans, including counselling employees, interpreting employee benefits programmes, handling records, enrolling, terminating or cancelling employees in specified plans on a timely basis, etc.

Employee Benefit Programmes: Programmes designed to benefit employees, arranged by the employer, which are not paid for primarily or directly by the employee, including for instance group life insurance and group Accident and/ or health insurance; profit sharing plans; employee stock subscription plans; workers' compensation; unemployment insurance; social security benefits; disability benefits, etc.

Employee Dishonesty Coverage Form: Commercial crime insurance form drafted by the insurance services office that covers the loss of money, securities, and other covered property because of any dishonest act of a covered employee or employees.

Employee Dishonesty Insurance: Coverage designed to protect an employer from financial loss due to the fraudulent activities of one or more employees. The coverage includes protection for loss of money, securities, and other property of the insured. Some scheduled policies are still available, but the majority are written on a blanket basis. This provides coverage for all employees, subject to the policy definitions. The limit of liability is "per loss" and is applied on an occurrence basis. All acts involving the same employee or group of employees is considered one occurrence.

Employee Retirement Income Security Act (ERISA): Legislation passed in 1974 applying to most private pension and welfare plans that requires certain minimum standards to protect participating employees.

Employment Practices Liability Insurance: Coverage designed to protect the corporation, directors and officers and employees for claims resulting from wrongful termination, discrimination, sexual harassment, wrongful discipline and failure to employ or promote.

Employment Stock Ownership Plan (ESOP): A defined contribution pension plan which is designed to invest primarily in securities of the employer, such as common stock and debentures.

EMS: See Emergency Medical Service.

Endorsement: The transfer of the right to obtain delivery of the goods of the carrier by means of the consignee's signature on the reverse side of a bill of lading. If the name of the new consignee (transferee) is not stated, the endorsement is an open one which means that every holder of the document is entitled to obtain delivery of the goods.

Endorsements: An additional piece of paper, not a part of the original contract, which cites certain terms and which, when attached to the original contract, becomes a legal part of that contract. See Rider.

Endowment: Life insurance payable to the policy-holder if living, on the maturity date stated in the policy, or to a beneficiary if the insured dies prior to that date.

English Jurisdiction Clause: A condition, printed in the MAR form of policy, whereby Underwriters agree to recognise judgements only from courts convened within English jurisdiction. Subscribing Underwriters may agree to replace this clause with a foreign jurisdiction clause. Please note this is not applicable to business emanating from the United States of America (USA) which is subject to the Service of Suit Clause appearing in the Standard Conditions.

English Law and Practice Clause: This clause appears in Institute clauses published for use with the MAR form of policy. It applies where a foreign jurisdiction clause attaches to the policy and requires that the foreign court shall base its decisions on English law and practice.

Enquiry: Document issued by a party interested in the purchase of goods specified therein and indicating particular, desirable conditions regarding delivery terms, etc., addressed to a prospective supplier with a view to obtaining an offer.

Enrolled Actuary: A person who performs actuarial service for a plan and who is enrolled with the Federal Joint Board for the Enrollment of Actuaries.

Enrollment Card: A document signed by an employee as notice of his/her desire to participate in the benefits of a group insurance plan.

Enterprise: An organization created to provide products and/or services to customers.

Enterprise Resource Planning (ERP): Complex applications used by large enterprises to manage inventory and integrate business processes across multiple divisions and organizational boundaries, frequently the application backbone in many large enterprises.

Entire Contract Clause: Provision in life insurance policies stating that the policy and attached application constitute the entire contract between the parties.

Entity Purchase Agreement: The terms for the business to buy back a deceased's share of the business's ownership.

Entry: It can be defined as: (*a*) The admittance of goods across the barrier and into Australia. (*b*) An ACS/AQIS electronic document which details information relating to consignments of goods imported into Australia. Entries are generated using ICS.

Environmental Damage: The injurious presence in or on land, the atmosphere, or any water course or body of water of solid, liquid, gaseous, or thermal contaminants, irritants, or pollutants.

Environmental Impairment Liability Insurance: Coverage designed to cover losses and liabilities arising from damage to property by pollution.

Equipment: Material resources necessary to facilitate the transport and handling of cargo. Transport equipment does under the given circumstances not have the ability to move by its own propulsion (e.g., sea container, trailer, unit load device, pallet).

Equipment Damage Report: *Abbreviation*: EDR—Written statement concerning damage to equipment, based on a physical inspection.

Equipment Interchange Receipt: *Abbreviation*: EIR—Physical inspection and transfer receipt.

Equities: Investments in the form of ownership of property, usually common stocks, as distinguished from fixed income bearing securities, such as bonds or mortgages.

Equity in the Unearned Premium Reserve: Amount by which an unearned premium reserve is overstated because it is established on the basis of gross premium rather than net premium.

Erasures and Alterations: Any changes made to a document after the original/first signature has been applied to that document.

ERISA: See Employee Retirement Income Security Act.

Errors and Omissions Insurance: Coverage designed to protect an insured against loss due to a claim of some negligent act, error, or omission by the insured.

Establishment: Perpetuation of a pest or disease for the foreseeable future, after its entry into Australia.

Likelihood of Establishment—The likelihood that a viable exotic pest or disease infects a susceptible host in Australia.

Estate: The assets and liabilities of a person left at death.

Estate Planning: The process of developing a plan to transfer property from one generation to the next, or within a generation (e.g., from husband to wife).

Estimated Delivery Date: The date and time a package or shipment is expected to be delivered to a given destination. *Acronym*: EDD.

Estimated Time of Arrival: *Abbreviation*: ETA—The expected date and time of arrival in a certain port. *Synonym*: Expected time of arrival.

Estimated Time of Departure: *Abbreviation*: ETD—The expected date and time when a certain port is left. *Synonym*: Expected time of departure.

Estoppel: Legal doctrine that prevents a person from denying the truth of a previous representation of fact, especially when such representation has been relied on by the one to whom the statement was made.

Ethylene Oxide (ETO): This is a gas that may be used to destroy pests in some classes of products.

European Article Numbering Association: *Abbreviation*: EAN—An international body responsible for administering the European Article Numbering system. It has affiliates in many countries such as: CCG in West Germany, DCC in Japan, ANA in the United Kingdom. *Note*: The North American body responsible for the Uniform Product Code (UPC) coding is the Uniform Code Council. (UPC is considered a subset of EAN).

European Pallet Pool: Pool for the exchange of standard size pallets (the so-called Europallets) in European cargo traffic, formed in 1961 by a number of European rail administrators.

European Zone Charge: *Abbreviation*: EZC—A charge for inland haulage transport in case of carrier haulage in Europe.

Even Keel: Said of a vessel which is balanced in such a way that the draft forward and aft is the same as the draft in the midship of the vessel on both sides.

Event: An occurrence.

Evidence of Insurability: Any statement of proof of a person's physical condition and/or other factual information affecting his/her acceptance for insurance.

Ex Works (...named place): "Ex works" means that the seller fulfils his obligation to deliver when he has made the goods available at his premises (i.e. works, factory, warehouse, etc.) to the buyer. In particular, he is not responsible for loading the goods on the vehicle provided by the buyer or for clearing the goods for export, unless otherwise agreed. The buyer bears all costs and risks involved in taking the goods from the seller's premises to the desired destination. This term thus represents the minimum obligation for the seller. This term should not be used when the buyer cannot carry out directly or indirectly the export formalities. In such circumstances, the FCA term should be used.

Examine: Includes: (*a*) in relation to an animal—carry out tests on, take samples from, or carry out a veterinary procedure on, the animal; (*b*) in relation to a plant—carry out tests on, take samples from, establish, cultivate, or undertake procedures for the diagnosis of a disease of, the plant; and (*c*) in relation to any other goods—carry out tests on, or take samples from, the goods; and (*d*) in relation to a vessel, installation or premises —carry out tests on, or take samples from, the vessel, installation or premises.

Excess: Going over the prescribed amount or degree e.g., excess luggage is luggage of which the weight is over the weight for free carriage.

Excess and Surplus Insurance: (1) Coverage designed to protect against losses above a certain amount, with losses below that amount usually covered by a regular policy. (2) Insurance for a risk for which coverage is unavailable in the normal market. Such risks are frequently unusual, e.g., damage to a musician's hands or the multiple perils of a convention.

Excess Stock: That portion of stock on hand which is over and above the desired stock level.

Exchange Rate: The rate at which one currency can be exchanged for another, usually expressed as the value of the one in terms of the other.

Exchanges: Two-sided marketplaces where buyers and suppliers negotiate prices, usually with a bid and ask system, and where prices move both up and down. Work best with easily definable products without complicated attributes—commodities, perishable items such as food, or intangibles such as electric power. Produce fluctuating, sometimes volatile prices. Particularly appropriate if a true market price is difficult to discover. Also work where brokers make high margins by buying low and selling high to purchasers who don't know the original sellers. Examples: Altra (energy), Paper Exchange (paper products), GoFish.com (frozen fish), Arbinet (telecommunications bandwidth). *Synonyms*: digital exchange, online exchange, dynamic exchange, dynamic trading exchange.

Exclusion or Exception: Specified conditions or circumstances, listed in the policy, for which the policy will not provide benefits.

Exclusion Ratio: The portion of an annuity payment, considered by tax law to be a return of your initial investment, that is not subject to income tax when received.

Exclusions: Specific conditions or circumstances listed in the policy for which the policy will not provide benefit payments.

Exclusive Agent: An agent who is employed by one and only one insurance company and who solicits business exclusively for that company.

Exclusive Provider Organization (EPO): People who belong to an EPO must receive their care from affiliated providers; services rendered by unaffiliated providers are not reimbursed.

Exclusive Remedy Doctrine: Doctrine in Workers Compensation Insurance which states that workers compensation benefits should be the exclusive or sole source of recovery for workers who have a job-related accident or disease. The doctrine has been eroded by legal decisions.

Execution: The actual act of carrying out a task.

Exempt Carrier: Company which transports commodities exempted from Interstate Commerce Commission (ICC) economic regulation.

Exemption Clause: A clause in a contract, which relieves the carrier's responsibility for certain events. *Synonym*: Exceptions Clause.

Expected: Likely to occur or appear.

Expediting: The 'rushing' or 'chasing' of production or purchase orders which are needed in less than the normal lead time.

Expendable Pallet: See disposable pallet. *Synonym*: One Way Pallet.

Expense Loading: See Loading.

Expense Ratio: The ratio of a company's operating expenses including acquisition costs to premiums written or earned.

Expenses: Costs paid out in connection with booking of cargo and arranging transport (e.g., commission).

Experience: A term used to describe the relationship, usually expressed as a percent or ratio, of premium to claims for a plan, coverage, or benefits for a stated time period.

Experience Modification Factor: Used in workers compensation rating to reflect the degree to which a particular employer has experience that is better or worse than expected for that industry. Weighted by employer's credibility factor.

Experience Rating: The process of determining the premium rate for a group risk, wholly or partially on the basis of that group's experience.

Experience Refund: A provision in most group policies for the return of premium to the policyholder because of lower than anticipated claims.

Explosion: A violent expansion, with force and noise, generally due to rapid chemical change; term covered under various property/casualty Insurance policies.

Exponential Market: Where one party can be both a buyer and seller.Both buyers and sellers benefit when a new participant joins because fewer participants are needed to create higher volumes. Grow faster than linear markets. Require well-defined or commoditized products to make purchase and sale easy. Transaction costs must be low to keep the market liquid. *Examples*: Altra (energy), e-Steel, MetalSite. *Synonym*: circular market. Antonym: linear market.

Export: The process of carrying or sending goods to another country or countries, especially for purposes of use or sale in the country of destination. The sale of products to clients abroad.

Export Declaration: A document required by the U.S. Treasury Department and completed by a shipper indicating the contents, value, and destination of an export shipment.

Exporter: The party responsible for the export of goods.

Export Licence: Document granting permission to export as detailed within a specified time.

Export Packer: Company, packing goods for export.

Exposure Unit: Unit of measurement used in insurance pricing.

Extended Coverage Insurance: Protection for the insured against property damage caused by windstorm, hail, smoke, explosion, riot, riot attending a strike, civil commotion, vehicle and aircraft. This is provided in conjunction with the Fire Insurance policy and the various package policies.

Extended Nonowned Coverage: Endorsement that can be added to an automobile liability insurance policy that covers the insured while driving any non-owned automobile on a regular basis.

Extended Reporting Period: An additional period of time after policy expiration during which valid claims will be paid under a claims-made policy of liability insurance.

Extended Reporting Period Endorsement: Added to a claims-made policy of liability insurance to provide an additional period of time during which valid claims will be paid.

Extended Term Insurance: A form of insurance available as a non-forfeiture option. It provides the original amount of insurance for a limited period of time.

Extended Unemployment Insurance Benefits: Additional cash benefits paid by federal-state unemployment insurance programmes to workers who are involuntarily unemployed and who have exhausted their regular weekly cash benefits during periods of high unemployment.

Extra Expense Insurance: Type of business income insurance that covers the extra expenses incurred to continue operations after a loss has occurred.

Extract: Summary or copy of something written, e.g. used in connection with the log book.

EXW: See Ex Works (...named place).

EZC: See European Zone Charge.

Fabrication: A term used to distinguish manufacturing operations for components as opposed to assembly operations.

FAC: Incoterm- Free carrier.

Face Amount: The amount stated on the face of the policy that will be paid in case of death or at the maturity of the policy. It does not include additional amounts payable under accidental death or other special provisions, or acquired through the application of policy dividends.

Facility: (1) A pooling mechanism for insureds not able to obtain insurance in the voluntary market. Insurers write and issue policies but cede premium and losses on those policies to a central pool in which all insurers share. (2) Quarantine Approved Premises criteria uses the term 'facility' or 'containment facility' when referring to Quarantine Approved Premises.

Facility of Payment: A contractual provision that allows the insurer, under stated conditions, to pay insurance benefits of up to $1,000 to a person or persons other than the insured, the designated beneficiary, or the insured's estate.

Factory Delivery: The delivery of goods by a factory whereby the goods are put at the disposal of another (internal) party such as a commercial department.

Factory Mutual: Mutual insurance company that aims to insure only properties that meet high underwriting standards. Emphasizes loss prevention.

Facultative Reinsurance: A type of reinsurance in which the reinsurer can accept or reject any risk presented by an insurance company seeking reinsurance.

Failure: Goods or vessels that do not meet the AQIS inspection, regulation or documentation requirements.

FAIR Plan: A facility, operating under a government-insurance industry cooperative programme, to make fire insurance and other forms of property insurance readily available to persons or in locations that have difficulty obtaining such coverage.

Fair Rental Value: Amount payable to an insured homeowner for loss of rental income due to damage that makes an insured premises uninhabitable.

Fairway: A navigable channel for vessels, often the regular or prescribed track a vessel will follow in order to avoid dangerous circumstances.

FAK: See Freight All Kinds.

FAL: Facilitation Committee of the IMO.

Family Expense Policy: A policy which insures both the policy-holder and his/her immediate dependents (usually spouse and children).

Family Income Policy: Special life insurance policy combining decreasing term and whole life insurance that pays a reduced monthly income (e.g., $10 for each $1000 of life insurance) if the insured dies within the specified period. The monthly income is paid to the end of the period, at which time the face amount of insurance is paid.

Family Policy: A life insurance policy providing insurance on all or several family members in one contract, generally whole life insurance on the principal breadwinner and small amounts of Term Insurance on the other spouse and children, including those born after the policy is issued.

Family Purpose Doctrine: Concept that imputes negligence committed by immediate family members while operating a family car to the owner of the car.

Fantainer: Identical to a GP but is fitted with an electric extraction fan for carriage of cargoes prone to condensation. 20′ only.

Farm Mutual: Local mutual insurance company that insures farm property in a limited geographical area primarily through assessable policies.

Farmowners-Ranchowners Policy: A Package Policy for a farm or a ranch, providing Property and liability coverages against personal and business losses.

FAS: See Free Alongside Ship (...named port of shipment).

Fashion Transport: Transport of clothing and/or garments including shoes, belts and handbags in dedicated means of transport.

FCA: See Free Carrier (...named place).

FCC: See Fully Cellular Containership.

FCL: See Full Container Load.

FCL/X: Full Container Load containing multiple bills of lading (see FCL and FCX).

FCX: An Australian Customs Service term referring to Full Container Loads with multiple Bills of Lading destined for the one unpack address. For quarantine purposes this is the same as FCL.

Federal Crime Insurance: Insurance against burglary, larceny, and robbery losses offered by the federal government where the Federal Insurance Administration has determined that an insurance availability problem exists.

Federal Crop Insurance: Comprehensive coverage at rates subsidized by the federal government for unavoidable crop losses, including those that result from hail, wind, excessive rain, drought, freezes, plant disease, snow, floods and earthquake.

Federal Flood Insurance: Insurance sold by private insurers with rates subsidized by the federal government to persons who reside in flood zones and whose community joins the programme and agrees to establish and enforce flood control and land-use measures.

Federal-Servant Doctrine: Common law defense blocking an injured employee from collecting Workers Compensation benefits if he or she sustained an injury caused in any way by the negligence of a fellow worker.

Federal Surety Bond: Type of Surety Bond required by federal agencies that regulates the actions of business firms. It guarantees that the bonded party will comply with federal standards, pay all taxes or duties accrued, or pay any penalty if the bondholder fails to pay.

Feed Back: The flow of information back into the control system so that actual performance can be compared with planned performance.

Feeder: A vessel normally used for local or coastal transport (for carriage of cargo and/or containers) to and from ports not scheduled to be called by the main (ocean) vessel, directly connecting these ports to the main (ocean) vessel.

Fender: An appliance made of rubber, timber and/or rope or other materials normally attached to a dock or quay used to prevent damage to the hull of a vessel especially during mooring and un-mooring operations.

FEU: See Forty Foot Equivalent Unit.

Fidelity Bond: Bond designed to protect an employer against dishonest or fraudulent acts of employees, such as embezzlement, fraud or theft of money.

Fiduciary: A person who holds something in trust for another.

Fiduciary Liability Insurance: Coverage designed to protect against loss for any alleged wrongful act by an insured or by any other person for whom the insured is legally responsible. It also covers the defense costs in connection with a covered claim. The policy is written on a claims made form. A wrongful act includes any violation of the responsibilities, obligations, or duties imposed on fiduciaries by the Employee Retirement Income Security Act (ERISA), as well as acts, errors, or omissions in the performance of the duties of the plan administrator. Also known as *Pension Trust Liability*.

FIFO: See First In First Out.

Fifth Wheel: Circular or wheel-shaped bearing mechanism, secured on the rear of the chassis of a truck-tractorm that engages the semi-trailer king pin with a spring lock device and supports the weight of the front end of the semi-trailer.

FILO: See Free In Liner Out.

Final Average Formula: A pension plan formula that bases retirement benefits on earnings during the final years (e.g., 3 years or 5 years) of employment.

Financial Responsibility Law: A state law which may require motorists to furnish evidence, either before or after involvement in an auto accident (depending on the individual state's law), of ability to pay for damages up to certain minimum dollar limits. These requirements commonly are met by carrying auto liability insurance with specified minimum limits or more.

FIO: See Free In and Out.

Fire: A combustion accompanied by a flame or glow, which escapes its normal confines to cause damage.

Fire Insurance: Coverage designed to protect against losses caused by fire and lightning, plus resultant damage caused by smoke and water.

Fire Legal Liability: Liability of a firm or person for fire or explosion damage caused by negligence of and damage to property of others. Coverage is needed for leased or rented property for which the insured could be held legally liable for damage to the property.

First In First Out: *Abbreviation*: FIFO—The method whereby the goods which have been longest in stock (first in) are used, delivered (sold) and/or consumed first (first out).

First Party Claim: A demand for payment under an insurance policy made by a policy-holder reporting an insured event directly to his company.

First Party Coverage: An insurance coverage under which the policy-holder collects for losses from the Insured's own insurer rather than from the insurer of the person who caused an accident.

Fixed Amount Option: Life insurance settlement option in which the policy proceeds are paid out in fixed amounts.

Fixed Annuity: Annuity whose periodic payment is a guaranteed fixed amount.

Fixed Crane: A crane of which the principal structure is mounted on permanent or semi-permanent foundations.

Fixed Height Load-carrying Truck: Truck carrying its load on a non-elevating platform. *Synonym*: Fixed platform truck.

Fixed Period Option: Life insurance settlement option in which the policy proceeds are paid out in fixed amounts.

Fixed Platform Truck: See Fixed Height Load-carrying Truck.

Flag: An indication of the country in which a means of transport is registered through a reference to the ensign of this country.

Flammable: Capable to be set on fire under given circumstances. (Amendment 25 IMO DGS).

Flash Point: The lowest temperature at which a good produces enough vapour to form a flammable mixture with air.

Flat: See Flat Rack.

Flat Bed Trailer: A wheeled trailer or a semi-trailer with a flat cargo carrying surface or deck and without any superstructure.

Flat Pack: Garments packed in cardboard boxes.

Flat Rack: A flat bed with fixed ends suitable for the carriage of cargo of excessive width and plated for carriage of heavy loads. 20′ and 40′.

Flat Schedule: A type of schedule in Group Insurance under which everyone is insured for the same benefits regardless of salary, position, or other circumstances.

Fleet : Any group of means of transport acting together or under one control.

Flexibility: The extent to which and the rate at which adjustments to changed circumstances are possible.

Flexible Computer Integrated Manufacturing: FCIM is the integration of equipment, software, communication, human resources, and business practices within an enterprise to rapidly manufacture, repair, and deliver items on demand with continuous improvements in the processes. The FCIM initiative is a Joint Service and Agency effort to establish and implement the procedures and processes needed. *Acronym*: FCIM.

Flexible Premium Policy or Annuity: A life accident policy or Annuity under which the policyholder or contract holder may vary the amounts or timing of premium payments.

Flexible Premium Variable Life Insurance: A life insurance policy that combines the premium flexibility feature of Universal Life Insurance with the equity-based benefit feature of Variable Life Insurance.

Flexitanks: A large polythene liner which can be fitted inside a 20'GP for the transportation of non-hazardous liquids.

Flex-Rating Law: Type of rating law in which prior approval of the rates is required only if the rates exceed a certain percentage above and below the rates previously filed.

Flight Member: A licensed crew member charged with duties essential to the operation of an aircraft during flight time.

Flight Number: A combination of two letters, indicating the airline, and three or four digits indicating the number of the voyage. *Synonym*: Line Number.

Floaters: Insurance policies designed to cover property that can be moved from one location to another for both transportation perils and perils affecting property at a fixed location.

Floating: Freely suspending in water of an object.

Floating Crane: A crane mounted on a barge or pontoon, which can be towed or is self propelled.

Floating Dock: A floating structure that can be partially submerged to enable vessels to enter and to leave and which can be raised for use as a dry dock.

Floating Stock: See Pipeline Inventory.

Flood Insurance: Coverage against loss resulting from the flood peril, widely available at low cost under a programme developed by the private industry and the federal government.

Flow Chart: A diagram, using symbols and depicting the sequence of events that should take place in a complex set of tasks.

Flow Control: A term often used to describe a specific production control system.

Flow Line: The direction of flow in which e.g., pallets have been positioned and stowed.

Flow of Materials: The flow of materials and components which goes to and through the factory for the production process.

FMC: Federal Maritime Commission (Control of shipping acts USA).

Fo'c's'le: See Forecastle.

FOB: See Free On Board (...named port of shipment).

Force Majeure: Circumstance which is beyond the control of one of the parties to a contract and which may, according to the terms and conditions, relieve that party of liability for failing to execute the contract. *Synonym*: Act of God.

Fore and Aft Stowage: Stowage from the bow to the stern (lengthwise), as opposed to stowage athwartships.

Forecast: An estimation or calculation in advance; a prediction. The amount of cargo expected to be booked for a certain sailing of a vessel. The number of containers expected to be used in a certain area, for steering purposes.

Forecastle: *Abbreviation*: Fo'c's'le. Forward part of a vessel where stores, ropes and anchor chains are located.

Foreign Insurer: An insurer is a foreign company in any state other than the one in which it is incorporated.

Forfeitures: Amounts contributed on behalf of terminated, non-vested participants. In a pension plan, such amounts must be applied to reducing future employer contributions. In a profit-sharing plan, such amounts may be allocated to the accounts of remaining participants.

Forgery or Alteration Coverage Form: Commercial Crime Insurance form by the Insurance Services Office that covers loss resulting from the forgery or alteration of checks, drafts, bills of exchange, promissory notes, and similar instruments.

Forgery or Alteration Insurance: Coverage designed to protect from loss sustained through forgery or alteration of outgoing negotiable instruments made or drawn by or on the accounts of the insured, or made or drawn by one acting as the insured's agent. This includes loss caused by (1) checks or drafts made or drawn in the insured's name, payable to a fictitious entity, (2) checks or drafts, including payroll checks, executed through forged endorsements, and (3) alteration of the amount of a check or draft.

Fork Lift Pockets: See Fork Pockets.

Fork Lift Truck: A three or four wheeled mechanical truck with forks at the front designed for lifting, carrying and stowing cargo.

Fork Pockets: Openings or recesses in a side of a container for the entry of the forks of a fork lift truck. *Synonym*: Fork Lift Pockets.

Formula of Camp: A mathematical formula on behalf of inventory management for calculating the optimum order quantity.

Fortuitous Loss: Unforeseen and unexpected loss that occurs as a result of chance.

Forty Foot Equivalent Unit: *Abbreviation*: FEU—Unit of measurement equivalent to one forty feet shipping container.

Forward: At, near or towards the bow or front of a vessel or an aircraft.

Forwarder: The party arranging the carriage of goods including connected services and/or associated formalities on behalf of a shipper or consignee. *Synonym*: Freight Forwarder.

Forwarding Instruction: Document issued to a freight forwarder, giving instructions to the forwarder for the forwarding of goods described therein.

Four Way Pallet: A pallet of which the frame permits the entry of forks of e.g., a fork lift truck at all four sides.

FPA: Free of Particular Average.

Fragile: Easily breakable. Term denoting that goods should be handled with care.

Fragmentation: Market condition when there is no dominant group of buyers or suppliers, but where many buyers are chasing many suppliers, often inefficiently.

Franchise: A provision in freight insurance conditions which exempts the insurer from particular average losses, in any one accident, under 3 per cent. The provision is waived if the loss is caused by fire, or by the ship stranding, sinking or being in collision.

Franchise Deductible: Deductible commonly found in Marine Insurance contracts in which the insurer has no liability if the loss is under a certain amount, but once this amount is exceeded, the entire loss is paid in full.

Franchise Insurance: Insurance under individual contracts issued to the employees of a common employer or the members of an association under an arrangement by which the employer or association agrees to collect the premiums and remit them to the insurer.

Fraternal Insurance: A cooperative type of insurance provided by social organizations for their members.

Fraternal Life Insurance: Life Insurance provided by fraternal orders or societies to their members.

Fraternal Society: A social organization that provides insurance for its members.

Free Airport: See Free Trade Zone.

Free Alongside Ship (...named port of shipment): *Abbreviation*: FAS.

Free Carrier (...named place): "Free Carrier" means that the seller fulfils his obligation to deliver when he has handed over the goods, cleared for export, into the charge of the carrier named by the buyer at the named place or point. If no precise point is indicated by the buyer, the seller may choose within the place or range stipulated where the carrier shall take the goods into his charge. When, according to commercial practice, the seller's assistance is required in making the contract with the carrier (such as in rail or air transport) the seller may act at the buyer's risk and expense. This term may be used for any mode of transport, including multimodal transport. "Carrier" means any person who, in a contract of carriage, undertakes to perform or to procure the performance of carriage by rail, road, sea, air, inland waterway or by a combination of such modes. If the buyer instructs the seller to deliver the cargo to a person, e.g., a freight forwarder who is not a "carrier", the seller is deemed to have fulfilled his obligation to deliver the goods when they are in the custody of that person.

Free Circulation, Libre Circulation: The movement of goods within the European Community without the need to pay any duty.

Free House Unclear: Delivered at a certain destination without payment of certain duties or incurred costs.

Free In and Out: *Abbreviation*: FIO—Transport condition denoting that the freight rate excludes the costs of loading and discharging and, if appropriate, stowage and lashing.

Free In Liner Out: *Abbreviation*: FILO—Transport condition denoting that the freight rate is inclusive of the sea carriage and the cost of discharging, the latter as per the custom of the port. It excludes the cost of loading and, if appropriate, stowage and lashing.

Free Lift: The maximum elevation of the forks of a fork lift truck.

Free On Board (...named port of shipment): "Free on Board" means that the seller fulfils his obligation to deliver when the goods have passed over the ship's rail at the named port of shipment. This means that the buyer has to bear all costs and risks of loss of or damage to the goods from that point. The FOB term requires the seller to clear the goods for export. This term can only be used for sea or inland waterway transport. When the ship's rail serves no practical purpose, such as in the case of roll-on/roll-off transport, the FCA term is more appropriate to use.

Free Port: An international port or an area within an international port at which, crew, passengers, baggage, cargo, mail and stores may be disembarked or unloaded, may remain and may be transhipped, without being subjected to any customs charges or duties. (Examination is possible for instance to meet security or narcotics control requirements.) *Source*: IMO.

Free Pratique: Permission granted by local medical authorities, denoting that the vessel has a clean Bill of Health so that people may embark and disembark.

Free Trade Zone: *Abbreviation*: FTZ—A part of the territory of a state where any goods introduced are generally regarded, in-so-far as import duties and taxes are concerned, as being exempted (Kyoto Convention). *Synonym*: Free Port, Free Airport.

Freeboard of a Vessel: Vertical distance from the main deck to the surface of the water measured at the middle of the vessel's length.

Freight: (1) The amount of money due for the carriage of goods and payable either in advance or upon delivery. (2) The remuneration earned by a shipowner or manager for the carriage of goods; including the profit derived from carrying his own goods.

Freight All Kinds: *Abbreviation*: FAK— Single freight which is charged irrespective of the commodity.

Freight Collect: Freight and charges be paid by the consignee.

Freight Container: See Container.

Freight Costs: Costs incurred by the merchant in moving goods, by whatever means, from one place to another under the terms of the contract of carriage. In addition to transport costs this may include such elements as packing, documentation, loading, unloading and transport insurance.

Freighter: A vessel or an aircraft used for the carriage of cargo.

Freight Forwarder: See Forwarder.

Freight Invoice: An itemized list of goods shipped and services rendered stating fees and charges.

Freight Manifest: A (cargo) manifest including all freight particulars.

Freight Prepaid: Freight and charges to be paid by the consignor.

Freight Ton: A unit for freighting cargo according to weight and/or cubic measurement. *Synonyms*: Revenue ton, Bill of Lading ton.

Fronting Company: A domestic insurance company that provides claims or administrative services to a captive.

FTL: Full Truck Load, an indication for a truck transporting cargo directly from supplier to receiver.

FTZ: See Free Trade Zone.

Full Container Load (FCL): (1) Refers to a full container consigned from one sender to one receiver. (2) A container stuffed or stripped under risk and for account of the shipper and/or the consignee. A general reference for identifying container loads of cargo loaded and/or discharged at merchants' premises.

Full Trailer: A truck trailer constructed in such way that its own weight and that of the cargo rest upon its own wheels, instead of being supported by e.g., a tractor.

Fully Cellular Containership: *Abbreviation*: FCC—A vessel specially designed to carry containers, with cell-guides under deck and necessary fittings and equipment on deck.

Fully Insured: Insured status of a covered person under the Old-Age, Survivors, and Disability Insurance (OASDI) programme if he or she meets certain criteria: forty quarters of coverage or one quarter of coverage for each year after 1950 (or after age twenty-one, if later) upto the year of death, disability or attainment of age sixty-two.

Fumigant: A chemical that at a particular temperature and pressure can exist in a gaseous state in sufficient concentration and for sufficient time to be lethal to insects or other pests.

Fumigation: (1) Application of a fumigant to a fumigation enclosure to eradicate pests. (2) Treating of cargoes with gases to exterminate unwanted life forms.

Fumigation Area: The portion of a QAP where goods are fumigated.

Fumigation Certificate: Documentation certifying that a fumigation treatment has been undertaken in compliance with AQIS requirements.

Funded Retirement Plan: A plan under which funds are set aside in advance to provide expected benefits.

Funding Agency: A financial institution or individual that provides for the accumulation or administration of the pension contributions that will be used to pay pension benefits.

Funding Instrument: An insurance contract or trust agreement that states the terms under which the funding agency will accumulate, administer and disburse pension funds.

Future Increase Option: A provision found in some policies that allows the insured to purchase additional Disability Income Insurance at specified future dates regardless of the insured's physical condition.

GAAP: See Generally Accepted Accounting Principles.

G.A. in Full: An agreement in a cargo insurance whereby underwriters do not reduce a claim for general average contribution in event of under insurance.

Gantry Crane: A crane or hoisting machine mounted on a frame or structure spanning an intervening space, which often travels on rails.

Gas Impervious Material: Includes plastic wrapping or laminated plastic films, lacquers or painted surfaces, aluminium foil, tarred or waxed paper.

Gateway: A point at which cargo is interchanged between carriers or modes of transport. A means of access, an entry.

GATT: See General Agreement on Tariffs and Trade.

GCR: See General Cargo Rate and General Commodity Rate.

General Agency System: Type of Life Insurance marketing system in which the General Agent is an independent businessperson who represents only one insurer, is in charge of a territory, and is responsible for hiring, training, and motivating new agents.

General Agreement on Tariffs and Trade: *Abbreviation*: GATT—Major international agreement on trade and tariffs between many nations all over the world.

General Average: In Ocean Marine Insurance, a loss incurred for the common good that is shared by all parties to the venture.

General Average Act (York-Antwerp Rules): There is a general average act when, and only when any extraordinary sacrifice or expenditure is intentionally and reasonably made or incurred for the common safety for the purpose of preserving from peril the property involved in a common maritime adventure.

General Average Contribution: The proportion paid or payable by a saved interest involved in a general average act.

General Average Deposit: Paid by a consignee to obtain release of the cargo from the carrier following a general average act. This may be replaced by an Underwriter's guarantee.

General Average Guarantee: An undertaking by Underwriters to pay the contribution due from a cargo assured on completion of the general average adjustment.

General Average Statement: This shows in detail all general average costs and expenses and the contribution of each interest in the general average in proportion to its value.

General Cargo: Cargo, consisting of goods, unpacked or packed, for example in cartons, crates, bags or bales, often palletized. General cargo can be shipped either in breakbulk or containerized. Any consignment other than a consignment containing valuable cargo and charged for transport at general cargo rates (aircargo).

General Cargo Rate: Abbreviation: GCR. Synonym: General Commodity Rate. The rate for the carriage of cargo other than a class rate or specific commodity rate.

General Commodity Rate: See General Cargo Rate.

General Damages: Damages awarded to an injured person for intangible loss which cannot be measured directly by dollars. Frequently called pain and suffering. General damages are distinguished from special damages which are awarded for actual economic loss, such as medical costs, loss of income, etc.

General Exclusions Clause: A clause in the Institute Cargo Clauses 1982, which specifies risks that are excluded, irrespective of the risks covered elsewhere in the wording.

General Liability Insurance: Coverage that pertains, for the most part, to claims arising out of the Insured's liability for injuries or damage caused by ownership of property, manufacturing operations, contracting operations, sale or distribution of products, and the operation of machinery, as well as professional services.

General Partner Liability Insurance: Coverage designed to protect against claims of loss against a general partner, for failure to properly exercise his fiduciary duty. Also known as General Partners' Liability and Limited Partnership Reimbursement coverage. A general partner's management and fiduciary responsibilities to a limited partnership closely parallel the director's or officer's to a corporation. Exposure occurs when general partners become the financial managers of a limited partnership. The directors and officers of corporate general partners share this type of exposure.

General Purpose Container: A container used for the carriage of general cargo without any special requirements for the transport and or the conditioning of the goods.

Generally Accepted Accounting Principles (GAAP): Principles of accounting and reporting business results developed by the American Institute of Public Accountants.

Generation Skipping Tax: A transfer tax imposed on gift or inheritance to those at least two generations younger than the person making the transfer.

Gen-set: Motor generator set as power source for e.g., thermal containers.

Germanischer Lloyd: German classification society.

Glass Insurance: Protection for loss of or damage to glass and its appurtenances.

Godown: A warehouse or cargo shed. This term is often used in the Far East.

Good Faith: A basic principle of insurance. The Assured and his broker must disclose and truly represent every material circumstance to the Underwriter before acceptance of the risk. A breach of good faith entitles the Underwriter to avoid the contract. (Proposed changes in law may affect this definition.)

Good Student Discount: Reduction of automobile premium for a young driver at least sixteen who ranks in the upper 20 per cent of his or her class, has a B or 3.0 average, or is on the Dean's List or Honour Roll. It is based on the premise that good students are better drivers.

Goods: (1) Common term indicating movable property, merchandise or wares. All materials which can be used to satisfy demands. Whole or part of the cargo received from the shipper, including any equipment supplied by the shipper. (2) Includes: (a) An animal; (b) A plant (whether moveable or not); and (c) Any other article, substance or thing (including but not limited to, any kind of moveable property; and, to remove any doubt, includes mail of any kind and ballast water.

Goods Control Certificate: Document issued by a competent body evidencing the quality of goods described therein, in accordance with national or international standards, or conforming to legislation in the importing country, or as specified in the contract.

Goods Flow: The direction and path of the movement of goods and sequence of placement of those goods in a supply chain.

Goods in Transit: The goods which have departed from the initial loading point and not yet arrived at the final unloading point. *Synonyms*: Stock in Transit, in Transit Inventory, Transportation Inventory.

Goods Item: A separate identifiable quantity of products or articles of a single type.

Goods Receipt: Document issued by a port, warehouse, shed, or terminal operator acknowledging receipt of goods specified therein on conditions stated or referred to in the document.

Gooseneck: Gooseneck shaped front end of a trailer or chassis. Recess front bottom of a container to reduce the total height of the chassis plus container.

Grace Period: A specified period after a premium payment is due, in which the policy-holder may make such payment, and during which the protection of the policy continues.

Graded Commission Scale: A commission scale providing for payment of a high first-year commission and lower renewal commissions.

Grid Number: An indication of the position of a container in a bay plan by means of a combination of page number, column and line. The page number often represents the bay number.

Gross Estate: All of the assets and liabilities owned at death.

Gross Manifest: A manifest containing freight details without any appropriate disbursements.

Gross Negligence: The intentional failure to perform a manifest duty in reckless disregard of the consequences as affecting the life or property of another.

Gross Premium: The premium paid by the policy-holder.

Gross Rate: The sum of the pure premium and a loading element.

Gross Tonnage: *Abbreviation*: GRT—The measure of the overall size of a vessel determined in accordance with the provisions of the international convention on measurement of vessels usually expressed in register ton.

Gross Weight: (1) Weight (mass) of goods including packing, but excluding the carrier's equipment expressed in whole kilograms. (2) The weight of a shipment including materials necessary for blocking etc.

Gross Weight of Container: Total weight of container including cargo (in kilograms).

Group Annuity: A pension plan providing annuities at retirement to a group of people under a master contract. It is usually issued to an employer for the benefit of employees. The individual members of the group hold certificates as evidence of their annuities.

Group Annuity Contract: A contract issued by a life insurance company that may be used as the funding instrument for benefits to be made in accordance with a pension plan. A single master contract provides that the group of persons participating in the plan will receive annuities during retirement. Individual certificates stating coverage may be issued to members of the group.

Group Contract: A contract of insurance made with an employer or other entity that covers a group of persons identified as individuals by reference to their relationship to the entity.

Group Creditor Life Insurance: Life insurance provided to debtors by a lending institution to provide for the cancellation of any outstanding debt should the borrower die. Normally Term Insurance limited to the amount of the loan.

Group Insurance: Insurance written on a number of people under a single master policy, issued to their employer or to an association with which they are affiliated.

Group Life Insurance: Life insurance usually without medical examination, on a group of people under a master policy. It is typically issued to an employer for the benefit of employees, or to members of an association, for example, a professional membership group. The individual members of the group hold certificates as evidence of their insurance.

Group Ordinary Life Insurance: Group insurance plan providing life insurance for employees. traditional whole life policy is split into decreasing insurance protection and increasing cash values.

Group Paid-up Life Insurance: Accumulating units of single premium whole life Insurance and decreasing Term Insurance, which together equal the face amount of the policy. Provided through a Group Life Insurance plan.

Group Permanent Plan: Type of pension plan in which cash value life insurance is issued on a group basis and cash values in each policy are used to pay retirement benefits when a worker retires.

Group Term Life Insurance: Most common form of group life insurance. Yearly renewable Term Insurance on employees during their working careers.

Group Universal Life Products (GULP): Universal life insurance plans sold to members of a group, such as individual employees of an employer. There are some differences between GULP plans and individual universal life plans; for instance, GULP expense charges generally are lower than those assessed against individual policies.

Groupage Agent, Groupeur (Fr): One who consolidates LCL consignments to offer to a carrier as an FCL.

Groupage Centre: A location where group-age takes place (roadcargo).

Groupage: The collection of several small consignments and the formation of one large shipment thereof (road cargo).

Guaranteed Insurability Option: See: Future Increase Option.

Guaranteed Investment Contract: An investment contract with an insurer in which the insurer guarantees both principal and interest on a pension contribution.

Guaranteed Purchase Option: Benefit that can be added to a life insurance policy permitting the insured to purchase additional amounts of life insurance at specified times in the future without requiring evidence of insurability.

Guaranteed Renewable Contract: A provision in an insurance policy that gives the insured the right to continue the policy in force by the timely payment of premiums for a substantial period of time, during which period the insurer is prohibited from making unilaterally any change in any provision of the contract, while the contract is in force, other than a change in the premium rate for classes of policy-holders.

Guaranty Fund: A fund, derived from assessments against solvent insurance companies, to absorb losses of claimants against insolvent insurance companies.

Hague Rules: International convention for the unification of certain rules, relating to Bills of Lading (1924). These Rules include the description of responsibilities of ocean carriers.

Hague-Visby Rules: Set of rules, published in 1968, amending the Hague Rules.

Half Height: Identical to the open top, but with 4'3" ends and not the standard 8'6". Suitable for the carriage of heavy cargo as the box weight is considerably less. 20' only.

Hamburg Rules: United Nations Convention on the carriage of goods by sea of 1978 adopted in 1992.

Handling Instructions: Indication how cargo is to be handled.

Handling Service: Service concerning the physical handling of cargo.

Harbour: Place of shelter for vessels. Most of the time used as an indication for the geographical location.

Hard Market: That part of the insurance sales cycle in which competitive pricing is at a minimum as companies charge the premiums necessary to meet their underwriting losses in order to avoid insolvency and boost capacity; usually associated with a sharp decline in capacity.

Harmonized System: *Abbreviation*: HS.—A numeric multi-purpose system, developed by the Customs Cooperation Council, for the classification of goods with its six digits it covers about 5000 descriptions of the products or groups of products most commonly produced and traded. It is designed for customs services, but can also be used for statistics, transport purposes, export, import and manufacturing.

Hatch Cover: Watertight means of closing the hatchway of a vessel.

Hatch Way: Opening in the deck of a vessel through which cargo is loaded into, or discharged from the hold and which is closed by means of a hatch cover.

Haulage: The inland carriage of cargo or containers between named locations/points. *Synonym*: Cartage.

Haulier: Road carrier. H/C-High Cube Identical to the GP, but with 9′6″ sides and not the standard 8′6″. 40′ only.

Hazard: (1) A pest or disease threat. (2) Condition that creates or increases the chance of loss.

Health Insurance: Coverage designed to protect against financial losses resulting from sickness or accidental bodily injury. Health insurance coverages include accident insurance, disability income insurance, medical expense insurance, and accidental death and dismemberment insurance.

Health Maintenance Organization (HMO): An organization that provides a wide range of comprehensive health care services for a specified group at a fixed periodic payment. The HMO can be contracted with and sponsored by the Government, medical schools, hospitals, employers, labour unions, consumer groups, insurance companies and hospital-medical plans.

Heated Container: Thermal container served by a heat producing appliance.

Heavy Lift: Single commodity exceeding the capacity of normal loading equipment and requiring special equipment and rigging methods for handling.

Heavy Lift Vessel: A vessel specially designed and equipped for the carriage of heavy cargo.

Hedging: Buying or selling earlier and more than really needed in order to protect the company against price increases or shortages of commodities or components to realize profits when prices fluctuate.

Held Covered: A provisional acceptance of risk, subject to confirmation at a later date that the agreed cover is needed. Where applicable to an existing insurance, cover is conditional, in practice, on prompt advice to the Underwriter as soon as the Assured is aware of the circumstances to be held covered coming into effect, and a reasonable additional premium is payable if the risk held covered comes into effect.

Heuristic: The process of solving problems by evaluating each step in the progress, searching for satisfactory solutions rather than optimal solutions. It comprises a form of problem-solving where the results are determined by experience or intuition instead of by optimization.

High-Risk Automobile Insurer: Company that specializes in insuring motorists who have poor driving records or have been canceled or refused insurance.

High Volume Specialist Operator (HVSO): A household goods and personal effects forwarder (HGF), which has been granted a Depot licence by the Australian Customs Service.

Hinterland: The inland area served by a certain port.

Hitchment Cargo: An amount of goods which is added to an original consignment as the owner and the destination are the same as those of the original consignment.

Hogged: Loading condition of a vessel in such a way that the centre of the vessel is slightly raised (arch-wise in the centre).

Hold: The space below the deck of a vessel, used to carry cargo.

Hold-Harmless Clause: Clause written into a contract by which one party agrees to release another party from all legal liability, such as a retailer who agrees to release the manufacturer from legal liability if the product injures someone.

Home Port: The port of registration of a vessel.

Home Service Life Insurance: Industrial life insurance and monthly debit ordinary life insurance contracts that are serviced by agents who call on the policy-owners at their homes to collect the premiums. The amount of life insurance per policy generally is larger than $1,000.

Homeowners Policy: A package of insurance designed to provide homeowners with a broad range of Property and Liability coverages, pertaining to events at home as well as away from home (although not automobile-related).

Horizontal Market: Sell materials or services that any company needs, not those used for manufacturing or production. Services include MRO, benefits management, and procurement process management. Examples: Ariba Network, CommerceOne's MarketSite.net, EmployEase. *Synonyms*: functional market, hub. (See MRO.)

Hospice: Health care facility providing medical care and support services such as counselling to terminally ill persons.

Hospital Admissions Programme: An arrangement to facilitate admission of persons covered by health insurance to hospitals and to assure the prompt payment of applicable insurance benefits to hospitals.

Hospital Expense Insurance: A form of health insurance designed to provide specific benefits for daily hospital room and board and hospital services during hospital confinement. Generally the policy also provides benefits for surgical operations and for in-hospital doctor's visits, in which case the policy is referred to as a Hospital and Surgical Expense Policy.

Hospital Indemnity: A form of health insurance which provides a stipulated daily, weekly, or monthly indemnity during hospital confinement. The indemnity is payable on an unallocated basis without regard to the actual expense of hospital confinement.

Hospital Medical Insurance: A term used to indicate protection which provides benefits for the cost of any or all of the numerous health care services normally covered under various health care plans.

Hospital Miscellaneous Services: Services other than room and board and general nursing services provided by a hospital during hospital confinement. Included are such items as x- ray examinations, laboratory tests, medicines, surgical dressings, anesthetics (including the administration thereof), and use of operating room.

House Address: Place of receipt respectively delivery (name and address) in case of carrier haulage.

Household Goods and Personal Effects Forwarder (HGF): An entity involved in facilitating the international movement of household goods and unaccompanied personal effects. Many HGFs are also High Volume Specialist Operators (HVSO) of

QAPs.

Household Goods and Unaccompanied Personal Effects: These consist of: (*a*) Consignments of less than 1m^3 which may consist of clothing, books, food and souvenirs; or (*b*) Consignments greater than 1m^3 consisting of part or whole contents of a household. Household goods may comprise furniture, clothing, manchester, electrical goods, tools and garden equipment, animal equipment and kitchen goods.

HS: See Harmonized System.

Hub: The central transhipment point in a transport structure, serving a number of consignees and/or consignors by means of spokes. The stretches between hubs mutually are referred to as trunks.

Hull: (1) Basically anything that floats and moves, from rowing boats to ultra-large ocean-going tankers, is defined as Hull. In terms of carrying capacity, usually expressed in Dead Weight Tons (DWT), this may cover a wide range, starting at a few hundred kilos and going as high as 5,60,000 tons for the largest of the Ultra-Large Crude oil Carries (ULCC) ever built.

The reference to "hull" i.e. the ship's outer skin needs to be understood in the historical context of marine insurance. Initially, when agreeing to insure a vessel, one was only covered for the ship and its masts, rather than for the whole package including stores, nets, ropes, equipment, bunkers etc. To make this intention clear, the object covered was referred to as the "hull".

Today the term has been widened to "Hull and Machinery" (H + M). The term Hull is also quite commonly deemed to embrace two other major groups of vessel owners' interests: "Disbursements and Collision Liability". Disbursements includes the ship's stores, bunker fuels and freight-earnings capacity up to an agreed maximum of 25 per cent of the total value for Hull and Machinery. The second, "Running Down Collision" liability (RDC), provides cover to the ship-owner for ¾ of liability to other ships in the event of collision.

A further important part of Hull business is construction and conversion of ships. These involve risks encountered in the actual building of ships, commencing the day the keel is laid up to the day the ship is delivered.

Risk Factors: The risk factors associated with Hull insurance are wide-ranging and include:

- The age of year of construction/refitting of the vessel, which may be indicative of its condition and risk susceptibility.
- The type of vessel such as bulker, tanker, gas carrier, ferry, tug etc.
- Tonnage—larger ships may be more stable in rough seas, but are at the same time more susceptible to metal fatigue when wave-oscillation is particularly adverse.
- Construction. Some materials are obviously preferable to others when it comes to certain jobs.
- The ship-owner's decision as to under which country's flag the ship sails has a bearing on risk. The decision may be determined by such factors as lower taxes

levied by some countries or less stringent regulations. The credibility of the ship's ownership also pays a part in assessing this risk.

- The type of product carried may have quite an influence on the longevity of the ship.
- Trading limits, such as coastal trade, river trade, North Atlantic, South Pacific, Cape Horn, typhoon areas, ice conditions etc., all play a part is assessing risk.
- Propulsion—sails, diesel engines, turbines, may have an influence on reliability, maneuverability and therefore influence risk.
- Socio-economic environment—this is probably the most difficult of all risk factors to assess adequately, as it involves the human element, also known as moral hazard.

(2) Outer shell of a vessel, made of steel plates or other suitable material to keep water outside the vessel.

Hull Insurance: (1) Class of Ocean Marine Insurance that covers physical damage to the ship or vessel insured. Typically written on an "all-risks" basis. (2) Physical Damage Insurance on aircraft, similar to Collision Insurance in an Automobile Policy.

Human Life Value: For purposes of Life Insurance, the net present value of the family's share of the deceased breadwinner's future earnings.

Hurricane: A tropical storm marked by extremely low barometric pressure and circular winds with a velocity of 75 miles an hour or more.

Husbanding: Taking care of a vessel's non-cargo related operations as instructed the by the master or owner of such vessel.

IACS: See International Association of Classification Societies.

IATA: See International Air Transport Association.

IATA Cargo Agent: An agent approved by IATA and registered in the IATA Cargo Agency List. This enables the agent, upon authorization of the IATA carrier, to receive shipments, to execute Air Waybills and to collect charges (aircargo).

IATA Member: An airline which is a member of IATA (aircargo).

IBNR: See: Incurred but not Reported.

ICAO: See International Civil Aviation Organization.

ICD: See Inland Clearance Depot.

ICHCA: International Cargo Handling Coordinating Association.

ICS: See International Chamber of Shipping.

Identification: The unique data, e.g. name, number or code, determining a certain object or person.

Idle Time: The amount of ineffective time whereby the available resources are not used e.g., a container in a yard.

IFC Act: Imported Food Act, 1992.

Ignition: Setting on fire or catching fire. The point at which a market gains momentum, liquidity is achieved, and the Net market becomes a more efficient means of buying and selling than the traditional physical market or channel. (Related term: Critical mass, liquidity, network effect.)

ILO: See International Labour Organization.

IMDG Code: See International Maritime Dangerous Goods Code.

IMGS: See International Medical Guide for Ships.

Immediate Annuity: An annuity providing for payment to begin immediately.

Immediate Participation Guarantee Plan (IPG): Type of pension plan in which all pension contributions are deposited in an unallocated fund and used directly to pay benefits to retirees.

IMO: See International Maritime Organization.

Import Conditions Database (ICON): An AQIS database that holds the conditions for the import of goods, including permit conditions, risk, legislation and treatments.

Importer: The party responsible for the import of goods. For customs purposes it is the party who makes, or on whose behalf an agent makes, an import declaration. This party may be the party who has possession of the goods or to whom the goods are consigned.

Import Permit: A permit issued to an importer of quarantine material pursuant to the *Act*.

Imputed Negligence: Case in which responsibility for damage can be transferred from the negligent party to another person, such as an employer.

Incontestability: A provision in Life Insurance policies that states that, except for non-payment of premiums and certain other circumstances, the policy shall be incontestable during the lifetime of the Insured after the policy has been in force for two years.

Incontestable Clause: An optional clause which may be used in non-cancelable or guaranteed renewable health insurance contracts providing that the insurer may not contest the validity of the contract after it has been in force for two (sometimes three) years.

Incoterms: Trade terms in coded form as established by the International Chamber of Commerce in 1953, whereafter they have been regularly updated. (Last update 1990). The terms represent a set of international rules for the interpretation of the principal terms of delivery used in trade contracts.

Incurred Losses: Expense account in an insurance company's Income Statement reflecting the claims paid during the policy year plus the loss reserves as of the end of the policy year, minus the corresponding reserves as of the beginning of the policy year. The difference between the year end and beginning of the year claim reserves is called the increase in reserves and may be added directly to the paid claims to produce the incurred losses.

Incurred-But-Not-Reported (IBNR) Reserves: Liability account on an insurer's balance sheet reflecting claims that are expected based upon statistical projections but which have not yet been reported to the insurer.

Incursion: The infestation or infection, post border and post barrier, by a viable exotic pest or disease.

Indemnification: (1) Compensation for a loss and/or the expenses incurred. (2) Compensation to the victim of a loss, in whole or in part, by payment, repair, or replacement.

Indemnity: Legal principle that specifies an Insured should not collect more than the actual cash value of a loss but should be restored to approximately the same financial position that existed before the loss.

Independent Adjustor: Claims adjustor who offers his or her services to insurance companies and is compensated by a fee.

Independent Agency System: Type of Property and Liability Insurance marketing system, sometimes called the American Agency System, in which the agent is an independent business person representing several companies. The Agency has legal right to income from the expirations and renewal rights to the business, and the agent is compensated by commissions.

Independent Agent: An independent business person who usually represents two or more insurance companies in a sales and service capacity and who is compensated by commissions.

Independent Demand: A demand which is unrelated to demand for other products. Demand for finished goods, parts required for destructive testing and service parts requirements are examples of independent demand.

Indeterminate Premium Whole Life Insurance: Non-participating whole life policy that permits the insurer to adjust premiums based on anticipated future experience. Initial premiums are guaranteed for a certain period. After the initial guaranteed period expires, the insurer can increase premiums up to some maximum limit.

Indirect Loss: See: Consequential Loss.

Indirect Route: Any route other than the direct route.

Individual Contract: A contract of Health Insurance made with an individual called the policy-holder or the Insured, which normally covers the individual and, in certain instances, members of his family.

Individual Deductible: Amount that an Insured and each person of his or her family covered by the policy must pay before the group or individual medical insurance policy begins to pay for medical expenses.

Individual Insurance: Policies which provide protection to the policy-holder and/or his/her family. Sometimes called Personal Insurance as distinct from group and Blanket Insurance.

Individual Policy Pension Trust: A type of pension plan, frequently used for small groups, administered by trustees who are authorized to purchase individual Level Premium Policies or Annuity contracts for each member of the plan. The polices usually provide both Life Insurance and retirement benefits.

Individual Retirement Account (IRA): An account to which an individual can make annual contributions of 100 per cent of earnings up to $2,000 ($2,250 for a one-income married couple). These contributions are tax deductible for most workers, and income earned in the account is deferred until withdrawn.

Industrial Life Insurance: Life insurance issued in small amounts with premiums payable on a weekly or monthly basis. The premiums are generally collected at the insured's home each week by an agent of the company. Sometimes referred to as Debit Insurance.

Infestation: The presence of live insects, mites, spiders or other animals.

Inflation-Guard Endorsement: Endorsement added at the Insured's request to a Homeowners Policy to increase periodically the face amount of insurance of the dwelling and other policy coverages by a specified percentage.

Infomediary (Business): Third party that provides research, competitive information, and advice on products or services to help buyers make informed buying decisions. TestMart, for example, tells engineers whether a test and measurement device is Y2K compliant, whether manuals are in stock, warranties available on secondary equipment, etc. *Synonyms*: lead generator, vertical portal.

Infomediary (Consumer): Trusted third parties that act as custodian, agent, or broker of customer information, marketing it to businesses on the consumer's behalf while protecting consumer privacy.

Information Portal: Create, install. and host personalized Yahoo-like information portals for enterprises and their employees. *Suppliers*: Aeneid, Moreover. *Synonym*: vertical portal.

Infrastructure: System of roads, waterways, airfields, ports and/or telecommunication networks in a certain area.

Inherent Vice: A property in cargo which causes, or is liable to cause, loss or damage to the cargo, without any accident occurring (e.g., spontaneous combustion). It is always excluded by the insurers of the cargo because of its inevitable nature.

Inheritance Tax: A tax on the estate of a deceased person.

Initial Audit: An audit conducted to assess whether the Other Party meets the requirements for a Schedule with AQIS. This audit may provide guidance to the Other Party in order to meet the outcomes and procedural requirements of the Scheme.

Initial Past Service Liability: The actuarial value (single sum) of the past service benefits as of the effective date of the establishment of a retirement plan, or at the date of the latest adjustment.

Initial Reserve: In life insurance, the reserve at the beginning of any policy year.

Inland Clearance Depot: *Abbreviation*: ICD—Inland location where cargo, particularly containerized, may be cleared by customs.

Inland Marine Insurance: A form of insurance designed to cover articles in transit as well as bridges, tunnels and other means of transportation and communication. Besides goods in transit (generally excepting *ocean cargo*), it includes numerous

Floater policies, such as those covering personal effects, personal property, jewellery, furs, fine arts and other items.

Inland Waterways Bill of Lading: Transport document made out to a named person, to order or to bearer, signed by the carrier and handed to the sender after receipt of the goods.

Insolvent: Having insufficient financial resources (assets) to meet financial obligations (liabilities).

Inspection: An examination of documentation and/or goods to determine whether or not goods meet AQIS requirements. Examination may include tests, taking samples, or undertaking procedures for diagnosis.

Inspection Field: The field in ICS where an Accredited Person enters the three character code that relates to the Quarantine Approved Premises (QAPs) where the particular activity for the consignment is to take place.

Inspection Report: A report (usually written) of an investigation of an applicant, generally conducted by an independent agency that specializes in insurance investigations. The report covers such matters as occupation, financial status, health history and moral problems.

Institute Cargo Clauses (ICC): There are three basic sets of these clauses (A, B and C). The A clauses cover "all risks", subject to specified exclusions. The B and C clauses cover specified "risks", subject to specified exclusions.

Insulated Container: Thermal container without the use of devices for cooling and/or heating.

Insulated Tank Container: Container frame holding one or more thermal insulated tanks for liquids.

Insurability: Acceptability to the company of an applicant for insurance.

Insurable Interest: It is illegal for anyone to insure without an insurable interest or, in the case of marine insurance, a reasonable expectation of acquiring such interest. In general one has such interest when his relationship to property at risk may expose him to loss or liability where he stands to gain by the safety of such property.

Insurable Risk: The conditions that make a risk insurable are (*a*) the peril insured against must produce a definite loss not under the control of the insured, (*b*) there must be a large number of homogeneous exposures subject to the same perils, (*c*) the loss must be calculable and the cost of insuring it must be economically feasible, (*d*) the peril must be unlikely to affect all insureds simultaneously, and (*e*) the loss produced by a risk must be definite and have a potential to be financially serious.

Insurance: An arrangement under which individuals, businesses, and other organizations or entities, in exchange for payment of a premium, are guaranteed compensation for losses resulting from certain perils under specified conditions.

Insurance Certificate: Proof of an insurance contract.

Insurance Commissioner: The top insurance regulatory official in a state.

Insurance Company: The party covering the risks of the issued goods and/or services that are insured.

Insurance Examiner: The representative of a state insurance department assigned to participate in the official audit and examination of the affairs of an insurance company.

Insurance Exchange: Term used to describe a facility that exists in a few states to provide a market for reinsurance and for the insurance of large or unusual domestic and foreign risks that are difficult to insure in the normal markets. Examples are the New York Insurance Exchange, the Insurance Exchange of the Americas, and the Illinois Insurance Exchange.

Insurance Guaranty Funds: State Funds that provide for the payment of unpaid claims of insolvent insurers. Such funds are frequently notional, in that they are commingled as part of a state government's general funds.

Insurance Services Offices (ISO): Major rating organization in Property and Liability Insurance that drafts policy forms for personal and commercial lines of insurance and provides rate data on loss costs for property and liability insurance lines.

Insured Life: The person on whose life the policy is issued.

Insured: A person or organization covered by an insurance policy.

Insurer: The party to the insurance contract who promises to pay losses or benefits. Also, any corporation engaged primarily in the business of furnishing insurance to the public.

Insuring Agreement: That part of an insurance contract that states the promises of the insurer.

Insuring Clause: The clause in an insurance contract which sets forth the type of loss being covered by the policy and the parties to the insurance contract.

Integrated Logistics Support: The systematic approach applied to simultaneous management and acquisition of equipment and related logistics support, in order to provide the customer with a desired level of availability. Resulting in an optimum life cycle cost and to maintain this level through the entire life cycle.

Integration: A coordination of pension, disability or other benefit with the other sources of income, such as Social Security benefit, through a specific formula designed to ensure reasonable income replacement. Qualified plans must integrate so that total benefits are non-discriminatory between rank and file employees and owners, officers or highly compensated employees.

***Inter Vivos* Trust:** A trust created while the creator of the trust is living. Also known as a *Living Trust*.

Interception: Goods of quarantine interest, detected as a result of an inspection.

Interchange: Reciprocal exchange of e.g., information between two or more parties.

Intercoastal: As opposite to coastal water operations, intercoastal refers to water transport carried out between coasts (e.g., between pacific and atlantic coasts).

Intercontainer: A co-operative formed by 19 European Railways, for the management of international rail container traffic in Europe.

Interest: Money paid for the use of money, generally calculated as a percentage per annum.

Interest Option: Life insurance settlement option in which the principal is retained by the insurer and interest is paid periodically.

Interest-Adjusted Method: Method of determining cost to an insured of a life insurance policy that considers the time cost of money by applying an interest factor to each element of cost.

Interline: Two or more road transport companies joining operations to bring cargo to a certain destination.

Intermediary: Aggregates data and facilitates transactions by bringing buyers and sellers together. Internet-based intermediaries create multivendor, multiproduct marketplaces.

Intermodal Transport: The movement of goods (containers) in one and the same loading unit or vehicle which uses successively several modes of transport without handling of the goods themselves in changing modes.

International Air Transport Association: *Abbreviation*: IATA—An international organization of airlines, founded in 1945, with the aim of promoting the commercial air traffic. This should be achieved by cooperation between parties concerned and by performance of certain rules, procedures and tariffs, regarding both cargo and passengers, by those parties.

International Association of Classification Societies: *Abbreviation*: IACS—An organization in which the major classification societies, among others American Bureau of Shipping, Lloyd's Register of Shipping and Germanischer Lloyd, are joined, whose principal aim is the improvement of standards concerning safety at sea.

International Carriage: Carriage whereby the place of departure and any place of landing are situated in more than one country (aircargo).

International Chamber of Shipping: *Abbreviation*: ICS—A voluntary organization of national shipowner' associations with the objective to promote interests of its members, primarily in the technical and legal fields of shipping operations.

International Civil Aviation Organization: *Abbreviation*: ICAO—An international organization of governments, dealing with search and rescue in distress, weather information, telecommunications and navigational requirements.

International Labour Organization: *Abbreviation*: ILO—An United Nations agency, dealing with employment rights and working conditions, covering work at sea and in ports.

International Maritime Dangerous Goods Code: *Abbreviation*: IMDG—Code. A code, representing the classification of dangerous goods as defined by the International Maritime Organization (IMO) in compliance with international legal requirements.

International Maritime Organization: *Abbreviation*: IMO—An United Nations agency concerned with safety at sea. Its work includes codes and rules relating to tonnage measurement of vessels, load lines, pollution and the carriage of dangerous goods. Its previous name was the Inter-Governmental Maritime Consultative Organization (IMCO).

International Medical Guide for Ships: *Abbreviation*: IMGS—'The doctor at sea'.

International Organization for Standardization: *Abbreviation*: ISO—A worldwide federation of national standards institutes (ISO member bodies).

International Safety Management Code: This international standard for the safe management and operation of ships prescribes rules for the organization of a shipping company management in the context of safety and pollution prevention and requires the development and implementation of a safety management system.

International Transport and Information System: *Abbreviation*: INTIS—An organization with the aim to improve the position of the port of Rotterdam by the development, realization and exploitation of a communication—and information network for computers.

Intervention: Application of any activity by a Quarantine Officer to determine if the goods are subject to quarantine.

Intestate: Without a will.

INTIS: See International Transport and Information System.

In Transit: The status of goods or persons between the outwards customs clearance and inwards customs clearance.

Introduction: The entry of a pest or disease resulting in its establishment.

Inventory: A detailed list of goods located in a certain space or belonging to a specified object. Goods available for satisfying certain demands. Inventories may consist of finished goods ready for sale, they may be parts or intermediate items, they may be work in process, or they may be raw materials. *Synonym*: Stock.

Investment Income: Line reported in the Income Statement of a company's financial statements that states the income generated by a company's portfolio of investments (such as in bonds, stocks, or other financial ventures).

Investment Only Contract: Type of funding instrument that uses only the investment services of an insurer.

Invoice: An account from the supplier, for goods and/or services supplied by him.

IPG Plan: See Immediate Participation Guarantee Plan.

IRA: See Individual Retirement Account.

Irrevocable Beneficiary: Beneficiary designation allowing no change to be made in the beneficiary of an insurance policy without the beneficiary's consent.

Irrevocable Trust: A trust in which the creator does not reserve the right to reacquire the trust property.

ISO: (1) See International Organization for Standardization. (2) Insurance Services Office.

Item: Separate article or unit.

Itinerary: The route of a means of transport, indicated by the names of the ports of call or other locations, often including estimated arrival and departure dates.

Jettison: (1) Hazard covered under a Marine Cargo Insurance policy, defined as the throwing overboard of cargo when done to preserve property from loss. Coverage is not provided under this clause for goods jettisoned because of spoilage, such as foods, plants, hides, etc. (The spoilage may be covered under another clause, or another policy, which can be determined by consulting with your insurance agent.) (2) The act of intentionally throwing cargo overboard e.g. with the objective of lightening a vessel, which has run aground, such for the common good of all interests: vessel, crew and remaining cargo (see GA).

Jetty: A mole or breakwater, running out into the sea to protect harbour or coast. It is sometimes used as a landing-pier.

Jeweller's Block Insurance: Coverage designed to protect the Insured's stock, property left with the insured for repair or other purposes, and the insured's interest in and legal liability for property on consignment from others in the jewellery trade. The policy is written on a special form. Some of the more prevalent perils covered are fire, open stock burglary, inside and outside holdup, safe burglary, theft, pilferage, kidnapping, shoplifting, window smashing, damage or loss of salesman's samples in transit, loss in transit by registered mail, water damage, sprinkler leakage and smoke damage.

Jib: Projecting arm of a crane. Attachment connected to the top of a crane boom.

JIT: See Just In Time.

Job: That work which is undertaken to meet a customer or production order and, for production control purposes, has a unique identification.

Joint Tenants: A form of joint property ownership with right of survivorship, i.e., in which the survivors automatically own the share of a deceased co-owner.

Joint Underwriting Association: A device used to provide insurance to those who cannot obtain insurance in the voluntary market. Certain companies (called carriers) issue policies at one rate and handle claims, but the ultimate costs are borne by all companies writing insurance in that state.

Joint Venture: A joint activity of two or more companies, usually performed under a common name.

Joint-and-Several Liability: A legal principle that permits the injured party in a tort action to recover the entire amount of compensation due for injuries from any defendant who is able to pay, regardless of the degree of that party's negligence, once any liability by that defendant has been established.

Joint-and-Survivor Annuity: A contract that provides income periodically, payable during the longer lifetime of two persons. The amount payable may decrease at the death of one or the other (See: Contingent Annuity Option).

Judgment Rating: Rate-making method for which each exposure is individually evaluated and the rate is determined largely by the underwriter's judgment.

Judicial Bond: Type of Surety Bond used for court proceedings and guaranteeing that the party bonded will fulfill certain obligations specified by law, for example, fiduciary responsibilities.

Jumbo Risk: A risk involving exceptionally high limits.

Jumping Juvenile Insurance Policy: Life insurance purchased by parents for children under a specified age. Provides permanent life insurance that increases in face value five times at age 21, with no increase in premium.

Jurisprudence: Juridical decisions used for explanation and meaning of law.

Just In Time: *Abbreviation:* JIT—The movement of material/goods at the necessary place at the necessary time. The implication is that each operation is closely synchronized with the subsequent ones to make that possible. A method of inventory control that brings stock into the production process, warehouse or to the customer just in time to be used, thus reducing stock piling.

Kanban: A method which during storage uses standard units or lot sizes with a single card attached to each. A pull system used at a stock point in which a supply batch is ordered only when a previous batch is withdrawn. *Note*: Kanban in Japanese means loosely translated 'card or sign'.

Keel: Longitudinal girder at the lowest point of a vessel from which the framework is built.

Kenney Rule: Concept permitting a Property/Casualty insurer to write $2 of new net premiums for each $1 of policy-holders surplus.

Keogh (HR 10) Account: An account to which a self-employed person can make annual tax deductible contributions and which may be withdrawn without penalty after the age of 59 1/2. Income generated in the account accumulates tax-deferred.

Key-Person Insurance: Insurance designed to protect a business firm against the loss of income resulting from the death or disability of a key employee.

Kind of Packing: Description of the packaging material used for goods to be transported.

King Pin: The coupling pin, welded or bolted in the centre of the front underside of a semi-trailer chassis, which couples to the fifth wheel of the towing tractor or dolly convertor.

Knot: Unit of measurement for the speed (of a vessel) equal to a nautical mile (= 1852 metres) per hour.

Known Loss: A loss known to one or both parties when a broker and Underwriter are negotiating a placing.

Kyoto Convention: The convention for the International Customs Cooperation Council held in Kyoto in 1973 for the simplification and harmonization of national customs procedures.

L/C: See Letter of Credit.

Label: A slip of e.g., paper or metal attached to an object to indicate the nature, ownership, destination, contents and/or other particulars of the object.

Labor-Management Relations Act of 1947 (Taft-Hartley Act): Law which controls conditions under which an employer may pay any money to a representative (e.g., union representative) of employees.

Laden Vessel: See Loaden Vessel.

Land Bridge: Overland transport between following and/or preceding sea transport of goods and/or containers.

Lapse: The termination or discontinuance of an insurance policy due to non-payment of a premium.

Lapsed Policy: (1) A policy terminated for non-payment of premiums. (2) A policy terminated for non-payment occurring before the policy has a cash or other surrender value.

Larceny: The unlawful taking, carrying, leading or riding away of another person's property.

Lash: To hold goods in position by the use of e.g., wires, ropes, chains and straps. See Lighter Aboard Ship.

Lashing Point: Point on a means of transport to which wires, chains, ropes or straps, which are used to hold goods in position, are attached.

Last Clear Chance Rule: Statutory modification of the contributory negligence law allowing the claimant endangered by his or her own negligence to recover damages from a defendant if the defendant has a last clear chance to avoid the accident but fails to do so.

Last In First Out: *Abbreviation*: LIFO—A method of which the assumption is that the most recently received (last in) is the first to be used or sold (first out).

Lateral and Front Stacking Truck: High-lift stacking truck capable of stacking and retrieving loads ahead and on either or both sides of the driving direction.

Latitude: The angular distance of a position on its meridian north or south from the equator, measured in degrees ('a vessel at 25 degrees north latitude').

Lattice Vortex Network: Term coined by Mohanbir Sawhney and Steven Kaplan to describe how vertical and functional markets intersect and partner.

Law of Large Numbers: Concept that the greater the number of exposures, the more closely will actual results approach the probable results expected from an infinite number of exposures.

Lay Days: The number of days allowed in a charter party for the loading and discharging of cargo. Lay days may be indicated in different ways e.g., consecutive days, working days, weather working days.

Lay Up a Vessel: Temporary cessation of trading of a vessel by the shipowner.

Layout Key: See United Nations Layout Key.

Lead Generation: Typically seller-driven, they derive revenue from ads, commissions on sales, or fees for delivering qualified leads to suppliers. Also may generate RFPs (requests for proposals) and RFQs (requests for quotes) for buyers. Provide value by understanding information needs of their users and integrating and aggregating content, information and transactions for buyers and sellers. Most lead generation markets seek to migrate to transaction-oriented catalog aggregation model. Examples: PhotonicsOnline.com (lasers), SolidwasteOnline.com (sewage treatment systems), PlasticsNet.com, Questlink.com (electronic components).

Lead Time: The amount of time between the request of a service and the actual provision of this service. A span of time required to perform an activity. In a logistics context, the time between the initiation of a process and its completion.

Leakage: The movement of goods subject to quarantine undetected through the barrier.

Lease: A contract by which one party gives to another party the use of property or equipment, e.g., containers, for a specified time against fixed payments.

Leasehold Interest Insurance: Coverage designed to protect a tenant in the event his or her lease is terminated. It is a form of Time Element Coverage that serves to provide coverage for the difference between the old rental and a new, likely more expensive rental.

Leasing Company: The company from which property or equipment is taken on lease.

Leasing Contract: A contract for the leasing of property or equipment.

Legal Reserve Life Insurance Company: A life insurance company operating under state insurance laws specifying the minimum basis for the reserves the company must maintain on its policies.

Legal Reserve: The minimum reserve which a company must keep to meet future claims and obligations as they are calculated under state insurance regulations.

Less than Container Load (LCL): (1) These consignments have multiple suppliers, importers and brokers. (2) *Abbreviation:* LCL. A general reference for identifying cargo in any quantity intended for carriage in a container, where the Carrier is responsible for packing and/or unpacking the container. For operational purposes a LCL (less than full container load) container is considered a container in which multiple consignments or parts thereof are shipped.

Less than Truck Load: *Abbreviation:* LTL—A term used if the quantity or volume of one or more consignment(s) does not fill a standard truck.

Lessee: The party to whom the possession of specified property has been conveyed for a period of time in return for rental payments.

Lessor: The party who conveys specified property to another for a period of time in return for the receipt of rent.

Letter of Credit: *Abbreviation*: L/C—A written undertaking by a bank (issuing bank) given to the seller (beneficiary) at the request, and on the instructions of the buyer (applicant) to pay at sight or at a determinable future date up to a stated sum of money, within a prescribed time limit and against stipulated documents.

Level Commission Scale: A commission scale providing for payment of Commissions at the same rate every year the policy is in force.

Level Premium: A premium which remains unchanged throughout the life of a policy.

Level Premium Life Insurance: Life insurance for which the premium remains the same from year to year. The premium is more than the actual cost of protection during the earlier years of the policy and less than the actual cost in the later years. The building of a reserve is a natural result of level premiums. The overpayments in the early years, together with the interest that is earned, serve to balance out the underpayments of the later years.

Liabilities: Portion of an insurer's balance sheet which denotes legal obligations of the company, including anticipated future payments of losses covered under policies issued.

Liability: Any legally enforceable obligation.

Liability Insurance: Insurance designed to protect the policy-holder from financial loss due to liability resulting from injuries to other persons or damage to their property.

Liability Limits: The sum or sums stipulated in an insurance contract beyond which an insurance company is not liable to protect the insured.

Liability Without Fault: Principle on which Workers Compensation is based, holding the employer absolutely liable for occupational injuries or disease suffered by workers, regardless of who is at fault.

License and Permit Bond: Type of Surety Bond guaranteeing that the person bonded will comply with all laws and regulations that govern his or her activities.

Lien: A legal claim upon real or personal property to pay a debt or duty.

Life Annuity: A contract that provides for a series of payments under which payments, once begun, continue throughout the remaining lifetime of the Annuitant but not beyond.

Life Annuity with 10 Years Certain: A annuity contract which pays an income for as long as the annuitant lives, but if death occurs within 10 years after the annuity payments begin, payments are continued to a named beneficiary for the remainder of the 10 years.

Life Cycle Cost: Encompasses all costs associated with the product's life cycle. These include all costs involved in acquisition (research and development, design, production and construction, and phase-in), operation, support and disposal of the product.

Life Expectancy: The average number of years of life remaining for a group of persons of a given age according to a particular Mortality Table.

Life Income Option: Life insurance settlement option in which the policy proceeds are paid during the lifetime of the beneficiary. A certain number of guaranteed payments may also be payable.

Life Insurance in Force: Amount reported in an insurance company's financial statements that sets out the sum of the face amounts, plus dividend additions, of life insurance polices outstanding at a given time. Additional amounts payable under accidental death or other special provisions are not included.

Life Insurance Programming: Systematic method of determining the insured's financial goals, which are translated into specific amounts of life insurance, then periodically reviewed for possible changes.

Life Insurance: Insurance providing for payment of a specified amount on the insured's death, either to his or her estate or to a designated beneficiary; or in certain cases to the policy-holder at a specified date.

Lifetime Disability Benefit: (1) A benefit to help replace income lost by an insured person as long as he/she is totally disabled. (2) Disability Income payable for the life of the insured as long as he is totally disabled.

Lifetime Value of the Customer: The amount a customer spends over time with a supplier minus the cost of acquiring the customer. Both vertical and horizontal net markets have promised investors they will "own" the b2b customer, become the default buying option, and thus have customers with a higher lifetime value than consumer e-commerce businesses. That promise has slowed development of partnerships between vertical and horizontal markets.

LIFO: See Last In First Out. See Liner In Free Out.

Lift-On Lift-Off Vessel: *Abbreviation*: LOLO—Vessel of which the loading and discharging operations are carried out by cranes and derricks.

Lighter: See Barge. Lighter Aboard Ship. *Abbreviation*: Lash—A vessel which carries barges.

Lighterage: The carriage of goods within a port area by a barge, e.g., from a vessel to a quay.

Lightweight: Weight of an empty vessel including equipment and outfit, spare parts required by the regulatory bodies, machinery in working condition and liquids in the systems, but excluding liquids in the storage tanks, stores and crew.

Limited Payment Life Insurance: Whole Life Insurance on which premiums are payable for a specified number of years or until death (if death occurs before the end of the specified period).

Limited Policy: An insurance contract which covers only certain specified diseases or accidents.

Line Item: See Order Line.

Line Number: See Flight Number.

Linear Market: When products move from one end of the supply chain to the other, typical of traditional markets and manufactured goods. Adding a seller primarily benefits buyers, and adding a buyer mainly benefits sellers. *Antonym*: exponential market.

Linear Programming: A mathematical procedure for minimizing or maximizing a linear function of several variables, subject to a finite number of linear restrictions on these variables.

Liner Conference: A group of two or more vessel-operating carriers, which provides international liner services for the carriage of cargo on a particular trade route and which has an agreement or arrangement to operate under uniform or common freight rates and any other agreed conditions (e.g. FEFC = Far Eastern Freight Conference).

Liner In Free Out: *Abbreviation*: LIFO—Transport condition denoting that the freight rate is inclusive of the sea carriage and the cost of loading, the latter as per the custom of the port. It excludes the cost of discharging.

Liner Service: The connection through vessels between ports within a trade.

Liner Shipping Company: A company transporting goods over sea in a regular service.

Liner Terms: Condition of carriage denoting that costs for loading and unloading are borne by the carrier subject the custom of the port concerned.

Liquidation: The process of dissolving a company by selling its assets for cash.

Liquidity: Volume of transactions. With enough buyers and sellers, a market has continuous bidding, offers, and consummated transactions, and market liquidity is achieved. (See critical mass, network effect.)

Liquor Liability Insurance: Coverage designed to protect an individual or entity for bodily injury or property damage to another for which an insured may be held liable by reason of causing or contributing to the intoxication of any person; furnishing alcoholic beverages to a person under the legal drinking age or under the influence of alcohol; or violating any statute, ordinance, or regulation relating to the sale, gift, distribution, or use of alcoholic beverages.

Liquor Liability Law: See: Dramshop Law.

Live Stock: Cargo consisting of live animals, such as horses, cows, sheep and chickens.

Living Benefits Rider: A rider that allows Insureds who are terminally ill or who suffer from certain catastrophic diseases to collect part of their Life Insurance benefits before they die, primarily to pay for the care they require.

Living Trust: A trust created while the creator of the trust is living. Also known as an *Inter Vivos* Trust.

Load: Quantity or nature of what is being carried. This term normally refers to transport by truck.

Load Factor Management: The process of maximising the utilization of the (slot) capacity of vessels and or other means of transport.

Loaden Vessel: Vessel where cargo has been put on board. *Synonym*: Laden Vessel.

Loading: The process of bringing cargo into a means of transport or equipment.

Loading Platform: A flat surface to facilitate loading usually alongside a warehouse.

Loadmaster: A loadcalculator designed for a vessel approved by a classification bureau for the calculation of the vessels stability.

Locating Pin: See Cones.

Location: Any named geographical place, recognized by a competent national body, with permanent facilities used for goods movements associated with international trade, and used frequently for these purposes.

Geographical place such as a port, an airport, an inland freight terminal, a container freight station, a container yard, a container depot, a terminal or any other place where customs clearance and/or regular receipt or delivery of goods can take place. An area (e.g., in a warehouse) marked off or designated for a specific purpose.

Location Clause: Used in cargo open covers this limits Underwriters' liability in any one location.

Location Code: The code added to the *Inspection Field* on the JEMS entry by an Accredited Person. This code indicates to AQIS the Accredited Person's preferred Quarantine Approved Premises (QAP) where the activity is to be performed.

Lock: For marine purposes: A space, enclosed at the sides by walls and at each end by gates, by which a vessel can be floated up or down to a different level.

Locker: A compartment, in a shed or on board of a vessel, used as a safekeeping place to stow valuable goods, which can be secured by means of a lock.

Log Book: The daily report of all events and other relevant particulars of a vessel and attested by the proper authorities as a true record.

Logistics (CEN): The planning, execution and control:

- of the movement and placement of people and/or goods;
- and of the supporting activities related to such movement and placement within a system organized to achieve specific objectives

Logistics Chain: All successive links involved in the logistic process.

LOLO: See Lift-On Lift-Off Vessel.

Longitude: The angular distance of a position on the equator east or west of the standard Greenwich meridian up to 180° east or west.

Long-term Care: The continuum of broad-ranged maintenance and health services to the chronically ill, disabled, or retarded. Services may be provided on an inpatient (rehabilitation facility, nursing home, mental hospital), outpatient, or at-home basis.

Long-term Disability Income Insurance: Insurance issued to an employer (group) or individual to provide a reasonable replacement of a portion of an employee's earned income lost through serious and prolonged illness or injury during the normal work career.

Lorry: Motor truck used for transport of goods. Note: Motor truck is an American term. British synonym for motor truck is Heavy Goods Vehicle. This British term means any vehicle exceeding 7.5 metric tons maximum laden weight.

Loss: The Occurrence of the event for which insurance pays.

Loss Avoidance: A risk management technique whereby a situation or activity that may result in a loss for a firm is avoided or abandoned.

Loss Control: Any conscious action (or decision not to act) intended to reduce the frequency, severity, or unpredictability of accidental losses.

Loss Expense—Allocated: Handling expenses, such as legal or independent adjuster fees, paid by an insurance company in settling a claim which can be definitely charged to that particular claim.

Loss Expense—Unallocated: Salaries and other expenses incurred in connection with the operation of a claim department of an insurance carrier which cannot be charged to individual claims.

Loss of Maintenance Fees Insurance: Coverage designed to protect an association (such as a condominium association) against the loss of maintenance fees when occupancies have been interrupted or impaired by the occurrence of any insured peril. This is a form of Business Interruption Insurance for the association. It assures continuous income while a building is untenantable.

Loss Payable Clause: Means of protecting a mortgagee's interest in property by directing the insurer to make a loss payment to the mortgagee in the event of a loss.

Loss Prevention: Any measure which reduces the probability or frequency of a particular loss but does not eliminate completely all possibility of that loss.

Loss Ratio: The percent which losses bear to premiums (either earned or written) for a given period.

Loss Reserve: The amount set up as the estimated cost of a claim. (See: IBNR Reserve)

LTL: See Less than Truck Load.

Luffing Crane: A crane with which the load can be moved to or from the crane horizontally.

Luggage: Travellers' baggage, suitcases, boxes etc., normally accompanied by a passenger.

Lump-Sum: An agreed sum of money, which is paid in full settlement at one time. This term is often used in connection with charter parties.

Lump-Sum Charter: A voyage charter whereby the shipowner agrees to place the whole or a part of the vessel's capacity at the charterer's disposal for which a lump-sum freight is being paid.

Lump-Sum Distribution: Payment within one taxable year of the entire balance payable to an employee from a trust which forms part of a qualified pension or employee annuity plan on account of that person's death, separation from service or attainment of age 59 1/2.

Macro Non-Conformity: A less serious breach of the procedures and/or failure to meet the outcomes set out in the Processes and Outcomes Document. *Note*: Two *MINOR* non-conformities equal a *MAJOR* non conformity and may result in an increased level of review.

Mafi Trailer: German brand name of a roll trailer used for RoRo purposes.

Maiden Trip: First voyage of a vessel or aircraft after delivery from new-building to her owner(s).

Mail Order Insurer: Type of insurance company that sells policies through the mail or other mass media, eliminating need for agents.

Main-Line Operator: *Abbreviation*: MLO—A carrier employing vessel(s) in the main or principal routes in a trade but not participating within a consortium.

Maintenance Chain: A sequence of events in a goods flow which preserves and/or restores the value of a specific good. This may include: Repair.

Major Medical Expense Insurance: A form of Health Insurance that provides benefits for most types of medical expense up to a high maximum benefit, such as $250,000 or higher after a substantial deductible, such as $500 or more. Such contracts may contain internal limits and are normally subject to coinsurance.

Major Medical Insurance: Health insurance designed to finance the expense of major illness and injury. Characterized by large benefit maximums ranging up to $250,000 or higher above an initial deductible, which reimburses the major part of all charges for hospital, doctor, private nurses, medical appliances, prescribed out-of-hospital treatment, drugs and medicines. The insured person pays the remainder.

Major Non-Conformity: A breach of the procedures set out in the Processes and Outcomes Document, and/or failure to meet the outcomes and responsibilities as described in the Processes and Outcomes Document. The accrual of a major non-conformity will result in AQIS imposing an increased level of review on the Other Party.

Malicious Damage Clause: A clause published by the Institute of London Underwriters for use in a cargo policy that is subject to the Institute Cargo Clauses (1982) B or C. It adds the risks of malicious acts, vandalism and sabotage to the cargo policy.

Malingering: The practice of feigning illness or inability to work in order to collect insurance benefits.

Malpractice Insurance: Coverage for a professional practitioner, such as a doctor or a lawyer, against liability claims resulting from alleged malpractice in the performance of professional services.

Managed Care: Health care systems that integrate the financing and delivery of appropriate health care services to covered individuals by arrangements with selected providers to furnish a comprehensive set of health care services.

Manifest: Document which lists the specifications of goods loaded in a means of transport or equipment for transportation purposes. As a rule cargo manifests are drawn up by the agents in the place of loading. *Note*: For shipping a manifest represents a cumulation of Bills of Lading for official and administrative purposes.

Manual Rate: The premium rate developed for a group's insurance coverage from the company's standard rate tables normally referred to as its rate manual or underwriting manual.

Manufacturers Plate: A plate indicating the name and address of the container manufacturer and particulars of the container.

Manufacturing Process: The producing of goods or wares by manual labour or machinery, often on a large scale and with division of labour.

Manufacturing Resource Planning: *Abbreviation*: MRP-II—A method for the effective planning of a manufacturing company, being a direct out-growth and extension of MRP-I.

Manuscript Policy: Policy designed for a firm's specific needs and requirements.

MAR Policy: A market term for the form of marine policy used by Lloyd's and the London company market. It is a basic contract form to which the conditions agreed by the insurers subscribing a marine insurance contract are attached.

Marine Insurance: A form of insurance primarily concerned with means of transportation and communication, and with goods in transit (See: Inland Marine Insurance and Ocean Marine Insurance).

Marine Insurance Policy: An insurance policy protecting the insured against loss or damage to his goods occurred during ocean transport.

Marine Liability: This is a fairly young chapter in the history of marine insurance. Traditionally the term Marine Liability (apart from the collision liability covered under "Hull") is used to embrace straightforward professional, legal liabilities of such people as carriers, forwarders, wharfingers, stevedores, ship repairers etc. In other words, cover is provided for a rather well-defined and limited group of professionals all engaged in an occupation closely related to maritime trade, against legal liability claims arising out of the operation of their business.

Another group included under Marine Liability is the owners of small vessels such as yachts, speedboats, harbourcraft and the like. The reason for this is that small vessels cannot join one of the so-called P and I clubs (Protection and Indemnity) which traditionally provide the liability cover not obtainable in the Marine market.

Marital Deduction: A reduction of an estate for estate tax purposes, which is available if the deceased is survived by his or her spouse.

Market Analysis: Systematic investigation of the growth and the composition of a market.

Marketing: The process of organizing and directing all the company activities which relate to determining the market demand and converting the customers buying power into an effective demand for a service and bringing that service to the customer.

Market Maker: In a stock exchange, market makers take ownership of shares, allowing people to buy and sell those goods from them. They also can make or lose money from price movements. Outside the financial community, market makers help match buyers and sellers, regardless of whether or not they take possession or own goods. (See Net market maker.)

Market Price (or Market Value): The price at which a security can be bought or sold at any particular time.

Marks: See Shipping Marks.

Master Policy: A policy that is issued to an employer or trustee, establishing a group insurance plan for designated members of an eligible group.

Master Production Schedule: *Abbreviation*: MPS—A realistic, detailed, manufacturing plan for which all possible demands upon the manufacturing facilities [such as available personnel, working hours, (management) policy and goals] have been considered and are visualized. The MPS is a statement of what the company expects to produce and purchase expressed in selected items, specific quantities and dates.

Mate's Receipt: A document signed by the chief officer of a vessel acknowledging the receipt of a certain consignment on board of that vessel. On this document, remarks can be made as to the order and condition of the consignment.

Material Damage: Automobile insurance designed to provide financial protection against damage to an insured vehicle. It includes automobile comprehensive, collision, fire and theft. Material damage and physical damage are terms that often are used interchangeably.

Material Requirements Planning: *Abbreviation*: MRP-I—An inventory and purchasing planning system that integrates product components, lead times and deadlines.

Materials Handling: The activities of loading, unloading, placing and manipulating material and of in-process movement.

Materials Management: The planning and control of the activities related to the materials flow from the suppliers up to the end of the conversion/production process.

Maximum Family Benefit: The largest amount in Social Security benefits that will be paid to any family unit.

McCarran-Ferguson Act: Federal law passed in 1945 stating that continued regulation of the insurance industry by the states is in the public interest and that federal antitrust laws apply to insurance only to the extent that the industry is not regulated by state law.

MCO: See Miscellaneous Charge Order.

Means of Transport: Type of vehicle used for the transport of goods (e.g. aircraft, barge, truck, vessel or train).

Measurement Ton: A ton of one cubic meter water.

Mechanics Lien: The legal enforceable claim which a person who has performed work or provided materials is permitted to make against title to the property or as a preferential person in the event the estate or business is liquidated.

Medicaid: State programmes of public assistance to persons whose income and resources are insufficient to pay for health care. Title XIX of the federal Social Security Act provides matching federal funds for financing state Medicaid programmes, effective January 1, 1966.

Medical Examination: The examination given by a qualified physician to determine the insurability of an applicant. A medical examination may also be used to determine whether an insured claiming disability is actually disabled.

Medical Expense Insurance: A form of health insurance that provides benefits for expenses incurred for medical care. This form of Health Insurance provides benefits for expenses of physicians, hospital, nursing, and related health services, and supplies. These benefits may be related to actual expense, specified sums, or services rendered. Such insurance sometimes includes benefits for prevention and diagnosis as well as treatment.

Medical Expense Liability Insurance: A General Liability Coverage in which the insurer reimburses, without regard to the Insured's liability, the Insured and others (as specifically provided in the policy) for medical and funeral expenses incurred by such persons as a result of bodily injury or death sustained by accident under the conditions specified in the policy.

Medical First Aid Guide: *Abbreviation*: MFAG—Instructions to be consulted in case of accidents involving dangerous goods.

Medical Malpractice: Improper care or treatment by a physician, hospital, or other provider of health care.

Medical Payments Insurance: A coverage, available in various liability insurance policies, in which their insurer agrees to reimburse the insured and others, without regard for the Insured's liability, for medical or funeral expenses incurred as the result of bodily injury or death by accident under specified conditions.

Medicare: A programme of Hospital Insurance (Part A) and Supplementary Medical Insurance (Part B) protection provided under the Social Security Act.

Medigap: A term sometimes applied to private insurance products that supplement Medicare insurance benefits.

Memo Bill: See Service Bill of Lading.

Merchant: For cargo carried under the terms and conditions of the Carrier's Bill of Lading and of a tariff, it means any trader or persons (e.g. Shipper, Consignee) and including anyone acting on their behalf, owning or entitled to possession of the goods.

Merchant Haulage: Inland transport of cargo in shipping containers arranged by the Merchant. It includes empty container-moves to and from hand-over points in respect of containers released by the Carrier to Merchants. *Note*: Carrier's responsibility under the Bill of Lading does not include the inland transport stretch under Merchant Haulage.

Merchant Inspired Carrier Haulage: Carrier haulage by a carrier, which is nominated by the shipper or receiver of the goods, but paid by the carrier.

Meta-Centric Height: The distance between the centre of gravity of a vessel and a fictitious point. If the metra-centric height is zero or negative, the vessel will heel or capsize.

Metamediary: Besides providing a multi-vendor, multi-product marketplace, the metamediary provides additional services for market participants. These services can be offered directly by the metamediary, or the metamediary can invite third party service providers into its marketplace. Services provided could include quality assurance, procurement management, fulfillment, or payment settlement.

Metropolitan Area: The suburban area around a Designated Port, for example around Sydney, Port Kembia, Newcastle, Brisbane, Melbourne, Adelaide and Perth. The limits of the Metropolitan Area for any Designated Port are determined by assessment by AQIS Canberra. Areas that are not located within the AQIS Metropolitan Postcodes List supplied with the QAP Criteria are deemed as Non-Metropolitan or rural.

MFAG: See Medical First Aid Guide.

Micro-Organism: Means protozoa, fungi, free-living bacteria, cell dependent bacteria and viruses.

Minimum Benefits: A provision that a minimum amount of annuity will be paid if the regular benefit formula produces less. This minimum is usually payable only if certain service requirements are met at retirement.

Minimum Charge: The lowest amount which applies to the transport of a consignment, irrespective of weight or volume (aircargo, shipping).

Minimum Group: The least number of employees permitted under a state law to effect a group for insurance purposes; the purpose is to maintain some sort of proper division between individual policy insurance and the group forms.

Minimum Inventory: The planned minimum allowable inventory for an independent demand item.

Minimum Premium Plan (MPP): An arrangement under which an insurance carrier will, for a fee, handle the administration of claims and insure against large claims for a self-insured group.

Minor Non-conformity: A less serious breach of the procedures and/or failure to meet the outcomes set out in the Processes and Outcomes Document.
Note: Two *Minor* non-conformities equal a *Major* non-conformity and may result in an increased level of review.

Minor Unit: Unit of recorded value (i.e. as recorded by banks) which is a division of the respective unit of currency. Examples are the cent being a one hundredth part of the US dollar. *Note*: Some countries have minor units that are used in low-value coinage within a country or locality, but which are not used by the international banking system in making formal records of value. *Examples*: Belgium, Greece and Spain.

Miscellaneous Charge Order: *Abbreviation*: MCO—A document issued by a carrier or his agent requesting the issue of an appropriate passenger ticket and baggage cheque or revision of services to the person named in such document.

Miscellaneous Expenses: Expenses in connection with Hospital Insurance, hospital charges other than room and board, such as X-rays, drugs, laboratory fees, and other ancillary charges. (Sometimes referred to as ancillary charges.)

Miscellaneous Hospital Expense Benefit: A provision in a Hospital Expense Policy providing for the payment of a benefit for expenses for necessary hospital services and supplies during a period of hospital confinement. Expenses commonly covered under this benefit include those for x-ray examinations, laboratory tests, medicines, surgical dressings, anesthetics (including administration thereof), and use of operating room.

Misrepresentation: A false, incorrect, improper, or incomplete statement of a material fact, made in the application for an insurance policy.

Mixed Consignment: A consignment of different commodities, articles or goods, packed or tied together or contained in separate packages (aircargo).

Mode of Premium Payment: The frequency with which premiums are paid: monthly, quarterly, semiannually, or annually.

Mode of Transport: Method of transport used for the conveyance of goods, (e.g. by rail, by road, by sea).

Model: A representation of a process or system that attempts to relate the post important variables in the system in such a way that analysis of the model leads to insights into the system.

Module: A separate and distinct unit of hardware or software that may be used as a component in a system.

Moral Hazard: Hazard arising from any non-physical, personal characteristic of a risk that increases the possibility of loss or may intensify the severity of loss, for instance, bad habits, low integrity or poor financial standing.

Morbidity: The incidence and severity of sicknesses and accidents in a defined class or classes or persons.

Morbidity Tables: Actuarial statistics showing the frequency and duration of disability.

Mortality: The rate at which members of a group die in a specified period of time. Actual mortality rates are compared to the mortality table.

Mortality Table: A chart showing how many members of a group, starting at a certain age, will be alive at each succeeding age. It is used to calculate the probability of dying in, or surviving through, any period, and for determining the value of an annuity. To be appropriate for a specific group, it should be based on the experience of individuals having common characteristics, including such variables as sex and occupation.

Movement: The act or process of changing the position of an object and or people.

Movement Inventory: The inventory during a production process caused by the time required to move goods from one place to another.

MPC: See Multi Purpose Carrier.

MPS: See Master Production Schedule.

MRO (Maintenance, Repair and Operating equipment): Routine purchases such as office supplies, travel services, or computers needed to run a business but not central to the business's output. Ariba and CommerceOne sell buy-side procurement software for MRO. (See horizontal market.)

MRP-I: See Material Requirements Planning.

MRP-II: See Manufacturing Resource Planning.

MTO/Carrier: See Multimodal Transport Operator/Carrier.

Multi-Employer Plan: A plan maintained according to a collective bargaining agreement, to which more than one employer contributes (e.g., multiple school districts). Under ERISA, at the beginning of the plan, no single employer may contribute as much as 50 per cent of the total, and thereafter as much as 75 per cent. An employee may change employers within the group without losing retirement benefits unless a break in service (under the plan) cancels credits earned before the break.

Multi Purpose Carrier: See Multi Purpose Vessel.

Multi Purpose Vessel: Vessel designed for the carriage of different types of cargo: general, bulk, heavy and/or containerized cargo. *Synonym*: Multi Purpose Carrier (MPC).

Multimodal Transport: The carriage of goods (containers) by at least two different modes of transport.

Multimodal Transport Document: See Combined Transport Document.

Multimodal Transport Operator/Carrier: *Abbreviation*: MTO/Carrier. The person on whose behalf the transport document or any document evidencing a contract of multimodal carriage of goods is issued and who is responsible for the carriage of goods pursuant to the contract of carriage.

Multi-Peril Policy: A Package Policy which provides protection against a number of separate perils. Multi-Peril Policies are not necessarily multiple line policies, since the combined perils may be all within one insurance line.

Multiple Employer Trust (MET): A legal trust established by a plan sponsor that brings together a number of small, unrelated employers for the purpose of providing group medical coverage on an insured or self-funded basis.

Multiple Sourcing: Selecting of and working with more than two equivalent suppliers for a certain product.

Mutual Insurance Company: An insurance company in which ownership and control is vested in the policyholders and a portion of surplus earnings may return to policyholders in the form of dividends. No capital stock (e.g., common stock) exists.

Named Perils: Coverage in a Property Policy that provides protection against loss from only the perils specifically listed in the policy (rather than protection from physical loss). Examples of named perils are fire, windstorm, theft, smoke, etc.

National Association of Insurance Commissioners (NAIC): The association of insurance commissioners of various states formed to promote national uniformity in the regulation of insurance.

Navigation: The act of determining position, location and course to the destination of an aircraft or a vessel.

Negligence: Imprudent action or omission which may cause injury, damage or loss.

Negotiable: In terms of documents, 'negotiable' means that e.g. a Bill of Lading is handed over/transferred in the right manner (viz. proper endorsement) to another person either endorsed in blank or endorsed to a person and that person acquires, by this transfer certain rights vis-a-vis the goods e.g. is entitled to take possession of the goods.

Net Manifest: A manifest containing all freight details including negotiated disbursements.

Net Market: An online intermediary that connects fragmented buyers and sellers. Net markets eliminate inefficiencies by aggregating offerings from many sellers or by matching buyers and sellers in an exchange or auction. For buyers, they lower purchasing costs while reaching new suppliers. For suppliers, they lower sales cost and reach new customers. A central hub where a trusted intermediary integrates both procedures and technology can save costs. *Synonyms*: infomediary, metamediary, electronic markets, e-markets, Internet markets, I-markets, vertical hubs, e-hubs, butterfly markets, vortex businesses, digital exchanges, online exchanges, fat butterfly.

Net Market Maker: A company creating an Internet market to match buyers and sellers. Doesn't necessarily own goods. (See market maker.)

Net Premium: (1) The portion of the premium rate which is designed to cover benefits of the policy, but not expenses, contingencies, or profit. (2) The portion of the premium remitted to the home office by an agent after deduction of the agent's commission. (3) Net written premium.

Net Present Value: The value today of an asset to be received in the future, either as a single payment or a series of payments (such as an annuity). The value is considered to be different if received at a later date because of the time value of money.

Net Tonnage: The measure of the useful capacity of a vessel determined in accordance with the provisions of the international convention on tonnage measurement of vessels.

Net Weight: The weight of the goods, excluding all packing.

Network Effect: Describes how all buyers and sellers benefit when a new market participant is added. The network effect produces a cycle with more buyers attracting more sellers and more sellers attracting more buyers. Robert Metcalfe created the notion that the value of a network grows by the square of the number of participants. *Synonym*: Metcalfe's Law. (See liquidity, critical mass.)

Network Planning System: A technique for making a time schedule for the implementation of a project.

Net Written Premiums: Premium income retained by insurance companies, directly or through reinsurance, after payments made for reinsurance.

No-Fault Automobile Insurance: A form of insurance by which a person's financial losses resulting from an automobile accident are paid by his or her own insurer regardless of who was at fault.

Non-Admitted Insurance Company: An insurance company not licensed to do business in a particular state; such a company may sell excess and surplus insurance in the state if admitted insurers decline to write a risk.

Noncancellable: A clause stating that the insured has the right to continue a policy in force by the timely payments of premiums set forth in the contract for some extended period of time specified, during which period the insurer has no right to make unilaterally any change in any provision of the contract while the contract is in force.

Non-Commodity Documentation: Any document that contains information used in making an assessment in respect of non-commodity concerns.

Non-Commodity: Non-commodity issues relate to any matter that is not directly related to the actual goods within a consignment. Non-commodity issues include (but are not restricted to) soil contamination, animal/plant trash, Giant African Snail (GAS) issues and the presence of untreated wooden packing.

Non-Commodity Risk: The quarantine risk associated with those goods that are not commodities.

Nonconfining Sickness: A sickness that disables the insured person but does not confine him to his home or a hospital.

Non-Conformity/Non-Conformities: A deviation or multiple deviations from the documented procedures, which is confirmed through the collection of objective evidence that shows discrepancies or lapses in discipline relating directly to either AQIS requirements or legislative requirements, and which may compromise the overall effectiveness of the Scheme and Processes and Outcomes Document without breachins legislation.

Non-Contributory: A term applied to employee benefit plans under which the employer bears the full cost of the benefits for the employees. Generally, under noncontributory policies one hundred percent of the eligible employees must be insured.

Non-Disabling Injury Benefit: A benefit in some Disability Income Policies providing payment for medical expense due to injury when medical care is necessary but the Insured is not totally disabled.

Non-Disabling Injury: An injury which may require medical care, but does not result in loss of working time or income.

Non-Forfeiture Option: One of the choices available in many Life Insurance policies if the policy-holder discontinues premium payments on a policy with a cash value. This, if any, may be taken in cash, as extended Term Insurance or as reduced paid-up insurance.

Non-Medical Limit: The maximum face value of a policy that a given company will issue without the applicant taking a medical examination.

Non-Occupational Disability Policy: Contract which insures a person against off-the-job accident or sickness. It does not cover disability resulting from injury or sickness covered by Workers' Compensation. Group accident and sickness policies are frequently non-occupational.

Non-Participating Insurance: Plan of insurance under which the policyholder is not entitled to share in the dividend distribution of the company.

Non-Participating Policy: A Life Insurance policy, generally issued only by mutual insurance companies, in which the company does not distribute to policyholders any part of its surplus. Premiums for nonparticipating polices are usually initially lower than for comparable participating polices, but premiums can be varied. The current premium reflects anticipated experience that is more favorable than the company is willing to guarantee, and it may be changed from time to time.

Non-Profit Insurers: Persons organized under special state laws to provide hospital, medical, or dental insurance on a nonprofit basis. The laws exempt them from certain types of taxes.

Non-Vessel Operating Common Carrier: *Abbreviation:* NVOCC—A party who undertakes to carry goods and issues in his own name a Bill of Lading for such carriage, without having the availability of any own means of transport.

Normal Charge: The specified general cargo rate without any quantity discount (aircargo).

Normal General Cargo Rate: The under 45 kgs rate or, if no under 45 kgs rate exists, the under 100 kgs rate (aircargo). *Synonym*: Normal Rate.

Normalize: To create a consistent set of terms and product descriptions, often using industry-specific translation software. Primarily used by catalog aggregators, normalization technology requires translating schema or structures in product databases. (See ontology.)

Notice of Readiness: Written document or telex issued by the master of a vessel to the charterers advising them the moment when a vessel is ready to load or discharge. Document advising a consignee or his agent that cargo has arrived and is ready for delivery.

Notify Address: Address of the party other than the consignee to be advised of the arrival of the goods.

Not Subject to Quarantine (NSTQ): Goods that are of no quarantine concern and do not require mandatory AQIS inspection are described as Not Subject to Quarantine.

Notify Party: The party to be notified of arrival of goods.

Nouvelles Frontiéres: A 1986 ruling by the Court of Justice which ruled that air transport was not exempt from EC competition policy.

NVOCC: See Non-Vessel Operating Common Carrier.

Obsolete Stock: The products or materials that cannot be or is unlikely to be used in future processes and which is to be sold or disposed of through the usual outlets.

Occupational Hazards: Occupations which expose the Insured to greater than normal physical danger by the very nature of the work in which the insured is engaged, and the varying periods of absence from the occupation, due to the disability, that can be expected.

Occurrence: An accident, including continuous or repeated exposure to substantially the same general, harmful conditions, that results in bodily injury or property damage during the period of an insurance policy.

Occurrence Policy: A liability insurance policy that covers claims arising out of occurrences that take place during the policy period, regardless of when the claim is filed.

Ocean Marine Insurance: Coverage on all types of vessels, including liabilities connected with them, and on their cargoes.

Offshore: Contracting work carried out at sea (e.g., drilling for oil).

Oil Bulk Ore-Vessel: *Abbreviation*: OBO-Vessel—A vessel, designed for the carriage of either dry or liquid bulk cargo.

On-Board Computer: Cab-mounted device which electronically or mechanically records data such as truck speed, engine rpm, idle time and other information useful to trucking management.

Oncarriage: The carriage of goods (containers) by any mode of transport to the place of delivery after discharge from the ocean vessel (main means of transport) at the port (place) of discharge.

One Way Pallet: See disposable pallet. *Note*: The addition 'One Way' has nothing to do with the number of pallet sides in which the forks of e.g., a fork lift can enter, as opposed to the two and four way pallets.

Ontology: A Yahoo-like hierarchy of relationships and a glossary used as a standardization device to describe goods and services and to facilitate commerce in a Net market. (See normalize.)

Open Cover: An agreement whereby the Assured undertakes to declare every item (e.g., shipment, vessel, etc., as appropriate) that comes within the scope of the cover in the order in which the risk attaches. The insurer agrees, at the time of concluding the contract, to accept all valid declarations up to the agreed limit for each declaration. An open cover may be for a fixed period or always open; subject to a cancellation clause.

Open Order: See Backlog.

Open Sided Container: Shipping container with frames with wire-mesh at the sides covered by means of a tarpaulin which can be dropped down to give unrestricted access to the sides of the container for loading or discharging.

Open Top Container: A freight container similar in all respects to a general purpose container except that it has no rigid roof but may have a flexible and movable or removable cover, for example one made of canvas or plastic or reinforced plastic material normally supported on movable or removable roof bows.

Operating Efficiency: A ratio of the actual output of a piece of equipment, department, or plant as compared to the planned or standard output.

Operating Ratio: The sum of expenses and losses expressed as a percent of earned premium.

Operations Research: The development and application of quantitative techniques to the solution of problems. More specifically, theory and methodology in mathematics, statistics, and computing are adapted and applied to the identification, formulation, solution, validation, implementation and control of decision-making problems.

Operator: The party responsible for the day to day operational management of certain premises such as ware-houses, terminals and vessels.

Optimal Trim: The best calculated TRIM related to speed engine capacity, fuel consumption for a specific sailing condition.

Optimization: Achieving the best possible solution to a problem in terms of a specified objective function.

Option: One of a limited range of choices or features that is offered to a customer when purchasing an otherwise basic standard product and that has to be an integral part of the product (used in commercial trading).

Optional Cargo: Cargo of which the final destination is not known at the moment of booking but will be indicated during the transport.

Optional Port: A port of which it is not known whether or not it will be called by a vessel during a voyage.

Optionally Renewable Contract: A contract of Health Insurance in which the insurer reserves the right to terminate the coverage at any anniversary or, in some cases, at any premium due date, but does not have the right to terminate coverage between such dates.

Order: A request to deliver specified quantities of goods or to render specific services. Order line. Each line on a customer's purchase order. An order line always contains one Stock Keeping Unit (SKU) only, but the number may vary.

Order Into Quarantine (OIQ): The process of detaining goods, to isolate quarantine risk. Also, a form used to direct goods to treatment premises, under Section 55A of the *Quarantine Act 1908 (Cth)*. Also, the rifle of the forms used to order goods into quarantine.

Ordinance or Law Insurance: Coverage designed to provide protection against financial loss for (1) the loss of value of an undamaged portion of the existing building which must be demolished and/or removed to conform with municipal ordinance, code, etc.; (2) the cost of demolition of the undamaged portions of the building necessitated by the enforcement of building, zoning or land use ordinance or law; (3) any increased expenses incurred to replace the building with one conforming to building laws or ordinances, or to repair the damaged building so that it meets the specifications of current building laws or ordinances.

Ordinary Life Insurance: Life Insurance usually issued in amounts of $1,000 or more with premiums payable on an annual, semi-annual, quarterly or monthly basis. Compare Whole Life and Straight Life. The three terms are applied to the type of policy which continues during the whole of the insured's life and provides for the payment at death of an amount insured.

Organization: An identifiable social unit with a particular responsibility which endeavour to achieve multiple goals by coordinated activities and relationships between members and objects.

Other Car Insurance: Coverage designed to protect employees or executives of a company or any other person who is supplied a company vehicle, but who does not own a his or her own vehicle, therefore not having personal automobile coverage. The coverage is generally added by endorsement to the Automobile Policy of the company that furnishes the automobile, giving protection while the named individual or a member of his family is driving a car borrowed from a third party (other than the vehicle named in the policy).

Out of Gauge Cargo: Cargo which dimensions are exceeding the normal dimensions of a 20 or 40 feet container, e.g., overlength, overwidth, overheight, or combinations thereof.

Outsider: A carrier, which operates on a route served by a liner conference but which is not a member of that conference.

Outward Handling: The operations to be performed on outgoing goods from a production unit, both administrative and physical, starting at the moment forwarding orders can be executed to the moment of actual departure of the goods.

Overage: An additional premium charged on a cargo open cover declaration because the carrying vessel is outside the scope of the classification clause.

Overcarrier: A carrier within a consortium who carries cargo beyond the allotment distributed to him.

Overhaul: To extensively inspect and repair a system or component.

Overhead Expense Insurance: A special form of Health Insurance designed to help offset overhead expenses such as office rent, utilities, employees' wages, and auditors' fees, incurred during total disability. The monthly payments during disability are not a fixed amount of indemnity as on regular disability polices, but the amount of overhead expense actually incurred, or a percentage thereof, up to the limit specified in the policy.

Overhead Insurance: A type of short-term Disability Income contract that reimburses the insured person for specified, fixed monthly expenses, normal and customary in the operation and conduct of his/her business or office.

Overlength Cargo: Cargo, exceeding the standard length.

Overpack: A unit used by a single shipper to contain one or more packages and to form one handling unit for convenience of handling and stowage. Dangerous goods packages contained in the overpack must be properly packed, marked, labelled and in proper condition as required by the Regulations regarding dangerous goods (aircargo).

Overriding Commission (Overwrite): A commission paid to General Agents or agency managers in addition to the commission paid to the soliciting agent or broker.

Over-the Counter Market: A means of buying and selling securities that are not listed on a stock exchange. Negotiations are carried out by telephone or computer network.

Overtime: Work beyond normal established working hours that usually requires a premium to be paid to the employees concerned.

Overwidth Cargo: Cargo, exceeding the standard width.

Owner: The legal owner of cargo, equipment or means of transport.

Owner's Container Code: See Container Prefix.

Owner's or Contractor's Protective Liability Insurance: Coverage designed to provide for payment on behalf of the Insured all damages the insured becomes legally obligated to pay due to bodily injury or property damage caused by an occurrence arising from (1) operations performed for the named Insured by independent contractors, (2) acts or omissions of the named insured in connection with his/her general supervision of such operations. This does not include maintenance and repair at premises owned by or rented to the named insured, or structural alterations at such premises that do not involve changing the size of or moving buildings or other structures.

Owner-Operator: Trucker who owns and operates his own truck(s).

Package: Any physical piece of cargo in relation to transport consisting of the contents and its packing for the purpose of ease of handling by manual or mechanical means. The final product of the packing operation consisting of the packing and its contents to facilitate manual or mechanical handling. *Synonym*: Parcel.

Package Policy: A combination of two or more individual policies or coverages into a single policy. A home-owners policy, for example, is a package combining property, liability and theft coverages for the home-owner.

Packaging: Material intrinsically associated with cargo such as wooden pallets, crates, skids, etc., attached to the goods during transportation.

Packing Declaration: A declaration completed by the overseas packer/supplier that describes how the goods in a container were packed and whether the container was clean prior to packing.

Packing: Any container or other covering in which goods are packed.

Packing Instruction: Document issued within an enterprise giving instructions on how goods are to be packed.

Packing List: Document specifying the contents of each individual package.

Packing Unit: A type of package where a standard quantity of products of a specific product type can be packed and that requires no additional packaging for storage and shipment.

Paid-up Insurance: (1) Insurance on which all required premiums have been paid. (2) The reduced paid-up insurance available as a non-forfeiture option.

Pallet: A platform used to support cargo during shipment. Generally of standard dimensions to allow for easy stacking. Pallets used in shipping are generally made of timber, plywood, metal, plastic or moulded fiberboard.

Pallet Convertor: Superstructure which can be applied to a pallet to convert it into either a box or post pallet.

Pallet Rack: A skeleton framework, of fixed or adjustable design, to support a number of individual pallet loads.

Pallet Truck: Pedestrian- or rider-controlled non-stacking lift truck fitted with forks.

Panamax Size: The maximum measurements and dimensions of a vessel capable to pass the Panama Canal.

Paramedical Examination: Physical examination of an applicant by a trained person other than a physician.

Parcel: See Package.

Partial Disability Benefits: A benefit sometimes found in Disability Income Policies providing for the payment of reduced monthly income in the event the insured cannot work full time and/or is prevented from performing one or more important daily duties pertaining to his occupation.

Partial Disability: The result of an illness or injury which prevents an insured from performing one or more of the functions of his/her regular job.

Participating Insurance: Life insurance under which an insurance company agrees to distribute to policyholders the part of its surplus which its Board of Directors determines is not needed at the end of the business year. Such a distribution serves to reduce the premium the policyholder had paid.

Particular Average: (1) A fortuitous partial loss to the subject- matter insured, proximately caused by an insured peril but which is not a general average loss. Particular average only relates to damage and/or expenses which are exclusively borne by the owners of a vessel which has sustained damage as a result of e.g., heavy weather or by the owners of the cargo, which has been damaged in transit. (2) Accidental partial loss of subject-matter insured proximately caused by an insured peril. In a freight at risk policy the term may be applied to a claim for loss of freight following particular average loss of goods.

Partition: See Divider.

Pathogen: A micro-organism capable of causing disease in a host.

Payee: A party to whom a payment is made or owed.

Payer: A party who pays or is to pay.

Payload: The revenue-producing load carried by a means of transport.

Payment: That which discharges a debt.

Payment Against Documents: Instructions given by a seller to a bank to the effect that the buyer may collect the documents necessary to obtain delivery of the goods only upon actual payment of the invoice.

Pension Benefit Guaranty Corporation (PBGC): The federal body responsible for administering retirement insurance programmes, under ERISA.

Pension Benefits: A series of payments to be provided to past employees in accordance with the rules of pension plan of a company or other organization.

Pension Plan: A plan established and maintained by an employer, group of employers, union or any combination, primarily to provide for the payment of definitely determinable benefits to participants after retirement.

Percentage Participation: A provision in a health insurance contract that the insurer and insured will share covered losses in agreed proportions. Also see: Coinsurance.

Performance Bond: Bond issued by a surety or insurance company to guarantee performance under or in conjunction with a contract.

Performance Indicator: A variable indicating the effectiveness and/or efficiency of a process.

Performance Measurement: The comparison of the results of business processes with each other or with standards in order to know the effectiveness of these processes and/or the supportive actions.

Peril: The cause of a possible loss, such as fire, windstorm, theft, explosion, or riot, covered in an insurance policy.

Perils of the Sea: All perils which are unique to transportation and which could not be prevented by reasonable efforts, including sinking of the vessel, stranding, heavy weather, lightning, collision with other vessels or submerged objects (such as Titanic's iceberg), and damage by sea water when caused by an insured peril.

Permanent Life Insurance: A phrase used to cover any form of Life Insurance except Term Life; generally accrues cash value, such as Whole Life or Endowment.

Persistency: A term used to refer to the length of time insurance remains continuously in force.

Personal Articles Floater: A form of coverage designed to meet the needs for insurance on moveable property. The coverage usually protects against all physical loss, subject to specific exclusions and conditions. Examples of property that can be covered include jewelry, furs, silverware and fine arts.

Personal Effects (PEs): Non-commercial goods imported by private individuals, often with the assistance of a HGF, freight forwarder or similar. PEs include "household goods" and "unaccompanied baggage".

Personal Injury Liability Insurance: Coverage designed to protect against false arrest, detention or imprisonment, or malicious prosecution; libel, slander, defamation, or violation of right of privacy; and wrongful entry, eviction, or other invasion of right of private occupancy.

Personal Injury Protection (PIP): First-party no-fault coverage in an Automobile Insurance Policy in which an insurer pays, within the specified limits, the wage loss, medical, hospital and funeral expenses of the Insured.

Personal Lines: Those types of insurance, such as Auto or Home Insurance, for individuals or families rather than for businesses or organizations.

Personal Representative: A person appointed through the will of a deceased or by a court to settle the estate of one who dies.

Pest: Any species, strain orbiotype of plant, animal or pathogenic agent injurious to humans, plants, animals or the environment.

Physical Damage: Damage to or loss of the auto resulting from collision, fire, theft or other perils.

Physical Distribution: Those activities related to the flow of goods from the end of conversion to the customer.

Physical Distribution Management: The planning execution and control of those activities which are related to the flow of goods from the end of conversion to the customer.

Physician's Expense Insurance: Coverage which provides benefits toward the cost of such services as doctor's fees for nonsurgical care in the hospital, at home or in a physician's office, and X-rays or laboratory tests performed outside the hospital. (Also called Regular Medical Expense Insurance.)

Phytotoxic: Poisonous to plants.

Pick and Pack: Taking goods out of a stock and packing them according to customer conditions.

Pick Order: An order to pick certain quantities of goods out of a stock.

Pick Up and Delivery: A service concerning the collection of cargo from the premises of the consignor and the delivery to the premises of the consignee.

Picking: Taking products or components out of a stock.

Picking List: A list used to collect items from stores needed to fulfil an order. Synonym: Material issue list, Kitting list.

Pier: See Quay.

Piggyback: The carriage of road vehicles and trailers on railway wagons. *Synonym*: Huckepack Carriage.

Pilferage: Petty stealing of goods from a ship's hold, cargo shed or warehouse.

Pipeline: A line of pipes for conveying liquids and gasses. The physical goods flow from a supplying organization to a receiving organization.

Pipeline Inventory: The amount of goods in a pipeline: the sum of loading stock, goods in transit and receiving stock. *Synonym*: Floating Stock.

Place of Acceptance: See place of receipt.

Place of Delivery: The location where a consignment (shipment) is delivered to the consignee viz., the place where the carrier's liability ends for the transport venture.

Place of Receipt: The location where a consignment (shipment) is received by the carrier from the shipper viz., the place where the carrier's liability for transport venture commences. *Synonym*: Place of Acceptance.

Placement: The activity of positioning an object or goods in a chosen location or position.

Plan Administrator: The person or persons controlling the money or property contributed to a pension, health or other plan, usually designated in the plan agreement.

Planning: The setting of goals over a certain time and the determination of how to achieve these goals and with what resource.

Planning Horizon: The period of time to which a certain particular plan relates.

Plate Glass Insurance: Coverage designed to provide special protection, except for the perils of war, nuclear reaction and fire. (Fire is covered under the building policy.) This coverage is for full replacement cost and covers the expense of repairing frames, installing temporary plates or boarding up openings of plate glass windows.

Platform: (1) The area on an airport where aircrafts are parked for embarkation and/or loading and discharging purposes (aircargo). *Synonym*: Apron, Ramp. (2) The bare floor of a container, suitable for the carriage of uncontainerable cargo, as several platforms can be placed together to provide a larger base. Plated for the carriage of heavy goods. 20′ and 40′.

Platform Body: A truck or trailer without ends, sides or top but with only a floor.

Plimsoll Mark: A mark, welded on both sides of the vessel, which gives the limit to which a vessel may be loaded, depending on the specific gravity of the water in which the vessel is situated.

Point-of-Service Plans: Often known as open-ended HMOs or PPOs, these plans permit Insureds to choose providers outside the plan yet are designed to encourage the use of network providers.

Point Value: The point value can be seen as the relative value of an empty container of a certain size type in a depot location. The system serves to quantify the imbalance costs resulting from a full container move and are the result of empty optimization calculations.

Point values are created on forecasted container flows between depot locations. They are calculated taking into account a.o. the forecasted imbalances plus repositioning, storage and container costs for empty moves and expressed in USD.

Note: In the various computer systems point values are used to calculate the imbalance charge or credit for a particular container flow. This charge or credit is the difference in point values between start and end depot location.

Policy: The legal document issued by an insurance company to a policyholder, which outlines the conditions and terms of the insurance; also called the policy contract or the contract.

Policy Dividend: A refund of part of the premium on a Participating Life Insurance policy reflecting the difference between the premium charged and actual experience.

Policy Loan: A loan made by a life insurance company from its general funds to a policyholder on the security of the cash value of a policy.

Policy Reserves: The measure of the funds that a Life Insurance company holds specifically for fulfillment of its policy obligations. Reserves are required by law to be so calculated that, together with future premium payments and anticipated interest earnings, they will enable the company to pay all future claims. Compare Reserves.

Policy Term: That period for which an insurance policy provides coverage.

Policyholder: A person who pays a premium to an insurance company in exchange for the insurance protection provided by a policy of insurance.

Policyholders' Surplus: Sum left after liabilities are deducted from assets. Sums such as paid-in capital and special voluntary reserves are included in this term. This surplus is an additional financial protection to policyholders in the event a company suffers unexpected or catastrophic losses.

Pollution Legal Liability Insurance: Coverage designed (1) to protect all sums the Insured is legally obligated to pay as a result of emission, discharge, release, or escape of any contaminants, irritants, or pollutants into or on land, the atmosphere, or any water course or body of water, provided this results in environmental damage; (2) to reimburse reasonable and necessary cleanup costs incurred in the discharge of a legal obligation validly imposed through governmental action, provided such expense is incurred because of environmental damage; and (3) for the defense of any claim or suit that is the subject of this insurance.

Pollution Liability: Exposure to lawsuits for injury or cleanup costs that result from pollution damage.

Pontoon: A vessel with flat deck and a shallow draft.

Pool: (1) An organization of insurers or reinsurers through which particular types of risk are underwritten and premiums, losses and expenses are shared in agreed-upon amounts. (2) The shared use of e.g., equipment by a number of companies, which make together the investments in the equipment mentioned.

Poop: Aft part of a vessel where the steering engine is located.

Port: Harbour having facilities for vessels to moor and load or discharge. Left side of a vessel when facing towards the front or forward end.

Port of Call: Place where a vessel actually drops anchor or moors during a certain voyage.

Port of Discharge: The port where the cargo is actually discharged (unloaded) from the sea (ocean) going vessel.

Port of Loading: The port where the cargo is actually loaded on board the sea (ocean) going vessel.

Portability: The right to transfer pension rights and credits when a worker changes jobs.

Portal Crane: A type of gantry crane with vertical legs of sufficient height and width to permit vehicles or railroad equipment to pass between the legs.

Portlog: A statement concerning a vessel containing the actual arrival and departure time used tugs, draft, deadweight, quantity of discharged and loaded goods/ containers and any other important particulars.

Positioning: The transport of empty equipment from a depot to shipper's premises or from consignee's premises back to a depot as the empty leg of a carrier haulage transport.

Postal Code: A national code maintained by the Postal Authorities designed to indicate areas and accumulated addresses to facilitate sorting and the delivery of mail and other goods. Note: The coding system is different in the various countries throughout the world. In the Netherlands the code consists of 4 figures and 2 characters.

Preadmission Certification: Process in which a health care professional evaluates an attending physician's request for a patient's admission to a hospital by using established medical criteria.

Precarriage: The carriage of goods (containers) by any mode of transport from the place of receipt to the port (place) of loading into the ocean vessel (main means of transport).

Precarrier: The carrier by which the goods are moved prior to the main transport.

Preexisting Condition: A physical and/or mental condition of an Insured which first manifested itself prior to the issuance of his/her policy or which existed prior to issuance and for which treatment was received.

Preferred Provider Organization (PPO): An arrangement whereby a third-party payer contracts with a group of medical care providers who furnish services at lower than usual fees in return for prompt payment and a certain volume of patients.

Preferred Stock: Evidence of ownership which entitles the holders to receive dividends from the corporation before the common stockholders, but after bondholders, and which usually also provides a claim prior to common holders to corporate assets if the corporation is dissolved.

Premium: The sum paid by a policy-holder to keep an insurance policy in force.

Premium Finance: Payment terms that allow the insured to pay part of the premium when coverage takes effect and pay the rest during the policy period.

Premium Loan: A loan, sometimes made by a third party, made for the purpose of paying premiums to the insurer.

Premium Tax: A tax, imposed by each state, on the premium income of insurers doing business in the state.

Prepaid Group Practice Plan: A plan under which specified health services are rendered by participating physicians to an enrolled group of persons, with a fixed periodic payment in advance made by or on behalf of each person or family. If a health insurance carrier is involved, a contract to pay in advance for the full range of health services to which the insured is entitled under the terms of the health insurance contract. Such a plan is one form of Health Maintenance Organization (HMO).

Preshipment Inspection: *Abbreviation*: PSI—The checking of goods before shipment for the purpose of determining the quantity and/or quality of said goods by an independent surveyor (inspection company) for phytosanitary, sanitary and veterinary controls.

Presently there is a tendency by developing countries to use the inspection also for the purpose of determining whether the price charged for certain goods is correct.

Pre-slinging: The act of placing goods in slings which are left in position and used for loading into and discharging from a conventional vessel.

Pre-trip Inspection: *Abbreviation*: PTI—A technical inspection of Reefer containers prior to positioning for stuffing.

Price Transparency: When both buyer and seller know pricing. Net markets can eliminate arbitrage situations when only a broker knows the price. Net markets can result in sellers making more money and buyers paying a lower price, since broker margins are reduced.

Primary Insurance: Insurance that pays compensation for a loss ahead of any other insurance coverages the policy-holder may have.

Principal: Person for whom another acts as agent.

Principal Carrier: See Responsible Carrier.

Principal Corporate Body: The company that owns the various subsidiary companies or branches acting as customers on their own and is registered as the corporate customer for statistical purposes.

Principal Sum: The amount payable, under Life and Health Insurance policies, in one sum in the event of accidental death and in, some cases, accidental dismemberment. When a contract provides benefits for both accidental death and accidental dismemberment, each dismemberment benefit is an amount equal to the principal sum or some fraction thereof.

Priority Order: An order which is identified as taking precedence over other orders to ensure its completion in the minimum time. *Synonym*: Urgent order, Rush order.

Private Carrier: Business which operates trucks primarily for the purpose of transporting its own products and raw materials. The principle business activity of a private carrier is not transportation.

Private Warehouse: A warehouse operated by the owner of the goods stored there.

Probate: The court-supervised process of validating or establishing a distribution for assets of a deceased including the payment of outstanding obligations.

Probate Estate: That portion of the assets and liabilities whose distribution is supervised by the courts in the probate process.

Probationary Period: A period from the policy date to a specified time, usually 15 to 30 days, during which no sickness coverage is effective. It is designed to eliminate a sickness actually contracted before the policy went into effect.

Procurement: The activities which ensure the availability of the material and or services in the desired quantity, quality, place and time from the supplier.

Procurement Hub: An MRO procurement marketplace for routine purchases such as office supplies, travel services, or computers needed to run a business but not central to the business's output. A type of horizontal or functional market. Examples: Ariba, Commerce One.

Procurement Logistics: Control of the flow of materials up to the manufacturing process.

Product: A result, end item or output from a certain process.

Product Chain: All phases in the transformation- or production process of one product.

Product Liability: Legal liability incurred by a manufacturer, merchant, or distributor because of injury or damage resulting from the use of its product.

Product Liability Insurance: Coverage designed to provide protection against financial loss arising out of the legal liability incurred by a manufacturer, merchant or distributor because of injury or damage resulting from the use of a covered product.

Product Life Cycle: The period of time between the introduction date and end date of a product in the market. *Note*: Phases are introduction, growth, maturity, saturation, decline & end.

Production: The conversion of materials and or assembly of components to manufacture goods, products or services. The total quantity of goods manufactured or to be manufactured in a particular period of time expressed in quantitative or financial terms. (The term manufacturing is often used specifically for physical operations resulting in a product).

Productivity: Relative measure of output of labour hour or machine hour.

Professional Review Organization (PRO): An organization in which practicing physicians assume responsibility for reviewing the propriety and quality of health care services provided under Medicare and Medicaid.

Profile: A set of characteristics used to target incoming risk items.

Profit Centre: An organizational unit which will be held responsible for its own profits and losses.

Pro Forma Invoice: Draft invoice sent to an importer by the exporter prior to order confirmation and shipment to assist in matters relating to obtaining import licences or foreign exchange allocations, or simply to advise the value of a consignment so that letters of credit can be opened.

Project Cargo: Quantity of goods connected to the same project and often carried on different moments and from various places.

Proof of Delivery: The receipt signed by the consignee upon delivery.

Proof of Loss: Documentary evidence required by an insurer to prove a valid claim exists. It usually consists of a claim form completed by the insured, and for health insurance claims by the insured's attending physician. for medical expense insurance itemized bills must also be included.

Proper Shipping Name: A name to be used to describe particular goods on all shipping documents and notifications and, if appropriate, on the goods.

Property Damage Coverage: An agreement by an insurance carrier to protect an insured against legal liability for damage by an insured automobile to the property of another.

Property Insurance: Insurance providing financial protection against the loss of, or damage to, real and personal property caused by such perils as fire, theft, windstorm, hail, explosion, riot, aircraft, motor vehicles, vandalism, malicious mischief, riot and civil commotion and smoke. Available on Special and All-risk forms, depending on the property being insured.

Property Management Errors and Omissions Insurance: Coverage designed to pay on behalf of the insured all sums he/she becomes legally obligated to pay by reason of any act, error, or omission arising out of services rendered or that were failed to be rendered. Such services include arranging for property maintenance, renting or leasing, construction, alteration, land development, etc. Coverage also provides for defense of any claim or suit that is the subject of this insurance.

Propriety Standard: A standard which has been endorsed by industry or government as the accepted international standard, but not officially approved by an accredited standards body such as ISO.

Proration: The adjustment of benefits paid because of a mistake in the amount of the premiums paid or the existence of other insurance covering the same accident or disability.

Prospective Payment: An advancement of payment for health care charges that are likely to occur.

Protection and Indemnity Club: *Abbreviation*: P & I club—A mutual association of shipowners who provide protection against liabilities by means of contributions.

Protocol: A statement drawn up to attest certain events.

Prototype Plan: A standardized life insurance plan, approved and qualified as to its concept by the internal revenue service, which is made available by companies, banks and mutual funds for employers' use.

Provision: A clause, sentence or paragraph of an insurance contract that describes or explains a feature, benefit, condition, requirement, etc., of the insurance protection afforded by the contract.

Proximate Cause: The most direct cause of loss, that is, the most effective and dominant cause in a chain of events which ends in the loss.

Public Authorities: The agencies or officials in a state responsible for the application and enforcement of the laws and regulations of that state. *Source*: IMO.

Public Warehouse: A warehouse which is available to all companies and persons who wish to make use of the services offered.

Pull Distribution System: A system to provide warehouses with new stock on request of the warehouse management.

Punitive Damages: A court-awarded amount that exceeds the economic losses and general damages of a defendant and is intended solely to punish the plaintiff.

Purchase Order: A definite order for one or more deliveries by the supplier to the customer of a specific quantity of goods, materials, services or products under agreed terms of delivery and prices.

Purchasing Hub: Buyer-centric mediators that aggregate demand from small buyers to negotiate better terms with large sellers. Can be horizontal (operating supplies) or vertical manufacturing. Used for spot purchasing (using exchange or auction) or systematic purchasing (catalog mechanism). The horizontal purchasing hubs use horizontal logistics (UPS, for example), while the vertical purchasing hubs generally need vertical logistics (for hazardous chemicals, for example) work with existing distributors.

Push Distribution System: A system to provide warehouses with new stock upon decision of the supplier of the goods.

Qualification Period: The period during which the insured must be totally disabled before becoming eligible for Residual Disability benefits.

Qualified Impairment Insurance: A form of Substandard or Special Class Insurance, which restricts benefits for the insured person's particular condition.

Qualified Plan: A plan which the Internal Revenue Service approves as meeting the requirements of Section 401(a) of the 1954 Internal Revenue Code. Such plans receive tax advantages.

Qualified Terminable Interest Property: A category of property, created by the Economic Recovery Tax Act, which by a deceased spouse's will entitles the surviving spouse to all income from the property for life, with that income payable at least annually, and precludes anyone including the spouse from appointing the property to anyone else during the spouse's life.

Qualifier: A data element whose value shall be expressed as a code that gives specific meaning to the function of another data element or a segment.

Quality (ISO8402): The totality of features and characteristics of a product or service that bear on its ability to satisfy stated or implied needs. *Note*: The ISO9000 standards on quality management and quality assurance consists of 4 standards: 9000 guidelines for selection and use, 9001 model for quality assurance in design/development 9002 model for quality assurance in production and installation, 9003 model for quality assurance in final inspection and test, and 9004 guidelines for quality management and quality system elements, part 2 are guidelines for services.

Quality Assurance (ISO8402): All those planned and systematic actions necessary to provide adequate confidence that a product or service will satisfy given requirements for quality.

Quality Control (ISO8402): The operational techniques and activities that are used to fulfill requirements for quality.

Quantity Charge: The unit rate which is lower than the normal rate and applies to shipments meeting specific weight requirements (aircargo).

Quantity Discount: A proportional reduction of a rate based on quantity (aircargo).

Quarantinable Goods: Any imported goods that are subject to quarantine.

Quarantine: The period during which an arriving vessel, including its equipment, cargo, crew or passengers, suspected to carry or carrying a contagious disease is detained in strict isolation to prevent the spread of such a disease.

Quarantine Approved Premises (QAP): Facilities that are approved by AQIS for the performance of quarantine under section 46A of the *Quarantine Act 1908 (Cth).* For the purpose of this document, the term 'Quarantine Approved Premises' will be taken to mean the area specifically meeting the necessary standards for the Class of QAP.

Quarantine Area: The designated area within a QAP where goods subject to quarantine are stored, handled and/or treated. This area may also be used for the collection and temporary storage of quarantine waste and dunnage. The Quarantine Area and the QAP may be synonymous.

Quarantine Containment: The safe methods for managing goods within a Quarantine Approved Premises environment where they are being handled or maintained. Quarantine containment reduces or eliminates the exposure of persons and the outside environment to potentially hazardous quarantine risk material.

Quarantine Entry: An ACS/AQIS electronic document which details information relating to consignments of goods imported into Australia. Entries are generated using ICS.

Quarantine Fumigation: The fumigation of goods to meet quarantine clearance requirements.

Quarantine Inspection Area: That portion of a Quarantine Area designated for use by AQIS officers for performing detailed inspections of goods subject to quarantine.

Quarantine Interest: Any goods, vectors, receptacles or locations subject to the *Quarantine Act 1908 (Cth).*

Quarantine Non-commodity Concern: Quarantine risk that is imposed by anything other than the cargo itself and includes packing or contamination.

Quarantine Pest: A pest of potential economic and/or environmental importance to an area where it is not yet present, or is present but not widely distributed and being officially controlled.

Quarantine Risk Material (QRM): Includes but is not limited to live insects, seeds, soil, dirt, clay, animal material, plant material such as straw, twigs, leaves, roots, bark, food refuse and other debris.

Quarantine Waste: May include, but is not limited to: (*a*) Material used to pack or stabilise cargo; and (*b*) Galley and food waste; and (*c*) Human, animal or plant waste; and (*d*) Refuse or sweepings from the holds or decks of a vessel or installation. Quarantine waste also includes the accumulated solids from any process that separates larger solid particles of material fromwastewater or from any other quarantine operation. Further, examples of quarantine waste include solid material such as dead bodies, tissues, unhatched eggs, microbiological waste or residues of imported material and packaging of quarantine concern.
Quarantine waste excludes excrement from imported circus animals, horses, dogs, cats or animals held at QC1 facilities that are considered to pose a minimal risk to quarantine.

Quarantine Wastewater: The liquid portion of the residue associated with any quarantine operation at an approved quarantine facility. Quarantine wastewater excludes excrement from imported circus animals, horses, cats, dogs and animals held at QC1 facilities, which are considered to pose a minimal risk to quarantine.

Quay: That part of a wharf which is intended for the mooring of vessels. *Synonym*: pier.

Queue: A stored arrangement of computer data, programmes or messages, waiting to be processed in the order in which they were submitted.

Quoin: Timber wedge used to secure drums against movement.

Quota Restrictions: Restraints upon trade which limit the volume of exports into a country, abolished within the EC by 1968, and removed in many of the international agreements to which the EC is party.

Quotas: A system of controlling imports, exports or production by specifying a certain limitation.

Quotation: Amount stated as the price according to tariff for certain services to be provided or issued to a customer with specification on conditions for carriage.

Quotation Expiration Date: The date as from which a quotation price is no longer valid.

Rail Car: A wheeled wagon used for the carriage of cargo by rail.

Rail Consignment Note: A document evidencing a contract for the transport of goods by rail.

Ramp: An artificial inclined path, road or track along which wheeled vehicles, cargo and trailers may pass for the purpose of changing their elevation and facilitating the loading and unloading operation (e.g. an entrance way into a Roll-on Roll-off vessel). For aircargo see Platform.

Rate: (1) The price of a transport service.
Quantity, amount or degree measured or applied.
(2) The pricing factor upon which the insurance buyer's premium is based.

Rate of Calculation: A factor for the calculation of an amount.

Rate of Turn: The figure indicating the speed of a change of course of a means of transport expressed in degrees per minute.

Rated Policy: An insurance policy issued at a higher-than-standard premium rate to cover a higher-than-standard risk; for example, for an insured who has impaired health or a hazardous occupation.

Ratemaking: The statistical process by which insurers determine probability of loss and pricing for the basic classes of insurance.

Rating: A class to which an article is assigned.

Rating Territory: A geographical grouping in which like hazards tend to equalize and permit the establishment of an equitable rate for the territory.

Raw Timber: Unfinished timber, including furniture and wooden articles. Does not include dunnage or wooden packing materials.

Real-Time: The description for an operating system that responds to an external event within a short and predictable time frame. Unlike a batch or time-sharing operating system, a real-time operating system provides services or control to independent ongoing physical processes.

Reasonable and Customary Charge: A charge for health care which is consistent with the going rate or charge in a certain geographical area for identical or similar services.

Rebate: That part of a transport charge which the carrier agrees to return.

Rebating: Giving any valuable consideration, usually all or part of the commission, to the prospect or Insured as an inducement to buy or renew. Rebating is illegal.

Receipt: A written acknowledgement, that something has been received.

Receiving Carrier: The carrier receiving a consignment on behalf of a carrier, agent or shipper for onward transport (aircargo).

Receiving Stock: The stock comprising all the goods that have arrived at the door of the receiving organization and which is not yet available in the stock of that organization.

Receptacle: Non-commodity goods that are used to carry commodity goods. Receptacles for different programmes are:

Programme—Airport, International mail, Import clearance, Seaport.

Receptacle—Passenger, Parcels letter etc., Containers, Pallets, vessels ate.

Reconditioning: All activities connected with restoring and or adjusting the packaging of a product. In such manner that it can be presented to the customer in the requested form.

Reconditioning of Garments: The act or process of bringing garments after transport in shop's condition.

Recovery: Amount recovered from a third party responsible for a loss on which a claim has been paid.

Recurring Claim Provision: A provision in some health insurance policies which specifies a length of time during which the recurrence of a condition is considered to be a continuation of a previous period of disability or hospital confinement. Also known as a Recurring Clause.

Redelivery: Return of a shipment to the party who originally delivered it to the carrier (aircargo). Return of a charter vessel to the owners.

Reduced Paid-Up Insurance: A form of insurance available as a non-forfeiture option. It provides for continuation of the original insurance plan, but for a reduced amount.

Reefer: Refrigerated trailer with insulated walls and a self-powered refrigeration unit. Most commonly used for transporting food.

Reefer Cargo: Cargo requiring temperature control.

Reefer Container: A thermal container with refrigerating appliances (mechanical compressor unit, absorption unit etc.) to control the temperature of cargo.

Reforwarding Charge: Charges paid or to be paid for subsequent surface or air transport from the airport of destination by a forwarder, but not by a carrier under the Air Waybill (aircargo).

Refund: The repayment to the purchaser of the total charge or a portion of that charge for unused carriage.

Region: Specified geographical area for operational purposes.

Register Ton: The unit of measurement for the internal capacity of a vessel whereby one register ton equals 100 cubic feet (2.83 cubic meter). The gross (bruto) tonnage comprises all spaces below the main (tonnage) deck and the enclosed spaces above the main (tonnage) deck less exempted spaces. The net tonnage consists of the gross tonnage less exemptions like ballast tanks, engine room, living quarters etc. The register tonnages are mentioned on the tonnage certificate.

Regroupage: The process of splitting up shipments into various consignments (degroupage) and combining these small consignments into other shipments (groupage).

Regulation: Supervision of business practices by a governmental entity. Regulation of insurance companies is through respective state insurance commissioners.

Rehabilitation: (1) Restoration of a totally disabled person to a meaningful occupation. (2) A provision in some Long-term Disability Policies that provides for continuation of benefits or other financial assistance while a totally disabled insured is retraining or attempting to resume productive employment.

Reimbursement: The payment of the expenses actually incurred as a result of an accident or sickness, but not to exceed any amount specified in the policy.

Reinstatement: The resumption of coverage under a policy which has lapsed.

Reinstatement Audit: An audit scheduled and conducted by a Quarantine Officer following an Other Party's period of suspension from a Scheme.

Reinsurance: The acceptance by one or more insurers, called reinsurers, of a portion of the risk accepted by another insurer who has contracted for the entire coverage. Reinsurance can be treaty or facultative.

Reinsurance Facility: An alternative mechanism to service those insureds who cannot obtain insurance in the voluntary market. Premiums and losses for the business that is ceded to the facility are pooled and all insurers share according to their proportion of the voluntary market.

Re-invoicing: The procedure whereby goods shipped directly from a supplier to the customer are invoiced in two stages: at first by the supplier to an intermediary and subsequently by the intermediary to the customer.

Rejection: Non-acceptance of e.g., cargo.

Relay: Common practice in the less-than-truckload industry, in which one driver takes a truck for 8 to 10 hours, then turns the truck over to another driver, pony express style.

Release: Authorisation for release from quarantine after all AQIS impediments lifted.

Reliability of Delivery: The reliability of a supplier concerning the agreed terms of delivery with regard to the quality, quantity, delivery time, conditions and price.

Renewable Term Insurance: Term insurance which can be renewed at the end of the term, at the option of the policy-holder and without evidence of insurability, for a limited number of successive terms. The rates increase at each renewal as the age of the insured increases.

Renewal: Continuance of coverage under a policy beyond its original term by the insurer's acceptance of the premium for a new policy term.

Rent Insurance: A form of Business Interruption Insurance for a landlord, designed to protect building owners against loss of income when rentals have been interrupted or rental value has been impaired by the occurrence of any of the insured perils. It assures continuous income while an Insured's building is untenantable.

Renter's Policy: A package type of insurance that includes coverage similar to a homeowners policy to cover the personal property of a renter or tenant in a building.

Replacement: Indicating that a subject is interchangeable with another subject, but which differs physically from the original subject in that the installation of the replacement subject requires extra machining or provisions in addition to the normal application and methods of attachment.

Replacement Clause: A clause limiting Underwriters' liability for damage to machinery cargo.

Replacement Cost Insurance: Insurance designed to provide coverage on the basis of full replacement cost without deduction for depreciation on any loss sustained, subject to the terms of the co-insurance clause. This coverage applies to both building and contents items as specified on the face of the policy. No deduction is taken for depreciation in arriving at the proper amount of insurance needed to comply with the coinsurance clause.

Replacement Cost: The cost to repair or replace property at construction costs prevailing at time of loss; the cost to repair or rebuild property without considering depreciation. Contrast Actual Cash Value.

Replacement Ratio: The percentage of income before retirement that is required to be replaced to maintain the same standard of living after retirement.

Replenishment: Completion of stock.

Representation: Statements made by an applicant in an insurance application, which he represents as being substantially true to the best of his knowledge and belief, but which are not warranted as exact in every detail.

Request for Proposals (RFP): Invitation to suppliers to bid on supplying products or services that are difficult to describe for a company or public agency.

Request for Quotation (RFQ): Invitation to suppliers to bid on supplying easily described products or services needed by a company or public agency.

Rescission: Termination of an insurance contract by the insurer on the grounds of material misstatement on the application for insurance. The action of rescission must take place within the contestable period or Time Limit on Certain Defenses clause set forth in the policy, but takes effect as of the effective date of the policy, thus voiding the contract from its inception.

Reservation: Allotment in advance of space or weight capacity. Also referred to as 'booking'.

Reservation of Rights: An arrangement whereby an insurer defends a case without commitment to provide coverage in the event that the facts disclosed during the trial reveal that the occurrence is not covered.

Reserve: (1) An amount representing an insurer's estimate of its liabilities on future commitments under policies outstanding. (2) An amount allocated for a special purpose.

Reserve Inventory: See Safety Stock.

Residual Disability Benefits: A provision in an insurance policy that provides benefits in proportion to a reduction of earnings as a result of disability, as opposed to the inability to work full-time.

Residual Disability: A period of partial disability that immediately follows a period of total disability. Benefits for residual disability are paid on a pro-rata basis, depending on the percentage of earnings loss.

Residual Market: A source of insurance available to applicants who are unable to obtain insurance through ordinary methods in the voluntary market. (See: Automobile Insurance Plan, Joint Underwriting Association).

Responsible Carrier: (1) The carrier liable under the terms of a consortium Bill of Lading. (2) Carrier responsible for the transport of goods as indicated in the transport document (aircargo). *Synonym*: Principal Carrier.

Retention: The net amount of risk retained by an insurance company for its own account or that of specified others, and not reinsured.

Retrocession: The process by which a reinsurer obtains reinsurance from another company.

Retrospective Date: The first date for which claims will be paid under a Claims-Made Policy of Liability Insurance.

Retrospective Rating: Rating procedure which allows adjustment of an Insured's final rate on the basis of the Insured's own loss experience.

Returns: Goods returned to their place of acceptance.

Revenue: Amounts of income stemming from the provision of transport services.

Reverse Auctions: Buyers post their need for a product or service, then suppliers bid to fulfill that need. Unlike an auction, prices only move down. FreeMarkets (industrial parts, raw materials) uses reverse auctions as its primary market mechanism, serving large buyers. Since buyer power is key to reverse auctions, they work either for large enterprises or when practiced by intermediaries like KillerBiz andBizBuyer, which aggregate demand of many small buyers. Reverse auctions also are becoming common features of many Net markets.

Reverse Distribution: The collection of used, damaged, or outdated products and/or packaging from end-users.

Review Level: The level at which an Other Party will be monitored for its performance against a Scheme and under its Compliance Agreement.

Review Period: The review period is the time each review level is applicable for.

Revocable Trust: A trust that can be terminated or revoked by its creator.

Rider: A document that modifies an insurance policy. It may increase or decrease benefits, waive a condition or coverage, or in any other way amend the original contract. See Endorsement.

Right of Survivorship: Legal rule which states that at the death of one co-owner of property, that person's interest in the property automatically passes to the surviving joint tenant or tenants.

Rinacertificate: Certificate issued by the Italian Government for carrying dangerous goods in Italian Waters.

Risk: (1) A fortuity. It does not embrace inevitable loss. The term is used to define causes of loss covered by a policy. (a) The chance of loss; (b) The insured or property covered by a policy or application.
(2) The probability of an exotic pest or disease establishing in Australia. Risk may take account of the likelihood of exposure of the goods to an exotic pest or disease in the originating country or on the import pathway, the likelihood of leakage, the likelihood of exposure to a susceptible host, the likelihood of establishment and spread of a pathogen, and the likely consequences of its establishment.

Risk Classification: The process by which a company decides how its premium rates for life insurance should differ according to the risk characteristics of individuals insured (e.g., age, occupation, sex, state of health) and then applies the resulting rules to individual applications.

Risk Control: Any conscious action (or decision not to act) intended to reduce the frequency, severity, or unpredictability of accidental losses.

Risk Retention Group: An alternative form of insurance in which members of a similar profession or business band together to self-insure their risks.

Road Carrier: Party undertaking transport by road of goods from one point to another such as indicated in the contract. *Synonym*: Haulier.

RoadRailer: Semitrailer specially designed to travel both on highway and on rails. Manufactured by Wabash Corp.

Road Vehicle: A means of transport capable and allowed to move over public roads and other landways.

Robbery: The taking of property from a person by force or threat of violence.

Roll Trailer: Special trailer for terminal haulage and stowage on board of Roll-on Roll-off vessels. Also referred to as Mafi Trailer.

Rolling Resistance: The total frictional force that a tyre, a set of tyres or all the tyres on a vehicle is developing with the road.

Roll-on Roll-off: *Abbreviation*: RoRo—System of loading and discharging a vessel whereby the cargo is driven on and off by means of a ramp.

Rollover: Transfer of IRA or other qualified pension funds from one financial institution to another.

RoRo: See Roll-on Roll-off.

Rotation: Sequence in which a vessel calls at the ports on her itinerary.

Round Trip: A voyage, a journey etc., to a certain place, port or country and back again.

Route: The track along which goods are (to be) transported.

Routing: The determination of the most efficient route(s) that people, goods, materials and or means of transport have to follow. The process of determining how a shipment will be moved between consignor and consignee or between place of acceptance by the carrier and place of delivery to the consignee. The process of aiding a vessel's navigation by supplying long range weather forecasts and indicating the most economic and save sailing route.

Row: A vertical division of a vessel from starboard to portside, used as a part of the indication of a stowage place for containers. The numbers run from midships to both sides.

SAD: See Single Administrative Document.

Safe Working Load: *Abbreviation*: SWL—The maximum load any lifting appliance may handle.

Safety Stock: In general, a quantity of stock planned to be in inventory to protect against fluctuations in demand and/or supply. In the context of master production scheduling, safety stock can refer to additional inventory and/or capacity planned as protection against forecast errors and/or short terms changes in the backlog. Also referred to as 'overplanning' or a 'market hedge'. *Synonym*: Reserve Inventory.

Said to Contain: *Abbreviation*: STC—Term in a Bill of Lading signifying that the master and the carrier are unaware of the nature or quantity of the contents of e.g., a carton, crate, container or bundle and are relying on the description furnished by the shipper.

Sales Cycle: Condition seen in the selling of insurance in which premium prices rise and fall over time in relation to capacity. The sales cycle is generally completed over several of years.

Salvage Charges: The award due to a salvor for services rendered in saving the insured property.

Salvage Loss: Occurs when the Underwriter agrees to settle a cargo claim by paying the difference between the insured value and the proceeds realised by selling the damaged goods.

Salvage: The saving or rescue of a vessel and/or the cargo from loss and/or damage at sea.

Sanctions: A range of penalties that may be imposed for non-compliance under a Compliance Agreement.

Scale Ton: Freighting measurement used in certain trades for various commodities.

Schedule: A list attached to a slip, open cover, policy or other document, usually detailing the rates of premium for various voyages, interests and risks.

Scheduled Insurance: An insurance policy amendment or endorsement that specifies items covered, in contrast to blanket coverage, which would cover all items fitting a given description. Auto insurance is the principal scheduled insurance purchased by consumers.

SCP Simplified Clearance Procedure: A procedure covering non-restricted goods which enables approved exporters or agents to export goods on presentation of minimum information. The full statistical information is supplied within 14 days of shipment.

SCR: See Specific Commodity Rate.

SDR: See Special Drawing Rights.

Seal: A device used for containers, lockers, trucks or lorries to proof relevant parties that they have remained closed during transport.

Seal Log: A document used to record seal numbers.

Seals Intact: Often heard in the phrase "Deliver seals intact." This means that a consignment has been permitted to move from one place to another under seal. The inspector at the receiving end is to check to ensure that the seals have not been broken in transit.

Seasonal Inventory: Inventory built up in anticipation of a seasonal peak of demand in order to smooth production.

Seaworthiness: Fitness of a vessel to travel in open sea mostly related to a particular voyage with a particular cargo.

Seaworthiness Warranty: There is an implied warranty in every voyage policy that the ship must be seaworthy at the commencement of the insured voyage or, if the voyage is carried out in stages, at the commencement of each stage of the voyage. To be seaworthy, the ship must be reasonably fit in all respects to encounter the ordinary perils of the contemplated voyage, property crewed, fuelled and provisioned, and with all her equipment in proper working order. Cargo policies waive breach of the warranty, except where the Assured or their servants are privy to the unseaworthiness. Breach of the warranty is not excused in a hull voyage policy, literal compliance therewith being required. Although there is no warranty of seaworthiness in a hull time policy, claims arising from unseaworthiness may be prejudiced if the ship sails in an unseaworthy condition with the knowledge of the Assured.

Sectional Rate: The rate established by scheduled air carrier(s) for a section of a through route (aircargo).

Security: The Underwriters subscribing a risk.

SED: See Shipper's Export Declaration. See Bill of Lading.

Segregation: Distance required by the rules of IMDG or BC codes between the various commodities of dangerous and or bulk cargoes.

Self- Administered (Trusteed or Directly Invested) Plan: A plan funded through a fiduciary, generally a bank, but sometimes a group of individuals, which directly invests the accumulated funds. Retirement payments are made from the fund as they fall due.

Self-Administration: The procedure where an employer maintains all records regarding the employees covered under a Group Insurance Plan.

Self-Insurance: A form of risk management through which a firm assumes all or a part of its own losses.

Seller's Market: A 'seller's market' is considered to exist when goods cannot easily be secured and when the economic forces of business tend to be priced at the vendor's estimate of value. In other words, a state of trade favourable to the seller, with relatively great demand and high prices of something for sale.

Selling Price Insurance: Coverage which applies to the value of goods which have been damaged or destroyed by an insured peril. The purpose is to assure the profit that would have been incurred through a sale. It defines the insurable value of merchandise which has been sold, but not delivered, at the amount at which it was sold, less any charges not incurred.

Semi Trailer: A vehicle without motive power and with one or more axles designed to be drawn by a truck tractor and constructed in such way that a portion of its weight and that of its load rest upon e.g., the fifth wheel of the towing vehicle.

Sender: See Shipper.

Senior Citizen Policies: Contracts insuring persons 65 years of age or more. In most cases, these policies supplement the coverage afforded by the government under the Medicare programme. For example, see Medigap.

Separate Account: An asset account established by a life insurance company separate from other funds, used to match specific assets with corresponding liabilities such as pension plans and variable life products. This arrangement permits wider latitude in the choice of investments, particularly in equities.

Service Bill: A service bill (of lading) is a contract of carriage issued by one carrier to another for documentary and internal control purposes. For internal documentary and control purposes a so-called participating agent in a consortium uses some kind of document which, depending on the trade, is referred to as 'Memo Bill' which will among others state:

- Name of Carrier on whose behalf the original document (Way Bill, Bill of Lading, etc.) was issued.
- The original document number.
- The agent who issued the original document and his opponent at the discharging side.
- The number of packages, weight and measurement, marks and numbers and goods description.
- Further mandatory details in case of special cargo.
- No freight details will be mentioned and the Memo Bill is not a contract of carriage.

Service Level: A measure for the extent to which the customer orders can be executed at delivery conditions normally accepted in the market.

Service-Type Plans: Plans that provide their benefits in the form of services rendered rather than cash (for example, Blue Cross and Blue Shield).

Setting/Air Delivery Temperature: An indication in the documents (B/L) stating the air supply temperature to the container.

Note: No other details than this temperature shall be included in the Bill of Lading.

Settlement Options: The several ways, other than immediate payment in cash, which a policy-holder or beneficiary may choose to have policy benefits paid.

Shed: See Warehouse.

Shelf Life: The specified length of time prior to use for which items which are inherently subject to deterioration are deemed to remain fit for use under prescribed conditions. *Synonym*: Storage life.

Shift: Part of the work-programme of a stevedoring company (a working day can have up to 3 shifts {24 hours}).

Ship: See Vessel.

Ship Broker: Acts as intermediary between shipowners or carriers by sea on the one hand and cargo interests on the other. The functions are to act as forwarding agent or custom broker, fixing of charters, and acting as chartering agent.

Ship's Protest: Statement of the master of a vessel before (in the presence of) competent authorities, concerning exceptional events which occurred during a voyage.

Shipment: A separately identifiable collection of goods to be carried. See Consignment. *Note*: In the United States of America the word shipment is used instead of the word consignment.

Shipoperator: A ship operator is either the shipowner or the (legal) person responsible for the actual management of the vessel and its crew.

Shipowner: The (legal) person officially registered as such in the certificate of registry where the following particulars are contained.

- Name of vessel and port of registry.
- Details contained in surveyors certificate.
- The particulars respecting the origin stated in the declaration of ownership. The name and description of the registered owner, if more than one owner the proportionate share of each.

Shipper: The merchant (person) by whom, in whose name or on whose behalf a contract of carriage of goods has been concluded with a carrier or any party by whom, in whose name or on whose behalf the goods are actually delivered to the carrier in relation to the contract of carriage. *Synonym*: Consignor, Sender.

Shipper's Export Declaration: *Abbreviation*: SED—A United States customs form to be completed for all exports to assist the government in compiling export statistics.

Shipper's Letter of Instruction: *Abbreviation*: SLI—A document containing instructions given by the shipper or the shipper's agent for preparing documents and forwarding (aircargo).

Shipping Aids: Material used in sea freight containers to prevent cargo dislodging in transit.

Shipping Container: Standard-sized rectangular box used to transport freight by ship, rail and highway. International shipping containers are 20 or 40 feet long, conform to International Standards Organization (ISO) standards and are designed to fit in ships' holds. Containers are transported on public roads atop a container chassis towed by a tractor.

Shipping Documents: Documents required for the carriage of goods. *Synonym*: Transport Documents.

Shipping Instruction: Document advising details of cargo and exporter's requirements of its physical movement.

Shipping Label: A label attached to a shipping unit, containing certain data.

Shipping Marks: The identification shown on individual packages in order to help in moving it without delay or confusion to its final destination and to enable the checking of cargo against documents. *Synonym*: Marks.

Shipping Note: Document provided by the shipper or his agent to the carrier : ultimodal transport operator, terminal or other receiving authority, giving information about export consignments offered for transport, and providing for the necessary receipts and declarations of liability.

Shipping Weight: "Dry" weight of a truck including all standard equipment, but excluding fuel and coolant.

Shortage: The negative difference between actual available or delivered quantity and the required quantity.

Short-term Disability Income Insurance: Coverage designed to cover a disabled person as long as he/she remains disabled up to a specified period not exceeding two years.

Shrink Wrapping: Heat treatment that shrinks an envelope of polyethylene or similar substance around several units, thus forming one unit. It is used e.g., to secure packages on a pallet.

Shut-out: Containers not carried on intended vessel.

Shuttle Service: The carriage back and forth over an often short route between two points.

SIC: See Standard Industrial Classification.

Sickness Insurance: A form of Health Insurance providing benefits for loss resulting from illness or disease.

Siding: A short railroad track connected with a main track by a switch : to serve a warehouse or an industrial area.

Simulation: The imitation of the reality for studying the effect of changing parameters in a model as a means of preparing a decision.

Single Administrative Document: *Abbreviation*: SAD—A set of documents, replacing the various (national) forms for customs declaration within European Community, implemented on January 1st, 1988. The introduction of the SAD constitutes an intermediate stage in the abolition of all administrative documentation in intra European Community trade in goods between member states.

Single Market: In which the twelve member states of the European Community form a Single Market in which there is free movement of goods, persons, services and capital. Came into being 01 01 1993, when export and import Custom entries were abolished for intra-community trade.

SITPRO: National organization for the simplification of International Trade PROcedures in the United Kingdom (e.g. in The Netherlands SITPRO is called 'Sitproneth', in France 'Simprofrance' and in Japan 'Jastpro').

Skeleton Trailer: Road trailer consisting of a frame and wheels, specially designed to carry containers. See Chassis.

Skid: Support placed under cargo to make it easier to manoeuvre. Generally consists of two pieces of timber placed under cargo to allow a forklift to raise or slide the cargo.

Skids: Battens fitted underneath frames, boxes or packages to raise them off the floor and allow easy access for fork lift trucks, slings or other handling equipment.

Skip Person: A beneficiary who is at least two generations younger than the person making the transfer.

Sleeper: Sleeping compartment mounted behind a truck cab, sometimes attached to the cab or even designed to be an integral part of it.

Sleeper Team: Team of two drivers who alternative driving and resting.

SLI: See Shipper's Letter of Instruction.

Sliding Tandem: An undercarriage with a subframe having provision for convenient fore and aft adjustment of its position on the chassis/semi-trailer. The purpose being to be able to shift part of the load to either the king pin or the suspension to maximize legally permitted axle loads (road cargo).

Sling: Special chain, wire rope, synthetic fibre strap or ropes used for cargo handling purposes.

Slot: The space on board a vessel, required by one TEU, mainly used for administrative purposes.

Slot Charter: A voyage charter whereby the shipowner agrees to place a certain number of container slots (TEU and/or FEU) at the charterer's disposal.

SOB (Shipped On Board): An endorsment on a B/L confirming loading of goods on the vessel.

Social Security Freeze: A Long-Term Disability Policy provision which establishes that the subtraction from benefits paid by Social Security will not be changed regardless of subsequent changes in the Social Security Law.

Social Security Option: An option available in some annuity contracts under which the employee may elect that monthly payments of an annuity before a specified age (62 or 65) be increased, and that payments thereafter be decreased to produce, as nearly as practical, level total annual payments, including Social Security benefits when they become due.

Soft Market: That part of the insurance sales cycle in which competition is at a maximum as insurance companies use their excess capacity to sell more policies at lower prices.

Space Charter: A voyage charter whereby the shipowner agrees to place part of the vessels capacity at the charterers disposal.

Special Damages: Compensation awarded for actual economic losses, such as medical expenses and lost wages.

Special Drawing Rights: *Abbreviation*: SDR—Unit of account from the International Monetary Fund (IMF), i.e. used to express the amount of the limitations of a carrier's liability.

Special Rate: A rate other than a normal rate (aircargo).

Special Risk Insurance: Coverage designed to provide financial protection against risks or hazards of a special or unusual nature.

Specific Commodity Rate: *Abbreviation*: SCR—A rate applicable to carriage of specifically designated commodities (aircargo).

Specified Rate: A rate specified in an IATA Cargo Tariff Coordination Conference resolution (aircargo).

Speedability: Top speed a vehicle can attain as determined by engine power, engine governed speed, gross weight, driveline efficiency, air resistance, grade and load.

Split Funding: The use of two or more funding agencies for the same pension plan. An arrangement whereby a portion of the contributions to the pension plan are paid to a life insurance company and the remainder of the contributions invested through a corporate trustee, primarily in equities.

Spoke: The stretch between a hub and one of the group of consignees and/or consignors being served by the hub.

Spontaneous Ignition Temperature: The lowest temperature at which a substance will start burning spontaneously without an external source of ignition.

Spot Market: A market for unplanned purchases not made under contract terms. Transactions usually made on a one-time basis. Related terms: spot buy, spot demand.

Spouse's Benefit: Payments to the surviving spouse of a deceased employee, usually in the form of a series of payments upon meeting certain requirements and usually terminating with the survivor's remarriage or death.

Spread: The movement of a pest or disease beyond the initial incursion.

Spreader: Device used for lifting containers and unitized cargo. Beam or frame that holds the slings vertical when hoisting a load, to prevent damage to cargo.

Stability: The capacity of a vessel to return to its original position after having been displaced by external forces. The stability of a vessel depends on the meta-centric height.

Stack: An identifiable amount of containers stowed in a orderly way in one specified place on an (ocean) terminal, container freight station, container yard or depot (see container stack).

Stacking: To pile boxes, bags, containers etc., on top of each other.

Stackweight: The total weight of the containers and cargo in a certain row.

Standard Costs: A carefully prepared estimate of the cost of performing a given operation under specified conditions. *Note*: A standard work order describes a standard operation for which a standard cost is to be established.

Standard Industrial Classification: *Abbreviation*: SIC—A method, used in the United States, to categorize companies into different industrial groupings.

Standard Insurance: Life insurance written on the basis of regular morbidity underwriting assumptions used by an insurance company and issued at normal rates.

Standard Markets: Insurance companies for which the majority of people or organizations qualify.

Standard Product Module: *Abbreviation*: SPM—The building blocks used by business management to define services (shipment products) which can be offered to customers. They describe a more or less isolated set of activities with a standard cost attached to it. For operations management each module defines a combination of standard operations that needs to be carried out for a customer. *Note*: SPM's can be regarded as the interface between business and operations management.

Standard Provisions: A set of provisions set forth in laws that prescribed certain rights and obligations of both the insured and the company under personal health insurance policies. These were originally introduced in 1912 and have now been replaced by the Uniform Provisions.

Standard Risk: A person who, according to a company's underwriting standards, is entitled to purchase insurance protection without extra rating or special restrictions.

Standards: Efforts to create wide use of specific protocols so software from different vendors can interoperate more easily, particularly within a vertical industry. Standards bodies or efforts often work more slowly than entrepreneurial companies in setting up interoperable terms of trade. Many e-commerce standards today are based on XML (eXtensible Markup Language), which provides a flexible way to describe product specifications or business terms. Relevant b2b e-commerce standards efforts include BizTalk, promoted by Microsoft so different industries can communicate online with each other; Open Buying on the Internet (OBI), overseen by trade group CommerceNet; and RosettaNet, an effort within the computer manufacturing industry.

Standards Testing: Determines whether the national, international, or military standards and specifications) are viable and implementable.

Starboard: Right side of a vessel when facing towards the front or forward end.

State Disability Plan: A plan for accident and sickness, or Disability Insurance required by state legislation of those employers doing business in that particular state.

State Fund: A fund set up by a state government to provide a specific line or lines of insurance.

State Insurance Department: A department of a state government whose duty is to regulate the business of insurance and give the public information on insurance.

State-of-the-Art Defense: An argument used in product liability cases that the technology needed to avoid the loss in a particular case did not exist at the time of the product's manufacture.

Statutory Accounting: Special accounting practices for insurance companies required by state law, prescribing a greater level of detail than required by GAAP and designed to provide greater protection for the public against potential insolvency of these essential institutions.

Statutory Accounting Principles (SAP): Rules of financial computation and presentation required by statute which must be followed by an insurance company when submitting its financial statements to state insurance departments. Such principles differ from Generally Accepted Accounting Principles (GAAP).

Statutory Underwriting Profit or Loss: Premiums earned less losses and expenses, as calculated under Statutory Accounting Principles.

STC: See Said To Contain.

Steering of Containers: The function, with the aid of specific software for tracking and forecasting (IRMA, MINKA), to direct empty containers to demanding areas at minimum costs.

Stem: The foremost part of a vessel.

Step-Rate Premium: A rating structure in which the premiums increase periodically at pre-determined times such as policy years or attained ages.

Step-Up In Basis: An increase in the tax basis of property to the value claimed in the taxable estate of a decedent.

Stern: The aftermost part of a vessel.

Sticky, Stickiness: The ability to retain participants. (See switching costs, lifetime value of the customer.)

Stock: The materials in a supply chain or in a segment of a supply chain, expressed in quantities, locations and or values. *Synonym*: Inventory when used as a generic term, common in the USA and extensive in the UK.

Stock Company: A company organized and owned by stockholders, as distinguished from the mutual form of company which is owned by its policy-holders.

Stock Control: The systematic administration of stocklevels with respect to quantity at all times.

Stock Exchange: An organization that provides a facility for buyers and sellers of listed securities to come together to make trades in those securities.

Stock Insurance Company: A company in which the legal ownership and control is vested in the stockholders.

Stock Keeping Unit: The description of the unit of measurement by which the stock items are recorded on the stock record.

Stock Life Insurance Company: A life insurance company owned by stockholders who elect a board to direct the company's management. Stock companies, in general, issue Nonparticipating Insurance, but may also issue Participating Insurance.

Stock Locator System: A system in which all places within a warehouse are named or numbered.

Stock Point: A point in the supply chain meant to keep materials available.

Stock Record: A record of the quantity of stock of a single item, often containing a history of recent transactions and information for controlling the replenishment of stock.

Stock Redemption Plan: An entity purchase form of Buy-Sell Agreement within a corporation that involves the corporation buying back shares from a departing owner.

Stockholder: A person who owns shares of stock in a corporation.

Storage: The activity of placing goods into a store or the state of being in store (e.g., a warehouse).

Storage Charge: The fee for keeping goods in a warehouse.

Stores: Provisions and supplies on board required for running a vessel.

Stowage: The placing and securing of cargo or containers on board a vessel or an aircraft or of cargo in a container.

Stowage Factor: Ratio of a cargo's cubic measurement to its weight, expressed in cubic feet to the ton or cubic metres to the tonne, used in order to determine the total quantity of cargo which can be loaded in a certain space.

Stowage Instructions: Imperative details about the way certain cargo is to be stowed, given by the shipper or his agent.

Stowage Plan: A plan indicating the locations on the vessel of all the consignments for the benefit of stevedores and vessel's officers.

Stowaway: An unwanted person who hides on board of a vessel or an aircraft to get free passage, to evade port officials etc.

Straddle Carrier: Wheeled vehicle designed to lift and carry shipping containers within its own framework. It is used for moving, and sometimes stacking, shipping containers at a container terminal.

Straddle Crane: A crane usually running on rails and spanning an open area such as rail-tracks or roadways.

Straight Life Insurance: Whole life insurance on which premiums are payable for life.

Straight Truck: Vehicle which carries cargo in a body mounted to its chassis, rather than on a trailer towed by the vehicle.

Strange Attractor: A key feature that causes buyers and sellers to use a Net market, often eliminating a transaction cost in a specific industry. Examples: CarStation (locating, then obtaining auto body parts), e-Chemical (distributing industrial chemicals), Chemdex (comparing chemical reagents from different vendors), Floraplex (paying sellers in seven days, not 45).

Strap: A band of metal, plastic or other flexible material used to hold cargo or cases together.

Straw: Includes straw, cereal, rice hulls, and other unprocessed plant materials.

Stretch: The leg between two points.

Strict Liability: Liability for damages even though fault or negligence cannot be proven.

Stripping: The unloading of cargo out of a container. *Synonym*: Devanning, Unstuffing, Unpacking.

Stuffing: The loading of cargo into a container. *Synonym*: Vanning, Packing.

Subject To Quarantine (STQ): Goods requiring AQIS inspection and possible remedial action. Goods may be subject to quarantine if they are dirty or the goods are viewed as of quarantine concern.

Suboptimizing: Striving for optimum performance in one element of an organization disregarding the effects this may cause to the performance of the other elements. In other words, a solution for a problem that is best from a narrow point of view but not from a higher or overall company point of view.

Subrogation: (1) Process by which one insurance company seeks reimbursement from another company or person for a claim it has already paid. (2) The right of the Underwriter to step into the shoes of the Assured following payment of a claim to recover the payment from another party who was responsible for the loss. Limited to the amount paid on the policy.

Substandard (Impaired) Risk: A risk that cannot meet the normal requirements of a standard insurance policy. Protection is provided in consideration of a waiver, a special policy form, or a higher premium charge.

Substandard Insurance: Insurance issued with an extra premium or special restriction to those persons who do not qualify for insurance at standard rates.

Substretch: Part of a stretch. This term is used if it is necessary to distinguish between a stretch and a part thereof.

Sue and Labour (Marine): Expenses incurred by the assured or their representatives with the intention of preventing or minimising a loss for which the Underwriter would have been liable. They do not include expenses incurred in general average or salvage acts; these being recoverable under the policy only as part of the Underwriters' liability for contribution to general average or salvage, if any. Sue and labour charges are recoverable under a policy that incorporates a sue and labour clause (SG policy), or in accordance with the wording of the policy (e.g. under the "duty of the assured" clause attached to a MAR policy).

Supercargo: Experienced officer assigned by the charterer of a vessel to advise the management of the vessel and protect the interests of the charterer.

Supplementary Contract: An agreement between a life insurance company and a policy-holder or beneficiary by which the company retains the cash sum payable under an insurance policy and makes payments in accordance with the settlement option chosen.

Supply Chain: A sequence of events in a goods flow which adds to the value of a specific good. These events may include:

- conversion.
- assembling and/or disassembling.
- movements and placements.

Supply Chain Management: An attempt to coordinate processes involved in producing, shipping and distributing products, generally with large suppliers. Net markets can extend supply chain management to all trading partners regardless of size because they provide a central hub to integrate information from buyers and sellers.

Supply Vessel: Vessel which carries stock and stores to offshore drilling rigs, platforms.

Surcharge: An additional charge added to the usual or customary freight.

Surety Bond: An agreement providing for monetary compensation in the event of a failure to perform specified acts within a stated period. The surety company, for example, becomes responsible for fulfillment of a contract if the contractor defaults.

Surgical Expense Insurance: Health insurance, which provide benefits toward the physician's or surgeon's operating fees. Benefits may consist of scheduled amounts for each surgical procedure.

Surgical Schedule: A list of maximum amounts payable by the policy for various types of surgery, with the amount based on the severity or complexity of the operation.

Surplus: The net worth of a company, equal to the amount by which assets exceed liabilities.

Surplus Lines: (1) A risk or a part of a risk for which there is no standard insurance market available. (2) Insurance written by non-admitted insurance companies.

Surveillance: The active observance by a Quarantine Officer of activities and environments that may pose a quarantine concern to ensure quarantine integrity is maintained.

Survey: An inspection of a certain item or object by a recognized specialist.

Surveyor: A specialist who carries out surveys. *Note*: A surveyor is quite representing a classification bureau or a governmental body.

Susceptible Host: A plant, human, animal or the environment that could be infected by an exotic pest or disease.

Switching Costs: Costs incurred in changing suppliers or marketplaces. Net markets often seek to re-architect procurement, search, and other processes so buyers stay put, a key reason switching costs are higher in business-to-business than consumer e-commerce. (See lifetime value of the customer, churn).

SWL: See Safe Working Load.

Swop Body: Separate unit without wheels to carry cargo via road sometimes equipped with legs to be used to carry cargo intermodal within Europe. The advantage being that this unit can be left behind to load or discharge whilst the driver with the truck/chassis can change to another unit. These units are not used for sea transport.

Synergy: The simultaneous joint action of separate parties which, together, have greater total effect than the sum of their individual effects. *Synonym*: Header Board.

System: A whole body of connected elements which influence each other and have specific relations with the environment.

T1: Goods that are not in free circulation are assigned the EC Customs code T1.

T2: Goods that are in free circulation are assigned the EC Customs code T2.

Table of Multiples: The life expectancy figures provided by the Internal Revenue Service to be used in calculating the exclusion ratio for life contingent annuities after June 30, 1986. Separate tables provide the figures for joint and last survivor annuities, annuities that contain a refund or minimum payment guarantee, and for annuities that pay quarterly, semi-annually, or annually.

Tailgate Inspection: This inspection is undertaken to visually verify some aspect of the contents of a container such as packing or to establish whether the goods in the container have been satisfactorily fumigated. A Quarantine Officer at the opened container doors performs this without entering the container.

Tallyman: A person who records the number of cargo items together with the condition thereof at the time it is loaded into or discharged from a vessel.

Tank Container: A tank, surrounded by a framework with the overall dimensions of a container for the transport of liquids or gasses in bulk.

Tanker: A vessel designed for the carriage of liquid cargo in bulk.

Tare Mass of Container: See Tare Weight of Container.

Tare Weight of Container: Mass of an empty container including all fittings and appliances associated with that particular type of container on its normal operating condition. *Synonym*: Tare Mass of Container.

Tariff: The schedule of rates, charges and related transport conditions.

Tarpaulin: Waterproof material, e.g., canvas, to spread over cargo to protect it from getting wet.

Tax Basis: The cost from which your profits or losses are calculated for income tax purposes.

Taxable Estate: The value upon which estate taxes are calculated by the federal government.

Taxonomy: A classification system for items based on their relationship to one another. *Related terms*: ontology, normalize.

Temporary Life Annuity: An annuity payable while the annuitant lives but not beyond a specified period, such as five years. No payments are to be made after the end of the stipulated temporary period or the death of the annuitant.

Ten Day Free Look: A notice on the first page of health insurance policies that the insured has ten days in which to examine the policy and return it for a refund of premium if he is not satisfied with the policy.

Tenants in Common: A form of joint property ownership in which the owners may have unequal shares and which does not involve a right of survivorship.

Term Insurance: Life insurance payable to a beneficiary only when an insured dies within a specified period. The coverage expires without value if the insured survives the stated period.

Terminal: A location on either end of a transportation line including servicing and handling facilities.

Terms of Delivery: All the conditions agreed upon between trading partners regarding the delivery of goods and the related services. *Note*: Under normal circumstances the INCO terms are used to prevent any misunderstandings.

Terms of Freight: All the conditions agreed upon between a carrier and a merchant about the type of freight and charges due to the carrier and whether these are prepaid or are to be collected. *Note*: The so-called Combi terms based on the INCO terms do make a distinction what of the freight and related costs is to be paid by the seller and what by the buyer. In the UN recommendation 23 a coding system is recommended to recognize the various items.

Testamentary Trust: A trust created through the will of its creator.

TEU: See Twenty Foot Equivalent Unit. The concept should be used in combination with load factor management. The landing gear of an aircraft.

Theft, Disappearance and Destruction of Money and Securities Insurance: Coverage designed to provide protection against financial loss for loss of money and securities resulting directly from theft (any act of stealing), disappearance and destruction. Coverage applies while the money and securities are on the insured's premises, while in the custody of the insured or the insured's messenger while conducting business at the bank, and while off the insured's premises in the custody of the insured or the insured's messenger.

Thermal Container: A container built with insulating walls, doors, floor and roof by which heat exchange with the environment is minimized thus limiting temperature variations of the cargo.

Third Party: The claimant under a Liability Policy. So-called because the person making the claim is not one of the two parties, insured and insurer, to the insurance contract.

Third Party Claim: A demand made by a third party against a policy-holder of an insurer and any payment that will be made by that company.

Third Party Logistics: Supply of logistics related operations between traders by an independent organization.

Third-Party Over Suit: A lawsuit where a third-party tries to recover damages assessed against that party by bringing suit against his or her employer.

Threshold: The point, measured in money, time or other ways, beyond which tort liability can be established. Until that point is reached, reparations must be paid within the provisions of the no-fault plan, with no recourse to the Courts.

Through Charge: The total rate from point of departure to point of destination. It may be a joint rate or a combination of rates (aircargo). *Synonym*: Through Rate.

Through Rate: See Through Charge.

Through Route: The total route from point of departure to point of destination (aircargo).

Tier: A horizontal division of a vessel from bottom to top. The numbers run from bottom to deck and from deck upwards and are used as a part of the indication of a stowage place for containers.

Tilt Transport: Roadtransport whereby the cargo area is protected against the elements by means of a tilt made of canvas or other pliable material.

Timber: Also known as lumber; a term of commerce for wood, either in natural form as logs or in sawn units.

Time Charter: A contract whereby a vessel is let to a charterer for a stipulated period of time or voyage, for a remuneration known as hire, generally a monthly rate per ton deadweight or a daily rate. The charterer is free to employ the vessel as he thinks fit within the terms as agreed, but the shipowner continues to manage his own vessel through the master and crew who remain his servants.

Time Element Insurance: Coverage designed to provide insurance for a covered incident resulting in loss of use of property for a period of time. For example, Business Interruption and Extra Expense Insurance.

Time Limit: The period of time during which a notice of claim or proof of loss must be filed.

Time Limit on Certain Defenses: The 2-year or 3-year time period in health insurance policies after which the insurer cannot deny a claim or void a policy because of pre-existing conditions or misstatements on the application.

Time Sheet: Statement, drawn-up by the ship's agent at the loading and discharging ports, which details the time worked in loading and discharging the cargo together with the amount of laytime used.

Time Value of Money: The income that can be gained over time by holding money, such as interest income or dividends.

TIR: Transport International des Merchandises par la Route.

TOFC: See Trailer on Flat Car.

To Pay as Cargo: Used in an ancillary insurances relating to the cargo (e.g., increased value) when the Assured is not required to show evidence of loss or interest and can claim on the policy if he can show that a corresponding loss has been settled on the main cargo policy. Today the term has been widened to "Hull and Machinery" (H+M). The term Hull is also quite commonly deemed to embrace two other major groups of vessel owners' interests: "Disbursements and Collision Liability." Disbursements includes the ship's stores, bunker fuels and freight-earnings capacity up to an agreed maximum of 25 per cent of the total value for Hull and Machinery. The second, "Running Down Collision" liability (RDC), provides cover to the ship-owner for ¾ of liability to other ships in the event of collision.

Ton: Unit of weight measurement: 1000 kilograms (metric ton) or 2,240 lbs (long ton).

Unit of cubic measurement, mainly used to express the cubic capacity of a vessel. Unit of weight or measurement used as a basis for the calculation of freights (freight ton).

Tonnage: Cubic capacity of a merchant vessel. Total weight or amount of cargo expressed in tons. The displacement of a vessel in tons of water; or a duty charged per ton of cargo at a port, pier, dock or canal.

Tornado: A whirling wind over land, accompanied by a funnel-shaped cloud. It is usually very violent and destructive in a narrow path, often for many miles.

Tort: A civil wrong, other than a breach of contract, for which a court of law will afford legal relief, e.g., harming another by an act of negligence in driving an auto.

Total Disability: An illness or injury which prevents an insured person from continuously performing every duty pertaining to his/her occupation or engaging in any other type of work.

Total Loss: This can be actual total loss or constructive total loss.

Tracing: The action of retrieving information concerning the whereabouts of cargo, cargo items, consignments or equipment.

Tracking: The function of maintaining status information, including current location, of cargo, cargo items, consignments or containers either full or empty.

Traction: The power to grip or hold to a surface while moving without slipping.

Tractor: A powered vehicle designed and used for towing other vehicles.

Trade: (*a*) The exchange of goods, funds, services or information with value to the parties involved. This value is either previously agreed or established during business. (*b*) A commercial connection between two or more individual markets.

Traffic: The number of passengers, quantity of cargo etc., carried over a certain route.

Trailer: A vehicle without motive power, designed for the carriage of cargo and to be towed by a motor vehicle.

Trailer on Flat Car: *Abbreviation*: TOFC—Carriage of piggyback highway trailers on specially equipped railway wagons.

Tramp Vessel: A vessel not operating under a regular schedule.

Trans Siberian Landbridge: Overland route from Europe to the Far East via the Trans Siberian Railway (TSR).

Transfer Cargo: Cargo arriving at a point by one flight and continuing there-from by another flight (aircargo).

Transferability: Any arrangement under which the accumulated benefit credits of a terminating participant, or their actuarial value, are transmitted from one plan to another, or to a central agency.

Transferring Carrier: A participating carrier who delivers the consignment to another carrier at a transfer point (aircargo).

Transit Cargo: Cargo between outwards customs clearance and inwards customs clearance. Cargo arriving at a point and departing there from by the same through flight (aircargo).

Transit Clause: A clause in the Institute Cargo Clauses, specifying the attachment and termination of cover.

Transit Insurance: Coverage of the Insured's property while in transit over land from one location to another. Property Insurance Policies typically provide coverage only at locations identified in the policy.

Transit Shipment: A shipment passing between one port and another, or between a port and a final destination.

Transmission Control Protocol/Internet Protocol: A compilation of network and transport level protocols that allow a PC to speak the same language as other PCs on the internet or other networks. Acronym: TCP/IP.

Transponder: A device (chip) used for identification, which automatically transmits certain coded data when actuated by a special signal from an interrogator.

Transport: The assisted movement of people and or goods. *Synonym*: Carriage. *Note*: Transport is often used as a generic term for various means of transport, and is distinguished from 'movement' in that it requires such means.

Transport Documents: See Shipping Documents.

Transport International by Road: *Abbreviation*: TIR—A set of rules following a customs convention to facilitate the international, European transport of goods by road with minimal interference under cover of TIR-carnets.

Transport Policy: The subject of several legislative decisions since 1983, but while regulations apply to several different transport sectors, there is as yet no common transport policy.

Travel Accident Policy: A limited contract covering only accidents while an insured person is travelling, usually on a commercial airline carrier.

Treatment: Any process for controlling or eliminating a disease or pest and: (*a*) In relation to a vessel, installation or premises, includes examination, spraying, fumigation, disinfection, denaturing and cleaning; and (*b*) In relation to a person, includes examination, spraying, fumigation, disinfection and cleaning; and (*c*) In relation to an animal, includes examination, disinfection, denaturing, vaccination, testing and veterinary treatment; and (*d*) In relation to a plant or other goods, includes examination, spraying, fumigation, and disinfection, denaturing, sorting, cleaning and repacking.

Treatment Certificate: A certificate that specifies the treatment applied to goods within a specific consignment to destroy any pests that may be present.

Treaty: An agreement between a reinsurer and a ceding insurer setting forth details of the reinsurance arrangement.

Trip: See Voyage.

Trip Leasing: Leasing a company's vehicle to another transportation provider for a single trip.

Trip Recorder: Cab-mounted device which electronically or mechanically records data such as truck speed, engine rpm, idle time and other information useful to trucking management.

Truck: Class of automotive vehicles of various sizes and designs for transporting goods.

Truckload: The quantity of freight required to fill a trailer; usually more than 10,000 pounds. *Acronym*: TL.

Trunk: The stretch between two hubs mutually.

Trunking: Movement of containers between terminal and carrier's inland facilities.

Trust: A legal instrument allowing one party to control property for the benefit of another.

Tugmaster: Brand name of tractor unit used in ports to pull trailers. They are equipped with a fifth wheel or a gooseneck type of coupling.

Tweendeck: Cargo carrying surface below the main deck dividing a hold horizontally in an upper and a lower compartment.

Twenty Foot Equivalent Unit: *Abbreviation*: TEU—Unit of measurement equivalent to one twenty foot shipping container.

Twisting: The practice of inducing by misrepresentation, or inaccurate or incomplete comparison, a policy-holder in one company to lapse, forfeit or surrender his insurance for the purpose of taking out a policy in another company.

Twistlock: Device which has to be inserted into the corner fittings of a shipping container and is turned or twisted, thus locking the container for the purpose of securing or lifting.

Two Way Pallet: A pallet of which the frame permits the entry of forks of (e.g., a fork lift at two opposite sides).

Type of Cargo: An indication of the sort of cargo to be transported, (e.g. Break Bulk, Containerized, RoRo).

Type of Equipment: The type of material used, e.g. 40 feet container, four way pallet or mafi trailer.

Type of Facility: 'Type' refers to the kind of Quarantine Approved Premises that a containment facility will fall into. The facility will be one of four 'types'—Microbiological, Animal, Plant or Invertebrate.

Type of Load Indicator: A general reference or a classification of loads of cargo like 'FCL', 'LCL', 'unpacked' and even ship's convenience container, though this is rarely used nowadays.

Type of Means of Transport: The type of vehicle used in the transport process, e.g. wide-body aircraft, tank truck or passenger vessel.

Type of Movement: Description of the service for movement of containers. *Note*: The following type of movement can be indicated on B/L and Manifest all combinations of FCL and LCL and break bulk and RoRo. Whilst only on the manifest combinations of House, Yard and CFS can be mentioned.

Type of Packing: Description of the packaging material used to wrap, contain and protect goods to be transported. *Synonym*: Kind of Packing, Package Type.

Type of Transport: The indication whether the carrier or the merchant effects and bears the responsibility for inland transport of cargo in containers i.e., a differentiation between the logistical and legal responsibility. *Note*: Values are Carrier haulage and Merchant haulage, whilst in this context special cases are carrier-nominated merchant haulage, and merchant nominated carrier haulage.

Type of Vessel: The sort of vessel used in the transport process e.g. Container, RoRo, or Multi Purpose.

UCP 500: See Uniform Customs and Practice for Documentary Credits.

UIC: See Union Internationale des Chemins de Fer.

ULCC: See Ultra Large Crude Carrier.

ULD: See Unit Load Device.

Ullage: Free space above a liquid contained in a tank, drum or tank-container, expressed as a percentage of the total capacity. Ullage is often used to leave room for possible expansion of the liquid.

Ultra Large Crude Carrier (ULCC): A vessel designed for the carriage of liquid cargo in bulk with a loading capacity from 250.000 till 500.000 DWT.

Umbrella Liability Insurance: Coverage designed to protect for losses in excess of amounts covered by other Liability Insurance Policies; in some cases, may also protect the Insured not covered by the usual Liability Polices. This type of Liability Insurance provides excess liability protection. Businesses and individuals need this coverage for its provision of excess coverage over the underlying Liability Insurance they maintain. Various extensions are available for Umbrella Coverages.

Unallocated Benefit: A policy provision providing reimbursement up to a maximum amount for the cost of all extra miscellaneous hospital services, but not specifying how much will be paid for each type of service.

Unannounced Audit: An audit not scheduled by AQIS. These audits are conducted by a Quarantine Officer and occur in line with the prescribed audit rate for the Other Party.

UNCTAD: See United Nations Conference on Trade and Development.

Undercarriage: A supporting frame or structure of a wheeled vehicle.

Undercarrier: A carrier in a conference or consortium who carries less cargo than the allotment distributed to him.

Underwriter: (1) A company that receives the premiums and accepts responsibility for the fulfillment of the policy contract; (2) the company employee who decides whether or not a particular risk meets the insurance company's underwriting guidelines; (3) the agent who sells the policy.

Underwriting: The process of selecting risks for insurance and determining in what amounts and on what terms the insurance company will accept the risk.

Underwriting Profit or Loss: The amount of money which an insurance company gains or loses as a result of its insurance operations. It excludes investment transactions and federal income taxes.

UNDG Number: See United Nations Dangerous Goods Number.

Unearned Premium: The portion of a premium that a company has collected but has yet to earn because the policy still has unexpired time to run.

UNECE: See United Nations Economic Commission for Europe.

Unified Credit: A one-time credit, usually applied against Federal Estate Taxes, that is available to every individual's estate. The credit also can be used for payment of Federal Gift Taxes during that individual's lifetime.

Uniform Customs and Practice for Documentary Credits: The in 1993 revized rules of the International Chamber of Commerce (ICC) governing a letter of credit issued in respect of goods shipped applicable as from 1-1-1994.

Uniform Premium: A rating structure in which one premium applies to all insureds, regardless of age, sex, or occupation.

Uniform Provisions: Statutory policy provisions of Health Insurance Policies which specify some of the rights and obligations of the Insured and the company. These provisions, with some modifications, are part of the insurance laws of all 50 states and the District of Columbia.

Uninsurable Risk: A risk that is not acceptable for insurance due to excessive risk, moral hazard or other factor.

Uninsured/Underinsured Motorist Coverage: A form of insurance that pays the policy-holder and passengers for bodily injury caused by the owner or operator of an uninsured or inadequately insured automobile.

Union Internationale des Chemins de Fer (UIC): International railway union, in which most of the European national railway companies are united.

Unit Load Device (ULD): Any type of container or pallet, in which a consignment can be transported by air whether or not such a container is considered aircraft equipment.

Unit Load: A number of individual packages bonded, palletized or strapped together to form a single unit for more efficient handling by mechanical equipment.

Unit Owner's Excess Insurance: Coverage, generally added by endorsement, which expands the Insured's coverage to include damage or loss to alterations, fixtures, and improvements within individual units owned by the unit owner, caused by the insured perils. This includes damage to air conditioners, clothes washers, clothes dryers, cooking ovens, cooking ranges, dishwashers, floor coverings, countertops, kitchen cabinets, refrigerators and freezers. This coverage applies as excess insurance over any other valid and collectible insurance that would apply in the absence of this policy.

United Nations Conference on Trade and Development (UNCTAD): A United Nations agency whose work in shipping includes the liner code involving the sharing of cargoes between the shipping lines of the importing and exporting countries and third countries in the ratio 40:40:20.

United Nations Dangerous Goods Number (UNDG Number): The four-digit number assigned by the United Nations Committee of Experts on the Transport of Dangerous Goods to classify a substance or a particular groups of substances. *Note*: The prefix 'UN' must always be used in conjunction with these numbers.

United Nations Economic Commission for Europe (UN/ECE): The UN/ECE is one of a number of Economic and Social Commissions established by the General Assembly of the United Nations. Despite its name it embraces both Europe and North America. The UN/ECE comprises twenty nine core member states, as well as any country which is a member of the United Nations and which applies under Article 11 of the United Nations constitution for delegate status. The aim is to advance the economic development of Europe and associated countries through trade facilitation and common agreements.

United Nations Layout Key (UNLK): A standard (ISO6422) which lays down the basic principles for the design of the image area on documents for use in international trade. *Synonym*: Layout Key.

United Nations Standard Message (UNSM): A collection of structured data that is exchanged to convey information related to a specific transaction between partners engaged in electronic data interchange. Messages are composed of logically grouped segments required for the type of message transaction covered. *Note*: A set of segments in the order specified in a message directory starting with the message header and ending with the message trailer (ISO9735).

Universal Life Insurance: A flexible premium Life Insurance Policy under which the policy-holder may change the death benefit from time to time (with satisfactory evidence of insurability for increases) and vary the amount or timing of premium payments. Premiums (less expense charges) are credited to a policy account from which mortality charges are deducted and to which interest is credited at a rate which may change from time to time.

UNLK: See United Nations Layout Key.

UNSM: See United Nations Standard Message.

User Network: A public network made up of thousands of newsgroups and organized by topic.

Utilization Rate: The quotient of used capacity and available capacity.

Valuable Cargo: A consignment which contains one or more valuable articles (aircargo).

Valuation Charge: Transport charges for certain goods, based on the value declared for the carriage of such goods (aircargo).

Valuation: A clause in a marine policy that fixes the insured value.

Value Added Tax (VAT): A form of indirect sales tax paid on products and services at each stage of production or distribution, based on the value added at that stage and included in the cost to the ultimate customer.

Value Surcharge: A surcharge for the carriage of cargo having a value in excess of a specified amount per kilogram (aircargo).

Vanning: See Stuffing.

Variable Annuity: An annuity contract in which the amount of each periodic income payment may fluctuate. The fluctuation may be related to securities market values, a cost of living index, or some other variable factor. Variable annuity contracts are generally designed to minimize current taxes on the income derived from the investments in them; income taxes are then incurred when withdrawals are made from the annuity, for instance beginning after age 59 1/2.

Variable Life Insurance: Life insurance under which the benefits relate to the value of assets behind the contract at the time the benefit is paid. The amount of death benefit payable would generally not be less than the initial death benefit payable under the policy, depending on the terms outlined in the policy.

VAT: See Value Added Tax.

Vendee: Buyer.

Vendor: Seller.

Ventilated/Coffee: Identical to the GP, except for the inclusion of full length ventilation galleries sited along the top and bottom side rails, and thus ideal for the carriage of coffee, as condesation is prevented from accumulating. 20′ only

Verbal Threshold: Term in No-Fault Auto Insurance, applicable in some states, which states that victims are allowed to sue in tort only if their injuries meet certain verbal descriptions of the types of injuries that render one eligible to recover for pain and suffering.

Very Easy Rodent-Oriented Netwide Index to Computerized Archives: A search tool (like archie) that searches text that appears in Gopher menus.

Very Large Crude Carrier (VLCC): A vessel designed for the carriage of liquid cargo in bulk with a loading capacity from 50.000 till 250.000 DWT.

Vessel: (1) A floating structure designed for the transport of cargo and/or passengers. *Synonym*: Ship. Boiler, drum. (2) This can be defined as: (*a*) A ship, boat or other description of vessel used in navigation by sea; or (*b*) An aircraft; or (*c*) An aircushion vehicle; or (*d*) An offshore industry mobile unit.

Vested Commissions: Renewal commissions, generally related to Life insurance policies, payable to the writing agent or his estate, whether or not he remains with the company.

Vesting: A provision that a pension participant will, after meeting certain requirements, retain a right to all or part of the accrued benefits, even though the employee may leave the job before retirement.

Viatical Settlement: Payment of a portion of the proceeds from Life insurance to an insured who is terminally ill.

Viral: A self-propagating practice or pattern of internet use that moves from person to person. Works best in consumer e-commerce because of easy adoption. Longer sales cycle for b2b e-commerce makes viral practices less important. *Example*: HotMail's explosive growth.

Virtual Private Marketplace: A private market to enable approved suppliers to bid on a large buyer's business or to enable more cost-effective transactions under negotiated terms. Can be a hosted extranet or a feature a larger Net market. For example, National Transportation Exchange sets VPMs for large shippers to schedule and obtain bids from approved carriers, in addition to NTE's main spot market. FreeMarkets sets up VPMs for large buyers to interact with their suppliers through reverse auctions.

VLCC: See Very Large Crude Carrier.

Void Policy: One which is inadmissible as evidence in a court of law (e.g. P.P.I. policy).

Volatility Allowance: The largest difference in container availability taking into account past peaks in net demand after having removed the trend in container demand during the repositioning trade-off period.

Volume: Size or measure of anything in three dimensions.

Volume Charge A charge for carriage of goods based on their volume (aircargo).

Voluntary Market: The market where one seeking insurance obtains insurance in the open market with no help from the state, through an insurer of his or her own selection.

Voucher: A receipt, entry or other document which establish the accounts.

Voyage: A journey by sea from one port or country to another one or, in case of a round trip, to the same port. *Synonym*: Trip.

Voyage Charter: A contract under which the shipowner agrees to carry an agreed quantity of cargo from a specified port or ports to another port or ports for a remuneration called freight, which is calculated according to the quantity of cargo loaded, or sometimes at a lumpsum freight.

Voyage Number: Reference number assigned by the carrier or his agent to the voyage of the vessel.

Waiting Period: The length of time an employee must wait from his/her date of employment or application for coverage, to the date his/her insurance is effective.

Waiting Time: The period of time between the moment at which one is ready for an activity to start and the moment at which this activity can actually begin.

Waiver: An agreement attached to a Disability Policy which exempts from coverage certain disabilities or injuries that otherwise would be covered by the policy.

Waiver Clause: (1) Clause in a marine insurance policy stating that no acts of the insurer or insured in recovering, saving or preserving the property insured, shall be considered a dismissal from or acceptance of abandonment. (2) A clause which entitles both Underwriter and Assured to take measures to prevent or reduce loss without prejudice to the rights of either party.

Waiver of Premium: A provision in some policies to relieve the insured of premium payments falling due during a period of continuous total disability that has lasted for a specified length of time, such as three or six months.

Warehouse: A building specially designed for receipt, storage and handling of goods. *Synonyms*: Shed, Store.

Warehouse Keeper: Party who takes responsibility for goods entered into a warehouse.

Warehouse Receipt: Receipt for products deposited in a warehouse.

Warehousing: Those activities of holding and handling goods in a warehouse (store).

Warranty: An undertaking by the Assured whereby he promises to comply with the terms of the warranty. Non-compliance constitutes breach of warranty and the Underwriter is discharged from liability as from the date of the breach. Breach of warranty may be excused in certain circumstances, or where the breach is held covered under the policy conditions.

Warsaw Convention: The Convention for the Unification of Certain Rules Relating to International Carriage by Air, signed at Warsaw, 12 October 1929, or that Convention as amended by the Hague Protocol, 1955, stipulating obligations or parties and limitations and/or exonerations of carriers (aircargo).

Wash Bay: An area of a QAP to be used for the cleaning of goods contaminated with quarantinable material. All wash bays must conform to the relevant structural criteria for the class of QAP in which they are to be used.

Waste Disposal: Processing and or removal to final resting place or transfer to a place for re-use or recovering of waste.

Waste Logistics: The collection of used, damaged, or outdated products and or packaging from designated users. *Synonym*: Reverse Distribution.

Waterborne Agreement: A market understanding whereby Underwriters cover goods against war risks only whilst they are on the overseas vessel. This rule is relaxed only in the case of goods in a transhipping port for a short period awaiting onward carriage.

Waybill: Non-negotiable document evidencing the contract for the transport of cargo.

Wear and Tear: Loss or deterioration resulting from ordinary use.

Weight Ton: A ton of 1000 kilos.

Wharf: A place for berthing vessels to facilitate loading and discharging of cargo.

Wharfage: The fee charged for the use of a wharf for mooring, loading or discharging a vessel or for storing goods.

What can Go Wrong?: Hopefully nothing! But in the event of a loss, one of two types apply: total loss or partial loss.

Total loss can be one of the following:

- *Actual total loss*: when the assured's goods are no longer 'a thing of the kind insured' or are irretrievably removed from the assurer's use.
- *Constructive total loss*: when the goods are abandoned because their actual loss seems unavoidable, or the cost of recovering the goods would exceed the insured value.
- *Total loss of part*: when a part of the consignment is destroyed but the rest arrives

safely at its destination.

Partial loss can be:

General average loss General average loss refers to deliberate partial loss incurred as a result of the voluntary actions of the ship-owner, or the ship's master, to save the voyage if it is in danger. The voluntary actions might be, for example:

- Jettisoning cargo in order to lighten the ship which is stranded on a reef.
- Pumping water into the ship's hold to quench a fire. Having the ship towed to port for repairs as a result of engine failure.

Particular average loss: Particular average loss refers to a fortuitous partial loss which affects a particular cargo owner only, such as the owner of a crate which was dropped during the loading of the vessel. A claim for a particular average loss is based on the proportion of the invoiced value which has been lost. This proportion is applied to the insured value in order to arrive at the amount of compensation payable. These contributions are levied pro rata on all the parties who have an interest in the safety of the voyage. These include the owner and/or the charterer of the vessel, the master and crew, and each owner of cargo on board.

WHO: See World Health Organization.

Whole Life Insurance: Life insurance payable to a beneficiary at the death of the insured whenever that occurs. Premiums may be payable for a specified number of years (Limited Payment Life) or for life (Straight Life).

Wholesaler: An intermediary between manufacturers and retailers in various activities such as promotion, warehousing, and the arranging of transport and or distribution.

Will: The legal statement of a person's wishes concerning the disposal of his or her property after death.

Without Benefit of Salvage: A term in a marine insurance policy, whereby the Underwriters forgo their subrogation rights. A policy incorporating such a term is deemed to be a gambling policy in law, and is therefore invalid in a court of law.

Without Prejudice: The claim is paid on this occasion, although the Underwriter feels it does not attach to the policy, but this action must not be treated as a precedent for future similar claims.

Work Load: The quantity of work ahead assigned to a certain facility such as a work station, capacity group or a department respectively staff-member.

Workers Compensation: A system established under state law that provides payments, without regard to fault, to employees injured in the course and scope of their employment.

Workers' Compensation Insurance: Coverage designed to protect against financial loss to employers to pay benefits and furnish care to employees injured, and to pay benefits to dependents of employees killed in the course of or arising out of their employment.

Workflow Marketplace: Provides project tracking or collaboration services for complex, iterative, multi-party projects in construction, syndicated bank debt, or licensed trademarks. Charge subscriptions but add transaction fees, such as Bidcom.com charging a contractor to print project blueprints. Create an information-sharing network that gives all parties an appropriate view of the project. Examples: Bidcom (construction), Hurricane (intellectual property). Also, many Net markets incorporate workflow to hold onto users. Once a Net market becomes part of everyday business processes, the switching to another net market becomes much harder.

World Health Organization (WHO): The global agency linked with the United Nations and cooperating with other technical agencies relating to health matters at sea and on land.

Written Premiums: The entire amount of premiums due in a year for all polices bound or issued by an insurance company.

X, C and U Exclusions: Exclusions to Property Liability forms aimed principally at contractors and excavators. The exclusions deny payment for loss due to Explosion ("X"), Collapse ("C") or Underground Damage ("U"). Explosion includes property damage arising from blasting or explosion. Collapse includes structural property damage and property damage to any other property rising out of grading of land, excavating, burrowing, filling or backfilling, tunneling, pile driving, or coffer dam or caisson work, or moving, shoring, underpinning, razing or demolishing any building or structure. Underground damage includes damage to wires, conduits, pipes, mains, sewers, tanks, tunnels, or any similar property beneath the surface of the ground or water caused by and occurring during the use of mechanical equipment for the purpose of grading land, paving, excavating, drilling, burrowing, filling, backfilling, or pile driving.

X.25: International standard of the CCITT for packet switching.

X.400: A CCITT recommendation designed to facilitate international message and information exchange between subscribers of computer based store-and-forward services and office information systems in association with public and private data networks.

X.500: The CCITT now ITU recommendations (ISO9594) for the structure of directories for the maintenance of addresses used in electronic mail.

X-ray: High frequency electromagnetic ray of short wave-length, capable of penetrating most solid substances.

Yard: Fenced off, outdoor storage and repair area.

Yawl: A vessel's small boat moved by one oar. *Synonym*: a jolly-boat. A small sailboat rigged fore-and-aft, with a short mizzenmast astern of the cockpit; distinguished from ketch.

Yield Bucket: The remaining slot capacity for a trade/voyage in a certain port of loading after deduction of the allowance for specific contracts.

Yield Management: The process of maximising the contribution of every slot, vessel, trade and network. Basically it should be seen as the process of allocating the right type of capacity to the right kind of customer at the right price as to maximise revenue or yield. The concept should be used in combination with load factor management.

York-Antwerp Rules: See General Average Act.

Zodiac: A rubber dinghy. An inflatable craft for the transport of people.

Zone: Area, belt or district extending about a certain point defined for transport and/ or charge purpose.

Zone Haulage Rate: The rate for which the carrier will undertake the haulage of goods or containers between either the place of delivery and the carrier's appropriate terminal. Such haulage will be undertaken only subject to the terms and conditions of the tariff and of the carrier's Combined Transport Bill of Lading.

Zone Improvement Plan (ZIP): System to simplify sorting and delivery of mail, consisting of a number of five digits (the so-called ZIP-code) for identification of the state, city or district, and the postal zone in the U.S.A. delivery areas.

Index

Additional Protocol 112, 122-23
Agriculture Inspector 51, 53-55, 61-63, 66, 68, 70, 73, 75, 77, 89-90
Air Cargo 12, 87
  Management 43-71
Air Service 50, 53, 55-59, 61, 69, 73-74, 76
Air Transport 46-47, 101, 271, 308, 325
Aircraft Movements 51-63, 85, 90
Airport of Departure 115
Airport Ruzyne 62
All-cargo Carriers 74
Anchor 168, 173, 190, 196, 212, 317
Asia Pacific 137
Audit System 131
Australian Customs Service 208, 279
Automatic
  Identification 215
  Insurance Plan 214-15, 328
Automobile Reinsurance Facility 215
Average Customs Clearance Time 84, 87

Back-office System 36-38
Baggage 117-20, 122-23, 272, 298
Bailee Insurance 217
Ballast 217, 230-31
Bath Road 88-90
Benefit Period 207, 220
Billing Management 35
Brokers 12-14, 224, 231, 235, 253, 262, 275, 285, 291, 293, 311, 318
Bulk
  Cargo 1, 9, 224, 258, 331
  Carriers and Transport Contractors 22
  Container 224
Business and Corporate Services for Companies 149
Business Interruption Insurance 225, 238, 298, 326
Business Process Platform 31

Cargo
  Agency Registration Services 47
  Agency Rules 48
  Agent 20, 47-48
  Airline 43, 46
  and Shipping Agents 22
  Carriage
  Claims and Loss Prevention Handbook 49
  Claims Management, Effective 49
  Classification 1
  Handling 60, 65, 228
  Insurance 14-15, 97, 228, 233, 274
  Law Network 148-49, 150-55
  Loss Prevention Techniques 146, 152
  Loss, Photo Gallery of 150
  Management Policy and Law 125-53
  Space 50, 52-59, 61-63, 69, 76, 78
  Temperature of 237, 325
  Terminal 86, 92
Carriers 101, 111, 120
  Enablement 40-41
  Ply 94
Cathay Pacific 45
Cause 119-20, 267
Centros Logisticos Aeroportuarios 82-83
Certified Insurance Counsellors 231
China Airlines 45
Claims 14
Cold Store Liability Claims 148
Combined Transport Document 235, 246, 305
Comprehensive Personal Liability Insurance 237
Conditions of 105, 115-16, 220
Consignment 103-06
  Note 103
Container 224, 240, 272, 309
  Load Plan 96, 233, 240
  Owner 240, 255
Containerised Cargo Clearance 230, 241
Contractors Liability Insurance 242
Cost and Freight 231, 234, 243
Customer Service 30, 32, 38, 41, 247
Customs
  and Border Protection 125, 129
  Broker Legal Practice 147
  Broker Liability 148
  Clearance Time 51-55, 57-59, 61, 66, 68, 85, 90-92
  Trade Partnership 125, 128-29, 147

Damage 15, 106-09, 117-20, 212, 236, 238, 247, 267, 275
Damaged Cargo Report 247
Dangerous Goods 213, 238, 247, 288, 302, 311, 329, 350

Deadweight Tonnage 95
Death Benefit 248, 350-51
Declaration 247-48
Delivered Ex Ship 250-51
Delivery System 212
Depreciation 208, 251, 327
Designated Port 251, 302
Disability 28, 180, 211, 226, 247, 252-53, 258, 273, 287, 291, 304, 307-08, 311
  Benefit 253, 259
  Income Policies 307, 313
Discharging of 292, 353
Documentation
  Relating to Cargo 113
  of Carriage 102
Drop & Swap 38-39
Dunnage 256, 322, 324
Dwelling 256, 285
  Property 217, 256

Electronic Data Processing 257-58
Emergency Medical Service 258-59
Employee
  Benefit Programmes 226, 258-59, 307
  Dishonesty Coverage Form 259
  Dishonesty Insurance 259
  Performance Management 158, 167, 174, 191, 196
  Performance Goals 196
  Retirement Income Security Act 259, 261, 267
Employment of 20-21
Empty Containers 130, 239, 240-41, 251, 316, 342
Endorsement 209, 211, 246, 252, 259, 264, 285, 305, 310, 328, 330, 349
Environmental 260, 317
Equipment Damage Report 257, 260
Estate Planning and Special Service 147, 149
European Cargo Traffic 261
Evergreen Seal Management Policy 125, 129
Export Cargo Shipping Instruction 257

Fedex Express 11, 45, 97-99
Flat Bottomed Inland Cargo Vessel 217
Fleet 7
Floor 239-40
Foreign Trade Zone 52-53, 55
Forgery 270
Fork Lift Truck 270, 272, 335
Forwarders 14, 153, 270, 272, 300, 325
Free Carrier 266, 271
Free Trade Zone 82, 271-73
Freight
  Forwarder and General Logistics Legal Practice 14, 49-59, 62, 65-67, 70-71, 147, 270
  Shipments 12
Fulfillment Process 31-35
Full Container Loads 266, 273, 293
Full Truckload Carrier 16-17
Fumigation 273, 323, 346

GATI Cargo Management Services 141
Gauge 5, 311
General Average Act 274, 356
General Cargo Rate 274-75, 308
Global Cargo Management
  Acknowledgement of Receipt 208
  Addition 22
  Administrative Services 210
  Article 106, 112, 120
  Average 216
  Container Dimensions 2
  Edmonton Airport Authority 56
  Fax 72, 84, 88
  Forecast 270
  Identification 114
  Incursion 284
  Integrated Planning Solutions 30
  Issues 168
  Life 232
  Solution 34
  Phone 58, 64, 82
  Process 314
  Production 320
  Quotation 324
  Special Services 66, 70
  Strap 340
  Traffic 60
  Type of Transport 348
  Virtual Private Marketplace 352
  Yield Management 356
Goods Receipt 276
Group Insurance 214, 268, 277
Guadalajara Convention 123

Handling Equipment 140-41, 335
Health Insurance Contracts 211, 221, 226, 284, 310, 313, 318
Heathrow Point West 88-90
Heavy Cargo 278-79
High Contracting Parties 101-02, 109, 111-12, 114, 118-19
High Security Seal 125, 128-29
Hospital Confinement 280, 303, 325
Household Goods and Personal Effects Forwarder 280
Hull Insurance 281-82

Identification Number 240
Inland Transport of Cargo 302
Inland Waterway Port 53-55, 58, 60-62, 65-66, 68-72, 75
Insurance
  Benefits 208, 230, 265, 299

Carrier 209-10, 214, 298, 303, 320
Policy 209, 211-12, 214, 220-21, 226-27, 238, 251-52, 268-69, 316, 328
Underwriters 146, 150-51
Integrated Logistics Solutions 26, 30, 32, 35-38
Integrated Planning Solutions 30
Integrated Transportation Management Solutions 36-38
Intermediaries 4, 14-15
International Air Transport Association 46-48, 138, 282, 288
Cargo Agent 48, 282
Member 282
International Cargo Claims Information 49
International Carriage 101, 111-13, 120, 123, 213, 288, 353
International Character 102, 104
International Marine Insurance Managers 99-100
International Maritime
Dangerous Goods Code 283, 288
Organization 283, 288
International Monetary Fund 118-19, 336
International Organization for Standardization 239, 289
International Ship and Port Facility Security Code 125, 128-29
International Transport and Information System 289
Introduction to Cargo Classification and Management 1-21
ISO 3, 24, 127, 129, 239-40, 246, 287, 289, 320, 322, 333, 350, 355

Jet Fuel, Kerosene-type 97, 99

Keflavik Airport 72
Key-person Insurance 291

Labour Management 31, 33-35
Laden Vessel 292, 296
Largest Freight Carriers 45
Leasing Companies 7, 240
Liability
Claims, Completed Operations Property Damage 223
Coverages 223, 266, 280
Insurance 222-24, 231-32, 236-37, 242, 264, 294, 328, 348
Life and Health Insurance 231
Lift-on Lift-off Vessel 295, 297
Liquid Bulk Cargos 10, 309
Liquid Cargo 342, 348, 351
Litigation Services for Customs and Logistics Providers 147-48
Load Management 34-36
Loaden Vessel 292, 296
Logistics 2, 24-25, 140, 142, 144-45, 147, 225, 297, 343
Event Management Architecture 31
Management 23-41
Providers 148, 151
Service Providers 35-36, 41, 145
Services 144-45
Loss 14, 313
Avoidance 216, 297
Expense 297-98
Prevention 49, 265, 298
Reinsurance 211
Risk of 228-29, 232
Lufthansa Cargo 44-45

Major Medical Plan 243, 245
Management of Human Service Organizations 176
Manchester Airport 91
Manhattan Associates 26, 28-39, 41
Solutions 36-38
Component of 40-42
Marine Cargo
Insurance Policy 290
Policies 208, 213, 217
Ships and Ocean Shipping 94-121
Marine Insurance Act 227
Underwriters 147-48
Marine Liability 300
Material 301
Medical Expenses 204, 207, 221, 226, 254, 284, 299, 307, 336
Merchant Vessels 95, 345
Middlesex 88-90
Montreal Convention 93
Most Major Trading Nations 146, 148-50
Motor Truck Cargo Claims 148
Multimodal Transport Operator 235, 304-05

New Cargo Facilities 54-55, 71, 75, 80-81, 84, 87
Non-scheduled Charter 50, 53-56, 59, 61, 64, 70, 72, 74, 79, 84, 87, 91
Non-vessel Operating Common Carrier 308

Ocean Port 51, 53-54, 57, 60, 62-66, 70-72, 74-75
Online Marketplace Services 12
Operations Management 337
Organizational Policies 194

Parcel Carrier Operations 17
Payroll Information 204
Performance and Logistics Management 23-41
Performance Management 26-27, 34-36, 195, 197
Solutions 27
System, Complete Employee 183
Personal Auto Policies 245
Personal Insurance 284
Physical Loss 305, 314
Piracy 94, 210

Plan Document 163, 165
Policy Declarations 209
Processes and Outcomes Document 246, 298-99, 303
Professional Transport Errors and Omissions Liability Claims 148
Property and Liability Insurance 231-32
Property Damage 236, 242, 255, 257, 264, 296, 308, 312, 355
  Coverage 320
Property Insurance Coverage 248

Quarantine
  Act 222, 310, 322-23
  Approved Premises 265, 286, 322, 347
  Risk Material 233, 241, 323
  Wastewater 323

Rate 14, 246, 271-72, 296
Reefer Container 136, 318, 325
Refrigeration 50-51, 54, 58, 61-62, 66-67, 69-70, 72, 80, 82-83, 87
Reinsurance 227, 265, 287, 306, 326, 328
Republic of
  China 151, 153-54
  Poland 111-12
Reverse Logistics Management 29, 31
Risk Factors 227, 281-82
Road
  Cargo 225, 278, 335
  Carrier 279, 329
Roll-on Roll-off 324, 329

Sample List of Personnel Policies 203
Seal
  Discrepancies 126, 131, 133
  Management 125, 127-28
  Number Range 126-27
Secure Storage 56, 58, 61-62, 66-68, 70-72, 75, 80-83, 87
Semi Trailers 16, 332
Shipments 11, 14-15, 20
  Cost 12, 14
  Parcel 11
  Status 41
Shipper's Export Declaration 331, 333
Shipping Containers 6, 233, 302, 339
Singapore Airlines Cargo 44-45
Slotting Optimization 31, 34-35
Special Drawing Rights 118-19, 331
Specialized Types of Cargo Vessels 94
Statutory Policy Provisions of Health Insurance Policies 349
Stockholm-Arlanda Airport 83
Super Carriers Initiative Programme 125, 129
Supplier Enablement 39-40
Supply Chain 23-41, 338
  Management 25-26, 140, 341
Support Employee Motivation 194
Surcharge 13, 97-99

Tare Mass of Container 342
Tarmac Surface for Cargo Handling 52-55, 61, 64, 67, 69-70, 73, 76-80
Time Management 171, 173
Total Air Carriers 57, 70
Total Ramp Tarmac Surface for Cargo Handling 78
Trading Partner Management 31, 39-40
Transport
  Charges 324, 350
  Documents 229, 238, 286, 305, 328, 334, 346
  Equipment 239, 260
  Freight 16, 333
  Mode of 228-29, 239, 248, 271, 309, 317
  Multimodal 228-29, 235, 271, 305
  of Dangerous Goods 350
  Venture 315
Transportation
  Intermediaries 14
  Planning 26, 32, 37
Truck Terminal 51, 54, 57, 59, 63, 66-71, 74, 80, 88, 91

Ultra Large Crude Carrier 96, 348
Underground 355
Underwriters 152, 207, 218, 253, 256, 259, 274-75, 279, 290-91, 330, 340, 348, 353
Uniform Customs and Practice for Documentary Credits 348-49
United Arab Emirates 86-88
United Kingdom 88-89, 91-92, 151, 154, 261, 335
United Nations 121, 288, 349-50, 355
United Parcel Service 45
United States 3, 7, 10, 49, 146, 150-55, 333, 337
Uship 96

Vessels 94-95, 217, 219-20, 222, 230, 250, 253, 255, 272, 282, 296, 317, 333, 339, 344
  Capacity 296, 336
  Ocean 229, 242, 309, 318
  Tonnage Measurement of 288, 306

Warehouse 20, 22, 24, 26, 28, 32-34, 56, 87, 141, 230, 321, 339, 353
  and Cold Store Liability Claims 148
  Management 30, 33-35, 141, 321
  Space 50, 53-55, 57, 59, 69, 71, 78, 80-81, 84-85, 87, 90
Warsaw Convention 113, 120-24, 353
World Health Organization 354-55

Zipp 140, 142